Global Histories of Education

Series Editors
Diana Vidal
University of São Paulo, São Paulo, Brazil

Tim Allender
University of Sydney, NSW, Australia

Eckhardt Fuchs
Georg Eckert Institute for International
Textbook Research
Braunschweig, Germany

Noah W. Sobe
Loyola University Chicago
Chicago, IL, USA

We are very pleased to announce the ISCHE Global Histories of Education book series. The International Standing Conference for the History of Education has organized conferences in the field since 1978. Thanks to our collaboration with Palgrave Macmillan we now offer an edited book series for the publication of innovative scholarship in the history of education.

This series seeks to engage with historical scholarship that analyzes education within a global, world, or transnational perspective. Specifically, it seeks to examine the role of educational institutions, actors, technologies as well as pedagogical ideas that for centuries have crossed regional and national boundaries. Topics for publication may include the study of educational networks and practices that connect national and colonial domains, or those that range in time from the age of Empire to decolonization. These networks could concern the international movement of educational policies, curricula, pedagogies, or universities within and across different socio-political settings. The 'actors' under examination might include individuals and groups of people, but also educational apparatuses such as textbooks, built-environments, and bureaucratic paperwork situated within a global perspective. Books in the series may be single authored or edited volumes. The strong transnational dimension of the Global Histories of Education series means that many of the volumes should be based on archival research undertaken in more than one country and using documents written in multiple languages. All books in the series will be published in English, although we welcome English-language proposals for manuscripts which were initially written in other languages and which will be translated into English at the cost of the author. All submitted manuscripts will be blind peer-reviewed with editorial decisions to be made by the ISCHE series editors who themselves are appointed by the ISCHE Executive Committee to serve three to five year terms.

Full submissions should include: (1) a proposal aligned to the Palgrave Book Proposal form (downloadable here); (2) the CV of the author(s) or editor(s); and, (3) a cover letter that explains how the proposed book fits into the overall aims and framing of the ISCHE Global Histories of Education book series. Proposals and queries should be addressed to bookseries@ische.org. Preliminary inquiries are welcome and encouraged.

More information about this series at
http://www.palgrave.com/gp/series/15390

Damiano Matasci ·
Miguel Bandeira Jerónimo ·
Hugo Gonçalves Dores
Editors

Education and Development in Colonial and Postcolonial Africa

Policies, Paradigms, and Entanglements, 1890s–1980s

palgrave
macmillan

Editors
Damiano Matasci
University of Lausanne
Lausanne, Vaud, Switzerland

Hugo Gonçalves Dores
University of Coimbra
Coimbra, Baixo Mondego, Portugal

Miguel Bandeira Jerónimo
Center for Social Studies
University of Coimbra
Coimbra, Baixo Mondego, Portugal

Published with the support of the Swiss National Science Foundation

Global Histories of Education
ISBN 978-3-030-27800-7   ISBN 978-3-030-27801-4   (eBook)
https://doi.org/10.1007/978-3-030-27801-4

© The Editor(s) (if applicable) and The Author(s) 2020. This book is an open access publication.
Open Access This book is licensed under the terms of the Creative Commons Attribution 4.0 International License (http://creativecommons.org/licenses/by/4.0/), which permits use, sharing, adaptation, distribution and reproduction in any medium or format, as long as you give appropriate credit to the original author(s) and the source, provide a link to the Creative Commons license and indicate if changes were made.
The images or other third party material in this book are included in the book's Creative Commons license, unless indicated otherwise in a credit line to the material. If material is not included in the book's Creative Commons license and your intended use is not permitted by statutory regulation or exceeds the permitted use, you will need to obtain permission directly from the copyright holder.
The use of general descriptive names, registered names, trademarks, service marks, etc. in this publication does not imply, even in the absence of a specific statement, that such names are exempt from the relevant protective laws and regulations and therefore free for general use.
The publisher, the authors and the editors are safe to assume that the advice and information in this book are believed to be true and accurate at the date of publication. Neither the publisher nor the authors or the editors give a warranty, expressed or implied, with respect to the material contained herein or for any errors or omissions that may have been made. The publisher remains neutral with regard to jurisdictional claims in published maps and institutional affiliations.

Cover illustration: Ignacio Hennigs/Moment Open/gettyimages

This Palgrave Macmillan imprint is published by the registered company Springer Nature Switzerland AG
The registered company address is: Gewerbestrasse 11, 6330 Cham, Switzerland

ACKNOWLEDGEMENTS

This book is the result of an international conference held in Lausanne in September 2017 (*Shaping Education in the (Post) Colonial World, 1890s–1980s*), to which some individual papers have been added. The editors would like to thank the Institute of Political Studies of the University of Lausanne and the Centre for Social Studies of the University of Coimbra for their administrative and financial support. Funding has also been provided by the Swiss National Science Foundation (research project: *De la régulation au "développement". Modernisation, accès au savoir et politiques éducatives dans l'âge global (1929–1961)*, no. PZ00P1_161530) and the *Fundação para a Ciência e a Tecnologia* (Portugal), in association with the research project "The worlds of (under) development: processes and legacies of the Portuguese colonial empire in a comparative perspective (1945–1975)" (PTDC/HAR-HIS/31906/2017|POCI-01-0145-FEDER-031906).

Contents

1 Introduction: Historical Trajectories of Education and
  Development in (Post)Colonial Africa   1
  Damiano Matasci, Miguel Bandeira Jerónimo and
  Hugo Gonçalves Dores
  On Adaptability and "Useful Producers" (1900–1930)   6
  Development, After Depression (1930–1960)   12
  Competing Projects (1960–1990)   16
  Overview: Themes and Problems   19
  Bibliography   22

Part I Education, Living Standards and Social Development

2 Welfare and Education in British Colonial Africa,
  1918–1945   31
  Peter Kallaway
  Conceptualizing Colonial Education   33
  Welfare and Education   39
  Conclusion   47
  Bibliography   51

3 *Une aventure sociale et humaine*: The Service *des Centres Sociaux* in Algeria, 1955–1962   55
Brooke Durham
Fundamental Education at UNESCO and the Service des Centres Sociaux   58
The Structure and Organization of the Service des Centres Sociaux   62
The Centres Sociaux *in the Context of the Algerian War*   66
The Service des Centres Sociaux's *Innovative Pedagogy*   72
Conclusion: "An Educational Exception"   77
Bibliography   79

4 Education Through Labor: From the *deuxième portion du contingent* to the Youth Civic Service in West Africa (Senegal/Mali, 1920s–1960s)   83
Romain Tiquet
The deuxième portion du contingent: *A Disciplinary Heterotopia*   86
   Education Through Labor   86
Social Confinement and Hazardous Living Conditions   89
Civic Service: A Developmentalist Heterotopia   92
   Mobilize and Control the Youth   92
   The Senegalese and Malian Experiences of Civic Service   93
The More Things Change, the More They Stay the Same   97
   Legislative Legacies   97
   Obligation, Civic Duty, and Memory   99
Conclusion   101
Bibliography   103

Part II   Training Economic Actors

5 Becoming a Good Farmer—Becoming a Good Farm Worker: On Colonial Educational Policies in Germany and German South-West Africa, Circa 1890 to 1918   109
Jakob Zollmann
Conditions and Development Plans for Farming in GSWA—The Necessity for Agricultural Education   112

	Colonial Knowledge and Tropical Agriculture: A Research and Teaching Subject in Germany—An Administrative Task in GSWA	120
	"Germany Has the Education and not the Colonies." The Deutsche Kolonialschule für Landwirtschaft and the Colonial Women's School	125
	Educating Africans as Workers? Why or Why Not?	133
	Bibliography	138
6	Cruce et Aratro: *Fascism, Missionary Schools, and Labor in 1920s Italian Somalia*	143
	Caterina Scalvedi	
	Introduction	143
	Church–State Reconciliation	146
	The Shaping of Colonial Education Under De Vecchi (1923–28)	152
	Towards Adapted Education, 1930s	163
	Conclusion	166
	Bibliography	168
7	Becoming Workers of Greater France: Vocational Education in Colonial Morocco, 1912–1939	173
	Michael A. Kozakowski	
	The Politics of Muslim Vocational Education	177
	Vocational Education Beyond the Indigenous Classroom	185
	The Limits of Vocational Training	189
	Ineffective Reforms and Expansion	193
	Conclusion	198
	Bibliography	200
8	Engineering Socialism: The Faculty of Engineering at the University of Dar es Salaam (Tanzania) in the 1970s and 1980s	205
	Eric Burton	
	The International Roots of Tanzania's National Engineering Education	210
	Socializing Engineers: Protests and Transnational Technocracy	214

  Engineering Education Under Conditions of Dependency   220
  Engineering Socialism: Economization and the Undermining
  of Egalitarianism   223
  Conclusion: The Legacies and Inequalities of Technocraticizing
  Socialism   227
  Bibliography   230

Part III Entanglements and Competing Projects

9 **Enlightened Developments? Inter-imperial Organizations and the Issue of Colonial Education in Africa (1945–1957)**   237
  Miguel Bandeira Jerónimo and Hugo Gonçalves Dores
  Proclaiming an "Enlightened" Colonialism   237
  Education: "Moral Character," the Political Problem   243
  Creating the Conditions: Old Principles, New Drive,
  New Challenges   248
  New Data for a New Policy   255
  Conclusion   258
  Archival Sources   259

10 **The Fabric of Academic Communities at the Heart of the British Empire's Modernization Policies**   263
  Hélène Charton
  Universities to Reinvent the Empire   265
   Establishing New Links Within the Empire   265
   Training Academic Elites in and for the Colonies   268
  The Fabric of Imperial Academic Communities   272
   The Asquith Universities: Agents of a New Cultural
   Imperialism   272
   Integrating, Supporting, and Controlling Colonial
   Students in Great Britain   274
   Distinguishing Colonial Students from the Immigrant
   Population   275
  Training Allies—Academic Communities Serving the New
  British Imperial Project   278
   The Specter of Communism   278

	Highly Sought-After Colonial Elites	280
	Colonial Resistance	282
	Conclusion	285
	Bibliography	285
11	**Exploring "Socialist Solidarity" in Higher Education: East German Advisors in Post-Independence Mozambique (1975–1992)**	289
	Alexandra Piepiorka	
	How Does "Socialist Solidarity" Integrate into the Mozambican History of Education?	294
	Mozambican Ideas for Post-Independence Development in Higher Education	298
	East German Involvement in Mozambique's (Socialist) Development and International Cooperation in Higher Education	303
	East German Advisers at the UEM and Internationalist Practices "on the Ground"	306
	Intercultural Encounters	306
	Ideological Disputes	308
	Dialogue and Cooperative Attitude	309
	Wind of Change and the Legacy of "Socialist Solidarity" at the UEM	311
	Conclusion	313
	Bibliography	314
Index		319

Notes on Contributors

Eric Burton is Assistant Professor in contemporary history at the University of Innsbruck specializing in the entangled histories of development, socialisms, and anticolonial liberation struggles. Previously, he was a postdoctoral research associate in the project "Socialism goes global" at the University of Exeter, Leibniz EEGA guest scholar at Leipzig University, and lecturer at the University of Vienna in African Studies and Development Studies.

Hélène Charton is a full-time CNRS researcher currently working for *Les Afriques dans le monde* (LAM) at the University of Bordeaux, France. Her main area of research is education in Africa using historical and political science approaches.

Hugo Gonçalves Dores is a postdoctoral researcher at the Centre for Social Studies (University of Coimbra, Portugal). His research addresses educational policies, international organizations activities (CCTA and UNESCO) and State–Church relations in colonial contexts.

Brooke Durham is a Ph.D. candidate at Stanford University. Her dissertation investigates integration, international volunteering, and education policies in Algeria between 1945 and 1972.

Miguel Bandeira Jerónimo is a Senior Research Fellow at the Centre for Social Studies, University of Coimbra, Portugal. He has been working on the historical intersections between internationalism(s) and imperialism, and on the late colonial entanglements between idioms and repertoires of development and of control and coercion in European colonial empires. He recently co-edited *Internationalism, Imperialism and the Formation of the Contemporary World* (Palgrave, 2017). He coordinates the international research project entitled "The worlds of (under) development: processes and legacies of the Portuguese colonial empire in a comparative perspective (1945–1975)," funded by the Portuguese Foundation for Science and Technology.

Peter Kallaway is a historian and policy analyst who has been a member of staff at the University of the Witwatersrand, the University of the Western Cape, and the University of Cape Town since the 1980s. His publications include *Apartheid and Education* (Ravan Press, 1984), *Education Under Apartheid* (Peter Lang/2002), and *Empire and Education in Africa* (2016). He is the coordinator of a research group on Colonial Education in Africa.

Dr. Michael A. Kozakowski is Teaching Fellow of Modern History at Keele University. His research and publications address subjects including migration, vocational training, economic transitions, and conceptions of the Mediterranean. He is currently preparing a book manuscript entitled, *Migration and the Transformation of the Western Mediterranean: Economic Development, Decolonization, and European Integration, 1945–1975.*

Damiano Matasci holds a Ph.D. in history from the University of Geneva and EHESS in Paris. He is a SNF Research Fellow at the Institute of Political Studies of the University of Lausanne. His research focuses on the history of education in Europe and colonial Africa (nineteenth–twentieth centuries).

Alexandra Piepiorka is a research fellow at the Institute for Educational Science, University of Giessen, Germany. Her ongoing Ph.D. project focuses on socialist cooperation in higher education between the former GDR and post-independence Mozambique.

Caterina Scalvedi is a doctoral student in history at the University of Illinois at Chicago. In her Master's thesis (University of Rome "La Sapienza"), she explored the controversial relationship between the Italian administration and Protestant missions in colonial Eritrea and Ethiopia (1880s–1940s). Currently, she is conducting research on the social and cultural dimensions of education throughout the fascist Italian Empire.

Romain Tiquet is a postdoctoral researcher at the Department of History (Geneva). He holds a Ph.D. (Humboldt University Berlin) on the issue of forced labor in Senegal during the colonial and post-colonial period. He is currently working on a comparative approach of decolonization processes in West Africa.

Jakob Zollmann is researcher at the Center for Global Constitutionalism of the WZB Berlin Social Science Center. His research focuses on the history of international law and on the (legal and social) history of colonial Africa. He has published *Koloniale Herrschaft und ihre Grenzen. Die Kolonialpolizei in Deutsch-Südwestafrika, Vandenhoek&Ruprecht*, 2010 and *Naulila 1914. World War I in Angola and International Law, Nomos*, 2016.

List of Figures

Fig. 6.1	A class for metalworkers (Mogadishu, 1928?) (Courtesy of AFIMC)	159
Fig. 6.2	A sewing class (Mogadishu, 1928?) (Courtesy of AFIMC)	160
Fig. 6.3	A class for woodworkers (Mogadishu, 1928?) (Courtesy of AFIMC)	161
Fig. 6.4	A class for printers (Mogadishu, 1928?) (Courtesy of AFIMC)	161

List of Tables

Table 2.1	Welfare and education in colonial Africa and South Africa, 1910–1945	48
Table 6.1	School Enrolment in Italian Somalia, 1924–1940	155
Table 6.2	Baptisms in Italian Somalia, 1925–1929	157

CHAPTER 1

Introduction: Historical Trajectories of Education and Development in (Post)Colonial Africa

Damiano Matasci, Miguel Bandeira Jerónimo and Hugo Gonçalves Dores

"Among the many problems of Africa there is none that has attracted more discussion, and indeed more controversy, than that of the type of education which should be given to the African."[1] Thus stated William Malcolm Hailey in his famous report *An African Survey: A Study of Problems Arising in Africa South of the Sahara* published in 1938.

[1] Lord Hailey, *An African Survey: A Study of Problems Arising in Africa South of the Sahara* (Oxford: Oxford University Press, 1938), 1208.

D. Matasci (✉)
University of Lausanne, Lausanne, Switzerland
e-mail: Damiano.Matasci@unige.ch

M. B. Jerónimo · H. G. Dores
Centre for Social Studies, University of Coimbra, Coimbra, Portugal

H. G. Dores
e-mail: hugodores@ces.uc.pt

© The Author(s) 2020
D. Matasci et al. (eds.), *Education and Development in Colonial and Postcolonial Africa*, Global Histories of Education, https://doi.org/10.1007/978-3-030-27801-4_1

In this monumental work, which marked the starting point of a new orientation in British colonial policy, on many issues, the eminent former member of the Indian Civil Service noted the great diversity of policies that were in force not only in the British possessions in Africa but also in the French, Belgian, and Portuguese territories. Variation ruled (at least in the policies proclaimed to be implemented), but the centrality of education in the colonial project was highlighted, at least rhetorically. For sure, the "educability" of the native had been the subject of numerous debates and experiments since the late nineteenth century, frequently shaped by culturalist and racialist arguments in the aftermath of formal abolitionism. In the early twentieth century, they continued, with various motivations and purposes, in different international and colonial contexts.[2]

The same happened with the debates about the *usefulness* of "native education," at the metropoles and at the colonies. Problems such as the *necessity* and the *utility* of the provision of educational services in Africa, for settlers and for the colonial subjects, were the object of numerous appreciations. A diversity of arguments and positions emerged within imperial and international circles in relation to the role that education could or should play in the economic and social transformation of African societies.[3]

---

[2] For instance, for the French case, see Pascale Barthélémy, "L'enseignement dans l'Empire colonial français: une vieille histoire?" *Histoire de l'éducation*, no. 128 (2010): 5–28; for the British case see Clive Whitehead, "The Historiography of British Imperial Education Policy, Part II: Africa and the Rest of the Colonial Empire," *History of Education* 34, no. 4 (2005): 441–454; for the Portuguese case, see Miguel Bandeira Jerónimo, "Livros Brancos, Almas Negras. Programas e Discursos (1880–1930)," MA diss., New University of Lisbon, 2000; João Carlos Paulo, "What Does Indigenous Education Mean? Portuguese Colonial Thought and the Construction of Ethnicity and Education," *Paedagogica Historica* 37, no. 1 (2001): 231–250. See also Julie McLeod and Fiona Paisley, "The Modernization of Colonialism and the Educability of the 'Native': Transpacific Knowledge Networks and Education in the Interwar Years," *History of Education Quarterly* 56, no. 3 (2016): 473–502. For a landmark see Marc Depaepe and António Nóvoa (eds.), "The Colonial Experience in Education," *Paedagogica Historica* 31, supplement 1 (1995).

[3] Barnita Bagchi, Eckhardt Fuchs, and Kate Rousmaniere (eds.), *Connecting Histories of Education: Transnational and Cross-Cultural Exchanges in (Post)Colonial Education* (New York: Berghahn Books, 2014). For a comparative assessment, see Peter Kallaway and Rebecca Swartz (eds.), *Empire and Education in Africa: The Shaping of a Comparative Perspective* (New York: Peter Lang, 2016). On the postcolonial period, see Céline Labrune-Badiane, Marie-Albane de Suremain, and Pascal Bianchini (dir.), *L'école en situation postcoloniale* (Paris: L'Harmattan, 2012).

Paradigms such as "adapted," "vocational," "mass," or "fundamental" education, elaborated within long-standing and enduring racialized frameworks, had a significant role in the ways in which European colonial administrations strove to improve the living standards of local populations, so to legitimize imperial rule or even enable some forms of controlled self-government. Similarly, education was also a crucial realm for newly independent countries, as part of ambitious political and socioeconomic modernization schemes.

Despite the importance of these issues, the burgeoning historiography focused on "development"[4]—innovative, solid and compelling as it is— has not reflected this fact accordingly.[5] Admittedly, economic historians have attempted to assess the impact of education on current macroeconomic performances of African countries.[6] Using quantitative methods,

[4] "Development" is an ambiguous and contentious notion. According to Joseph Hodge, this notion refers to "an intentional, organized intervention in collective affairs according to a general (if not universal) standard of improvement." It encompasses two distinct poles: raising production and productivity, on the one hand, and raising the living standards of people regarded as backward or underdeveloped, on the other. Joseph M. Hodge, Gerald Hodl, and Martina Kopf (eds.), *Developing Africa: Concepts and Practices in Twentieth-Century Colonialism* (Manchester: Manchester University Press, 2014): 3.

[5] For some notable contributions on the history of development in Africa, see Hodge, Hodl, and Kopf (eds.), *Developing Africa*; Peter J. Bloom, Stephan F. Miescher, and Takyiwaa Manuh (eds.), *Modernization as Spectacle in Africa* (Bloomington and Indianapolis: Indiana University Press, 2014). For general assessments, see Erez Manela and Stephen Macekura (eds.), *The Development Century: A Global History* (Cambridge: Cambridge University Press, 2018); Frederick Cooper and Randall Packard (eds.), *International Development and the Social Sciences* (Berkeley: University of California Press, 1997). See also the synthesis provided by Corinna Unger, "Histories of Development and Modernization: Findings, Reflections, Future Research," *H-Soz-Kult*, 9.12.2010, http://hsozkult.geschichte.hu-berlin.de/forum/2010-12-001; Joseph M. Hodge, "Writing the History of Development (Part 1: The First Wave)," *Humanity* 6, no. 3 (2015): 429–463; Hodge, "Writing the History of Development (Part 2: Longer, Deeper, Wider)," *Humanity* 7, no. 1 (2016): 125–174. Another crucial text is Nick Cullather, "Development? It's History," *Diplomatic History* 24, no. 4 (2000): 641–653.

[6] Among other important contributions see Gareth Austin, "Développement économique et legs coloniaux en Afrique," *Revue internationale de politique de développement*, no. 1 (2010): 11–32; Ewout Frankema, "The Origins of Formal Education in Sub-Saharan Africa: Was British Rule More Benign?" *European Review of Economic History* 16, no. 4 (2012): 335–355; Ewout Frankema, "Colonial Education and Postcolonial Governance in the Congo and Indonesia," in *Colonial Exploitation and Economic Development: The Belgian Congo and the Netherlands Indies Compared*, ed. by Ewout Frankema and F. Buelens (London: Routledge, 2013): 153–177.

they have identified historical factors that could explain contemporary inequalities, such as transatlantic slavery trade, the presence of missions' stations or the degree of public investments in institutions like schools.[7] These studies demonstrate, among other things, the relevance of long-term historical analysis to the understanding of developmentalism.[8] However, they often fail to fully appreciate the complex, changing and sometimes contradictory processes that shaped the link between education and socioeconomic change.[9]

---

[7] The literature is already vast, and compelling. For some major references, see, among others, Daron Acemoglu, Simon H. Johnson, and James A. Robinson, "The Colonial Origins of Comparative Development: An Empirical Investigation," *American Economic Review* 91, no. 5 (2001): 1369–1401; Leander Heldring and James Robinson, "Colonialism and Development in Africa," NBER Working Paper, 18566 (2012); Emmanuel Akyeampong, Robert H. Bates, Nathan Nunn, and James A. Robinson (eds.), *Africa's Development in Historical Perspective* (New York: Cambridge University Press, 2014); Stelios Michalopoulos and Elias Papaioannou (eds.), *The Long Economic and Political Shadow of History*, vol. II: *Africa and Asia* (London: CEPR Press, 2017). On the role of the state, see Matthew Lange, *Lineages of Despotism and Development: British Colonialism and State Power* (Chicago: University of Chicago Press, 2009); Elise Huillery, "History Matters: The Long-Term Impact of Colonial Public Investments in French West Africa," *American Economic Journal: Applied Economics* 1, no. 2 (2009): 176–215; Denis Cogneau, Yannick Dupraz, and Sandrine Mesplé-Somps, "African States and Development in Historical Perspective: Colonial Public Finances in British and French West Africa," Paris School of Economics Working Paper (2018). On missions, central to understand the question of education, see Nathan Nunn, "Gender and Missionary Influence in Colonial Africa," in *Africa's Development in Historical Perspective*, ed. by E. Akyeampong, R. Bates, N. Nunn, and J. Robinson, 489–512; Johan Fourie and Christie Swanepoel, "When Selection Trumps Persistence: The Lasting Effect of Missionary Education in South Africa," *Tijdschrift voor Sociale en Economische Geschiedenis* 12, no. 1 (2015): 1–29; Julia Cagé and Valeria Rueda, "The Devil Is in the Detail: Christian Missions' Heterogeneous Effects on Development in Sub-Saharan Africa," in *The Long Economic and Political Shadow of History*, ed. by S. Michalopoulos and E. Papaioannou, vol. II, 98–108; Remi Jedwab, Felix Meier zu Selhausen, and Alexander Moradi, *The Economics of Missionary Expansion: Evidence from Africa and Implications for Development*. CSAE Working Paper, Centre for the Study of African Economies, University of Oxford, 2018; Francisco A. Gallego and Robert D. Woodberry, "Christian Missionaries and Education in Former African Colonies: How Competition Mattered," *Journal of African Economics*, no. 3 (2010): 294–329.

[8] Nathan Nunn, "The Importance of History for Economic Development," *Annual Review of Economics* 1, no. 1 (2009): 65–92.

[9] An important point here is, of course, the reliability of the sources, mainly statistical, upon which these important exercises are based on and, therefore, the robustness of their conclusions. From the accurate study of their production to the critical appreciation of

This collective edited volume aims to fill this gap. It contributes to a closer interaction between the historiographies and historical trajectories of education and development, pointing to the co-constitution of arguments, debates, and policies focused on both colonial and postcolonial Africa. Drawing on empirical and multilingual enquiries, the contributors examine a vast array of actors, discourses, and projects aiming at the *mise en valeur* and at the socioeconomic transformation—in some circles seen as "the theory of modernization"[10]—of the African continent and respective societies. Several key aspects of such a process will be highlighted, including transnational and inter-imperial entanglements, as well as continuities and ruptures between the colonial era and the post-independence years. The question at stake is to determine how and why the raise of educational standards of indigenous populations and the training of local elites became a key feature within imperial, national, and international agendas, in different ways and with distinct timings, as part of evolving development theses and projects produced by European administrations, missionaries, intergovernmental organizations, as well as African, Western, and Eastern countries.

During the twentieth century, three phases—or critical junctures—can be identified, during which the economic and social goals of education were profoundly reconfigured and its place in projects of societal and economic transformation evolved.[11]

---

their use in time, the quality of statistical information produced by empire states and colonial administrations needs to be constantly scrutinized. The thought-provoking arguments offered by Morten Jerven, *Poor Numbers: How We Are Misled by African Development Statistics and What to Do About It* (Ithaca, NY: Cornell University Press, 2013) can be useful on many ways.

[10] David C. Engerman and Corinna R. Unger, "Introduction: Towards a Global History of Modernization," *Diplomatic History* 33, no. 3 (2009): 375–385; David Ekbladh, *The Great American Mission: Modernization and the Construction of an American World Order, 1914 to the Present* (Princeton: Princeton University Press, 2010).

[11] Needless to say, this chronology does not aim at being exhaustive or to neatly organize the historical dynamics of the process under analysis. The political, sociocultural, and economic goals of education varied significantly from colonial empire to colonial empire, although some common features may be identified.

On Adaptability and "Useful Producers" (1900–1930)

The first phase, spanning the period between 1900 and 1930, coincided with the introduction of the first "native" educational systems in the wake of the scramble for Africa which had started in the last decades of the nineteenth century. These systems, which worked as such more de jure than de facto, were dominated by missionaries, widely acting in behalf of colonial authorities (although a clear distinction between Catholic and Protestant dynamics must be made in this respect).[12] From the beginning of modern missionary expansion (at least since the sixteenth century), education was an essential aspect of the activities of the missions, although conversion was surely more pivotal (in some cases, the two might be closely related). For Catholic and Protestant missionaries, conversion required learning local languages, teaching European languages, and adapting, sometimes forcefully, local concepts to Christian beliefs (and, often, vice versa). Missionaries carried more than a religious vision with them. They also embodied news ways of understanding sociocultural difference, and in different ways, they promoted a complex and multilayered set of assumptions commonly associated with the idea of "civilising mission." Furthermore, they often promoted a concept of "education through labour," intermingled with arguments of African purported laziness and idleness, which governed European perspective about African populations during colonial times. As some of the texts in this volume show, missions acquired a significant, frequently criticized, centrality in the provision of educational services to African populations, reproducing, at least on paper, European schooling models (see, for instance, the French and the Belgian cases). Needless to say,

---

[12] For the relationship between political and religious authorities in imperial and colonial contexts, see, among many others: Andrew Porter, *Religion Versus Empire? British Protestant Missionaries and Overseas Expansion, 1700–1914* (Manchester: Manchester University Press, 2004); Brian Stanley, *The Bible and the Flag: Protestant Missions and British Imperialism in the Nineteenth and Twentieth Centuries* (Leicester: Appollos, 1990); Norman Etherington (ed.), *Missions and Empire* (Oxford: Oxford University Press, 2005); Owen White and J. P. Daughton (eds.), *In God's Empire: French Missionaries and the Modern World* (Oxford: Oxford University Press, 2012); Miguel Bandeira Jerónimo, *A Diplomacia do Império. Política e Religião na partilha de África (1820–1890)* (Lisbon: Edições 70, 2012); Hugo Gonçalves Dores, *A missão da república: Política, religião e o império colonial Português (1910–1926)* (Lisbon: Edições 70, 2015).

and despite some perspectives that obscure this fact, their role varied in time and space, and it is not easily described and classified. Their actual intervention was diverse, and caution is needed when reading the existing statistics and reports. Like many other examples regarding imperial and colonial action, the rhetoric of "conversion" was frequently contradicted by closer inspections, including by the missionary or ecclesiastical actors themselves. The competition for "souls," among missionary societies, Christian denominations, and between Church and State, led to significant overestimations (some uncritically reproduced in contemporary assessments). Finally, their impact on forms of belief and social practices, on education and development, at the time and throughout time, was also plural, requiring much more than simple forms of causality.

The "effective occupation" proved hard to succeed, and clearly, the priorities of imperial governments and colonial administration rested not on the significant provision of educational services. Regarding the latter, this period was characterized not so much by the extent of practical achievements, despite the considerable, and formal, expansion of missionary schools, as by intense debates on the "content" of education and, in particular, its adaptation to the putative social, economic, and cultural specificities of African populations and territories.[13] The general goal was to strike a balance between the imperatives of "moral conquest"—as conceptualized in 1917 by Georges Hardy, Director of Education in West French Africa[14]—and the concerns linked to the "detribalization" and "social displacement" caused by a supposedly too abstract and literary education which emulated the metropolitan one. Given the need to sustain the efforts to foster "legitimate commerce," in relation to the protracted dynamics of abolition of slave trade and slavery, and the need to regulate the uses of coerced and "contract" labor, the ponderations about "native education" also appeared connected to the debates on how to guarantee the availability of African manpower. Faced with these problems, the solutions envisaged and the educational models put in place by European colonial powers were particularly diverse throughout

---

[13] For instance, Udo Bude, "The Adaptation Concept in British Colonial Education," *Comparative Education* 19, no. 3 (1983): 341–355.

[14] Georges Hardy, *Une conquête morale. L'enseignement en AOF* (Paris: Armand Colin, 1917).

the territories.[15] There was no coherent and unified educational project, but rather different and changing realities from one colony to another. The "moral conquest" meant slightly different things from colonial empire to colonial empire, from colony to colony, from administration to administration. Moreover, as happened with many other topics, the distance between proclaimed educational policies and the actual administrative practices was frequently unsurmountable.

After the First World War, colonial education progressively acquired new objectives, partially in response to the new League of Nations' concept of "trusteeship" and the growing native demand for education (which also varied from one context to another).[16] The French Minister for Colonies Albert Sarraut, for example, placed training and education in the program for the *mise en valeur* of African territories, which covered port and river development, railway and road construction, and also health care improvement. In this framework, education was supposed to not only be made widely available to the rural masses, but also be focused on practical objectives. It had to convey "practical experimental" notions, orient native children toward "manual trades," and prepare "useful producers" (*producteurs utiles*).[17] This practical emphasis was used by many, in diverse ways, some to justify the opposition to the role played by the religious entities in education in colonial contexts (partially a projection of ongoing conflicts at the metropole), while others to foster ideas of (forced) labor as quintessentially an educational instrument. This was noticeable at the metropoles but it was also manifest in the debates regarding the possibilities of economic change or the suppression of slavery and implementation of new forms of labor exaction within the League of Nations.[18] Similar considerations to those of Sarraut were also

---

[15] Ana Isabel Madeira, "Portuguese, French and British Discourses on Colonial Education: Church–State Relations, School Expansion and Missionary Competition in Africa, 1890–1930," *Paedagogica Historica* 41, nos. 1–2 (2005): 31–60.

[16] Susan Pedersen, *The Guardians: The League of Nations and the Crisis of Empire* (Oxford: Oxford University Press, 2015). On education, see J. M. Barrington, "The Permanent Mandates Commission and Educational Policy in Trust Territories," *International Review of Education* 22, no. 1 (1976): 88–94.

[17] Albert Sarraut, *La mise en valeur des colonies françaises* (Paris: Payot et Cie, 1923): 401.

[18] Miguel Bandeira Jerónimo, *The "Civilizing Mission" of Portuguese Colonialism, 1870–1930* (Basingstoke: Palgrave Macmillan, 2015), 147–150. See also Susan Pedersen, *The Guardians*. For a later period, see Frederick Cooper, *Décolonisation et travail en Afrique. L'Afrique britannique et française, 1935–1960* (Paris: Karthala, 2004).

expressed by Lord Lugard in his work *The Dual Mandate*, published in 1922. This influential volume stated that the goal of village schools was to "improve the village craftsmen and agriculturists, to raise the standard of life, comfort, and intelligence in the village community."[19]

The emergence of this "developmentalist" discourse accompanied the introduction of forms of *education through labour*, in a context marked by the intensification of the internationalization of imperial and colonial affairs, not least about the "conditions analogous to slavery."[20] For instance, those forms followed the example of the coercive measure called *deuxième portion du contingent* ("second part of the contingent") which was created in 1926 in French West Africa (see the chapter of Romain Tiquet). The first vocational and technical study programs were also established—for example, in North Africa (see the chapter of Michael A. Kozakowski) and in the German colonies (see the chapter of Jakob Zollmann)—even though they remained very limited and were sometimes restricted to white population.[21]

The publication in 1922 and 1925 of two reports on African education commissioned by the American philanthropic foundation Phelps-Stokes Fund (PSF) represented an important turning point in the international and (inter)imperial formulation of colonial educational policies, although its impact is yet to be comparatively studied. The transatlantic circulation of educational models and potential policies (and other

---

[19] Frederick Lugard, *The Dual Mandate in British Tropical Africa* (Edinburgh: William Blackwood and Sons, 1922): 444.

[20] Frederick Cooper, "Conditions Analogous to Slavery: Imperialism and Free Labor Ideology in Africa," in *Beyond Slavery: Explorations of Race, Labor, and Citizenship in Postemancipation Societies*, ed. by Frederick Cooper, Thomas C. Holt, and Rebecca J. Scott (Chapel Hill: University of North Carolina Press, 2000), 107–149; Miguel Bandeira Jerónimo, "A League of Empires: Imperial Political Imagination and Interwar Internationalisms," in *Internationalism, Imperialism and the Formation of the Contemporary World*, ed. by Miguel Bandeira Jerónimo and José Pedro Monteiro (London: Palgrave Macmillan, 2017), 87–126. For the dynamics of internationalization, see also, for instance, Pierre Singaravelou, "Les stratégies d'internationalisation de la question coloniale et la construction transnationale d'une science de la colonisation à la fin du XIXe siècle," *Monde(s)* 1, no. 1 (2012): 135–157; Veronique Dimier, "L'internationalisation du débat colonial: rivalités autour de la Commission Permanente des Mandats," *Outre-mers* 89, nos. 336–337 (2002): 333–360.

[21] Stéphane Lembré, "L'enseignement technique et professionnel dans l'Algérie coloniale, du territoire à l'atelier (1866–1958)," *Histoire de l'éducation*, no. 147 (2017): 91–117.

Alabamas in Africa) was differently engaged by different colonial powers.[22] Even those, such as the Portuguese, that were not the primordial focus of the study—not least because of the close connections between the state and the Catholic Church and of the convoluted relationship with foreign missions since the mid-nineteenth century—nonetheless reacted to the reports' findings.[23] Written in the wake of missions carried out by Thomas Jesse Jones, a leading member of the PSF and a former director of the Research Department of Hampton Institute in Virginia (one of the pioneer colleges for black students in the United States), the reports put forward precise suggestions with regard to adapting local schools systems to "the educational needs of Africa," in particular "those pertaining to the hygienic, economic, social, and religious conditions of the Native people."[24]

Taking up the educational model used with black Americans since the mid-nineteenth century, Jones's proposed policy could be summed up into four categories which he called "The Four Essentials of Education": health, home life training, industry (including agriculture), and recreation.[25] Education was meant to serve primarily the needs of the community, particularly agricultural and industrial ones, rather than provide literary knowledge that had supposedly little relevance or utility in African economic life. These utilitarian principles were embraced, directly or indirectly, by many colonial administrations (once again, for different reasons, with distinct aims).[26] In 1925, for example, the first report

---

[22] For a now classic study of these transatlantic connections, see Andrew Zimmerman, *Alabama in Africa: Booker T. Washington, the German Empire, and the Globalization of the New South* (Princeton: Princeton University Press, 2010).

[23] Thomas Jesse Jones, *Education in Africa: A Study of West, South, and Equatorial Africa by the African Education Commission* (New York: Phelps-Stokes Fund, 1922), and *Education in East Africa* (New York: Phelps-Stokes Fund, 1925).

[24] Jones, *Education in Africa*, xvi.

[25] Julia Bates, "U.S. Empire and the 'Adaptive Education' Model: The Global Production of Race," *Sociology of Race and Ethnicity* 5, no. 1 (2019): 41–54.

[26] Sybille Küster, "'Book Learning' Versus 'Adapted Education': The Impact of Phelps-Stokesism on Colonial Education Systems in Central Africa in the Interwar Period," *Paedagogica Historica* 43, no. 1 (2007): 79–97; Maud Seghers, "Phelps-Stokes in Congo: Transferring Educational Policy Discourse to Govern Metropole and Colony," *Paedagogica Historica* 40, no. 4 (2004): 455–477; Miguel Bandeira Jerónimo, *The "Civilizing Mission" of Portuguese Colonialism, 1870–1930* (Basingstoke: Palgrave Macmillan, 2015): 109–133.

submitted to the British Colonial Office by the Advisory Committee on Native Education in British Tropical Africa emphasized that education "should be adapted to the mentality, aptitudes, occupations and traditions of the various peoples"[27] and that it had to help improve agriculture, "native industries," and health. Adopting these principles, which were also amply discussed within international and intercolonial bodies,[28] new school institutions were created, some of them famous, such as the Achimota College in the Gold Coast.[29] In French West Africa, in the early 1930s, Governor General Jules Brévié and school inspector Albert Charton recommended changing "village schools" to "rural schools" *(écoles rurales)*, where an important place would be given to agricultural education (with the creation, for example, of school gardens) and to manual trades.[30]

This reorientation of educational policies came up against several problems. On the one hand, the paradigm of "adapted education" was often met with hostility among African elites, who saw it as education "on the cheap" devoid of attractiveness and any prospect of social promotion, as reported by Léopold Sédar Senghor in 1937.[31] Its "practical" positive consequences were questioned; its social, cultural, and economic effects criticized. What "development" would arise from it? Who would benefit from it? What did its implementation say about the ways the colonizers saw the colonized? On the other hand, there was no large-scale funding for the development of colonial school systems. Budgetary restrictions and policy options, for political but also sociocultural reasons, justified that fact, among other aspects. Overall, school-enrollment rates were very low, although

[27] Advisory Committee on Native Education in the British Tropical African Dependencies, *Education Policy in British Tropical Africa* (London: H. M. Stationery Office, 1925), 4.

[28] See Institut Colonial International, *L'enseignement aux indigènes. Rapports préliminaires, XXIe session, Paris, 5–8 mai 1931* (Bruxelles: Établissements généraux d'imprimerie, 1931).

[29] Gita Steiner-Khamsi and Hubert Quist, "The Politics of Educational Borrowing: Reopening the Case of Achimota in British Ghana," *Comparative Education Review* 44, no. 3 (2000): 272–299.

[30] Harry Gamble, "Peasants of the Empire. Rural Schools and the Colonial Imaginary in 1930s French West Africa," *Cahiers d'études africaines* 195 (2009): 775–804.

[31] See Paule Brasseur, "À propos du congrès de l'évolution culturelle des peuples coloniaux - Paris, 1937," *Journal des Africanistes* 49, no. 2 (1979): 145.

there were significant territorial differences.³² Despite the rhetoric around the *mise en valeur* of colonies, education remained a relatively neglected area of public investment, both for economic and political reasons. But the "educability" of the "natives" never ceased to be pondered.³³ This can be said of every European colonial empire in Africa. Arguments and debates abounded, numerous policies were proclaimed, but resources, human and financial, were scarce, and unevenly distributed. As a result, in a moment in which they were internally debating how to position themselves in the world born out of Versailles, missionaries continued to play a leading part, especially in British Africa, Belgian Congo, and the Italian East African colonies (see the chapter of Caterina Scalvedi). In the Portuguese case similar dynamics occurred, although the scarcity of educational services was matched by the feebleness of ecclesiastical and missionary ones, despite the rhetoric of the "civilizing mission."³⁴

Development, After Depression (1930–1960)

The debates on the content and goals of colonial education evolved in the 1930s. The decade marked the start of what can be seen as a second phase, lasting until independence. The effects of the Great Depression encouraged more attention being paid to education's economic and social repercussions, including in colonial realms. Together with the first signs of greater state intervention in colonial science research, new ideas on colonial education started to develop within many missionary and philanthropic circles (in this regard, see Peter Kallaway's timeline at the end of Chapter 2).³⁵ International missionary networks, grouped together within the International Missionary Council (1921) led by Joseph Oldham, devoted several of their conference sessions to

---

[32] Here, again, we should take into consideration the problematic reliability of colonial statistics.

[33] Clive Whitehead, "The Historiography of British Imperial Education Policy, Part II," 444.

[34] Ana Isabel Madeira, "Ler, escrever e orar: Uma análise histórica e comparada dos discursos sobre a educação, o ensino e a escola em Moçambique, 1850–1950," PhD diss., University of Lisbon, 2007; Miguel Bandeira Jerónimo, *A diplomacia do imperialismo*; Hugo Gonçalves Dores, *A missão da república*.

[35] Christopher Bonneuil, "Development as Experiment: Science and State Building in Late Colonial and Postcolonial Africa, 1930–1970," *Osiris* 15 (2000): 1501–1520.

the links between the education and welfare of African populations.[36] For instance, in 1926, in Le Zoute, Belgium, a meeting devoted to the "Christian mission" in Africa was clear on the statement that was widely acknowledged "not only by missionaries but by administrators" that "the future" of Africa was associated with "the moral, physical and intellectual development of the African peoples." As its reporter wrote, at the conference everyone "expressed its economic faith in this sentence." And he added, continuing to echo the general consensus at the meeting: "Europeans of themselves cannot carry out that development. The Africans as they were, and still are to a very large extent, cannot carry it out. Only by a process of education—which includes work, but much more—can they be fitted to take their share in developing Africa. Physical and moral improvement of the African is a necessary condition of the economic development of the continent."[37] On the Catholic side, similar points could be made, perhaps with more emphasis on religious education and conversion (see the chapter of Caterina Scalvedi). European humanitarian organizations too saw in the expansion of education a means to combine civilizational demands with native "well-being." At the 1931 International Conference on African Children held in Geneva by the Save the Children International Union, the Swiss missionary and ethnographer Henri-Alexandre Junod, president of the *Bureau international pour la défense des indigènes*, stated that education was an essential means not only for achieving economic progress in Africa, but also for "certain elements of civilization," following the example of norms of hygiene, to reach "as far as the lower levels of the population."[38]

---

[36] Peter Kallaway, "Education, Health, and Social Welfare in the Late Colonial Context: The International Missionary Council and Educational Transition in the Interwar Years with Specific Reference to Colonial Africa," *History of Education* 38, no. 2 (2009): 217–246.

[37] Edwin W. Smith, *The Christian Mission in Africa, a Study Based on the Work of the International Conference at Le Zoute, Belgium, September 14th to 21st, 1926* (London: International Missionary Council, 1926): 90.

[38] State Archives of the Canton of Geneva, Archives privées, 92-4-9. Conférence internationale pour l'enfance africaine. Compte rendu (1932): 55–60. On this conference, see Dominique Marshall, "Children's Rights in Imperial Political Cultures: Missionary and Humanitarian Contributions to the Conference on the African Child of 1931," *The International Journal of Children's Rights* 12, no. 3 (2004): 273–318.

This new outlook led the way to the great reorientations taking place in the 1940s. The *Mass Education in African Society* report published by the Colonial Office in 1944 provided a new conceptual basis for rethinking the role of education in raising living standards. As emphasized by one of its authors, Margaret Wrong, secretary to the International Committee on Christian Literature for Africa, "it has been proved that the attainment of literacy makes people aware of the need for social and economic improvements, and therefore they will co-operate more readily with welfare and other agencies working on these lines."[39] Thus, the spread of school education, the fight against illiteracy, and the improvement of adult education were directly linked with the economic and social modernization of African colonies, as attested also by the conclusions of the Brazzaville conference convened in 1944 by the authorities of Free France.[40] Thanks to the Colonial and Development Welfare Act (CDWA)—adopted in 1940 and revised in 1945—as well as the creation of the *Fonds d'investissement pour le développement économique et social* (FIDES) in France (1946) and the *Fonds du bien-être indigène* in Belgium (1947, followed by the *Plan décennal pour le développement économique et social du Congo belge* in 1949), significant financial resources were growingly invested in the educational sector. Education represented between 6 and 7% of the total budget of the FIDES, and about 20% of the budget of the CDWA (100 million pounds over 10 years). Part of a new "modernising mission,"[41] colonial development policies took shape around two major axes: on the one hand, building schools and expanding the educational offer, including at university level by creating of colonial universities and increasing the number of scholarships for studying in the metropole (see the chapter of Hélène Charton); on the other hand, European administrations carried out more delimited projects targeting the "community development" of towns and rural

---

[39] Margaret Wrong, "Mass Education in Africa," *African Affairs* 43, no. 172 (1944): 105–111.

[40] David E. Gardinier, "Les recommandations de la Conférence de Brazzaville sur les problèmes d'éducation," in *Brazzaville, janvier-février 1944: aux sources de la décolonisation*, ed. by Institut Charles-de-Gaulle (Paris: Plon, 1988): 170–180.

[41] See the Special Issue "Modernizing Missions: Approaches to the 'Developing' the Non-Western World After 1945," *Journal of Modern European History* 8, no. 1 (2010). For the French Empire, see Ed Naylor (ed.), *France's Modernising Mission: Citizenship, Welfare and the Ends of Empire* (Basingstoke: Palgrave Macmillan, 2018).

villages.⁴² Such was the case, for example, of the mass education and adult education experiments conducted in French and British Africa from the late 1940s, in rural centers in Belgium Congo, or in Algerian *Centres sociaux* which were created in 1955 and were active throughout the war (see the chapter of Brooke Durham).

These new priorities echoed the new international context emerging after the Second World War, and in particular the United Nations agenda. Indeed, UN specialized agencies, particularly the United Nations Educational, Scientific and Cultural Organization (UNESCO), embarked on ambitious programs for providing technical assistance to "underdeveloped" countries.⁴³ Naturally, education became a recurrent topic.⁴⁴ In this context, senior officials such as Julian Huxley (first Director General of UNESCO) and John Bowers (head of the Department of Fundamental Education) fostered a vast conceptual undertaking for the purpose of formulating an educational doctrine specially designed for countries of the Global South.⁴⁵ Known under the name of "Fundamental Education," it was tested beginning with 1947 within several pilot projects carried out in Haiti, Nyasaland, and China.⁴⁶ The introduction of a global agenda that was centered on the

---

⁴² For "community development," see Daniel Immerwahr, *Thinking Small: The United States and the Lure of Community Development* (Cambridge: Harvard University Press, 2014).

⁴³ Amy L. S. Staples, *The Birth of Development: How the World Bank, Food and Agriculture Organization, and World Health Organization Changed the World, 1945–1965* (Kent: Kent State University Press, 2006); Daniel Maul, *Human Rights, Development and Decolonization: The International Labour Organization, 1940–1970* (London: Palgrave Macmillan, 2012); Corinna R. Unger, Marc Frey, and Sonke Kunkel (eds.), *International Organizations and Development (1945–1990)* (Basingstoke: Palgrave Macmillan, 2014). See also Corinna Unger, *International Development: A Postwar History* (London: Bloomsbury, 2018).

⁴⁴ Phillip W. Jones, *International Policies for Third World Education: Unesco, Literacy, and Development* (London/New York: Routledge, 1988); Colette Chabbott, *Constructing Education for Development: International Organizations and Education for All* (New York: Routledge, 2003).

⁴⁵ UNESCO, *Fundamental Education: Common Ground for all Peoples: Report of a Special Committee to the Preparatory Commission of Unesco* (Paris: UNESCO, 1946).

⁴⁶ Joseph Watras, "UNESCO's Programme of Fundamental Education, 1946–1959," *History of Education* 39, no. 2 (2010): 219–237; For the Haiti's project (Marbial Valley), see: Chantalle F. Verna, "Haiti, the Rockefeller Foundation, and UNESCO's Pilot Project in Fundamental Education, 1948–1953," *Diplomatic History* 40, no. 2 (2016): 269–295.

fight against illiteracy and educational inequalities throughout the world, including "non-self-governing territories," stimulated the institutionalization of new forms of technical cooperation of an intercolonial nature which gained in importance beginning with the late 1940s (see the chapter of Hugo Gonçalves Dores and Miguel Bandeira Jerónimo).[47] Thus, in the context of a "crisis of the empires,"[48] education became an important area for certifying, within national and international circles, the metropoles' commitment to the "well-being" and living standards of the colonized populations.

COMPETING PROJECTS (1960–1990)

The independence wave sweeping over the early 1960s opened up a new phase marked by the political aspirations of the new independent states and Cold War tensions. Placed at the centre of the demands made by nationalist and pan-African movements, education became a priority for the new African governments. In this regard, decolonization raised specific problems: Low school-enrollment rates and high illiteracy rates, coupled with the departure of colonial senior staff, posed the immediate problem of a lack of qualified staff in administrations and certain economic sectors. Accordingly, the formation of a national elite and intelligentsia became a major goal in support of economic modernization and nation-building in African countries (see the chapter of Eric Burton), along with the promotion of mass schooling.

In a context that some sociologists have described as a "world educational revolution"[49] characterized by a spectacular increase in school-enrollment rates, development aid for Africa became a major issue in

[47] On education see Damiano Matasci, "Une 'UNESCO africaine'? Le ministère de la France d'Outre-mer, la coopération éducative intercoloniale et la défense de l'Empire, 1947–1957," *Monde(s)*, no. 13 (2018): 195–214, and "Assessing Needs, Fostering Development: UNESCO, Illiteracy and the Global Politics of Education (1945–1960)," *Comparative Education* 53, no. 1 (2017): 35–53; On health see Jessica Lynne Pearson, *The Colonial Politics of Global Health: France and the United Nations in Postwar Africa* (Harvard: Harvard University Press, 2018); Vincent Bonnecase, *La pauvreté au Sahel: du savoir colonial à la mesure internationale* (Paris: Karthala, 2011).

[48] Martin Thomas, Bob Moore, and Larry Butler, *Crises of Empire* (London: Hodder Education, 2008).

[49] John Meyer et al., "The World Educational Revolution, 1950–1970," *Sociology of Education* 50 (1977): 242–258.

North–South relations. Seeking to establish and defend their economic and cultural sphere of influence, the former metropoles quickly set up cooperation agreements which especially provided for financial contributions toward building schools or for sending European staff to secondary education and higher education institutions.[50] Foreign staff and *coopérants* occupied an important place within educational systems, in many countries reaching levels as high as 80–90%.[51] Starting with the early 1960s and the launch of the "Decade of Development," international organizations also played an important role in the assessment of educational needs, in the "africanization" of structures and programs, as well as the planning of long-term educational expansion, as attested by the plan developed at the Addis Ababa conference in May 1961.[52] Last but not least, the two superpowers—United States and Soviet Union— invested massively in programs meant to encourage the inflow of African students into their own countries. The philanthropic foundations Ford, Rockefeller, and Carnegie were particularly active in this respect.[53] Similarly, Eastern Bloc countries set up several programs for training future African elites.[54] Higher education in particular became one of the areas where "socialist solidarity" gained expression (as pointed out in the chapter of Alexandra Piepiorka), especially in the form of sending experts on-site or creating ad hoc institutions such as Patrice Lumumba University in Moscow in 1960.[55]

[50] Laurent Manière, "La politique française pour l'adaptation de l'enseignement en Afrique après les indépendances (1958–1964)," *Histoire de l'éducation*, no. 12 (2010): 163–190; Samy Mesli, "French Coopération in the Field of Education (1960–1980): A Story of Disillusionment," in *Francophone Africa at Fifty*, ed. by Tony Chafer and Alexander Keese (Manchester: Manchester University Press, 2013): 120–134.

[51] André Labrousse, "La France et l'aide à l'éducation aux États africains et malgache," *Cahiers de l'IIPE*, no. 22 (1971): 115–116.

[52] Jones, *International Policies for Third World Education*.

[53] Corinna Unger, "The United States, Decolonization and the Education of Third World Elites," in *Elites and Decolonization in the Twentieth Century*, ed. by Jost Dülffer and Marc Frey (Basingstoke: Palgrave Macmillan, 2011): 241–261; Ludovic Tournès and Giles Scott-Smith (eds.), *Global Exchanges: Scholarship Programs and Transnational Circulations in the Modern World* (New York: Berghahn Books, 2017).

[54] For case studies, see Eric Burton (ed.), "Socialisms in Development," *Journal für Entwicklungspolitik* XXXIII, no. 3 (2017).

[55] Constantin Katsakioris, "Creating a Socialist Intelligentsia: Soviet Educational Aid and Its Impact on Africa (1960–1991)," *Cahiers d'études africaines* 2, no. 226 (2017): 259–288.

Two aspects pertaining to the postcolonial period need to be emphasized. On the one hand, developmentalist discourses and practices were often part of a profound continuity with the colonial era. For instance, experts who had worked for colonial administrations in the 1940s and 1950s were, for example, mobilized as consultants by African governments or as specialists by international organizations.[56] In several respects, development aid, whether of a bilateral or multilateral nature, became a way to "recycle" the empire.[57] Similarly, the extracurricular measures for training young people and "getting them into work" that were put in place by African governments after independence drew directly on experiments carried out during the colonial period (as showed in the chapter of Romain Tiquet). On the other hand, development aid through education became one area where Cold War tensions and rivalries crystallized.[58] In this sense, postcolonial Africa represented an arena of competing projects which lay at the centre of global interactions between knowledge and players, where repertoires and paradigms that were tested there evolved based on the dealings between governments and foreign-aid players.

The contributions gathered in this volume deal with these long historical trajectories by drawing on several local case studies based on in-depth archival research. The authors have looked at various geographical spaces—ranging from the French, British, German, and Italian empires to independent countries such as Mali, Senegal, Mozambique, and Tanzania. All levels of education are investigated, from primary to university education, including extracurricular education. Taken as a whole, the chapters allow us to better understand the specificities of each of the three critical junctures presented above. Certainly, it would be possible to increase the number of case studies and territories under observation in order to identify other stakeholders, discourses, practices, and legacies. For example, the role of international organizations should be further examined, and the same goes for the postcolonial period, which would deserve more detailed case studies. Despite these aspects,

---

[56] Joseph M. Hodge, "British Colonial Expertise, Post-colonial Careering and the Early History of International Development," *Journal of Modern European History* 8, no. 1 (2010): 24–46.

[57] Véronique Dimier, *The Invention of a European Development Aid Bureaucracy: Recycling Empire* (Basingstoke: Palgrave Macmillan, 2014).

[58] Odd Arne Westad, *La guerre froide globale* (Paris: Payot, 2005).

this volume offers a renewed perspective on the successive reconfigurations of the relationship between education and development in Africa, thus helping to open up new research avenues, both on the historiography of development and on the one on colonial education.

Overview: Themes and Problems

This book is organized around three distinct, but complementary, sub-themes. The first part focuses on the link between education and the raise of living standards. The chapters investigate the ways in which education became increasingly linked to issues such as health, nutrition, agriculture, and social welfare, which were relevant topics in the debates on development and human progress of African colonized populations, but also in newly independent countries. In fact, different educational programs were substantially focused on these aspects, envisioning the organization of a new societal environment, with specific consequences in traditional societies. The first chapter, by Peter Kallaway, focuses on the relationships between education and social welfare in British Africa. By following the process of construction of a modern network of educational experts throughout the first half of twentieth century, he highlights different, but often correlated, backgrounds, and elucidates in which way they contributed to debates about colonial education. As Kallaway shows, government officials, missionary organizations (such as the International Missionary Council), and philanthropic institutions were key players in shaping development discourses and practices. Therefore, acknowledging the role of this multitude of actors is essential to understand the complexity and variety of proposals and objectives which dealt with education. Such perspective is emphasized by Brooke Durham. Her chapter focuses on the creation of *centres sociaux* in French Algeria right before independence. This government-sponsored development initiative pledged to provide "fundamental education" to adults and children, rudimentary medical services, and job training. The *centres sociaux* constitute one example of the attempts by the imperial and colonial administrations to transform different aspects related to the living of those under colonial rule. Durham explores the limits and possibilities of this initiative, which was supposedly apolitical, during a time of increasing conflict between imperial and nationalist forces. She clearly demonstrates that education was part of, and crucial to, a project of social control. This question is also discussed by Romain Tiquet's chapter, which investigates the legacies of French-established *second portion du contingent* of French West Africa in the youth civil service implemented in independent Mali and Senegal. Highlighting the "civilizing mission" rhetoric and its defense of *education through labour* for African populations, Tiquet also argues that postcolonial elites, in both countries, perpetuated these dynamics, in order to foster social control and economic development after independence.

The second part of the volume deals with issues related to the training of workers and future local elites. The chapters highlight the importance of technical and vocational curricula for urban and rural workers while many projects maintained the idea of *education through labour* and the long-standing racialized assertions of African "laziness" or "idleness." They also point out the ambiguities of that kind of colonial education, which was thought to serve imperial rule and to improve the economic productivity of colonial territories, but in many contexts became determinant to the increase of independence movements. Jakob Zollmann sheds light on agricultural education in German South West Africa, between the end of nineteenth century and the First World War. He examines the discussions about which education policy should be applied to European and African children, defining their role in society, economy, and, by extension, colonial development. The chapter by Caterina Scalvedi explores the monopolizing role played by Catholic missionaries in the building of the first state-sponsored school system in Italian Somalia during the interwar years. Having as background the emergence of a centralized and coercive colonial state, Scalvedi examines the different educational opportunities available to both Italian and African children and how school *curricula* were closely related to the economic needs of the colony. In this regard, technical and vocational education played a key role. In his contribution, Michael A. Kozakowski shows how French colonial administration sought to use technical and vocational education to induce economic transformation in interwar Morocco. As he argues, vocational education should produce loyal subjects, useful workers for the "Greater France," and, in some way, mitigate the dangers of new social aspirations and resulting conflicts brought by economic development and education. The training of competent economic actors was also a key issue in the postcolonial era, as Eric Burton demonstrates. His chapter analyzes the creation of the Faculty of Engineering of the University of Dar es Salaam as result of a pressing need of modernization and economic development in 1960s Tanzania. The faculty, which started as a Soviet endeavor and was later dominated by (West) German support, became an important place where the principles of Tanzanian socialist project—*ujamaa*—were undermined, throughout a process marked by ideological conflicts on the role of university education in society. If the University was seen as a "hotbed" of revolutionary fervor and leftist radicalism, the faculty was marked by technocratic considerations of manpower planning and careering.

The third and final part of the book examines how the circulation of ideas, people and practices between and beyond empires and nation-states contributed to forge the link between education and "development." It focuses on the ways Africa became an arena of competing projects devised by different actors, from intergovernmental organizations to imperial administrations and other European countries, against the background of the Cold War and decolonization. The chapters highlight the connections and rivalries among this multitude of actors, projects, and institutions, as well as the continuities and ruptures between the colonial and postcolonial periods. They also address education and its instrumental role in the overall developmentalist idea. Hugo Gonçalves Dores and Miguel Bandeira Jerónimo's chapter studies how the Commission for Technical Cooperation in Africa South of the Sahara (CCTA), an inter-imperial organization created in 1950, addressed the problem of colonial education. Tracing the renewed attempts launched by imperial powers to establish some forms of cooperation after the Second World War, the text scrutinizes in which way they sought to use education to reshape their developmentalist strategies, in social and economic fields, and to reinforce their arguments legitimizing imperial rule. Hélène Charton analyzes the university reforms designed by British imperial authorities in the 1940s and its impact on the new social and political agenda of British East Africa. These higher education projects, which include the creation of universities in African territories and the multiplication of scholarships in metropolitan institutions, were, as Charton states, at the heart of postwar modernization policies. By tracing new educational modalities, imperial administrations tried to forge a new local elite and deepen the links between metropole and colony. Finally, Alexandra Piepiorka's text focuses on postcolonial attempts to remodel the colonial university system and to readapt it to the new political and social context. Piepiorka uses the Eduardo Mondlane University (Mozambique) to trace the spirit of "socialist solidarity" in the context of educational aid coming from Eastern countries toward Africa's newly independent nations.

Bibliography

Acemoglu, Daron, Simon H. Johnson, and James A. Robinson. "The Colonial Origins of Comparative Development: An Empirical Investigation." *American Economic Review* 91, no. 5 (2001): 1369–1401.

Advisory Committee on Native Education in the British Tropical African Dependencies. *Education Policy in British Tropical Africa*. London: H. M. Stationery Office, 1925.

Akyeampong, Emmanuel, Robert H. Bates, Nathan Nunn, and James A. Robinson, eds. *Africa's Development in Historical Perspective*. New York: Cambridge University Press, 2014.

Austin, Gareth. "Développement économique et legs coloniaux en Afrique." *Revue internationale de politique de développement* 1, no. 1 (2010): 11–32.

Bagchi, Barnita, Eckhardt Fuchs, and Kate Rousmaniere, eds. *Connecting Histories of Education: Transnational and Cross-cultural Exchanges in (Post) Colonial Education*. New York: Berghahn Books, 2014.

Barrington, J. M. "The Permanent Mandates Commission and Educational Policy in Trust Territories." *International Review of Education* 22, no. 1 (1976): 88–94.

Barthélémy, Pascale. "L'enseignement dans l'Empire colonial français: une vieille histoire?" *Histoire de l'éducation*, no. 128 (2010): 5–28.

Bates, Julia. "U.S. Empire and the 'Adaptive Education' Model: The Global Production of Race." *Sociology of Race and Ethnicity* 5, no. 1 (2019): 41–54.

Bloom, Peter J, Stephan F. Miescher, and Takyiwaa Manuh, eds. *Modernization as Spectacle in Africa*. Bloomington and Indianapolis: Indiana University Press, 2014.

Bonnecase, Vincent. *La pauvreté au Sahel: du savoir colonial à la mesure internationale*. Paris: Karthala, 2011.

Bonneuil, Christophe. "Development as Experiment: Science and State Building in Late Colonial and Postcolonial Africa, 1930–1970." *Osiris* 15 (2000): 1501–1520.

Brasseur, Paule. "À propos du congrès de l'évolution culturelle des peuples coloniaux - Paris, 1937." *Journal des Africanistes* 49, no. 2 (1979): 143–150.

Bude, Udo. "The Adaptation Concept in British Colonial Education." *Comparative Education* 19, no. 3 (1983): 341–355.

Burton, Eric, ed. "Socialisms in Development." *Journal für Entwicklungspolitik* XXXIII, no. 3 (2017): 21–48.

Cagé, Julia, and Valeria Rueda. "The Devil Is in the Detail: Christian Missions' Heterogeneous Effects on Development in Sub-Saharan Africa." In *The Long Economic and Political Shadow of History*, edited by Stelios Michalopoulos and Elias Papaioannou, vol. II: *Africa and Asia*. London: CEPR Press, 2017.

Chabbott, Colette. *Constructing Education for Development: International Organizations and Education for All.* New York: Routledge, 2003.

Cogneau, Denis, Yannick Dupraz, and Sandrine Mesplé-Somps. "African States and Development in Historical Perspective: Colonial Public Finances in British and French West Africa." Paris School of Economics Working Paper (2018).

Cooper, Frederick. "Conditions Analogous to Slavery: Imperialism and Free Labor Ideology in Africa." In *Beyond Slavery: Explorations of Race, Labor, and Citizenship in Postemancipation Societies*, edited by Frederick Cooper, Thomas C. Holt, and Rebecca J. Scott, 107–149. Chapel Hill: University of North Carolina Press, 2000.

———. *Décolonisation et travail en Afrique. L'Afrique britannique et française, 1935–1960.* Paris: Karthala, 2004.

Cooper, Frederick, and Randall Packard, eds. *International Development and the Social Sciences.* Berkeley: University of California Press, 1997.

Cullather, Nick. "Development? It's History." *Diplomatic History* 24, no. 4 (2000): 641–653.

Depaepe, Marc, and António Nóvoa, eds. "The Colonial Experience in Education." *Paedagogica Historica* 31, supplement 1 (1995).

Dimier, Veronique. *The Invention of a European Development Aid Bureaucracy: Recycling Empire.* Basingstoke: Palgrave Macmillan, 2014.

———. "L'internationalisation du débat colonial: rivalités autour de la Commission Permanente des Mandats." *Outre-mers* 89, nos. 336–337 (2002): 333–360.

Dores, Hugo Gonçalves. *A missão da república: Política, religião e o império colonial Português (1910–1926).* Lisbon: Edições 70, 2015.

Ekbladh, David. *The Great American Mission: Modernization and the Construction of an American World Order, 1914 to the Present.* Princeton: Princeton University Press, 2010.

Engerman David C., and Corinna R. Unger. "Introduction: Towards a Global History of Modernization." *Diplomatic History* 33, no. 3 (2009): 375–385.

Etherington, Norman, ed. *Missions and Empire.* Oxford: Oxford University Press, 2005.

Fourie, Johan, and Christie Swanepoel. "When Selection Trumps Persistence: The Lasting Effect of Missionary Education in South Africa." *Tijdschrift voor Sociale en Economische Geschiedenis* 12, no. 1 (2015): 1–29.

Frankema, Ewout. "Colonial Education and Postcolonial Governance in the Congo and Indonesia." In *Colonial Exploitation and Economic Development: The Belgian Congo and the Netherlands Indies Compared*, edited by Ewout Frankema, and F. Buelens, 153–177. London: Routledge, 2013.

———. "The Origins of Formal Education in Sub-Saharan Africa: Was British Rule More Benign?" *European Review of Economic History* 16, no. 4 (2012): 335–355.
Gallego, Francisco A., and Robert D. Woodberry. "Christian Missionaries and Education in Former African Colonies: How Competition Mattered." *Journal of African Economics* 19, no. 3 (2010): 294–329.
Gamble, Harry. "Peasants of the Empire: Rural Schools and the Colonial Imaginary in 1930s French West Africa." *Cahiers d'études africaines* 195 (2009): 775–804.
Hailey, Lord. *An African Survey: A Study of Problems Arising in Africa South of the Sahara*. Oxford: Oxford University Press, 1938.
Hardy, Georges. *Une conquête morale. L'enseignement en AOF*. Paris: Armand Colin, 1917.
Heldring, Leander, and James Robinson. "Colonialism and Development in Africa." NBER Working Paper, 18566 (2012).
Hodge, Joseph M. "British Colonial Expertise, Post-colonial Careering and the Early History of International Development." *Journal of Modern European History* 8, no. 1 (2010): 24–46.
———. "Writing the History of Development (Part 1: The First Wave)." *Humanity* 6, no. 3 (2015): 429–463.
———. "Writing the History of Development (Part 2: Longer, Deeper, Wider)." *Humanity* 7, no. 1 (2016): 125–174.
Hodge, Joseph M., Gerald Hodl, and Martina Kopf, eds. *Developing Africa: Concepts and Practices in Twentieth-Century Colonialism*. Manchester: Manchester University Press, 2014.
Huillery, Elise. "History Matters: the Long-Term Impact of Colonial Public Investments in French West Africa." *American Economic Journal: Applied Economics* 1, no. 2 (2009): 176–215.
Immerwahr, Daniel. *Thinking Small: The United States and the Lure of Community Development*. Cambridge: Harvard University Press, 2014.
Institut Colonial International. *L'enseignement aux indigènes. Rapports préliminaires, XXIe session, Paris, 5–8 mai 1931*. Bruxelles: Établissements généraux d'imprimerie, 1931.
Jedwab, Remi, Felix Meier zu Selhausen, and Alexander Moradi. *The Economics of Missionary Expansion: Evidence from Africa and Implications for Development*. CSAE Working Paper, Centre for the Study of African Economies, University of Oxford, 2018.
Jerónimo, Miguel Bandeira. *The "Civilizing Mission" of Portuguese Colonialism, 1870–1930*. Basingstoke: Palgrave Macmillan, 2015.
———. *A diplomacia do império. Política e religião na partilha de África (1820–1890)*. Lisbon: Edições 70, 2012.

———. "A League of Empires: Imperial Political Imagination and Interwar Internationalisms." In *Internationalism, Imperialism and the Formation of the Contemporary World*, edited by Miguel Bandeira Jerónimo and José Pedro Monteiro, 87–126. London: Palgrave Macmillan, 2017.

———. "Livros Brancos, Almas Negras. Programas e Discursos (1880–1930)." MA diss., New University of Lisbon, 2000.

Jerven, Morten. *Poor Numbers: How We Are Misled by African Development Statistics and What to Do About It*. Ithaca, NY: Cornell University Press, 2013.

Jones, Phillip W. *International Policies for Third World Education: Unesco, Literacy, and Development*. London/New York: Routledge, 1988.

Jones, Thomas Jesse. *Education in Africa: A Study of West, South, and Equatorial Africa by the African Education Commission*. New York: Phelps-Stokes Fund, 1922.

———. *Education in East Africa*. New York: Phelps-Stokes Fund, 1925.

Kallaway, Peter. "Education, Health, and Social Welfare in the Late Colonial Context: The International Missionary Council and Educational Transition in the Interwar Years with Specific Reference to Colonial Africa." *History of Education* 38, no. 2 (2009): 217–246.

Kallaway, Peter, and Rebecca Swartz, eds. *Empire and Education in Africa: The Shaping of a Comparative Perspective*. New York: Peter Lang, 2016.

Katsakioris, Constantin. "Creating a Socialist Intelligentsia: Soviet Educational Aid and Its Impact on Africa (1960–1991)." *Cahiers d'études africaines* 2, no. 226 (2017): 259–288.

Küster, Sybille. "'Book Learning' Versus 'Adapted Education': The Impact of Phelps-Stokesism on Colonial Education Systems in Central Africa in the Interwar Period." *Paedagogica Historica* 43, no. 1 (2007): 79–97.

Labrousse, André. "La France et l'aide à l'éducation aux États africains et malgaxe." *Cahiers de l'IIPE*, no. 22 (1971): 115–116.

Labrune-Badiane, Céline, Marie-Albane de Suremain, and Pascal Bianchini, eds. *L'école en situation postcoloniale*. Paris: L'Harmattan, 2012.

Lange, Matthew. *Lineages of Despotism and Development: British Colonialism and State Power*. Chicago: University of Chicago Press, 2009.

Lembré, Stéphane. "L'enseignement technique et professionnel dans l'Algérie coloniale, du territoire à l'atelier (1866–1958)." *Histoire de l'éducation*, no. 147 (2017): 91–117.

Lugard, Frederick. *The Dual Mandate in British Tropical Africa*. Edinburgh: William Blackwood and Sons, 1922.

Madeira, Ana Isabel. "Ler, escrever e orar: Uma análise histórica e comparada dos discursos sobre a educação, o ensino e a escola em Moçambique, 1850–1950." PhD diss., University of Lisbon, 2007.

———. "Portuguese, French and British Discourses on Colonial Education: Church–State Relations, School Expansion and Missionary Competition in Africa, 1890–1930." *Paedagogica Historica* 41, nos. 1–2 (2005): 31–60.

Malinowski, Stephan, Andreas Eckert, and Corinna Unger, eds. "Modernizing Missions: Approaches to the 'Developing' the Non-Western World After 1945." *Journal of Modern European History* 8, no. 1 (2010): 35–63.

Manela, Erez, and Stephen Macekura, eds. *The Development Century: A Global History*. Cambridge: Cambridge University Press, 2018.

Manière, Laurent. "La politique française pour l'adaptation de l'enseignement en Afrique après les indépendances (1958–1964)." *Histoire de l'éducation*, no. 12 (2010): 163–190.

Marshall, Dominique. "Children's Rights in Imperial Political Cultures: Missionary and Humanitarian Contributions to the Conference on the African Child of 1931." *The International Journal of Children's Rights* 12, no. 3 (2004): 273–318.

Matasci, Damiano. "Assessing Needs, Fostering Development: UNESCO, Illiteracy and the Global Politics of Education (1945–1960)." *Comparative Education* 53, no. 1 (2017): 35–53.

———. "Une 'UNESCO africaine'? Le ministère de la France d'Outre-mer, la coopération éducative intercoloniale et la défense de l'Empire, 1947–1957." *Monde(s)*, no. 13 (2018): 195–214.

Maul, Daniel. *Human Rights, Development and Decolonization: The International Labour Organization, 1940–1970*. London: Palgrave Macmillan, 2012.

McLeod, Julie, and Fiona Paisley. "The Modernization of Colonialism and the Educability of the 'Native': Transpacific Knowledge Networks and Education in the Interwar Years." *History of Education Quarterly* 56, no. 3 (2016): 473–502.

Mesli, Samy. "French Coopération in the Field of Education (1960–1980): A Story of Disillusionment." In *Francophone Africa at Fifty*, edited by Tony Chafer and Alexander Keese, 120–134. Manchester: Manchester University Press, 2013.

Meyer, John, et al. "The World Educational Revolution, 1950–1970." *Sociology of Education* 50 (1977): 242–258.

Michalopoulos, Stelios, and Elias Papaioannou, eds. *The Long Economic and Political Shadow of History*, vol. II: *Africa and Asia*. London: CEPR Press, 2017.

Naylor, Ed, ed. *France's Modernising Mission: Citizenship, Welfare and the Ends of Empire*. Basingstoke: Palgrave Macmillan, 2018.

Nunn, Nathan. "Gender and Missionary Influence in Colonial Africa." In *Africa's Development in Historical Perspective*, edited by Emmanuel Akyeampong, Robert H. Bates, Nathan Nunn, and James A. Robinson, 489–512. New York: Cambridge University Press, 2014.

———. "The Importance of History for Economic Development." *Annual Review of Economics* 1, no. 1 (2009): 65–92.

Paulo, João Carlos. "What Does Indigenous Education Mean? Portuguese Colonial Thought and the Construction of Ethnicity and Education." *Paedagogica Historica* 37, no. 1 (2001): 231–250.

Pearson, Jessica Lynne. *The Colonial Politics of Global Health: France and the United Nations in Postwar Africa*. Harvard: Harvard University Press, 2018.

Pedersen, Susan. *The Guardians: The League of Nations and the Crisis of Empire*. Oxford: Oxford University Press, 2015.

Porter, Andrew. *Religion Versus Empire? British Protestant Missionaries and Overseas Expansion, 1700–1914*. Manchester: Manchester University Press, 2004.

Sarraut, Albert. *La mise en valeur des colonies françaises*. Paris: Payot et Cie, 1923.

Seghers, Maud. "Phelps-Stokes in Congo: Transferring Educational Policy Discourse to Govern Metropole and Colony." *Paedagogica Historica* 40, no. 4 (2004): 455–477.

Singaravelou, Pierre. "Les stratégies d'internationalisation de la question coloniale et la construction transnationale d'une science de la colonisation à la fin du XIXe siècle." *Monde(s)* 1, no. 1 (2012): 135–157.

Smith, Edwin W. *The Christian Mission in Africa, a Study Based on the Work of the International Conference at Le Zoute, Belgium, September 14th to 21st, 1926*. London: International Missionary Council, 1926.

Stanley, Brian. *The Bible and the Flag: Protestant Missions and British Imperialism in the Nineteenth and Twentieth Centuries*. Leicester: Appollos, 1990.

Staples, Amy L. S. *The Birth of Development: How the World Bank, Food and Agriculture Organization, and World Health Organization changed the World, 1945–1965*. Kent: Kent State University Press, 2006.

Steiner-Khamsi, Gita, and Hubert Quist. "The Politics of Educational Borrowing: Reopening the Case of Achimota in British Ghana." *Comparative Education Review* 44, no. 3 (2000): 272–299.

Thomas, Martin, Bob Moore, and Larry Butler. *Crises of Empire*. London: Hodder Education, 2008.

Tournès, Ludovic, and Giles Scott-Smith, eds. *Global Exchanges: Scholarship Programs and Transnational Circulations in the Modern World*. New York: Berghahn Books, 2017.

UNESCO. *Fundamental Education: Common Ground for All Peoples: Report of a Special Committee to the Preparatory Commission of Unesco*. Paris: UNESCO, 1946.

Unger, Corinna R., Marc Frey, and Sonke Kunkel, eds. "Histories of Development and Modernization: Findings, Reflections, Future Research." *H-Soz-Kult*, 9 December 2010. http://hsozkult.geschichte.hu-berlin.de/forum/2010-12-001.

———. *International Development: A Postwar History*. London: Bloomsbury, 2018.
———. *International Organizations and Development (1945–1990)*. Basingstoke: Palgrave Macmillan, 2014.
———. "The United States, Decolonization and the Education of Third World Elites." In *Elites and Decolonization in the Twentieth Century*, edited by Jost Dülffer and Marc Frey, 241–261. Basingstoke: Palgrave Macmillan, 2011.
Verna, Chantalle F. "Haiti, the Rockefeller Foundation, and UNESCO's Pilot Project in Fundamental Education, 1948–1953." *Diplomatic History* 40, no. 2 (2016): 269–295.
Watras, Joseph. "UNESCO's Programme of Fundamental Education, 1946–1959." *History of Education* 39, no. 2 (2010): 219–237.
Westad, Odd Arne. *La guerre froide globale*. Paris: Payot, 2005.
White, Owen, and J. P. Daughton, eds. *In God's Empire: French Missionaries and the Modern World*. Oxford: Oxford University Press, 2012.
Whitehead, Clive. "The Historiography of British Imperial Education Policy, Part II: Africa and the Rest of the Colonial Empire." *History of Education* 34, no. 4 (2005): 441–454.
Wrong, Margaret. "Mass Education in Africa." *African Affairs* 43, no. 172 (1944): 105–111.
Zimmerman, Andrew. *Alabama in Africa: Booker T. Washington, the German Empire, and the Globalization of the New South*. Princeton: Princeton University Press, 2010.

Open Access This chapter is licensed under the terms of the Creative Commons Attribution 4.0 International License (http://creativecommons.org/licenses/by/4.0/), which permits use, sharing, adaptation, distribution and reproduction in any medium or format, as long as you give appropriate credit to the original author(s) and the source, provide a link to the Creative Commons license and indicate if changes were made.

The images or other third party material in this chapter are included in the chapter's Creative Commons license, unless indicated otherwise in a credit line to the material. If material is not included in the chapter's Creative Commons license and your intended use is not permitted by statutory regulation or exceeds the permitted use, you will need to obtain permission directly from the copyright holder.

PART I

Education, Living Standards and Social Development

CHAPTER 2

Welfare and Education in British Colonial Africa, 1918–1945

Peter Kallaway

The relevance of historical research for an explanation of the roots of contemporary educational policy and its relationship to notions of equity, democracy and development has been sadly neglected in recent years. This means that policy makers have forfeited the advantages of reflecting on the traditions and experience of past endeavors and examining them critically for potential understandings of present and future policy making. The aim of this paper was to direct the attention of researchers to the complexities and multifaceted nature of educational policy development in inter-war era (1918–1945), with specific reference to British colonial Africa and South Africa. It will also hopefully provide a set of elementary tools for all of those interested in educational policy-making strategies that seek to promote meaningful social, economic and political change in an age of uncertainty.

Current discussion about the decolonization of education raises important questions about the nature of colonial education and requires researchers to avoid the reification of such notions if we are to gain an

P. Kallaway (✉)
University of Cape Town/University of the Western Cape,
Cape Town, South Africa
e-mail: peter.kallaway@uct.ac.za

© The Author(s) 2020
D. Matasci et al. (eds.), *Education and Development in Colonial and Postcolonial Africa*, Global Histories of Education,
https://doi.org/10.1007/978-3-030-27801-4_2

ample understanding of their meaning for the present. It is important therefore to understand the complexities of educational discourse, policy and practices in colonial contexts in precisely the same way that we need to understand the entanglements of education policy discussion at the present time. As stated by the editors in the introduction to this volume, it is essential to understand the *ambiguities* and *contradictions* of educational policy and practice, the variety of influences that informed such changes, and the changing nature of such discourses *over time* and in *different geographical locations*. We also need to be careful to distinguish between rhetoric and reality in education policy. What policy makers *say* about policy is not always the same as what they do in complex real-life situations.

The task of "development" in Africa in the post-World War II era was reconstituted within the frameworks that were evolved by the agencies of the United Nations Organization and the World Bank. Within the optimistic atmosphere of the post-colonial politics of the 1950s and 1960s, a new infrastructure of "development studies" was constructed, with the backing of generous donations of foreign aid—much of it coming from the former colonial powers. Since then, the works of Hetherington, Constantine, Hargreaves, Darwin, Cell, Hodge, Tilley and Cooper have helped us to understand more fully why that gap between intentions and outcomes was often so marked.[1] A key element of their work is to elucidate the nature of the rickety scaffolding of emergent state-sponsored welfarism, philanthropic humanitarianism, scientific management and research, upon which this emergent enterprise of "development" was built in the inter-war era. In that context, I wish to address some comments to the question of the conceptualization of colonial education during this period and then relate it to the wider issue of welfare policies that provided the backdrop to much of this work.

[1] Penelope Hetherington, *British Paternalism and Africa* (London: Frank Cass, 1978); John D. Hargreaves, *Decolonization in Africa* (London: Longman, 1988); Stephen Constantine, *The Making of British Colonial Development Policy 1914–1940* (London: Frank Cass, 1984); John Darwin, "Decolonization and the End of Empire," *Oxford History of the British Empire*, vol. V (Oxford: Oxford University Press, 1999), 541–557; John Cell, *Hailey: A Study of British Imperialism, 1872–1969* (Cambridge: Cambridge University Press, 1992); Joseph M. Hodge, *Triumph of the Expert: Agrarian Doctrines of Development and the Legacies of British Colonialism* (Athens, OH: University of Ohio Press, 2007); Helen Tilley, *Africa as a Living Laboratory* (Chicago: University of Chicago Press, 2011); Frederick Cooper, *Africa Since 1940: The Past of the Present* (Cambridge: Cambridge University Press, 1996).

Conceptualizing Colonial Education

It is not possible to gain a comprehensive understanding of the development of educational policy in colonial Africa without a detailed study of the complexities of colonial educational discourse as it played itself out in the context of a worldwide revolution in educational thinking between the mid-nineteenth century to the mid-twentieth century. The influence of humanism, the legacy of the French Revolution, the impact of the Industrial Revolution and the movements for political and social reform, the challenges of mass education for a newly urbanized working class, the advent of vocational and technical education, the impact of the vast changes in the nature of science and technology, all contributed to the ferment of ideas that informed "Progressive Education," "vocational education" and "radical education" during the late colonial era (see Chapter 5 by Jakob Zollmann and Chapter 7 by Michael A. Kozakowski). These all impacted on the manner in which education, pedagogy and curriculum were conceived globally by a variety of actors in various context at different times,[2] and more specifically in relation to the African colonial context.

The origins of the story of mass education in England are to be found in Sanderson's description of the central policy dispute over education in the nineteenth century which was waged between those who wished to explain the provision of mass education as part of an attempt to ward off radical political and economic change by an increasingly organized urban working class, and those who saw the social reforms through education as a means of extending democratic rights, social welfare and human dignity in modern society increasing divided by class divisions.[3] The essential ambiguities of mass education in industrial countries were reproduced in the colonial context. Was colonial education to be about creating African Christians/African workers/African subject/citizens who were to be the vanguard of social, economic and political modernization and perhaps Westernization (*assimilation* for the French) or was

---

[2] Andy Green, *Education and State Formation: The Rise of Education Systems in England, France and the USA* (London: Macmillan, 1990); David Tyack and Larry Cuban, *Tinkering Toward Utopia: A Century of Public School Reform* (Cambridge: Harvard University Press, 1995); Harold Silver, *Equal Opportunity in Education* (London: Methuen, 1973).

[3] Michael Sanderson, *Education, Economic Change and Society in England, 1780–1870* (London: Macmillan, 1983).

the role of the school and missions to *prevent* such modernization and radicalization by facilitating more productive life on the land for peasant farmers and contented "tribesmen" or educated indigenes who would not threaten the colonial order?[4]

My broad focus is on the construction of a modern network of educational experts drawn from missionary, state and philanthropic backgrounds, who framed a context for professional debate and policy practice in the inter-war era. The origins of many of these debates about colonial education can be traced to the great ecumenical Edinburgh International Missionary Council (IMC) conference in 1910.[5] From this time, there was an attempt to establish consultative networks of experts who would engage with issues of African education. For the most part, these experts were missionaries and government officials, but after World War I, the grid was expanded to include philanthropic contributions (mainly from American foundations like Carnegie, Rockefeller, Jeanes and Phelps Stokes) and a variety of progressive educators and university-based educators located mainly at institutions like Teachers College, Columbia University, the *Institut Jean-Jacques Rousseau* in Geneva, the *École Coloniale* in Paris, and, from the 1930s, and the *Institute of Education*, at London University. Through these networks which were crafted via various Imperial Education conferences between 1907 and the 1930s,[6] IMC congresses at Le Zoute, Belgium (1923), Jerusalem (1926), Tambaram, India (1938),[7] New Education Fellowship (NEF) meetings during the 1920–1930s in Europe, South Africa and

---

[4] Martin Carnoy, *Education and Cultural Imperialism* (New York: David McKay, 1974); Keith Watson (ed.), *Education in the Third World* (London: Croom Helm, 1982); Peter Kallaway and Rebecca Swartz (eds.), *Empire and Education in Africa* (New York: Peter Lang, 2017).

[5] Peter Kallaway, "Education, Health and Social Welfare in the Late Colonial Context: The International Missionary Council and Educational Transition in the Inter-War Years with Specific Reference to Colonial Africa," *History of Education* 38, no. 2 (2009): 217–246; Felicity Jensz, "The 1910 Edinburgh World Missionary Conference and Comparative Colonial Education," *History of Education* 47, no. 3 (2018): 399–414.

[6] British Parliamentary Papers (BPP) Col. 5666 (1911); BPP Col. 1990 (1923); BPP Col. 2009 (1924); BPP Cmd. 2883 (1927); BPP Cmd. 3628-9 (1930); W. Rawson (ed.), *Education in a Changing Commonwealth* (London: HMSO, 1931).

[7] Kallaway, "Education, Health," 217–246.

Australasia,[8] and the Yale Education conferences convened by the South African, C. T. Loram, with the assistance of American philanthropic foundations between 1934 and 1939,[9] a research community gradually emerged which had a degree of influence on colonial education policy and practice.

The origins of the scientific study of colonial education can be traced to this time and to this context. The variety of reports of the English Board of Education (1897–1914), which included a considerable contribution on colonial education,[10] and the Hamburg Colonial Institute's report on *Education in the German Empire* (the *Schlunk Report* of 1914),[11] were probably the first attempt to compile data and information on education on a large scale informed by modern statistical methods and a scientific approach to colonial educational policy.[12] These were followed by the two major Phelps Stokes Commission Reports on African education in 1922 and 1924, sponsored by an alliance of American missionary and philanthropic endeavor.[13] In a context where "the assumed stability of colonial rule became more questionable during the 1930s, a certain number of persons in Britain and France conceived programmes of reform and renewal which would eventually lead towards the

---

[8] Peter Kallaway, "Conference Litmus: The Development of a Conference and Policy Culture in the Inter-War Period with Special Reference to the New Education Fellowship and British Colonial Education in Southern Africa," in *Transformations in Schooling: Historical and Comparative Perspectives*, ed. by Kim Tolley (New York: Palgrave Macmillan, 2007), 123–149.

[9] These Conferences on colonial education were held in New Haven (1934), Salisbury, Southern Rhodesia (1935), Hawaii (1936); North Carolina/Colorado (1937), Toronto (1939).

[10] UK Board of Education, *Special Reports on Educational Subjects, 1897–1914*. The publication most relevant to this topic is vol. V: "Education Systems in the Chief British Colonies of the British Empire," *House of Commons Sessional Papers*, vol. XXII, p. 1/1 (1900).

[11] Martin Schlunk, *Die Schulen für Eingeborene in den deutschen Schutzgebieten* (Hamburg: Hamburgischen Kolonialinstituts/L. Freidrichsen & Co., 1914).

[12] It is important to note that the annual reports of the Department of Public Education in the Cape Colony also offer a remarkable depth of evidence from the middle of the nineteenth century.

[13] Thomas Jesse Jones, *Education in Africa* (New York: Phelps Stokes Fund, 1922); *Education in East Africa* (New York: Phelps Stokes Fund, 1924).

independence of the African colonies,"[14] but the pace of such reforms needs to be understood in incremental terms with only the gradual emergence of broad plans for social reform.

In the field of education, the first landmark in this regard took the form of the Colonial Office (CO) statement on *Education Policy in British Tropical Africa* (1925).[15] These initiatives provided the template for much debate into the 1930s regarding the nature of the school curriculum and the extent of state support for education. Here, the major emphasis was on *adapted education* to support Lord Lugard's policy of Indirect Rule[16] and a "Progressivist" agenda of rural community education that had initially been piloted in the postbellum South of the USA.[17] Out of these initiatives, there emerged the beginning of a "scientific approach" to education and policy development to replace the previous dependence on the field experience of missionaries and colonial officials. This new approach was based in part upon the linkages between management and science that were being forged in relation to business and education in the USA.[18] The move by the CO to establish the Advisory Committee on Native Education in Tropical Africa (ACNETA) in 1923, subsequently called the Advisory Committee for Education in the Colonies (ACEC), marked a clear, if tentative, initiative to formalize educational policy discussion in an age of increasing uncertainty. Other significant CO Memos which will be referred to below were: *The Place of the Vernacular in Native Education* (1927)[19]; *A Biological Approach*

---

[14] Hargreaves, *Decolonization in Africa*, 2.

[15] Colonial Office (CO) Cmd. 2347, 1925.

[16] Lord Lugard, *Dual Mandate in Tropical Africa* (London: Frank Cass, 1922). A parallel text for French Africa was Albert Sarraut, *La Mise en valeur des Colonies francaises* (Paris: Payot, 1923). See also Anon, "Indirect Rule in Africa and Its Bearing on Educational Development," *Overseas Education* IV, no. 1 (1932): 82–84.

[17] Kenneth King, *Pan-Africanism and Education: A Study of Race Philanthropy and Education in the Southern States of America and East Africa* (Oxford: Clarendon Press, 1971).

[18] Lawrence A. Cremin, *The Transformation of the School "Progressivism" in American Education 1876–1957* (New York: Vintage, 1964); David Labaree, *Education, Markets and the Public Good* (London: Routledge, 2007); Diane Ravitch, *Left Back: A Century of Failed School Reforms* (New York: Simons & Schuster, 2001).

[19] CO: ACNETA: Africa, No. 1110: 1927.

to *Native Education in East Africa* (1930)[20]; *Compulsory Education in the Colonies* (1930)[21]; *Grants-in-Aid to Education* (1930)[22]; *Education of African Communities* (1935)[23]; *Mass Education in African Societies* (1944)[24]; and *Education for Citizenship* (1948).[25]

This led to the emergence of further influences on policy development—namely its increasing association with science and research—the expanded role of Universities and "educational experts" in training educators and conducting research, with the gradual shaping of a research culture which was expected to be "relevant" to policy concerns. This demonstrated the first signs of state intervention in welfare and education issues, despite very constrained budgets for research, and demonstrated that mission and state were to forge new alliance to meet the increasing demand for education, health and welfare services, parallel to the increasingly complex issues raised by the volatile political atmosphere in the international arena and in the African colonial context from the 1930s.

The IMC launched its own initiatives in this regard by establishing a Department of Social and Industrial Research in 1930,[26] but it was mainly through the efforts of the International Institute of African Languages and Culture (IIALC),[27] funded by the Rockefeller Foundation, that most of this work was to be pursued.[28] In that context, it was widely held that the emergent discipline of social anthropology held the keys to the evolution of expertise which would enable more efficient, and perhaps even more just, government/governance of the empire. There was as a result an extended association between colonial

[20] CO: Africa (East) No. 1134 (1930).
[21] CO: ACEC 847/3/15 (1933).
[22] CO: ACEC Col. 84 (1933).
[23] CO: (ACEC) No. 103 (London: HMSO, 1935).
[24] London: HMSO, 1944.
[25] Col. 216-1948; London: HMSO, 1948.
[26] Kallaway, "Education, Health."
[27] Later to be called the International Africa Institute [IAI].
[28] It is important to note that the establishment of a variety of institutions contributed substantially to the emergence of the research culture under discussion. In Britain, the key institutions involved in this context were: The School of Oriental (and African) Studies; the London School of Hygiene and Tropical Medicine (LSHTM); the London School of Economics (LSE) and the Oversea Division of the Institute of Education, London University.

education and anthropology, though the outcomes of that exercise did not prove particularly promising from the point of view of the officials charged with framing and implementing policy.[29] For all that, leading anthropologists like Malinowski at the London School of Economics made great claims for the relevance of this research for addressing the issue of "culture contact" which he asserted was central to understanding the dynamic of the colonial situation.[30]

German missionaries, both under the Kaiser and from the 1920s when they returned to the African mission field, focussed on issues of culture in education which had played a dominant role in the establishment of a German national identity since the 1880s. They were better equipped with the scientific tools of modern research than most other missionaries, and particularly in the East African context, they argued for an increased focus on indigenous cultures and languages in the development of African education—in part because this was the most effective means for proselytization. This view was defended by a range of progressive education arguments in favor of the use of the vernacular as a medium of instruction in education. The work of German linguists like Diedrich Westermann, who had senior posts both at Berlin University and the IIALC in London, aimed at the promotion of African languages and securing the textbooks and materials to make indigenous language instruction viable in West, East and Southern Africa.[31]

Another theme that informed colonial education in East Africa in the early 1930s was the attempt to promote secular and scientific education in the schools. This was defended in terms of the need to 'modernize' education and strengthen modern secular knowledge in a field

---

[29] Peter Kallaway, "Science and Policy: Anthropology and Education in British Colonial Africa During the Inter-War Years," *Paedagogica Historica* 48, no. 3 (2012): 411–430.

[30] Bronislaw Malinowski, "The Rationalization of Anthropology and Administration," *Africa* 3, no. 4 (1930): 405–430; "Native Education and Culture Contact," *International Review of Missions* 25 (1936): 480–515.

[31] Peter Kallaway, "Volkskirche, Völkerkunde and Apartheid: Lutheran Missions, German Anthropology and Science in African Education," in *Contested Relations: Protestantism Between Southern Africa and Germany from the 1930s to the Apartheid Era*, ed. by Hanns Lessing, Tilman Dedering, Jürgen Kampmann, and Dirkie Smit (Wiesbaden: Harrassowitz Verlag, 2015), 155–176; "Diedrich Westermann and the Ambiguities of Colonial Science in the Inter-War Era," *Journal of Imperial and Commonwealth History* 45, no. 6 (2017): 871–893.

dominated by missions. The drafting of a Memo on *Biology and its place in Native Education in East Africa*,[32] promoted by the British Social Hygiene Council (BSHC), was also aimed at introducing a science-based core curriculum that would counter what were considered to be pagan beliefs or the promote healthcare and economic development. This secular/scientific approach to education was linked to international trends which highlighted progressive pedagogy and the promotion of student motivation which sought to move away from the older tradition of passive rote-learning. Educational curricula were to focus on environmental awareness—plants, animals, agriculture, hygiene, nutrition, economic environment—and the role of women and children in society. The linking of the politics and policy of education to wider issues of welfare and society, that were increasingly being stressed by the League of Nations, reflected contemporary political and economic concerns in Britain and Europe in the 1930s. As indicated above, they came to have a significant bearing on policy development in the colonial context.

Welfare and Education

It is important to see the increasing attention to education in the context of wider attempts by the actors referred to above to come to grips with the variety of challenges presented to colonial government in the interwar years. In this context, there was a broad attempt to establish the elements of a welfare system in British African colonies, by promoting research into areas such as health, child welfare, nutrition, juvenile delinquency, the education of women and girls, as well as adult and higher education from the time of the first Colonial Development Act (1929) to the Colonial Development and Welfare Act of 1940.[33] The establishment of an Advisory Committee on Social Welfare (1943) represented a colonial postscript to the wartime Beveridge Report on Social Welfare in

---

[32] Julian Huxley, *Biological Approaches to Native Education in East Africa* (CO Africa (East) No. 1134 (1930); *Biology and Its Place in Native Education in East Africa* (London: HMSO, 1930).

[33] BPP *Colonial Welfare and Development Act* (1940); Cmd. 6175-1940 *Statement of Policy on Colonial Development and Welfare* (London: HMSO, 1940). For the Reports of the Colonial Development Fund for 1929–1941 see BPP Cmd. 3540, 3876, 4079, 4316, 4634, 4916, 5202, 5537, 5789, 6062, 6298.

the UK.[34] The establishment of a Social Services Department at the CO in 1939 represented a milestone. Although little was achieved in terms of the implementation of broad welfare plans, given the weakness of colonial states and the shortage of financial resources due to the war, there is evidence of some degree of concern with issues that would be taken up more fully at a later time.[35] Following on the work of Hetherington, Hodge and Tilley, I will therefore attempt to identify those areas that were highlighted in the process in the hope that others will explore them further. As a supplement to this enquiry, I will also indicate to what extent such welfare measures were to influence South Africa during this period prior to the advent of apartheid from 1948. I will refer to the provisional proposal for a national health and welfare system from 1939, and concern for issues such as nutrition (school feeding schemes), juvenile delinquency and vocational education. The key references for these events are the report of the National Conference on Social Work (1937), the establishment of a Department of Social Welfare (1937), the report of the commission to investigate the feasibility of a National Health Service (the Gluckman Report, 1944) and a Report on Social Security (the Batson Report, 1944).[36]

It is important to note at the outset that the use of the term "development" changes during the time under review, and this has considerable

---

[34] UK. Cmd. 6404 (1942) *Report on Social Insurance and Allied Services* (Beveridge Report).

[35] BPP Cmd. 6175 (1940) *Statement of Policy on Colonial Development and Welfare* (London: HMSO, 1940). The report of Sir Frank Stockdale on *Development and Welfare in the West Indies* paved the way for further thinking about the African context. BPP Colonial No. 189/HMSO, 1945.

[36] Union of South Africa, *Report of the National Conference on Social Work* (Johannesburg: Government Printer, 1937); U.G. No. 30-1944: National Health Services Commission of South Africa (the Gluckman Report): UG No. 14-1944: *Report of the Inter-Departmental Committee on Social Security* (the Batson Report). For a comprehensive survey of these issues see Ellen Hellman (ed.), *Handbook on Race Relations in South Africa* (Johannesburg: SAIRR, 1949), Chs. XVI, XVII. See Shula Marks, "Industrialization, Rural Health, and the 1944 National Health Services Commission in South Africa," in *The Social Basis of Health and Healing in Africa*, ed. by Steven Frierman and John M. Janzen (Berkeley: UCLA Press, 1992), 132–161; David Duncan, "The Origins of the 'Welfare State' in Pre-apartheid South Africa," *ICS Collected Seminar Papers* (London University, 1992).

significance for this enquiry. The 1929 Colonial Development Act was entirely focussed on *economic* development, or growth, and essentially shared the ethos of the Empire Marketing Board (EMB, 1926) which stressed the expansion of the colonial economies as a contribution to the British exchequer and a direct solution to the economic woes of the Depression. It was only successful after a long battle with Treasury over its potential as an element of the solution to the problem of mass unemployment in Britain.[37] Only incrementally over the course of the 1930s did the term "development" come to take on its modern connotations which focus on the social or welfare aspects of the colonial situation—what Hodge terms "the 'human side' of development."[38] This was reflected in the remarks of Lord De La Warr, the Under-Secretary of State for the Colonies in the late 1930s, when he argued that "the real Development needed in Africa today is not the investment of large sums of capital but the improvement of human capital."[39] This took place in the context of challenges presented by emergent social policy discourse in Britain with the rise of the Labour Party and Fabian influence, the tensions over the meaning of the Empire generated by the Closer Union debate,[40] and Labour's experiment with the "Doctrine of Native Paramountcy" in East Africa[41]; the rise of fascism and communism in Europe, and, perhaps most significantly, the rise of African nationalism.

The focus on "the African child" and child welfare seems to present a potential litmus test for a sensitivity to wider welfare issues. It also highlights the influence of the League of Nations in focussing attention of the colonial powers on development and welfare issues. The initiative can be traced to the international conferences on the topic held under the aegis of the League of Nations. The CO sent delegates to the first International Congress on Child Welfare in 1925[42] and to the larger

---

[37] See Constantine, *The Making of British*, Chs. VI and VII. Constantine notes that the CO strongly resisted these policies based on economic criteria.

[38] Hodge, *Triumph of the Expert*, Chapter 4.

[39] Memo by Lord de la Warr, n.d. [1937] Co 852/118/15279/5 cited by Constantine, *The Making...*, 221, 230.

[40] See J. H. Oldham, *White and Black in Africa: A Critical Examination of the Rhodes Lectures of General Smuts* (London: Longmans, 1930).

[41] Robert G. Gregory, *Sydney Webb and East Africa* (Berkeley: University of California Press, 1962).

[42] PRO CO 854/61-1925.

International Conference on the African Child (1931), both held in Geneva. Here the issues of child rights and humanitarian concerns took center stage.[43] It does not seem as if this issue was taken up directly by colonial governments, but it was tackled obliquely in various ways and with varying degrees of success.

In general terms, the health and medical issues relating to the colonial context had focussed on specific issues like the treatment of sleeping sickness or yellow fever prior to 1920 when there was a comprehensive report by a Departmental Committee on Colonial Medical Services.[44] The CO created the post of a Chief Medical Officers and this remained part of its establishment from 1926 to 1961. In the 1930s, a Colonial Medical Research Fund was initiated with a Committee to oversee its affairs. This led to a joint initiative by the British Medical Association (BMA) and the CO to establish a Medical Research Board.[45] Two conferences took place in the wake of these moves: one on Medical Research in East Africa (1934) and a Pan-African Health Conference held in Johannesburg in 1935.[46] Only after World War II was a Director of Colonial Medical Research appointed by the CO. During the War, the South African government also established a Commission to report on the feasibility of a National Health Service on the Beveridge model under the future Minister of Health, Henry Gluckman.[47] One of the key issues of concern that emerged from these activities was the question of food security and nutrition in Africa. The League of Nations enquiry

---

[43] Save the Children's Fund, *International Conference on the African Child* (Geneva: League of Nations, 1931); Evelyn Sharp, *The African Child: An Account of the International Conference on African Children, Geneva* (S.I. Longman, 1931); Dominique Marshall, "Children's Rights in Imperial Political Cultures: Missionary and Humanitarian Contributions to the Conference on the African Child of 1931," *International Journal of Children's Rights* 12 (2004): 273–318.

[44] BPP. Cmd. 939, XII, 267, September 1920.

[45] See CO 1931: Papers on the Health and Progress of Native Populations; CO/BMA Report on *Health Services in the Empire*. See Hodge, *Triumph of the Expert*, 314; CO 323/1112/8.

[46] The Johannesburg event was reported in the *Quart. Bull. Hlth. Org., LoN*, 5 (1) (1936): 1–209. It was almost entirely concerned with infectious diseases, with few references to social issues.

[47] UG No. 30-1944; Hellman, *Handbook on Race*, Ch. XVI (see f. 37).

into this issue produced a comprehensive four-volume report in 1936,[48] which set the tone for a wealth of publications on the topic in the next few years, and this provided the foundation for a variety of initiatives in this field. This was followed by the establishment of Standing Committee on Nutrition in the Colonial Empire under the auspices of the CO Economic Advisory Committee. It produced a report on *Nutrition in the Colonial Empire* (1938–1939)[49] and another from the newly established CO Social Services Department in 1943.[50] Audrey Richards also conducted pathbreaking work in anthropology, by linking ethnographic work to economics and diet in Central Africa.[51] However, it is difficult to establish to what extent these initiatives were to influence policy in colonial Africa. In South Africa, these trends were reflected by the holding of a National Nutritional Conference hosted by the South African Institute of Race Relations (SAIRR) and the publication of findings on the topic in 1939.[52] One of the consequences of this event was the establishment of state-sponsored national school feeding scheme in 1941–1942 that was expanded to include black school children.[53] This policy was in

---

[48] League of Nations, *The Problem of Nutrition* (Geneva: LoN, 1936); *Final Report of the Mixed Committee of the League of Nations on the Relations of Nutrition to Health, Agriculture and Economic Policy* (Geneva: LoN, 1937).

[49] *First Report of the Economic Advisory Committee on Nutrition in the Colonial Empire*: Part I. Nutrition in the Colonial Empire, Part II. Summary of Information Regarding Nutrition in the Colonial Empire (BPP Pt I: Cmd. 6050; Part II Cmd. 6051) (London: HMSO, 1938–1939).

[50] CO Dept of Social Services, *Memo on Nutrition in the Colonial Empire* 1943; John Scott, "Education and Nutrition in the Colonies," *Oversea Education* IX, no. 1 (October 1937): 39–40.

[51] Audrey Richards, *Hunger and Work in a Savage Tribe: A Functional Study of Nutrition Among the Southern Bantu* (London: George Routledge, 1932); *Land, Labour and Diet in Northern Rhodesia: An Economic Study of the Bemba Tribe* (London: OUP/IAI, 1939). Reviewed by E. B. Worthington in *Africa* XIII, no. 1 (1940): 77–82.

[52] *SAIRR Journal* 6 (3)(1939); "Findings of the Council on Nutrition," SAIRR RR9/40.

[53] See Quentin Whyte, *Native School Feeding* (Johannesburg: SAIRR, 1949); Union of South Africa, *Report of a Committee of Enquiry into the Native School Feeding Scheme* (Cillie Commission), 1949.

operation until the 1950s when it was abandoned by the National Party government in terms of apartheid policy.[54]

Another area of focus in relation to health care, social welfare and education was associated with the role and place of Woman and Children in colonial society.[55] At one level, this was about the access of this group to welfare services and education. At another, it was concerned about the place of women in society, to what extent they were subject to indigenous law and practices, and to what extent they fell under the legal mandate of the colonial state. The Church Missionary Society conference on "The Education of Women and Girls" in 1925[56] was a precursor to much debate on the topic in the 1930s. In 1927, the Australian-born British educationalist, Amy Whitelaw, and Canon Broomfield reported to ACNETA on the *Education of Women and Girls in East Africa*. This was followed by a Memo on *Education of African Women* by Sara Burstall and Whitelaw to the ACEC. Mary Blacklock's work on "The Welfare of Women and Children in the Colonies" was pathbreaking, linking health to social issues and education.[57]

In 1937, the CO produced a document on the topic *Welfare of Women in Tropical Africa*.[58] The published correspondence on this paper

---

[54] Peter Kallaway, "Policy Challenges for Education in the 'New' South Africa: The Case for School Feeding in the Context of Social and Economic Construction," *Transformation* 31 (1996): 1–24.

[55] Clive Whitehead, "The Education of Women and Girls: An Aspect of British Colonial Policy," *Journal of Educational Administration and History* 16, no. 2 (1984): 24–34; Joanna Lewis, *Empire and State-Building: War and Welfare in Kenya, 1925–52* (Oxford: James Currey, 2000), Ch. 1; Janet Welch, "The Goal of Women's Education in Africa," *Oversea Education* XI, no. 2 (1940): 65–72; Margaret Wrong, "The Education of African Women in a Changing World," in *Yearbook of Education* (London: Evans Bros., 1940), 497–520.

[56] IMC/CBMS African Education Group, Box 207/243/258/1224/1231/; CO 859/4 [1-12] 4/7.

[57] Sara Burstall and A. Whitelaw, *Memo on the Education of African Women* (IMC/CBMS Box 224); Mary Blacklock, "The Welfare of Women and Children in the Colonies," *Annals of Tropical Medicine and Parasitology* 2 (1936): 221–265.

[58] CO, *Welfare of Women in Tropical* (London: HMSO, 1937). Also see Correspondence relating to the Welfare of Women in Tropical Africa BPP CO 859/4 [1-12]/ (London: HMSO, 1938).

reveals the complexities of the legal status of women in East Africa and the problem of how this was to be handled by the CO. Between 1940 and 1943, there were a number of reports on the education and welfare of women and girls in Africa including a comprehensive 1943 CO Memo on *Women's Education and Welfare in Africa* (1943).[59] Charlotte Hastings has completed an excellent study of the influence of these policies in the specific context of Southern Nigeria in the inter-war years.[60] In South Africa, there seems to have been little focus on these issues.

Reflecting international trends, the issue of juvenile delinquency attracted systematic attention in some area like Kenya and South Africa where youth crime and antisocial behavior among male Africans was defined as an important social problem in need to state intervention. As Ellen Hellman pointed out in relation to South Africa, this often represented "an attitude of defiance from African and Colored juveniles toward the existing social structure" that required intervention in the form of welfare of some kind.[61] Between 1933 and 1936, there were four reports on juvenile crime in Kenya which led to the passing of legislation to deal with the problems including the establishment of the Kabete Reformatory near Nairobi. There was also a CO report on *Juvenile Welfare in the Colonies* in 1942.[62] In South Africa, legislation was also passed to deal with this issue, but it was initially aimed at white juveniles. There was a government report on the topic in 1937 and a National Juvenile Delinquency conference held in Johannesburg under the auspices of the SAIRR in 1938.[63] Ellen Hellman's pamphlet on *Problems of Urban Bantu Youth*[64] led to an expansion of the system for dealing with these issues, including the passing of a revised Children's Act (UG No. 31-1937) with the extension of Industrial Schools for

---

[59] CO Report on *Education and Welfare of Women and Girls in Africa* in 1943. BPP Colonial, No. 1169.

[60] Charlotte Hastings, "Gendered Education Between Metropole and Colony: Sara Burstall, Margaret Faith Wordsworth and Girl's Schooling in Inter-War Southern Nigeria," PhD diss., University of Edinburgh, 2011.

[61] Ellen Hellman, *Problems of Urban Bantu Youth* (Johannesburg: SAIRR, 1949), 94.

[62] BPP CO 885/103; 859/73/12770/43 (1942); see Chloe Campbell, *Race and Empire: Eugenics in Colonial Kenya* (Manchester: Manchester University Press, 2006).

[63] UG 38-1937: Report of the Interdepartmental Committee on Destitute, Maladjusted and Delinquent Children and Young Persons, 1934–1937.

[64] Hellman, *Problem of Urban*.

whites, and the establishment of Ottery School of Industries for Colored boys in Cape Town and Diepkloof Reformatory in Johannesburg for Africans, but the facilities supplied for African and Colored youth were always grossly inadequate.[65]

In addition to the above measures, the provision of education gradually drew greater attention during from the 1930s. In addition to the four major Memos on topic in 1933, 1935, 1944, 1948, cited above, there were also a variety of attempt to focus on technical and vocational education[66] and higher education.[67] In South Africa, there was also a flurry of activity relating to these issues during the war years relating to adult education and technical/vocational education.[68] Much of this related to the provision for whites, but there were indications of the relaxation of the color bar in the interests of economic growth and a broadening of the social security net.

---

[65] Linda Chisholm, *Reformatories and Industrial Schools in South Africa: A Study of Class, Colour and Gender in the Period Between 1882 and 1939*, PhD diss., University of the Witwatersrand, 1989 (unpublished); Azeem Badroodien, *A History of the Ottery School of Industries in Cape Town: Race, Welfare and Social Order in the Period 1937 to 1968*, PhD diss., University of the Western Cape, 2000 (unpublished); Alan Paton, *Diepkloof: Reflections on Diepkloof Reformatory* (Cape Town: David Philip, 1987).

[66] Lord Hailey, *An African Survey* (Oxford: Oxford University Press, 1938), 1243–1248; *Survey of Vocational Agricultural Education in the Colonial Empire* (CO Col. 124) (HMSO, 1937); *Survey of Vocational in Colonial Empire* (Col. 177-1940) and *Survey of in the Colonies* (report by F. J. Harlow) ACEC (53)19: 1953. In 1960, William McLean prepared a briefing for parliament "Notes on in the Colonies" Memo. 24B (1960).

[67] Hailey, *An African Survey*, 1248–1250; CO ACEC Misc. 423: *Report on Higher Education in East Africa* (Currie Commission, 1932–1933); BPP Col. No. 142: *Report of the Commission on Higher Education in East Africa* (de la Warr Commission) (CO 8467/9/6 (1937), HMSO, 1937); *Report of the Commission in Higher Education in West Africa* (Elliott) (Cmd. 6647; 6654; 6655/HMSO, 1945); Report on *Higher Education in West Africa* (Ashby) (Lagos; Government Printer, 1960). It is important to note that some of this motivation for the expansion of HE in Africa came from the fear that Africans studying abroad, and particularly in the USA, might be exposed to radical influences inimical to colonial rule. See Appolos O. Nwauwa, "The British Establishment of Universities in Tropical Africa, 1920–48: A Reaction Against the Spread of American 'Radical' Influences," *Cahiers d'études africaines* 130 (1993): 1247–1274; Kenneth King, *Pan-Africanism and Education*.

[68] *Select Committee on Adult Education* (Eybers) (SA Official: UG 35-1945); *Select Committee on Technical and Vocational Education* (De Villiers), SA Official: UG 65-1948.

Conclusion

These various political, scientific, religious, philosophical and humanitarian themes contested the policy terrain in colonial Africa and were joined up in multiple ways against the background of the debates about Keynesian economics and social welfare that were the informing political debate about education in Europe and the America during the 1930s. Lord Hailey's great *An African Survey* made an effort to place all the debates about African development within a scientific and analytical framework.[69] Education was a key issue of contestation in the context of future policy concerns relating to the nature of "development." Although "adapted education" was not entirely abandoned, and although the culturalist vision of the German linguistics and anthropologists was not forsaken, formal curriculum models based on international norms for formal mass schooling retained their popularity with African educators, parents and students and had a conservative influence on the nature of the school and the curriculum in the years beyond 1945, inhibiting radical educational reform.

The goal of widening access to schooling was a constant refrain, but the lack of resources in these fragile colonial states restricted this expansion. By the advent of World War II, little had been accomplished with regard to the establishment of comprehensive welfare or schooling systems. Yet, as Hodge demonstrates, it was "on the basis of these fragile (policy) constructions that the key policy objectives on which the postwar colonial development offensive would hinge."[70] Although beyond the scope of this enquiry, recent research indicates that many of the initiatives which dated from this time provided the scaffolding for the task of "development" in the very different context of independent Africa from the 1950s referred to by Hans Weiler. The strands of development policy were subsequently reconstituted within the frameworks that were evolved by the agencies of the United Nations Organization and the World Bank. Within the optimistic atmosphere of the post-colonial politics of the 1950s and 1960s, a new infrastructure of "development studies" referred to above was created. Yet, as Hans Weiler noted graphically, that project was best understood as an aspect of an "Age of Innocence"

---

[69] Hailey, *An African Survey*; Hodge, *Triumph of the Expert*; Tilley, *Africa as a Living Laboratory* (2011).

[70] Hodge, *Triumph of the Expert*, 143.

Table 2.1 Welfare and education in colonial Africa and South Africa, 1910–1945

Date	Britain	British Africa	South Africa Union
1910	IMC Conference, Edinburgh		
1911	Imperial Education Conference		
1914–1918		World War I	
1917			C. T. Loram, *Native Education in South Africa*
1919		East African Education Commission	
1922		Lugard, *Dual Mandate in Tropical Africa*	
1921–1924		Phelps Stokes Commissions on *Education in Africa*	
1923	Imperial Education Conference Establishment of ACNETA		
1925	CO Memo on *Educational Policy in British Tropical Africa* IMC Conference on the Education of Women and Girls in Africa (London)	Establishment of *Jeanes Schools* in East and Central Africa	
1926	Establishment of the IIALC Le Zoute (IMC) Conference on Colonial Education		
1927	ACNETA report on Vernacular Languages in African education		
1929	Colonial Development Act (establishment of ACEC)		

(continued)

Table 2.1 (continued)

Date	Britain	British Africa	South Africa Union
1929–1930	Memo on *A Biological Approach to Education in East Africa* (J. Huxley) Memo on Grants-in Aid to Educational Institutions		
1931	International Conference on the African Child (LoN/Geneva) British Commonwealth Conference on Education		
1932–1934			Carnegie Commission on Poor Whites in SA
1932			Native Economic Commission
1934			New Era Fellowship Conference (NEF) in South Africa
1935		CO Memo on *Education in African Communities* (no. 103) Inter-Territorial *Jeanes Schools* Conference (Salisbury)	
1935–1936			Inter-Departmental Commission on Native Education
1936–1938		League of Nations Nutrition Reports CO Report on Nutrition in the Colonies	
1937		CO Report on Higher Education in East Africa	
1939		Establishment of Social Services Department at the CO	

(continued)

Table 2.1 (continued)

Date	Britain	British Africa	South Africa Union
1939–1945		World War II	
1940	UK Colonial Development and Welfare Act	CO Report on the Education of Women and Girls in Africa	
1941			School Feeding schemes in South Africa
1942	UK Beveridge Report on recommendations for Welfare State	CO Report on Juvenile Delinquents in the Colonies	
1943		CO Nutrition Committee of the British Empire Establishment of CO Advisory Committee on Social Welfare	Reports on Adult Education/Vocational and Technical Education/Welfare and Health commissions
1944	Butler Act—Free Secondary Education in the UK	CO Report on *Mass Education in African Society*	
1945		CO Report on Higher Education in the Colonies	
1948		CO Report on *Education for Citizenship in Africa*	

that characterized the post-colonial era. Looking back from what he saw as an "Age of Scepticism" in the late 1970s, Weiler sought to understand how the dreams of increasing equity had failed to be realized and why education had failed to contribute to the goals of equity in ways that had been taken for granted during the heyday of the "Development Decades."[71] This chapter hopes to provide preliminary answers to these challenging questions (Table 2.1).

---

[71] Hans N. Weiler. "Education and Development: From the Age of Innocence to the Age of Scepticism," *Comparative Education* 14, no. 3 (1978): 179–198.

Bibliography

Archival Sources

British Parliamentary Papers and Colonial Office documents and archival references, as well as references from the IMC/CBMS collection at SOAS library, are cited in the footnotes.
The same applies to South African government papers.

References

Badroodien, Azeem. "A History of the Ottery School of Industries in Cape Town: Race, Welfare and Social Order in the Period 1937 to 1968." PhD diss., University of the Western Cape, 2000.

Blacklock, Mary. "The Welfare of Women and Children in the Colonies." *Annals of Tropical Medicine and Parasitology* 2 (1936): 221–265.

Campbell, Chloe. *Race and Empire: Eugenics in Colonial Kenya.* Manchester: Manchester University Press, 2006.

Carnoy, Martin. *Education and Cultural Imperialism.* New York: David McKay, 1974.

Cell, John. *Hailey: A Study of British Imperialism, 1872–1969.* Cambridge: Cambridge University Press, 1992.

Chisholm, Linda. "Reformatories and Industrial Schools in South Africa: A Study of Class, Colour and Gender in the Period Between 1882 and 1939." PhD diss., University of the Witwatersrand, 2000.

Constantine, Stephen. *The Making of British Colonial Development Policy 1914–1940.* London: Frank Cass, 1984.

Cooper, Frederick. *Africa Since 1940: The Past of the Present.* Cambridge: Cambridge University Press, 1996.

Cremin, Lawrence A. *The Transformation of the School: Progressivism in American Education 1876–1957.* New York: Vintage, 1964.

Darwin, John. "Decolonization and the End of Empire." In *Oxford History of the British Empire*, edited by Robin W. Winks, vol. V, 541–557. Oxford: Oxford University Press, 1999.

Duncan, David. "The Origins of the 'Welfare State' in Pre-apartheid South Africa." Institute of Commonwealth Studies Collected Seminar Papers on *the Societies of Southern Africa*, 1992, 106–119.

Green, Andy. *Education and State Formation: The Rise of Education Systems in England, France and the USA.* London: Macmillan, 1990.

Gregory, Robert G. *Sydney Webb and East Africa.* Berkeley: University of California, 1962.

Hailey, Lord. *The African Survey.* Oxford: Oxford University Press, 1938.

Hargreaves, John D. *Decolonization in Africa.* London: Longman, 1988.
Hastings, Charlotte. "Gendered Education Between Metropole and Colony: Sara Burstall, Margaret Faith Wordsworth and Girl's Schooling in Inter-War Southern Nigeria." PhD diss., University of Edinburgh, 2011.
Hellman, Ellen, ed. *Handbook on Race Relations in South Africa.* Johannesburg: SAIRR, 1949.
Hetherington, Penelope. *British Paternalism and Africa.* London: Frank Cass, 1978.
Hodge, Joseph M. *Triumph of the Expert: Agrarian Doctrines of Development and the Legacies of British Colonialism.* Athens, OH: University of Ohio Press, 2007.
Huxley, Julian. *A Biological Approach to Native Education in East Africa,* CO Africa (East) No. 1134 (1930); *Biology and Its Place in Native Education in East Africa.* London: HMSO, 1930.
Jensz, Felicity. "The 1910 Edinburgh World Missionary Conference and Comparative Colonial Education." *History of Education* 47, no. 3 (May 2018): 399–414. Special section: edited by Rebecca Swartz and Peter Kallaway on "Imperial, Global and Local Histories of Colonial Educational."
Jones, Thomas Jesse. *Education in Africa.* New York: Phelps Stokes Fund, 1922.
———. *Education in East Africa.* New York: Phelps Stokes Fund, 1924.
Kallaway, Peter. "Conference Litmus: The Development of a Conference and Policy Culture in the Inter-War Period with Special Reference to the New Education Fellowship and British Colonial Education in Southern Africa." In *Transformations in Schooling: Historical and Comparative Perspectives,* edited by Kim Tolley, 123–149. New York: Palgrave Macmillan, 2006.
———. "Diedrich Westermann and the Ambiguities of Colonial Science in the Inter-War Era." *Journal of Imperial and Commonwealth History* 45, no. 6 (2017): 871–893.
———. "Education, Health and Social Welfare in the late Colonial Context: The International Missionary Council and Educational Transition in the Inter-War Years with Specific Reference to Colonial Africa." *History of Education* 38, no. 2 (2009): 217–246.
———. "Policy Challenges for Education in the 'New' South Africa: The Case for School Feeding in the Context of Social and Economic Construction." *Transformation* 31 (1996): 1–24.
———. "Science and Policy: Anthropology and Education in the British Colonial Africa During the Inter-War Years." *Pedagogica Historica* 48, no. 3 (2012): 411–430.
———. "Volkskirche, Völkerkunde and Apartheid: Lutheran Missions, German Anthropology and Science in African Education." In *Contested Relations: Protestantism Between Southern Africa and Germany from the 1930s to the Apartheid Era,* edited by Hanns Lessing, Tilman Dedering, Jürgen Kampmann, and Dirkie Smit, 55–176. Wiesbaden: Harrassowitz Verlag, 2015.

Kallaway, Peter, and Rebecca Swartz, eds. *Empire and Education in Africa*. New York: Peter Lang, 2017.

King, Kenneth. *Pan Africanism and Education*. Oxford: Clarendon Press, 1971.

Labaree, David. *Education: Markets and the Public Good*. New York: Routledge, 2007.

League of Nations. *Final Report of the Mixed Committee of the League of Nations on the Relations of Nutrition to Health, Agriculture and Economic Policy*. Geneva: LoN, 1937.

———. *The Problem of Nutrition*. Geneva: LoN, 1936.

Lewis, Joanna. *Empire and State-Building: War and Welfare in Kenya, 1925–52*. Oxford: James Currey, 2000.

Lugard, Lord. *Dual Mandate in Tropical Africa*. London: Frank Cass, 1922.

Malinowski, Bronislaw. "Native Education and Culture Contact." *International Review of Missions* 25 (1936): 480–515.

———. "The Rationalization of Anthropology and Administration." *Africa* 3, no. 4 (1930): 405–430.

Marks, Shula. "Industrialization, Rural Health, and the 1944 National Health Services Commission in South Africa." In *The Social Basis of Health and Healing in Africa*, edited by Steven Frierman and John M. Janzen, 132–161. Berkeley: UCLA Press, 1992.

Marshall, Dominique. "Children's Rights in Imperial Political Cultures: Missionary and Humanitarian Contributions to the Conference on the African Child of 1931." *International Journal of Children's Rights* 12 (2004): 273–318.

Nwauwa, Appolos O. "The British Establishment of Universities in Tropical Africa, 1920–48: A Reaction Against the Spread of American 'Radical' Influences." *Cahiers d'Etudes africaines* 130 (1993): 1247–1274.

Oldham, J. H. *White and Black in Africa: A Critical Examination of the Rhodes Lectures of General Smuts*. London: Longmans, 1930.

Paton, Alan. *Diepkloof: Reflections on Diepkloof Reformatory*. Cape Town: David Philip, 1987.

Ravitch, Diane. *Left Back: A Century of Failed School Reforms*. New York: Simons & Schuster, 2001.

Rawson, W., ed. *Education in a Changing Commonwealth*. London: HMSO, 1931.

Richards, Audrey. *Hunger and Work in a Savage Tribe: A Functional Study of Nutrition Among the Southern Bantu*. London: George Routledge, 1932.

———. *Land, Labour and Diet in Northern Rhodesia: An Economic Study of the Bemba Tribe*. London: OUP/IAI, 1939.

Sanderson, Michael. *Education, Economic Change and Society in England, 1780–1870*. London: Macmillan, 1983.

Sarraut, Albert. *La Mise en valeur des Colonies françaises*. Paris: Payot, 1923.

Schlunk, Martin. *Die Schulen für Eingeborene in den deutschen Schutzgebieten.* Hamburg: Hamburgischen Kolonialinstituts/L. Freidrichsen & Co., 1914.

Scott, John. "Education and Nutrition in the Colonies." *Oversea Education* IX, no. 1 (October 1937): 39–40.

Sharp, Evelyn. *The African Child: An Account of the International Conference on African Children.* Geneva: S.I. Longman, 1931.

Silver, Harold. *Equal Opportunity in Education.* London: Methuen, 1973.

Tilley, Helen. *Africa as a Living Laboratory.* Chicago: University of Chicago Press, 2011.

Tyack, David, and Larry Cuban. *Tinkering Towards Utopia: A Century of Public School Reform.* Cambridge, MA: Harvard University Press, 1995.

Watson, Keith, ed. *Education in the Third World.* London: Croom Helm, 1982.

Weiler, Hans N. "Education and Development: From the Age of Innocence to the Age of Scepticism." *Comparative Education* 14, no. 3 (1978): 179–198.

Whitehead, Clive. "The Education of Women and Girls: An Aspect of British Colonial Policy." *Journal of Educational Administration and History* 16, no. 2 (1984): 24–34.

Welch, Janet. "The Goal of Women's Education in Africa." *Oversea Education* XI, no. 2 (1940): 65–72.

Whyte, Quentin. *Native School Feeding.* Johannesburg: SAIRR, 1949.

Wrong, Margaret. "The Education of African Women in a Changing World." In *Yearbook of Education*, 497–520. London: Evans Bros., 1940.

Open Access This chapter is licensed under the terms of the Creative Commons Attribution 4.0 International License (http://creativecommons.org/licenses/by/4.0/), which permits use, sharing, adaptation, distribution and reproduction in any medium or format, as long as you give appropriate credit to the original author(s) and the source, provide a link to the Creative Commons license and indicate if changes were made.

The images or other third party material in this chapter are included in the chapter's Creative Commons license, unless indicated otherwise in a credit line to the material. If material is not included in the chapter's Creative Commons license and your intended use is not permitted by statutory regulation or exceeds the permitted use, you will need to obtain permission directly from the copyright holder.

CHAPTER 3

Une aventure sociale et humaine: The Service *des Centres Sociaux* in Algeria, 1955–1962

Brooke Durham

At ten o'clock in the morning on 15 March 1962, six *Services des centres sociaux* (Social Service Centers) directors met at Château-Royal on the outskirts of Algiers. Within minutes, armed commandos belonging to the Secret Army Organization (*Organisation de l'armée secrète*, OAS) suddenly interrupted the meeting, escorted the six directors outside, and murdered them in cold blood. These murders took place mere days before the signing of the Evian Accords, which ended the seven-year war between the French Army and the Algerian nationalist *Front de libération nationale* (National Liberation Front, FLN), and initiated the negotiation process for Algerian independence.[1] The OAS attack on the six

[1] Jean-Philippe Ould-Aoudia, *L'Assassinat de Château-Royal* (Paris: Éditions Tirésias, 1992); Association Les Amis de Max Marchand, de Mouloud Feraoun et de leurs

Thank you to the editors, JP Daughton, and Danielle Beaujon for their comments and suggestions.

B. Durham (✉)
Department of History, Stanford University, Stanford, CA, USA
e-mail: bdurham@stanford.edu

© The Author(s) 2020
D. Matasci et al. (eds.), *Education and Development in Colonial and Postcolonial Africa*, Global Histories of Education,
https://doi.org/10.1007/978-3-030-27801-4_3

directors in March 1962 effectively decapitated the *Service des Centres Sociaux* and cut short its potential recovery before official recognition of Algerian independence. This bloody bookend distorts what the *centres sociaux* represented and what they were able to accomplish during the tumultuous period between 1955 and 1962. These *centres* were much more than hapless victims of the military conflict in Algeria and represented more than a system of remedial schools and medical dispensaries. Bringing together the history of education, development, and decolonization in Algeria is crucial to this more complete understanding of the *centres sociaux* and the potential for integrating Algeria's Muslim and European communities after the Second World War.[2] The *centres sociaux*'s local and international dimensions make it an ideal institution for studying late colonial and early postcolonial development efforts, from mid-1950s integration to the 1958 Constantine Plan for Algerian development announced by President Charles de Gaulle.

On the local level, the *Service des centres sociaux* represented an official attempt sponsored by the Governor-General of Algeria, Jacques Soustelle, to modernize the Algerian masses through increasing literacy rates, improving hygiene practices, and increasing Muslim Algerians' access to medical and social services. Soustelle's vision for integration in Algeria emphasized social progress, modernity and political equality for disenfranchised Muslim Algerians, and the *centres sociaux* can be considered one of his most ambitious projects.[3] For Soustelle, integration would respect the "originality" or "personality" of Algeria and "all Algerians and French citizens would be considered part of the same greater Franco-Algerian nation" with the same rights and responsibilities.[4]

Compangons, "Le 15 mars 1962," http://max-marchand-mouloud-feraoun.fr/15-mars-1962/. On the OAS, see, Raphaëlle Branche, "FLN et OAS: Deux terrorismses en guerre d'Algérie," *European Review of History* 14, no. 3 (2007): 325–342; Arnaud Déroulède, "L'OAS étude d'une organisation clandestine," PhD diss., Paris 4, 1993.

[2] On education during the colonial period, see Alf Andrew Heggoy and Paul J. Zingg, "French Education in Revolutionary North Africa," *International Journal of Middle East Studies* 7, no. 4 (1976): 571–578; Hubert Desvages, "La scolarisation des musulmans en Algérie (1882–1962) dans l'enseignement primaire public français. Étude statistique," *Cahiers de la Méditerranée* 4, no. 1 (1972): 55–72; Ahmed Djebbar, "Éducation et société: Le cas de l'Algérie," *Revue internationale d'éducation de Sèvres* 24 (1999): 45–54.

[3] Stephen Tyre, "From Algérie Française to France Musulmane: Jacques Soustelle and the Myths and Realities of 'Integration,' 1955–1962," *French History* 20, no. 3 (September 2006): 283.

[4] Ibid., 278.

Of equal importance are the *Service des centres sociaux*'s international links to the United Nations Educational, Scientific and Cultural Organization's Fundamental Education Program, which was designed to promote world peace by helping poor and illiterate peoples survive in the modern world (on this issue, see Chapter 1 by Damiano Matasci in this book). The *centres sociaux* absorbed fundamental education's paternalist and nebulous approach to human development, but also its optimism. They manifested their commitment to integration by hiring a diverse staff of Muslims and Europeans and by producing pedagogical tools especially tailored to their Algerian situation.[5]

The *centres sociaux* and fundamental education efforts in Algeria provide insight into rapidly evolving late colonial reforms as France and other European Empires sought to reconfigure their relationship to their disintegrating empires after the Second World War (see Chapter 9 by Miguel Bandeira Jeronimo/Hugo Gonçalves Dores and Chapter 10 by Hélène Charton in this book).[6] The old colonial paradigms of the "civilizing mission," "the dual mandate," "*mise en valeur*," assimilation and association no longer passed muster in African colonial territories.[7] Simply ignoring and brutally repressing the rapidly increasing Muslim population in Algeria—as during the May 1945 protests against French rule and the outbreak of the Algerian War in 1954—proved equally insufficient. Founded at the start of the Algerian War and outlasting Soustelle's tenure as governor-general, the *centres* were restructured and renamed the *Service des Centres Sociaux Éducatifs* in 1959 to adhere to the modernization objectives of the Constantine Plan and eventual negotiations for Algerian independence. The *centres*' commitment to the integration of Algeria's Muslim and European communities remained apparent even after 1959 in the composition of their staff and in the

---

[5] Lists of *centres sociaux* employees demonstrate the diversity of the staff, see, for instance, the folders on *centres sociaux* personnel in Archives Nationales d'Outre Mer (ANOM) ALG Alger 3F/119; 3F/110.

[6] See Muriam Haleh Davis, "Restaging *Mise en valeur*: 'Postwar Imperialism' and the Plan de Constantine," *Review of Middle East Studies* 44, no. 2 (Winter 2010): 176–186.

[7] "Introduction," in *Developing Africa: Concepts and Practices in Twentieth Century Colonialism*, ed. by Martina Kopf, Gerald Hödel, and Joseph Morgan Hodge (Manchester, UK: Manchester University Press, 2014), 11–15. On Algerian postwar development, France and Europe, see, Davis, "Restaging *Mise en valeur*," 176–186; Mahfoud Bennoune, *The Making of Contemporary Algeria, 1830-1987: Colonial Upheavals and Post-independence Development* (Cambridge, UK: Cambridge University Press, 1988).

content and delivery of their pedagogical materials. Pairing the history of education with international development in Algeria offers fruitful terrain for studying local and international approaches to human development in the decade leading up to Algerian independence in 1962.[8]

Fundamental Education at UNESCO and the *Service des Centres Sociaux*

The concept of "fundamental education" was highly influential in the early days of the United Nations Educational, Scientific and Cultural Organization (UNESCO), and these ideas came to life in Algeria in the form of the *centres sociaux*. UNESCO's 1947 treatise on fundamental education defines it as "basic education," the education of the "masses," and as "an essential instrument for establishing democratic life."[9] For the UNESCO committee tasked with creating the program, fundamental education was deeply connected to social and economic development and lasting global peace. Fundamental education was intended to equip underprivileged peoples with literacy, good health, and state-of-the-art resource management to facilitate their participation in the United Nations' objective of global cooperation. Aimed at both adults and children, this program extended beyond basic reading, writing and arithmetic to include social improvements, like better hygiene, housing, and agricultural practices.[10] Economic development projects, such as improving the water supply, conserving forests, and exploiting mineral wealth, would accompany the implementation of this broad educational endeavor.[11] Fundamental education was supposed to facilitate and improve the interactions between underprivileged peoples and the modern world. This introduction to the wider world paired with technical knowledge to develop local resources was to help the underprivileged grasp the interdependent relationship between their own productive work and the global economy.[12]

[8] Amy Staples, *The Birth of Development: How the World Bank, Food and Agriculture Organization and the World Health Organization Changed the World, 1945–1965* (Kent, OH: Kent State University Press, 2006); Corinna Unger, *International Development: A Postwar History* (London: Bloomsbury, 2018).

[9] UNESCO, *Fundamental Education: Common Ground for All Peoples* (London: The Frederick Printing Co., 1947), 128.

[10] Joseph Watras, "UNESCO's Programme of Fundamental Education, 1946–1959," *History of Education* 39, no. 2 (March 2010): 219.

[11] UNESCO, *Fundamental Education*, 167.

[12] Ibid., 170–171.

Fundamental education was presented as a comprehensive approach to promote social progress while avoiding the scourge of war. In order for fundamental education to impart the ideals of human solidarity, dignity, and freedom, this type of education had to be made available to "the bright areas" and "among the most advanced peoples" in addition to the "dark areas" and "among backwards and illiterate people."[13] Fundamental education was not supposed to be inspired by charity, humanitarian zeal, or the desire to dominate or exploit; rather, the people themselves were to be the primary motivating force behind fundamental education programs.[14] The pilot Fundamental Education program took place in the Marbial valley in Haiti, and other projects took place in Senegal, Guinée, Cameroun, and Oubangui-Chari.[15] 1950s fundamental education programs eschewed elite-focused colonial assimilation and sought instead to integrate the masses on the "fringes of civilization"—i.e., the peasants, the illiterate, and the poor.[16] Colonial paternalism and condescension pervaded the idea that underprivileged people had to be *taught* to live better and adopt the "few common tools without which humanity is still practically at the level of the beast."[17] Fundamental Education unabashedly advocated changing people's behaviors to improve their standard of living on the most basic levels.

Throughout the 1950s, UNESCO drew attention to the shortcomings of colonial states by gathering statistics on social, economic, and educational inequalities that pointed to colonial possessions as the most

---

[13] Ibid., 178.

[14] Ibid., 260.

[15] In addition to Haiti, pilot fundamental education projects were proposed in China and in East Africa. See Chantalle F. Verna, "Haiti, the Rockefeller Foundation, and UNESCO's Pilot Project in Fundamental Education, 1948–1953," *Diplomatic History* 40, no. 2 (2016): 269–295; Gouverneur Deschamps, "L'Éducation de base," *La Nouvelle Revue Française d'Outre Mer*, no. 5 (May 1955, Nouvelle série): 213–217. In West Africa, the French colonial government sponsored their own basic education programs, see, Pauline Kusiak, "Instrumentalized Rationality, Cross-Cultural Mediators, and Civil Epistemologies of Late Colonialism," *Social Studies of Science* 40, no. 6 (2010): 871–902.

[16] Damiano Matasci, "Assessing Needs, Fostering Development: UNESCO, Illiteracy and the Global Politics of Education (1945–1960)," *Comparative Education* 53, no. 1 (2017): 42; UNESCO, "Experiments in Fundamental Education in French African Territories," *Educational Studies and Documents*, no. 9 (January 1955): 55.

[17] UNESCO, "Experiments in Fundamental Education in French African Territories," 55.

disproportionally underdeveloped.[18] The average living conditions of mid-twentieth-century Muslim Algerian families were equally dire. After a century of French colonial rule, an estimated 80% of urban Algerians lived in makeshift housing (*bidonvilles*).[19] Seven million out of eight and a half million Algerians lived well below the poverty line, in unsanitary conditions, without sewage and garbage collection systems, without running water and electricity, and without public services including schools, post offices, and medical dispensaries.[20] Algerian children were severely underserved by the colonial school system, and many had never received any kind of education. The 1944 reform of the Algerian public-school system projected the enrollment of one million Muslim students over the next two decades.[21] Yet by 1954, public schools in Algeria had room for only 300,000 pupils or a mere 15% of more than 2 million Algerian children of primary school age.[22] Pressure on colonial states to remedy the human consequences of these bleak statistics also came from below. In Algeria, public intellectuals including Albert Camus and Germaine Tillion expressed alarm over the rampant illiteracy and appalling living conditions Muslim Algerians faced; both included greater access to schooling as a solution to these pressing issues.[23] A small yet diverse committee of Muslim Algerian and French men and women, social workers and teachers formed the Algerian Committee for Fundamental Education (*Comité Algérien pour l'éducation de base*) and took up UNESCO's arguments for fundamental education as a development strategy to address the poor living conditions in Algeria.[24] This committee published tracts and appealed to educational and social organizations

---

[18] Matasci, "Assessing Needs, Fostering Development," 45.

[19] Nelly Forget, "Le Service des Centres Sociaux en Algérie," *Matériaux pour l'histoire de notres temps* 26 (1992): 37.

[20] Ibid.

[21] Heggoy and Zingg, "French Education in Revolutionary North Africa," 576.

[22] Ibid. The same year, Qur'anic schools enrolled approximately 40,000 pupils in 181 schools.

[23] Albert Camus, *Actuelles III: Chroniques Algériennes, 1939–1958* (Paris: Éditions Gallimard, 1958). Germaine Tillion used the term "pauperization" (*clochardisation*) to describe the poor living conditions of the Algerian Muslim population. Germaine Tillion, *Algeria, the Realities* (London: Eyre & Spottiswoode, 1958).

[24] Le Comité Algérien pour l'éducation de base, "Appel," Janvier 1951: 1. ANOM ALG Alger 4I/230. James Le Sueur, *Uncivil War: Intellectuals and Identity Politics During the Decolonization of Algeria* (Lincoln, NE: University of Nebraska Press, 2001), 64.

interested in improving Algerians' standard of living and combatting "all forms of ignorance," including illiteracy, lack of hygiene, infant mortality, women's inferior social status, and inefficient agricultural practices.[25] The committee highlighted the success of other fundamental education programs, and they hoped for the creation of combined social, medical, and educative services that could reach Algerian men, women, and children in both urban and rural areas.[26] These desires would come to fruition on October 27, 1955, when the Governor-General of Algeria, Jacques Soustelle, signed into law the creation of the *Service des centres sociaux*.[27] The new service's action plan mirrored UNESCO's (and the Algerian Committee for Fundamental Education's) prescription for multi-purpose fundamental education. The first and primary goal of the *centres sociaux* was to provide "fundamental education (*éducation de base*) for the male and female population" and to provide technical as well as agricultural education; the *centres sociaux* would also provide medical and social assistance and generally facilitate and support any initiatives that would ensure "the economic, social and cultural progress" of its constituent populations.[28] The *centres sociaux* both relied on UNESCO expertise and elaborated their own fundamental education pedagogy during their existence.[29]

Fundamental Education's idealistic hope for a modern world in which all people would be equal participants mirrored Governor-General Jacques Soustelle's push for integrating Algeria's Muslim and Europeans populations during early years of the Algerian War. The *Service des centres sociaux* merits study for its links to contemporary international development initiatives put forth by UNESCO and to local advocacy

---

[25] Le Comité Algérien pour l'éducation de base, "Appel"; Service des Liaisons Nord-Africaines, Préfecture d'Alger, "Notice: Comité Algérien pour l'éducation de base," 21 Mai 1952, ANOM ALG Alger 4I/230.

[26] Le Comité algérien pour l'éducation de base, "Appel."

[27] "Arrêté du 27 octobre 1955 Portant création du Service des Centres Sociaux et nomination du chef de service," *Journal Officiel de l'Algérie*, 4 Novembre 1955, p. 2118, ANOM ALG GGA 12 CAB/192.

[28] Ibid.

[29] André Lestage, an adult education and literacy specialist in UNESCO's Education Department, presented at the *centres sociaux*'s first staff training session in 1955. See "Algérie: Création d'un service des centres sociaux," *Bulletin de liaison d'informations sur l'éducation de base et l'éducation des adultes* 9 (1er trimestre 1956): 19; Isabelle Deblé, "Une exception éducative: Les centres sociaux en Algérie," *Esprit* (Octobre 2004): 5.

for improving Muslim Algerians' living conditions. The Algerian context of the 1950s and 1960s produced both innovative pedagogical tools to foster integration and spotlighted local solidarity between Muslims and Europeans as France grappled with its changing relationship to its empire.

THE STRUCTURE AND ORGANIZATION OF THE *SERVICE DES CENTRES SOCIAUX*

The *Service des centres sociaux* sought to improve literacy rates and to ensure that the newly literate profited from their education as productive workers and as members of healthy families. Established in urban and rural areas where there were no other local government institutions, the *centres sociaux* bridged the gap between "the illiterate masses" and existing socioeconomic institutions such as public and trade schools, as well as the health, agriculture, and labor administrations.[30] Typically, the *centres sociaux* were established in urban makeshift neighborhoods (*bidonvilles*), villages, and rural areas, where "unschooled children (*enfants non-scolarisés*), illiterate and untrained (*inadaptés*) adolescents, and adult men and women," had no other resources at their disposal.[31] In urban areas, the *centres sociaux* helped their constituents adapt to urban life and facilitated access to employment, while the rural *centres sociaux* focused on improving resource management and updating local practices without a "brutal break with tradition."[32] Both urban and rural *centres sociaux* taught the basics: simple arithmetic, "(some) reading, (some) writing," first aid skills, financial management, how to sign official documents, how to dress, how to eat a balanced diet, and how to "defend oneself" or get by in everyday life.[33] The *centres sociaux* ultimately aspired to set

---

[30] "Le Centre Social," n.d., p. 3 ANOM ALG GGA 14 CAB 192. According to director Ould Aoudia, "The centre social educatif is established where no other official institution exists and as close as possible to the poorest communities," "Exposé de Monsieur Ould Aoudia: L'Éducation de Base et les Centres Sociaux Éducatifs," n.d. [1959?] Bibliothèque du Centre diocésain les Glycines, Algiers, Algeria, p. 12.

[31] "Le Centre Social," n.d., p. 3 ANOM ALG GGA 14 CAB 192.

[32] Ibid.

[33] Direction Générale de l'Éducation Nationale en Algérie, *Le Service des Centres Sociaux en Algérie* (Alger, n.d.), 19.

up (and be a part of) the infrastructure that would assist those ready to help themselves.[34]

The typical *centre social* would serve 6000 people with a seven-person staff of educators, activists, and artists.[35] In addition to the director and his assistant(s), there were six critical roles to be filled at every *centre social*: a nurse; a social worker; a domestic arts instructor; a pre-professional training instructor or, in the rural *centres*, an agricultural instructor; general education instructors in charge of literacy acquisition, and civic and social education.[36] In accordance with a 1956 government decree requiring parity among employees hired by public institutions, the *centres* staff was composed of equal numbers of Muslim and European Algerians.[37] Charles Aguesse, as one of his first initiatives as the founding director of the *centres sociaux*, instituted bilingual publications of all *centres* materials, in both French and Arabic.[38] Arabic courses were provided during staff training for all employees without sufficient prior knowledge of the language.[39]

The *centres* were not affiliated with any religious orders, and they claimed political neutrality. Every *centre social* was to "situate its action on the human level, without connections to political preoccupations."[40] The second article in a series on the *centres sociaux* in the *Journal d'Alger* in July 1959 described the *centres*' political neutrality as an advantage, since it allowed the organization to focus instead on more enduring and "permanent" problems.[41] The "social" in the *centres*' name harkens back to the original intent of social assistance programs instituted in

---

[34] Ibid., 17–19.

[35] Ibid., 23.

[36] Ibid.

[37] Andrée Dore-Audibert, *Des Françaises d'Algérie dans la guerre de libération: Des oubliées de l'histoire* (Paris: Éditions Karthala, 1995), 62; Georges Garillon, *De la Lorraine à l'Algérie. Une aventure sociale et humaine au tournant des années soixante: Les Centres Sociaux Éducatifs* (Saint-Just-la-Pendue: La Bartavelle, 2008), 58–59.

[38] Nelly Forget, "Le Service des Centres Sociaux dans le parcours algérien de Germaine Tillion," in *La guerre d'Algérie: Ethnologues de l'ombre et de la lumière*, ed. by Michel Cornaton, Nelly Forget, and François Marquis (Paris: L'Harmattan, 2015), 45.

[39] Garillon, *De la Lorraine à l'Algérie*, 65.

[40] Direction Générale de l'Éducation Nationale en Algérie, *Le Service des Centres Sociaux en Algérie*, 17.

[41] Hossein Djebrane, "Les Centres Sociaux Contre L'Ignorance et la Misère," *Journal d'Alger*, 18 July 1959.

France in the nineteenth century: "the social question," forced recently industrialized French society to grapple with how to reconcile the most disenfranchised workers to themselves and to the rest of society in this new industrialized, capitalist economy.[42] Nineteenth-century social workers (*travailleurs sociaux*) sought to equip all citizens to face the exigencies of modern life and to contribute to their well-being and societal progress at large.[43] As *centres sociaux* sprung up in France throughout the late nineteenth and early twentieth centuries, it was not until the Brazzaville Conference of 1944 that the French colonial administration decided to ensure that similar social services be made available to all "indigenous" populations in Francophone Africa with specially trained staff.[44]

The first Algerian *centres sociaux* were expansions of existing operations in the suburbs of Algiers. Before 1950, Algerians seeking social services had to venture into the European neighborhoods since the *bidonvilles* were considered illegal settlements and thus not outfitted with the much-needed social services available in European neighborhoods.[45] Father Jean Scotto recruited French social worker, Marie-Renée Chéné, to come to Algeria and provide medical and social services in the Bérardi neighborhood (known as "Boubsila" to its Muslim inhabitants) in Hussein-Dey in 1950.[46] Two French Algerian social workers Emma Serra-Sanchez and Simone Gallice worked with Chéné and the Hussein-Dey municipality to fund two medical and social service centers in 1953.[47] These Hussein-Dey *centres sociaux* would be the first

---

[42] Robert Durand, *Histoire des Centres Sociaux: Du voisinage à la citoyenneté* (Paris: Éditions la découverte, 2006), 16.

[43] Ibid., 32.

[44] Dore-Audibert, *Des Françaises d'Algérie dans la guerre de libération*, 44. On the history of the centres sociaux in France, see Durand, *Histoire des Centres Sociaux: Du voisinage à la citoyenneté*; Martin Evans, *Algeria: France's Undeclared War* (Oxford, UK: Oxford University Press, 2012), 79 and 131–132.

[45] Dore-Audibert, *Des Françaises d'Algérie dans la guerre de libération*, 44–45.

[46] Pierre Couette, *Marie-Renée Chéné (1911–2000) pionnière de l'action sociale* (Pierre Couette, 2012), 53–56; Marie-Rénée Chéné, "Treize ans d'histoire d'un bidonville algérien 'Bubs'ila' 1950–1963," Mémoire École Pratique des Hautes Études, 1963, 174–180; Dore-Audibert, *Des Françaises d'Algérie dans la guerre de libération*, 45.

[47] Serra, Chéné, and Gallice created a medical dispensary, a social secretariat, and the Social Workers Association of Hussein-Dey (*L'association des travailleurs sociaux d'Hussein-Dey*) which included Christian activists, secularists (*laïques*), and Muslims who grasped the tough conditions and needs of the neighborhood. The *centre social* at Hussein-Dey

incorporated under Governor-General Jacques Soutelle's 1955 promulgation of the *Service des centres sociaux*. In mid-nineteenth-century France, significant political upheavals in 1848 and 1870 accompanied the establishment of social service centers to resolve the "social question." In Algeria, social services were established following the political failure of 1947: Algeria's status relative to France was unresolved and faith in domestic electoral politics crumbled in the face of rigged election results in 1948, resulting in the FLN fighting for Algerian independence in order to address Muslim Algerians' political, social, and economic disenfranchisement. For Governor-General Jacques Soustelle and the *centres sociaux*, Algeria's future remained French, albeit following significant structural reforms to facilitate Muslim Algerians cohabitation with their European counterparts. The *Service des centres sociaux* and its predecessors underscore that the impetus for finding solutions to Muslim Algerian's disenfranchisement—through a combination of basic literacy with social and medical services—came from a mixed community of male and female, Muslim and European Algerians and individuals from France who were interested in working across ethnic and cultural barriers. The *Service des centres sociaux* adopted UNESCO's fundamental education program to help Muslim adults and children adapt to modern Algerian life. Fundamental education and integration, unlike the colonial policy of assimilation, did not set out to "substitute a mode of civilization with another, but, according to a declaration from UNESCO itself, [fundamental education] is at the service of all regional and national cultures."[48] According to a *centre sociaux* director, "We can try and help people with the best of intentions, but if we consider them inferior, we are wasting our time."[49] Fundamental education as practiced by the *centres sociaux* was above all practical in terms of the goal of integration during Jacques Soustelle's tenure as governor-general, as demonstrated by the content

included a literacy center, housekeeping courses (*cours ménager*), job training for adolescents and women. According to Father Scotto, it was the popularity of these poorly funded, grassroots medical-social centers in the *bidonvilles* around Algiers that encouraged Germaine Tillion to create her *centres sociaux*. Dore-Audibert, *Des Françaises d'Algérie dans la guerre de libération*, 46–47 and 56–61.

[48] "Exposé de Monsieur Ould Aoudia: L'Éducation de Base et les Centres Sociaux Éducatifs," 5.

[49] Ibid., 7.

and dissemination of *centres sociaux* pedagogical materials. The *centres sociaux*'s efforts to integrate Algeria's European and Muslim communities through fundamental education would be put to the test during the Algerian War, starting in 1955 until the brutal conclusion of the *centres*' existence and the assassination of its six directors.

The *Centres Sociaux* in the Context of the Algerian War

In order to be effective in Muslim Algerian communities, the *centres sociaux* had to cultivate close and trusting relationships with their constituents without appearing too sympathetic to Algerian nationalism or to other so-called progressive ideologies. Yet close interactions between Muslims and Europeans of this nature were unprecedented in French Algeria. Although European and Muslim Algerians frequently came into contact with each other as intellectuals and professionals in schools and universities, in cafés and markets, and at particular moments such as the fervent mobilizations around the Popular Front in 1936, Muslim Algerians were mostly invisible to their European neighbors.[50] Between 1941 and 1943, there were lukewarm attempts at inter-communal meetings among secular (*laïc*), Catholic, Protestant, Jewish, and Muslim scout and guide troops, but these meetings were increasingly rare after 1945.[51] In 1952, some Muslim and Catholic scouts along and university students formed a new organization, the Association of Algerian Youth for Social Action (*Association de la Jeunesse Algérienne pour l'Action Sociale*, AJAAS), to openly discuss the economic and social problems plaguing Algeria in a politically neutral environment.[52] Around the same time, the *Mission de France* Catholic missionary team, under the leadership of Father Scotto, sought to convince the Christian population in Algeria to create more just and fraternal relationships with their Muslim neighbors.[53] It was the

[50] James McDougall, *A History of Algeria* (Cambridge: Cambridge University Press, 2017), 133–134.

[51] Pierre et Claudine Chaulet, *Le Choix de l'Algérie: Deux Voix, Une Mémoire* (Algiers: Éditions barzakh, 2012), 86.

[52] Ibid., 87–89; Darcie Fontaine, *Decolonizing Christianity: Religion and the End of Empire in France and in Algeria* (New York: Cambridge University Press, 2016), 47, Note 91.

[53] Fontaine, *Decolonizing Christianity*, 43–45. The *Mission De France*'s emphasis on pursuing relationships with the Muslim community attracted suspicion from Europeans, the military, and the colonial government.

university students, teachers, social workers, and nurses involved in the early social service efforts in the *bidonvilles*, the adherents of the Algerian Committee for Fundamental Education and AJAAS who came to work in the *centres sociaux* created by Jacques Soustelle and Germaine Tillion in 1955. Studying the *centres sociaux* brings this diverse community into focus during a time of mounting animosity between Europeans and Muslims in Algeria as the war for Algerian independence escalated.

The *centres sociaux* walked a fine line between adhering to their mission to help the most impoverished and illiterate Algerians, and fending off the French military's suspicions of being *too* close to Muslims and inevitably helping the FLN. For some, this neutrality was real and provided a way for them to take action in the face of incredible violence and to help the victims of the war without choosing a side.[54] Working for the *centres sociaux* was a commitment in itself: The mixed Muslim and European Algerian staff and the *centres sociaux*'s presence in the thick of Muslim-majority urban and rural areas provided proof that cohabitation and cooperation was possible in Algeria. Mohamed Sahnoun, a former employee of a *centre* near Algiers, believed that the *centres sociaux* initiated "processes of dialogue and inter-communal cooperation, that everyone believed to be urgent and vital."[55] According to Isabelle Deblé, the *centres sociaux* and brought together men and women, "*pieds-noirs*, Algerian activists and lay people, people from France, people from *l'Éducation nationale*, or from social work backgrounds, artists, cinematographers who attached themselves to this common cause."[56] Fettouma Medjoub and Simone Gallice fondly remembered their "*chez nous*," the *centre social* Bel-Air outside of Algiers, as an "isle of fraternity" where "each of us could be herself without fear and get her work done."[57]

In the climate of the Algerian War, however, the *centres sociaux*'s insistence on integration and neutrality rendered them suspicious in the eyes of the French Army. Governor-General Jacques Soustelle was replaced in 1956 by Robert Lacoste; as governor-general, Lacoste was granted the right to rule by decree and transferred police powers in

---

[54] Dore-Audibert, *Les Françaises dans la guerre d'Algérie*, 64.

[55] Mohamed Sahnoun, *Mémoire blessée: Algérie, 1957* (Paris: Presses de la Renaissance, 2007), 91.

[56] Dore-Audibert, *Les Françaises dans la guerre d'Algérie*, 65.

[57] Forget, "Le Service des centres sociaux dans le parcours algérien de Germaine Tillion," 76.

Algiers to the military, giving the army the right to arrest, detain, and interrogate suspects, thus increasing the civil authority of the French military.[58] French Army General Jacques Massu took on civilian authority in Algiers in 1957 and became convinced that the *centres sociaux* were rife with individuals harboring "separatist" and Algerian nationalist sympathies.[59] General Massu deeply distrusted the Ministry of Education and public school teachers.[60] It did not help that several *centres sociaux* employees had participated in the general strike called by the FLN in January 1957, and that *centres sociaux* social workers had refused to participate in a military search of family homes in the Casbah.[61] Since 1955, the French Army had been tracking individuals who belonged to the banned Algerian Communist Party, the FLN, as well as other liberals, progressive Christians, and *Service des Centres Sociaux* employees.[62] In May 1957, sixteen *centres sociaux* employees were arrested on charges of undermining state security and stood trial that July following detention and torture.[63] The Trial of Progressive Christians in July 1957 has been interpreted as indicative of the impossibility of cooperation between Europeans and Muslims during the Algerian War.[64] But *centres sociaux* employees were ready to prove that the goal of integrating European and Muslim communities in Algeria was an achievable and worthwhile endeavor. Integration did not fail because of a lack of individuals willing to break down social, economic, and cultural barriers; integration pursued by the *centres sociaux* failed because of the military's

[58] Evans, *Algeria*, 143 and 167–169.

[59] Letter from General Massu to Monsieur Delouvrier, Le Délégué Général du Gouvernement en Algérie, 4 Avril 1959. ANOM ALG Alger 1K/1275.

[60] Ibid.

[61] On the social workers in the Casbah, see ANOM ALG Alger 1K/1280, and, Pierre Couette, *Marie-Renée Chéné*, 72–76. On the centres sociaux and the grève scolaire, see Letter from Charles Aguesse, Le Chef du Service des centres sociaux to Monsieur le Recteur, Directeur Général de l'Éducation Nationale en Algérie, 8 Février 1957; and Charles Aguesse, "Etat Récapitulatif des absences pour grève," 5 February 1957, ANOM ALG Alger 1K/1264.

[62] Yves Goddard, *Les Paras dans la Ville*, Service Civil International (SCI) Archives, La Chaux-de-Fonds, Switzerland, 31702.2.

[63] Ibid. On 'Christian progressivism,' see, Fontaine, *Decolonizing Christianity*, 69–70, 83; LeSueur, *Uncivil War*, 71–72.

[64] LeSueur, *Uncivil War*, 77. Fontaine, *Decolonizing Christianity*, 69–70 and 87.

expansive authority over civilian matters and the climate of distrust surrounding the Algerian Muslim community and those who associated with them.[65]

New Years wishes from a group of officers from the FLN's military arm, the National Liberation Army (*Armée de Libération Nationale*, ALN) criticized the French Army's use of fear tactics in their efforts to rally Muslims to the French cause. The ALN officers praised the heartfelt actions of *centres sociaux* employee Nelly Forget, progressive catholic priest Father Barthez, and anticolonial intellectual André Mandouze as individuals who earned the friendship and trust of Muslim people through their generosity.[66] For them and many others, this Franco-Muslim community was "more than just a publicity slogan, an empty promise or a righteous wish," but an endeavor worth risking their lives to achieve.[67]

Following the drama of the Trial of Progressive Christians, the French Algerian Government decided to reform the *Service des Centres Sociaux*. Charles De Gaulle's return to power in 1958 was accompanied by the unveiling of the five-year Constantine Plan for Algerian development and the expansion of the education system to reach millions of unschooled and illiterate children.[68] The *centres sociaux* had a vital role to play in this expanded educational effort as a pathway to traditional schooling for all school-aged children. Re-branded as the *Service des Centres Sociaux Éducatifs*, the *centres* were placed under the authority of the *Rectorat* in Algiers to provide greater oversight over the *centres*' activities.[69] But another scandal erupted in 1959, when ten *centres sociaux* employees were arrested for alleged connections to FLN cells, collecting money

---

[65] See previous Note 63; Letter from General Massu to Monsieur Delouvrier Le Délégué Général du Gouvernement en Algérie, 4 Avril 1959; Goddard, *Les Paras dans la Ville*.

[66] "Janvier 1958: Les 'voeux' de nouvel an d'un groupe d'officiers de l'ALN," ANOM 114/APOM.

[67] Jean Gonnet, "Libres Opinions: L'Affaire des Libéraux d'Alger," *Le Monde*, 18 Juin 1957, ANOM 41/230.

[68] Ministère de l'Éducation Nationale, Académie d'Alger, "Ordonnance du 20 aout 1958 sur la scolarisation accélérée de l'Algérie pendant 8 ans," ANOM ALG GGA 14 CAB/135.

[69] L'Inspecteur d'Académie, Chef du Service des Centres Sociaux Éducatifs, "Une Institution d'Éducation de base en Algérie: Les Centres Sociaux Éducatifs," 11 March 1961, p. 2, ANOM ALG GGA 15 CAB/12.

or delivering medicine to nationalist fighters.[70] An article published in July 1959 in the conservative newspaper L'Echo d'Alger sought to turn public opinion against the *centres sociaux* and falsely reported that the French Army had arrested over 800 employees guilty of conspiring with the FLN and implicated in a bomb-making workshop.[71] With many staff members expulsed from Algeria or fired, the *centres sociaux* struggled to fill leadership positions. The increased bureaucratic oversight also made the hiring of new staff excruciatingly slow.[72] Longtime *centres sociaux* employee and assistant director Isabelle Deblé blamed the press for painting the *centres* in a bad light. Deblé conceded that there was likely some FLN infiltration into the *centres sociaux* but never to the point that it would compromise the *centres*' central mission: "We did not make bombs, not in my house, not in the centres sociaux, we made sure fraternity prevailed between members of this traumatized society."[73]

In August 1961, Kabyle author, schoolteacher, and *centres sociaux* director Mouloud Feraoun expressed his frustration with the poor timing of the *centres*' mission in a letter to a friend: "Three times alas! This had to be done in [1950] and now no one believes in it… No one wants to do anything good anymore."[74] Working at the *centre social* in Relizane, fellow schoolteacher Georges "Pierre" Garillon witnessed a similar disenchantment: The *centre*'s appearance was in disarray—trees and flowers died or were overgrown and the walls were defaced with graffiti—and the dynamism and *esprit de corps* of the staff had regressed as well.[75] The Franco-Muslim community that had supported the implantation of the *centres sociaux*, and its predecessors either sat in jail, left for France, or lived with

---

[70] Letter from Commissaire Divisionnaire chef du service départemental des renseignements Généraux d'Alger à Monsieur de Directeur de la Sûreté nationale en Algérie, 10 juin 1959 ANOM ALG Alger 3F/110. Letter from the Direction Générale de l'Éducation Nationale en Algérie Service des Centres Sociaux to Monsieur le Préfet d'Alger, 28 May 1959 ANOM ALG Alger 3F/110.

[71] Association Les Amis de Max Marchand, de Mouloud Feraoun et de leurs Compagnons, *L'École en Algérie*, 110.

[72] Letter from Max Marchand, Directeur du Service des Centres Sociaux Éducatifs to Monsieur le Délégué Général copied Monsieur le Recteur de l'Académie d'Alger, 21 November 1961, ANOM ALG GGA 15CAB/3.

[73] Deblé, "Une exception éducative," 21.

[74] Mouloud Feraoun, *Lettres à ses amis* (Alger: ENAG Éditions, 1998), 202 and 225.

[75] Garillon, *De la Lorraine à l'Algérie*, 179.

the perpetual threat of arrests and jail time hindering their activities. Yet the *centres sociaux* continued to innovate and expand their activities: In 1961, several directors and instructors formed the Association for the Development of Fundamental Education Cooperatives in Algeria with the conviction that co-ops would help teach democratic citizenship, responsibility, solidarity, camaraderie, and integrity.[76] These co-ops would take the form of workshops, agricultural schemes, and livestock farming.[77] In one of the last *centres sociaux* newsletters, director Max Marchand emphasized that the *centres sociaux*'s success could only be attributed to the employees' steadfast dedication to their task: "We have no room for the pessimists, the hesitant, and the skeptics. I know that all those who remain are sincerely convinced of the importance of the Centres Sociaux and are doing their very best to ensure their operation."[78]

The tense context of the Algerian War and De Gaulle's return to power shifted the meaning of integration and French conception of difference between Europeans and Muslims. Gaullists went from seeing Muslims in general and Muslim Algerians in particular as "presenting an opportunity for an inclusive project" toward a perception of Islam and Muslim Algerians as fundamentally different and threatening to France's postwar ambitions.[79] The Constantine Plan represented a significant financial investment in Algerian economic development closely aligned with the European common market.[80]

---

[76] Centres Sociaux Éducatifs, *Bulletin de liaison d'information et de documentation*, no. 19 (1961): 25.

[77] Ibid., 30.

[78] Centres Sociaux Éducatifs, *Bulletin de liaison d'information et de documentation*, no. 20 (1961): 1.

[79] Tyre attributes this shift in perception to the escalation of the war in Algeria and to the Suez crisis. Tyre, "From Algérie Française to France Musulmane," 291. See also, Todd Shepard, *The Invention of Decolonization: The Algerian War and the Remaking of France* (Ithaca, NY: Cornell University Press, 2006); Amelia Lyons, *The Civilizing Mission in the Metropole: Algerian Families and the French Welfare State During Decolonization* (Stanford, CA: Stanford University Press, 2013).

[80] Davis, "Restaging *Mise en Valeur*," 177.

The *Service des Centres Sociaux*'s Innovative Pedagogy

The *centres sociaux*'s pedagogical materials further solidify the organization's local and international connections and its place within a European and Algerian community willing to work together in solidarity toward integration. *Centres sociaux* materials needed to be easy to use for a rapidly trained employee and for someone who had just acquired basic literacy skills. The materials had to be efficient, and impart as much knowledge as possible as quickly as possible, since illiteracy and "ignorance of modern science, ignorance of the most basic hygiene practices, ignorance of laws and rules that regulate society" constituted a "dangerous plague for the illiterate themselves and for the world in general."[81] One of the *centres sociaux*'s pedagogical tools was small handbooks which reinforced newly acquired basic French proficiency; provided step-by-step instructions on how to navigate the colonial social and medical administrations; and served as aide-mémoire for employees.[82] "These simple texts referencing economic and real adult problems" would help acquaint the reader—or auditor, since these handbooks were likely used during classes—with what he or she would "be asked to read or perform in every life."[83] The handbook, *Day to Day in the City: Initiation Manual for Real Life* (*Au jour le jour à la ville; Manual d'initiation à la vie pratique*), features large illustrations and copies of administrative forms, and questions in footnotes invite the reader to engage with the information presented. Themes covered in *Day to Day in the City* include taking the train, getting a paycheck, going to the doctor, and finding employment. In terms of facilitating the rapid integration of a recent Muslim émigré from the Algerian countryside, this handbook provided a simple, but instructive, introduction to modern Algerian life in a diverse city.

In addition to the handbooks, the *centres sociaux* produced a monthly newspaper, entitled *Our First Paper* (*Notre Premier Journal*) with the goal of encouraging newly literate adults and adolescents to reinforce

---

[81] "Lutte contre l'analphabétisme: Exposé de M. Ould Aoudia," Mars 1956, Bibliothèque du Centre d'études diocésain Les Glycines, Algiers, Algeria, p. 1.

[82] Titles include, *Petit guide d'hygiène, Vos yeux, Le bain du bébé, Entretien du linge et des vêtements, Au jour le jour dans le Bled.*

[83] Éducation Nationale en Algérie, Service des Centres Sociaux Éducatifs, *Au jour le jour à la ville, Manuel d'initiation à la vie pratique* (Alger: Ancienne Imprimerie V. Heintz, 1961). Archives privées Nelly Forget.

their budding literacy through didactic and leisure texts.[84] Short articles accompanied by simple illustrations covered topics such as the history of writing and printing, the history of home heating—from cave fires to central electric radiators and gas stoves—as well as Algeria's booming oil and gas industry in the Sahara.[85] Following the article on the history of writing and printing is a short section that deploys Muslim devotion to the Qur'an to encourage learning to read other written materials:

> In addition to the BOOK, you see all around you a multitude of printed papers. You see them every day there where you are: at home, in the street, at the factory, at the office. They accompany you everywhere. They are there to guide you. You, whose faith is directed by GOD'S BOOK, learn also to read men's words. They will help you in our modern world![86]

Other sections of the paper contained recipes for crepes, instructions for building a simple shelf and for using a pattern to sew a pair of pants, how to find employment at the local *Bureau de Main d'Oeuvre*, in addition to drawing contests for children, and parables with animals. The *centres sociaux* inserted themselves into the articles, for instance, the aforementioned instructions for sewing a pair of pants for a three-year-old child begins with a *centre social* instructor giving "Ali's mom" the pattern pieces to make the pants.[87] In 1961, 200,000 copies of *Our First Paper* had been distributed to new literates.[88] Similar newspapers, such as the *Journal des Villages*, were also were used in fundamental education projects in Nyong and Sanaga in Cameroun.[89]

---

[84] "Note sur le périodique 'Notre Premier Journal'," n.d. (1960?) ANOM ALG GGA 14 CAB/196. L'inspecteur de l'académie, Chef du service des centres sociaux, "Quelques données numériques," 11 March 1961, ANOM ALG GGA 15CAB/12.

[85] *Notre Premier Journal*, no. 2 in ANOM ALG GGA 14CAB/196; nos. 3, 8, 12 of *Notre Premier Journal* are in Archives Archevêché Algiers (AAA), Algeria, Casier 522. So far, I have only located these 4 issues of the paper.

[86] "El Qoran, Le Livre," *Notre Premier Journal*, n.d., AAA Casier 522.

[87] "Un pantalon pour Ali," *Notre Premier Journal*, no. 3, 1 November 1960, AAA Casier 522.

[88] L'Inspecteur de l'académie, Chef du service des centres sociaux, "Quelques données numériques," 11 March 1961, ANOM ALG GGA 15CAB/12.

[89] "Notes de Lecture. Une intéressante publication camerounaise: Le Journal des villages du Nyong et Sanaga," *Bulletin de liaison du centre français d'information sur l'éducation de base et l'éducation des adultes* 5 (December 1954): 12–13.

Besides printed materials, the *centres sociaux* made use of the flannelgraph board and flat figures, as well as still films and moving pictures, audio recordings, and radio broadcasts. During the nine days of training for *centres sociaux* employees in February 1956, trainees spent a half an hour every morning learning how to use projectors, recording devices, and duplicating machines.[90] Audio-visual methods were integral to fundamental education pedagogy, since these methods relied on skills people already possessed: watching and listening. In the *centre sociaux*'s December 1956–January 1957 newsletter, an article on literacy acquisition pushed back against the notion that the ability to read was the only medium providing access to modern thoughts and ideas; why should the focus remain on written communication when new forms of communication would surely emerge with the spread of audio and visual technologies? The author of the article argued that audio and visual methods should not just be used to teach reading and writing—the old ways of imparting and accessing ideas—but should be embraced as a method of communication by themselves.[91]

French ethnologist Marceau Gast worked as a schoolteacher in the Sahara before joining the *centres sociaux* between 1956 and 1960 with the responsibility of overseeing the audio-visual division of the organization. With his team of twenty to thirty employees, Gast prepared several pedagogical materials, including still films on how to change and feed a baby, and how to build shacks (*gourbis*) in rural areas with readily available materials so that families would not be without a suitable home while waiting for the construction of housing developments.[92] Gast estimated that he and his team put together about 300 radio shows that were broadcast over Radio Alger in Arabic.[93] Audio technology was

---

[90] "Le Premier Stage de formation de moniteurs," *Bulletin de liaison d'information et de documentation*, no. 2 (Mai 1956): 5–6.

[91] "Libres propos sur l'analphabétisme," Le Service des Centres Sociaux, *Bulletin de Liaison d'information et de documentation*, no. 6 (Decembre 1956–Janvier 1957): 7–9. ANOM ALG GG 8X/272. Gouverneur Deschamps, "L'Éducation de base," *La Nouvelle Revue Française d'Outre Mer*, no. 5 (May 1955, Nouvelle série): 213.

[92] Marceau Gast, "Ethnologue, évoque l'expérience des Centres Sociaux Éducatifs d'Algérie (1955–1962) dans le contexte de la guerre d'indépendance algérienne," interview by Hélène Claudot-Hawad, 20 January 1998, D3087, no. 3383, Archives sonores Maison méditerranéenne des sciences de l'homme.

[93] Gast, "Ethnologue, évoque l'expérience des Centres Sociaux Éducatifs d'Algérie."

also frequently used in *centres sociaux* waiting rooms since the medical side of the *centres sociaux*'s mission was often their first point of contact with the families they served. In 1960 questionnaire, 32 (out of 45 *centres*) had used radio broadcasts as part of their pedagogy, reaching a total of 2666 auditors.[94] On the visual side, between 10 November 1960 and 23 March 1961 the *centres sociaux* produced 25 television episodes broadcasted on the *France 5* network.[95] Unfortunately, not all of the *centres sociaux* were equipped with televisions, and the organization's forays into audio-visual pedagogy were not well received by all.[96] Social work intern, Gaby Carlier spent the summer of 1960 at the Centre Social St. Maur near Oran, and in her report on her summer internship, she expressed her surprise at the use of tape recorders, record players, radios, and film projectors: "We do not want to dwell on the costliness of this equipment, but we wonder what purpose it might serve in such an establishment... Many villages and hamlets in France do not have such tools at their disposal."[97] While this young Frenchwoman saw the use of expensive audio-visual technology as wasteful, all of the *centres sociaux* pedagogical materials were based on the need to provide Muslim constituents with as much practical information as quickly and effectively as possible. In Algeria, these methods demonstrated the *centres*' commitment to integration even after De Gaulle's return to power and the difficulties inherent in maintaining close ties to Algeria's Muslim population.

As development strategies shifted in late colonial Algeria, the *centres sociaux* remained connected to other fundamental education projects around the world. In 1957 and 1958, several public and private organizations agreed to host a number of *centres sociaux* trainees, including the French UNESCO Commission and the French National Institute for

---

[94] "Enquête auprès des responsables de Centre sur les émissions radiodiffusées des C.S.E.," n.d. (1960?) Archives Privés Nelly Forget.

[95] C. Castagno, "Les émissions télévisées d'Éducation de base," Archives privées Nelly Forget. Of these broadcasts, eight were original productions, including titles such as, "L'Erosion," "La venue de l'enfant," "Soins et alimentation des bébés," "Les poules," "La maison," "Méfiez-vous du feu," "Un métier pour tous," "Reportage sur le Service des Centres Sociaux Éducatifs."

[96] Idem.

[97] Gaby Carlier, "Rapport de Stage," October 1960, ANOM ALG GGA 14 CAB 230.

Popular Education.[98] Trainees were introduced to UNESCO's fundamental education methods used in Algeria, in suburban Parisian neighborhoods, in Southeast Asia, India, Egypt, and South America.[99] A *centres sociaux* newsletter from 1958 featured the translation of a brochure by the Experimental Education Center in Patzcuaro, Mexico, in cooperation with the Latin American Popular Library on the topic of creating agricultural cooperatives.[100] Governor-General Jacques Soustelle had witnessed the "cultural missions," mobile, multi-function educational, and health services during his anthropology fieldwork in Mexico, and these inspired him to create the *centres sociaux* in Algeria with Tillion.[101] *Centres sociaux* employees were aware of the specificities of working in Algeria but also took interest in fundamental education initiatives in other parts of the world.

In addition to participating in and contributing to the international development community's interest in fundamental education, the *centres sociaux* sustained a supportive Franco-Muslim community in the midst of a divisive war between the French Army and the FLN. The pedagogical tools mentioned above not only link the *centres sociaux* to other international fundamental education efforts, but were also designed to reach as many Algerians as quickly as possible with a rapidly trained staff and to facilitate the integration of Algeria's Muslim and European communities. However, this close relationship with the Muslim population was seen as threatening to the military's aims of "pacification" and to conservatives uninterested in, and unconvinced of, the possibility of integration with their Muslim neighbors.

---

[98] Académie d'Alger, Service des Centres Sociaux d'Algérie, "Stage Pédagogique et social, 3 rue Marie-Jeanne Bassot, LEVALLOIS (Seine) (1957–1958), But et Organisation," 1 November 1957. Archives Privées Nelly Forget.

[99] Idem. Germaine Tillion gave a presentation during this training session on "Contacts et Civilisation." Académie d'Alger, Service des centres sociaux, "Stage de Formation Pédagogique et Sociale, Session Spéciale de l'année 1957–1958, Formation des Moniteurs et Adjoints, Rapport Final," n.d. Private Archives Nelly Forget.

[100] Service des Centres Sociaux, "Documentation. Brochures d'Éducation de base," *Bulletin intérieur*, no. 6 (1958). ANOM ALG Alger 3F/110.

[101] Nelly Forget, "Le Service des Centres Sociaux en Algérie," 40.

Conclusion: "An Educational Exception"

French President Charles De Gaulle recognized Algerian independence on 3 July 1962. Persecuted by the French Army and the OAS, following the March 1962 assassination of the six directors, the *centres sociaux* never fully recovered before official recognition of Algerian independence. By the end of the war, 120 *centres sociaux* had been built. Assuming that each *centre* reached 2000–3000 adults and children annually, it can be estimated that the *centres sociaux* served between 200,000 and 300,000 individuals. This was no small feat given that by 1962, the oldest *centre* was only six years old, thirty-five were less than four years old, a third had only been open for two years and a final third were just opening their doors. The *centres sociaux* employed approximately 2000 staff members by 1962. At the end of the war, most of the European staff—representing 20% of the total staff, but 50% of managers—left Algeria; approximately 300 total staff members transferred into the French civil service, some left fleeing for their lives. Of the staff members who stayed in Algeria, most continued to work in similar capacities as social workers, pedagogy researchers, and educators.[102] The Algerian Republic's Ministry of Youth, Sports, and Tourism took over most of the buildings and repurposed them to serve as Popular Education Centers (*Centres d'Éducation Populaire*) and as youth and community centers.[103] UNESCO abandoned fundamental education as a stand-alone project in 1958, and it was combined with the Division of Out-of-School Education. From the start, it was unclear how to determine the content, language, and style of reading materials for new literates and how to adapt visual and audio aids without leading people astray from the goal of global citizenship. Other scholars have cited

---

[102]Tillion and Soustelle initially planned for 1000 *centres sociaux* to be built by 1965. Forget, "Le Service des centres sociaux dans le parcours algérien de Germaine Tillion," 73; Forget, "Le Service des centres sociaux en Algérie," 44–45; Association Les Amis de Max Marchand, de Mouloud Feraoun et de leurs Compagnons, *L'École en Algérie*, 180–183.

[103]Association Les Amis de Max Marchand, de Mouloud Feraoun et de leurs Compagnons, *L'École en Algérie*, 180–183. After Algerian independence, the Director of Youth and Popular Education requested inventories of furniture available in former *centre sociaux* and other ventures operated by the French military. These assessments were important for budget predictions and for the "takeover of all the buildings disseminated throughout the country." H. Bourges, le Directeur de la Jeunesse et de l'Éducation Populaire, "Note," n.d. [1963?], AAA Casier 522.

the absence of a strong philosophical orientation, lack of funding, and failure to follow up on existing programs as hindering the effectiveness of Fundamental Education programs.[104]

Moreover, the term "fundamental education" often led to confusion and the delegates at UNESCO's General Conference in 1958 decided to discontinue the use of the term and to focus instead on advocating for universal, free, and compulsory education.[105] Yet the legacy of fundamental education persisted in the 1960s and 1970s as other national and international bodies expressed interest in the role of literacy in human development. The concept of education as an essential development tool became more widely accepted by the United Nations and its member states, and access to education has since been recognized as an essential human right.[106]

The history of the *centres sociaux* in Algeria brings together the question of integration, international development ideas about fundamental education, and the existence of a unified Franco-Muslim community during a divisive war. Issues surrounding integration and Muslim difference in France are still pertinent today.[107] This particular fundamental education project arose out of local initiatives to break down barriers between communities and to meet the needs of the most disenfranchised in the midst of great violence and injustice. Studying the history of decolonization and education in Algeria together highlights this community of European and Muslim male and female teachers, social workers, artists, and university students, their tenacity and devotion to each other and their constituents, and the potential for social cohesion and integration in the midst of violent decolonization.

---

[104] UNESCO, *Fundamental education*, 256–261; Watras, "UNESCO's Programme of Fundamental Education, 1946–1959," 236–237; Jens Boel, "UNESCO's Fundamental Education Program, 1946–1958: Vision, Actions and Impact," in *A History of UNESCO: Global Actions and Impacts*, ed. by Poul Duedahl (Palgrave Macmillan, 2016), 153–167.

[105] Watras, "UNESCO's Programme of Fundamental Education, 1946–1959," 237.

[106] The World Experimental Literacy Programme was adopted as a result of UN General Assembly resolutions in 1961, 1963, and 1965. Algeria participated in this experimental program along with 51 other member states. See UNESCO, "The Position as Regards Functional Literacy Pilot Projects. Summary," 12 September 1968.

[107] Shepard, *The Invention of Decolonization*; Amelia Lyons, *The Civilizing Mission in the Metropole*; Rita Chin, *The Crisis of Multiculturalism in Europe: A History* (Princeton, NJ: Princeton University Press, 2017).

Bibliography

Primary Sources

Camus, Albert. *Actuelles III: Chroniques Algériennes, 1939–1958*. Paris: Éditions Gallimard, 1958.
———. *Carnets III: Mars 1951–Décembre 1959*. Paris: Éditions Gallimard, 1989.
Chaulet, Pierre et Claudine. *Le Choix de l'Algérie: Deux Voix, Une Mémoire*. Algiers: Éditions Barzakh, 2012.
Chéné, Marie-Rénée. "Treize ans d'histoire d'un bidonville algérien 'Bubs'ila' 1950–1963." Mémoire École Pratique des Hautes Études, 1963.
Direction Générale de l'Éducation Nationale en Algérie. *Le Service des Centres Sociaux en Algérie*. Alger.
Feraoun, Mouloud. *Journal 1955–1962: Reflections on the French–Algerian War*. Lincoln: University of Nebraska Press, 2000.
———. *L'Anniversaire*. Alger: ENAG Éditions, 1998.
———. *Lettres à ses amis*. Alger: ENAG Éditions, 1998.
Garillon, Georges. *De la Lorraine à l'Algérie. Une aventure sociale et humaine au tournant des années soixante: Les Centres Sociaux Éducatifs*. Saint-Just-la-Pendue, France: La Bartavelle, 2008.
Gast, Marceau. "Ethnologue, évoque l'expérience des Centres Sociaux Éducatifs d'Algérie (1955–1962) dans le contexte de la guerre d'indépendance algérienne". Interview by Hélène Claudot-Hawad, 20 January 1998. D3087, no. 3383. Archives sonores Maison méditerranéenne des sciences de l'homme.
Nora, Pierre. *Les Français d'Algérie*. France: Christian Bourgois, 2012.
———. *Les Français d'Algérie*. Paris: Julliard, 1961.
Sahnoun, Mohamed. *Mémoire blessée*. Paris: Presses de la Renaissance, 2007.
Tillion, Germaine. *Algeria: The Realities*. London: Eyre & Spottiswoode, 1958.
United Nations Educational Scientific and Cultural Organization (UNESCO). *Fundamental Education: Common Ground for All Peoples*. London: The Frederick Printing Co., 1947.

Secondary Sources

Association Les Amis de Max Marchand, Mouloud Feraoun et de leurs compagnons. "Centre sociaux en Métropole et Centres sociaux en Algérie: deux histoires distinctes ou croisées?" Assemblée générale du 12 mars 2011, http://memoiresvives.centres-sociaux.fr/files/2014/09/CS-Alg%C3%A9rie-expos%C3%A9-V3-Pdf.pdf.
———. *L'École en Algérie: 1830–1962, De la Régence aux Centres sociaux éducatifs*. Paris: Éditions Publisud, 2001.

Bennoune, Mahfoud. *The Making of Contemporary Algeria, 1830–1987: Colonial Upheaveals and Post-independence Development.* Cambridge, UK: Cambridge University Press, 1988.

Branche, Raphaëlle. "FLN et OAS: Deux terrorismes en guerre d'Algérie." *European Review of History, Revue européenne d'histoire* 14, no. 3 (2007): 325–342.

———. *La Torture et l'armée pendant la guerre d'Algérie: 1954–1962.* Paris: Gallimard, 2001.

Chin, Rita. *The Crisis of Multiculturalism in Europe: A History.* Princeton, NJ: Princeton University Press, 2017.

Cornaton, Michel, Nelly Forget, and François Marquis, eds. *La Guerre d'Algérie: Ethnologues de l'ombre et de la lumière.* Paris: L'Harmattan, 2015.

Couette, Pierre. *Marie-Renée Chéné (1911–2000) pionnière de l'action sociale.* Pierre Couette, 2012.

Davis, Muriam Haleh. "Restaging *Mise en valeur*: 'Postwar Imperialism' and the Plan de Constantine." *Review of Middle East Studies* 44, no. 2 (Winter 2010): 176–186.

Deblé, Isabelle. "Une exception éducative: Les Centres Sociaux en Algérie." *Esprit* (Octobre 2004): 157–164.

Déroulède, Arnaud. "L'OAS étude d'une organisation clandestine." PhD diss., Paris 4, 1993.

Desvages, Hubert. "La scolarisation des musulmans en Algérie (1882–1962) dans l'enseignement primaire public français. Étude statistique." *Cahiers de la Méditerranée* 4, no. 1 (1972): 55–72.

Djebbar, Ahmed. "Éducation et société: Le cas de l'Algérie." *Revue internationale d'éducation de Sèvres* 24 (1999): 45–54.

Dore-Audibert, Andrée. *Des Françaises d'Algérie dans la guerre de libération: Des oubliées de l'histoire.* Paris: Éditions Karthala, 1995.

Duedahl, Poul, ed. *A History of UNESCO: Global Actions and Impacts.* New York: Palgrave Macmillan, 2016.

Durand, Robert. *Histoire des Centres Sociaux: Du voisinage à la citoyenneté.* Paris: Éditions la découverte, 2006.

Evans, Martin. *Algeria: France's Undeclared War.* Oxford: Oxford University Press, 2012.

Fontaine, Darcie. *Decolonizing Christianity: Religion and the End of Empire in France and Algeria.* New York: Cambridge University Press, 2016.

Forget, Nelly. "Le Service des Centres Sociaux en Algérie." *Matériaux pour l'histoire de notre temps* 26 (1992): 37–47.

Heggoy, Alf Andrew, and Paul J. Zingg. "French Education in Revolutionary North Africa." *International Journal of Middle East Studies* 7, no. 4 (1976): 571–578.

Kopf, Martina, Gerald Hödel, and Joseph Morgan Hodge, eds. *Developing Africa: Concepts and Practices in Twentieth Century Colonialism.* Manchester, UK: Manchester University Press, 2014.

Kusiak, Pauline. "Instrumentalized Rationality, Cross-Cultural Mediators, and Civil Epistemologies of Late Colonialism." *Social Studies of Science* 40, no. 6 (2010): 871–902.

Lacouture, Jean. *Le témoignage est un combat: Une biographie de Germaine Tillion.* Paris: Éditions du Seuil, 2000.

LeSueur, James. *Uncivil War: Intellectuals and Identity Politics During the Decolonization of Algeria.* Lincoln, NE: University of Nebraska Press, 2005.

Lyons, Amelia. *The Civilizing Mission in the Metropole: Algerian Families and the French Welfare State During Decolonization.* Stanford, CA: Stanford University Press, 2013.

Mabon, Armelle, and Gewndal Simon, eds. *L'Engagement à travers la vie de Germaine Tillion.* Paris: Riveneuve éditions, 2013.

Martin, Douglas. "Germaine Tillion, French Anthropologist and Resistance Figure, Dies at 100." *The New York Times,* April 25, 2008.

Matasci, Damiano. "Assessing Needs, Fostering Development: UNESCO, Illiteracy and the Global Politics of Education (1945–1960)." *Comparative Education* 53, no. 1 (2017): 35–53.

McDougall, James. *A History of Algeria.* Cambridge: Cambridge University Press, 2017.

Mestre, Claire, Hélène Aseni, and Marie Rose Moro, eds. *Vivre c'est résister: Textes pour Geramine Tillion et Aimé Césaire.* Grenoble, France: Éditions La Pensée Sauvage, 2010.

Ould-Aoudia, Jean-Philippe. *L'Assassinat de Château-Royal.* Paris: Éditions Tirésias, 1992.

Reynaud, Michel. *L'Enfant de la rue et la dame du siècle: Entretiens inédits avec Germaine Tillion.* Paris: Éditions Tirésias, 2010.

Shepard, Todd. *The Invention of Decolonization: The Algerian War and the Remaking of France.* Ithaca, NY: Cornell University Press, 2006.

Staples, Amy. *The Birth of Development: How the World Bank, Food and Agriculture Organization and the World Health Organization Changed the World, 1945–1965.* Kent, OH: Kent State University Press, 2006.

Thénault, Sylvie. *Une drôle de justice: Les magistrats dans la guerre d'Algérie.* Paris: Éditions la découverte, 2001.

Tyre, Stephen. "From Algérie Française to France Musulmane: Jacques Soustelle and the Myths and Realities of 'Integration,' 1955–1962." *French History* 20, no. 3 (September 2006): 276–296.

Unger, Corinna. *International Development: A Postwar History.* London: Bloomsbury, 2018.

Verna, Chantalle F. "Haiti, the Rockerfeller Foundation, and UNESCO's Pilot Project in Fundamental Education, 1948–1953." *Diplomatic History* 40, no. 2 (2016): 269–295.

Watras, Joseph. "UNESCO's Programme of Fundamental Education, 1946–1959." *History of Education* 39, no. 2 (March 2010): 219–237.

Open Access This chapter is licensed under the terms of the Creative Commons Attribution 4.0 International License (http://creativecommons.org/licenses/by/4.0/), which permits use, sharing, adaptation, distribution and reproduction in any medium or format, as long as you give appropriate credit to the original author(s) and the source, provide a link to the Creative Commons license and indicate if changes were made.

The images or other third party material in this chapter are included in the chapter's Creative Commons license, unless indicated otherwise in a credit line to the material. If material is not included in the chapter's Creative Commons license and your intended use is not permitted by statutory regulation or exceeds the permitted use, you will need to obtain permission directly from the copyright holder.

CHAPTER 4

Education Through Labor: From the *deuxième portion du contingent* to the Youth Civic Service in West Africa (Senegal/Mali, 1920s–1960s)

Romain Tiquet

This chapter focuses on two forms of participation and education through labor in Senegal and Mali: The *deuxième portion du contingent*, a form of forced labor used during the colonial period, and civic services for young people set up in the two countries after their independence in 1960. This chapter sheds light on the organization of these two forms of mobilization and education through work and aims at highlighting the differences but also the similarities and permanencies in their goals and functioning as well as in the discourses used by the (post)colonial authorities to justify them.

Research for this chapter was supported by the SNF Project "Decolonization as regional experience and global trend."

R. Tiquet (✉)
Humboldt University Berlin, Berlin, Germany

IMAF (CNRS), Aix-en-Provence, France

© The Author(s) 2020
D. Matasci et al. (eds.), *Education and Development in Colonial and Postcolonial Africa*, Global Histories of Education,
https://doi.org/10.1007/978-3-030-27801-4_4

Every year, throughout the Federation of French West Africa (FWA), military recruitment is divided between the first portion, which is meant to join the army, and a second portion, considered as a reserve of soldiers, brought to the Federation's public worksites for two years. This form of forced labor, regulated by the decree of October 31, 1926,[1] was abolished only in 1950. The recruitment is specific to the colonies and is not inspired by previous metropolitan experience. The *deuxième portion* has rarely been the core of detailed analyses—apart from the French Sudan (now Mali)[2]—because of its hybrid status, which put it at the crossroads of two historiographies: the history of forced labor and the history of West African soldiers.[3]

In the aftermath of African independence in 1960, in a context of national construction but also in the fight against unemployment and the deruralization of the youth, a national civic service is gradually being set up in Senegal and Mali to mobilize young people for the country's development and to provide them with physical, professional, and civic training. These initiatives are not isolated and are part of a broader movement to establish civic services in a majority of African countries during the 1960s.[4] While the historiography on young people in Africa

---

[1] This decree is inspired by an experiment launched a few months earlier in Madagascar, the *Service de la Main-d'oeuvre pour les Travaux d'Intérêt Général* (SMOTIG). However, it seems that in Senegal, the 1926 decree only legalizes a situation that has previously existed. A report by the Governor of Senegal on the availability of labor stipulates that more than 1000 men classified as *deuxième portion* had already been recruited in 1923 on the colony's construction sites. Archives Nationales du Sénégal (ANS), K58(19), Gouverneur du Sénégal au gouverneur de l'AOF, 14 August 1928.

[2] Myron Echenberg and Jean Filipovich, "African Military Labour and the Building of the 'Office du Niger' Installations, 1925–1950," *Journal of African History* 27, no. 3 (1986): 533–552; Catherine Bogosian, "Forced Labor, Resistance and Memory: The Deuxieme Portion in the French Soudan, 1926–1950," PhD in History, University of Pennsylvania, 2002.

[3] Romain Tiquet, "Enfermement ordinaire et éducation par le travail au Sénégal (1926–1950)," *Vingtième Siècle. Revue d'Histoire* 140, no. 4 (2018): 29–40.

[4] Jean-Luc Chapuis, "Les Mouvements de service civique en Afrique noire francophone: l'exemple centrafricain. Armée, jeunesse et développement," MA diss., University Paris 1, 1972; Jeffrey S. Ahlman, "A New Type of Citizen: Youth, Gender, and Generation in the Ghanaian Builders Brigade," *The Journal of African History* 53, no. 1 (2012): 87–105; Claire Nicolas, "Des corps connectés: les Ghana Young Pioneers, tête de proue de la mondialisation du nkrumahisme (1960–1966)," *Politique Africaine*, no. 147 (2017): 87–107.

is abundant,[5] very little has been written about the role played by the youth in the national construction of French-speaking African countries after independence. This observation is surprising when we consider that the youth of francophone West African countries constitute a central ideological category that the authorities wish to integrate and politically and socially control for the country's development.[6]

The focus of this chapter is twofold. First, while the *deuxième portion du contingent*, a form of forced labor, is justified as a means of education of colonized populations within the context of the "civilizing mission,"[7] youth national service emerging in the 1960s is conceived as means of civic and professional education but was rapidly transformed into pool of cheap workers for the national development. Second, the similarities between these two forms of education through work allow us to interrogate the weight of colonial legacies that influenced postcolonial elites.

This chapter proposes a comparison between two countries, Senegal and Mali, which share a common history in many aspects. Both countries were part of the FWA and the vast majority of the recruits of the *deuxième portion* came from Mali (call French Sudan at that time) for the colony's public works or sent to worksites in Senegal. In 1959, after the promulgation of the French Community which gave a share of autonomy to the FWA colonies, the ephemeral Federation of Mali was initiated by the representatives of Senegal, French Sudan, Upper Volta, and Dahomey. The Federation was recognized within the French Community by General De Gaulle in May 1959. However, after the withdrawal of Upper Volta and Dahomey, relations between the two enemy brothers, Senegal and French Sudan, quickly deteriorated regarding the further political development of the Federation. Senegal then proclaimed its independence on August 20, 1960, breaking up the

[5] Catherine D'Almeida-Topor (ed.), *Les jeunes en Afrique* (Paris: l'Harmattan, 1992); Filip De Boeck and Alcinda Honwana (eds.), *Makers and Breakers: Children and Youth in Postcolonial Africa* (Oxford/Dakar: J. Currey/Codesria, 2005).

[6] See on Mali Serge Nedelec, "Jeunesses, sociétés et État au Mali au XXe siècle," PhD diss., University Paris 7, 1994. On Senegal, see Mamadou Diouf, "Urban Youth and Senegalese Politics: Dakar 1988–1994," *Public Culture* 8 (1996): 225–249; Romain Tiquet, "Encadrement de la 'jeunesse' et service civique national au Sénégal: l'expérience limitée de Savoigne (1960–1968)," in *Décolonisation et enjeux post-coloniaux de l'enfance et de la jeunesse (1945–1980)*, ed. by Yves Denechère (Bruxelles: Peter Lang, 2019), 161–170.

[7] Alice L. Conklin, *A Mission to Civilize: The Republican Idea of Empire in France and West Africa, 1895–1930* (Stanford: Stanford University Press, 1997).

Federation of Mali. Léopold Sédar Senghor was declared President of the Republic and Mamadou Dia became President of the Council. Mali then proclaimed its independence on September 22, 1960, and Modibo Keita is elected President of the Republic.

First, this chapter sheds light on the *deuxième portion du contingent* which is designed primarily as a labor pool employing thousands of forced laborers in the FWA. The use of these labor brigades is then justified by colonial authorities as a means of education through work as part of the "mise en valeur"[8] (in this regard, see Chapter 5 by Jakob Zollmann, Chapter 6 by Caterina Scalvedi, and Chapter 7 by Michael A. Kozakowski in this book). Second, the establishment of civic services after independence is thought as a means for the rural and civic education of young people. Although education is the key word for the establishment of civic services in Senegal and Mali, they are quickly diverted to mobilize the young men for the country's economic development. Finally, without falling into a simplistic mimicry, the chapter raises three types of similarities between these two forms of mobilization: Legislative similarities, a legacy through the dialectic of civic obligation and duty, and finally the weight of the legacy of forced labor left by the second portion in populations' memories after independence.

THE *DEUXIÈME PORTION DU CONTINGENT*: A DISCIPLINARY HETEROTOPIA

Education Through Labor

In a context where labor appears as the cornerstone of colonial policy,[9] the *deuxième portion du contingent* represents in the eyes of colonial administrators an inexhaustible source of inactive men to be used on public worksites of the FWA. In addition to this important economic aspect, the *deuxième portion* is also conceived by colonial authorities as

---

[8] The "mise en valeur des colonies" was a political and economic plan launched in 1923 by Albert Sarraut, French minister of colonies. It was the basis of economic colonization, suggesting the use of a local workforce to "develop" the colonial territories. See Albert Sarraut, *La mise en valeur des colonies françaises* (Paris: Payot et Cie, 1923).

[9] Frederick Cooper, *Decolonization and African Society: The Labor Question in French and British Africa* (Cambridge: Cambridge University Press, 1996); Romain Tiquet, "Challenging Colonial Forced Labor? Resistance, Resilience, and Power in Senegal (1920s–1940s)," *Journal of International Labor and Working-Class History*, no. 93 (2018): 135–150.

a means of educating colonized populations through work, in the context of the so-called civilizing mission and in a broader international framework where forced labor started to attract widespread criticism in the 1920s.[10] The way in which this form of forced labor is thought and organized sums up a large part of the colonial *clichés* in that time regarding the fight against the so-called idleness and immaturity of colonized populations. For colonial authorities, "indigenous people" need to be educated in a strict but fair manner:

> The units of workers constituted under the 1926 decree do not only respond to an economic necessity; they also respond to a duty of the educating nation. It would be a failure of our civilizing mission to renounce defeating atavistic laziness and let millions of people languish in a miserable condition that generates physical decay that once caused so many murderous famines.[11]

Another interesting point linked with the will to educate the second portion is the implementation of a *pécule*, a salary deduction. The sums withheld, corresponding to a deduction of one-third of the pay, are recorded in a booklet given to the recruit at the time of his release.[12] The establishment of the *pécule* meets on a major objective that corresponds with the colonial ideology of education through work: to educate recruits to foresight through forced savings. The *deuxième portion du contingent* is then described and justified as a laboratory of civilization. It is depicted as an instrument of economic and social modernization of the populations, and as a means of social control and discipline of the workers during their two years of service. The Minister of Colonies Léon Perrier, in a report presented to the President of the Republic in 1926, insisted on this point:

---

[10] The International Labor Organization (ILO) enacted two conventions on Slavery (1926) and Forced Labor (1930) in order to abolish (but in reality, regulate) coercive form of labor recruitment.

[11] ANS, 2G29/13, L'utilisation de la deuxième portion du contingent en AOF, Memorandum du directeur des Affaires Politiques et Administratives, Dakar, 18 December 1929.

[12] Article 3. Archives Nationales d'Outre-Mer (ANOM), Affpol, Carton 2808, Dossier Activités économiques et main-d'œuvre, BIT Séries Législatives, Décret du ministère des Colonies du 22 octobre 1925 règlementant le travail indigène en AOF. The *pécule* should not overtake one quarter of the monthly salary in Senegal. Article 13 of decree of 4 December 1926.

[...] The serious problem of labor would be considerably reduced at the same time as the indigenous people of our West African colonies would benefit socially from their time in training courses where they would have acquired the notions of discipline, work and hygiene. When they return to their homes, they would benefit the populations of their home region from what they acquired.[13]

Between 1926 and 1950, when this form of forced labor was abolished, more than 10,000 men are recruited per year, mainly from French Sudan for various public works in the FWA and on the Dakar–Niger railway line. A 1935 political report indicates for instance that the French Sudan is "the only colony in which this recruitment system has really worked."[14] Indeed, in the 1920s, the colony set up a labor-intensive major works program, the *Service Temporaire d'Irrigation du Niger* (STIN). STIN or Office du Niger is a large-scale irrigation project in the Niger River Valley, with the aim of attracting African farmers from neighboring regions to the area to intensively cultivate cotton, rice, and other market gardening crops.[15] STIN yards employ the vast majority of the *deuxième portion du contingent* in FWA. In comparison, in 1933, the demand for workers from the *deuxième portion* was 900 men for the Dakar–Niger line in French Soudan and more than 3500 for Office du Niger.[16]

In Senegal, the use of the *deuxième portion du contingent* appears uneven. There was a low use of around 500 men in the 1930s in the colony. The majority of recruits were directed to the worksites of the Dakar–Niger line and came mainly from French Sudan. However, as part of the war effort, the employment of the *deuxième portion* in Senegal abruptly

---

[13] ANOM, 7affeco, Carton 31, Rapport du ministre des Colonies au président de la République, Exécution des travaux d'intérêt général en AOF par des travailleurs prélevés sur la deuxième portion du contingent indigène, 31 October 1926.

[14] ANS, 2G35/25, AOF Rapport annuel sur l'emploi de la main-d'œuvre, 1935.

[15] See, amongst other, Echenberg and Filipovich, "African Military Labour," 533–552; Monica M. Van Beusekom, *Negotiating Development: African Farmers and Colonial Experts at the Office du Niger, 1920–1960* (Portsmouth: Heinemann, 2002); Chéibane Coulibaly, Koffi Alinon, and Dave Benoît, *L'Office du Niger en question* (Bamako: Les cahiers de Mandé Bukari, no. 5, éditions Le Cauri d'Or, 2005).

[16] ANS, K226(26), Gouverneur général de l'AOF à Messieurs les gouverneurs de la Côte d'Ivoire, de la Guinée française et du Sénégal, Appel à la main-d'œuvre volontaire pour les grands travaux soudanais, 24 October 1933.

increased in the early 1940s to constitute the essential lever for recruiting forced laborers throughout the decade, as the territory undertook new public work projects, mainly in Dakar (Dakar harbor and airport). More than 3000 men from all over the FWA were mobilized on Dakar worksites.[17] In 1942, for the whole FWA, 3500 men were recruited in Senegal and more than 800 for French Sudan.[18] Nearly 13,500 men were even recruited in 1946 throughout the Federation, even though the Houphouët-Boigny law abolishing forced labor in the French colonies had just been enacted.[19]

Social Confinement and Hazardous Living Conditions

According to the 1926 regulations, the recruits of the *deuxième portion du contingent* were confined into work camps designed as a heterotopia, in the Foucauldian sense of the term: A space that would obey a precise and specific type of organization and sanitary and disciplinary rules.[20] In addition to the economic interest, these camps had a social objective: to promote a certain order and education at work. The 1926 decree organized the camp as the living space of the worker and his family, a disciplinary place where everything was codified.

Based on the model of the military camp, the workers' camps are organized around a central square where barracks, disciplinary rooms, kitchens, latrines, and an infirmary are arranged all around.[21] In Senegal, work camps for Dakar construction sites are located in the heart of the capital. The colonial authorities, for fear of collusion with the outside tried to avoid any contact between the workers and the rest of the city population by putting in place a "strict discipline[22]" and external

---

[17] ANS, K306(26), Mise au point, disposition en vue recours plus large aux travailleurs de la deuxième portion, 30 July 1943.

[18] Ibid.

[19] ANS, K374(26), Tableau général de répartition de la seconde portion en AOF, 10 May 1946.

[20] Michel Foucault, *Dits et écrits* (1984), T IV, "Des espaces autres" (Paris: Gallimard, 1994), 752–762.

[21] Archives Nationales d'Outre-Mer (ANOM), AGEFOM, Carton 381, Dossier 63bis/1 Travail Sénégal avant 1945, Camp des travailleurs de Yoff, Rapport médical annuel, 1944.

[22] ANS, K306(26), Lettre pour le directeur des travaux publics, visite camps travailleurs deuxième portion du contingent Yoff et zone nord port en compagnie de Monsieur l'inspecteur général des colonies Gayet et de Monsieur le gouverneur Martine inspecteur général du travail (19 juillet 1943), 23 July 1943.

fences that locked up the living space of the workers in the camp.[23] The organization of the workers day is strictly supervised, with 8 hours of activity, 6 days a week, with a rest day spent in the camp. However, the weekly rest period is not a space of free time, but rather a time of training and education. The workers are responsible for cleaning the camp and various *corvées* and receive basic hygiene training.[24]

The salary received by recruits is similar to the salary of *tirailleurs* serving in AOF, at 0.75 francs in 1934.[25] On Senegalese construction sites, a daily bonus of between 0.50 and 3 francs can be granted to workers to speed up the pace and guarantee maximum labor productivity.[26] On the other hand, workers in the *deuxième portion du contingent* can be sanctioned for 4 types of misconduct: negligence, laziness, unjustified absence, and refusal of obedience.[27] The reasons for the sanctions are essentially linked to the efficiency and effectiveness of the workers, recalling that the productivity of the worksites remains one of the priorities in the daily functioning of the *deuxième portion*.

The labor camp appears above all as a place of spatial and social confinement, with recruits living in a miserable environment, where insalubrious conditions and daily violence prevail, leading to many illnesses and deaths. Concerning the living conditions of the workers, the inspection reports are unanimous: The labor camp constitutes a space of alarming insalubrity and transmission of diseases, contrary to the hygienist project initially defended by colonial authorities. In 1944, in the Yoff camp devoted to the work at Dakar airport, there was no access to water.[28]

---

[23] ANS, K306(26), Gouverneur général de l'AOF à l'administrateur de la circonscription de Dakar et dépendances, A/S Travailleurs de la deuxième portion de contingent, 4 février 1944.

[24] In Senegal, local regulations stressed the need for soap distribution for cleaning workers and the construction of cemented spaces for ablutions and laundry washing. ANS, K393(26), Instruction pour l'emploi de la main-d'œuvre de la deuxième portion du contingent au Sénégal, non daté (mais vers le début des années 1940). See also Bogosian, *Forced Labor, Resistance and Memory*, 35.

[25] It corresponds to the half of the salary of a skilled worker at that time in FWA. Echenberg and Filipovich, "African Military Labour," 544.

[26] ANS, K335(26), Gouverneur général de l'AOF au gouverneur du Sénégal, Solde des travailleurs de la deuxième portion, 18 February 1946.

[27] Article 18 of decree of 4 December 1926.

[28] ANOM, AGEFOM, Carton 381, Dossier 63bis/1 Travail Sénégal avant 1945, Camp des travailleurs de Yoff, Rapport médical annuel, 1944.

Another example, among others, is the latrine system set up, which consists of trenches dug in the ground, covered with boards pierced with holes, hidden by branches. As a consequence, "numerous flies" were abounding in the camp.[29]

In addition to the insalubrious environment of the camp, the food of the recruits is also problematic. A minimum ration is theoretically provided to each worker under the 1926 regulations. However, many cases of malnutrition and weight loss are noted in inspection reports. In 1943, in the Yoff camp, the new recruits from Mauritania were in a "state of manifest malnutrition."[30] In addition to not being adequately fed, workers are often malnourished. On construction sites in French Sudan, workers even give a name in Bambara to the ration, often made up of millet or undercooked barley: *sakaroba*.[31]

Hygiene conditions and malnutrition have a direct impact on the daily health of the second portion. In Yoff, there is one doctor for every 2000 workers. Workers are being forced to heal their wounds with "makeshift bandages" made out of leaves.[32] Between September and December 1944, a medical report indicates that more than 1500 people were admitted to the infirmary of the Yoff camp for illnesses or accidents.[33] In 1943, Senegal's inspection reports noted nearly 54 deaths in Yoff camp, nearly 5 deaths per month, as a result of intestinal problems, general weakening of the nervous systems, and respiratory disorders, particularly tuberculosis.[34] However, the labor camp does not appear to be a "the

---

[29] ANS, K306(26), Lettre pour le directeur des travaux publics, Visite camps travailleurs deuxième portion du contingent Yoff et zone nord port en compagnie de Monsieur l'inspecteur général des colonies Gayet et de Monsieur le gouverneur Martine inspecteur général du travail (19 juillet 1943), 23 July 1943.

[30] ANS, K306(26), Pour le directeur des travaux publics, Visite chantiers aéroport Yoff et camps travailleurs, 24 May 1943.

[31] Bogosian, *Forced Labor, Resistance and Memory*, 38.

[32] ANS, K306(26), Lettre pour le directeur des travaux publics, Visite camps travailleurs seconde portion du contingent Yoff et zone nord port en compagnie de Monsieur l'inspecteur général des colonies Gayet et de Monsieur le gouverneur Martine inspecteur général du travail (19 juillet 1943), 23 July 1943.

[33] ANOM, AGEFOM, Carton 381, Dossier 63bis/1 Travail Sénégal avant 1945, Camp des travailleurs de Yoff, Rapport médical annuel, 1944.

[34] ANS, K306(26), Administrateur de la circonscription de Dakar et dépendances au gouverneur général de l'AOF, Deuxième portion du contingent, Décès survenus du 1er janvier 1943 au 1er mars 1944.

protected place of disciplinary monotony" dear to Foucault.³⁵ Living conditions in the camps lead to a number of reaction and resistance from workers: desertion, slower pace, feigned illness, refusal to receive pay, or collective work stoppages. These forms of protest increase in the aftermath of the Second World War, in a context of reconfiguration of colonial policy and political and social unrest that makes it possible to renegotiate the living and working conditions of recruits. These reactions push authorities to remove the last avatar of forced labor in 1950.

CIVIC SERVICE: A DEVELOPMENTALIST HETEROTOPIA

Mobilize and Control the Youth

The main ambition of the development programs set up by the Senegalese and Malian regimes after they gained independence in 1960 is primarily focused on the economic and social reconstruction of the territories and the promotion of the rural masses.³⁶ By restoring trust between rural populations and the State, the postcolonial authorities intend to initiate a new dialogue and encourage the populations to participate in national construction. In this context, the country's youth, which at the time represented nearly 60% of the total population under 25 years of age (the situation is similar in Senegal and Mali), is under the spotlight of the authorities.³⁷

Youth generation in West Africa embodies both the rupture with the colonial past and the starting point of national construction. It represents the possible but also and above all what is desirable for postcolonial authorities. The open call of the participation of the youth for the development of the countries is numerous. The Senegalese Ministry of Youth and Sports, for example, argues that the country "can count on

---

³⁵ Michel Foucault, *Surveiller et punir: naissance de la prison* (Paris: Gallimard, 1975), 54.

³⁶ Cissé Ben Mady, "L'Animation rurale base essentielle de tout développement. Où en est l'expérience sénégalaise?" *Afrique documents* (1963): 115–128; Daouda Gary-Tounkara, "Quand les migrants demandent la route, Modibo Keïta rétorque: 'retournez à la terre!': Les Baragnini et la désertion du 'chantier national' (1958–1968)," *Mande Studies*, no. 5 (2003): 49–64.

³⁷ UNESCO, *Sénégal. Plan d'un programme en faveur de l'éducation extrascolaire des jeunes* (Paris: UNESCO, 1969), 6.

its dynamic YOUTH, more dedicated than ever and ready to invest itself for the peace and prosperity of the nation."[38] In the same manner, in 1962, the Ministry of Information in Mali calls for the "participation of the Malian youth to the construction of the nation."[39] However, and it is an obvious anthropological truism, the youth, considered by postcolonial authorities as a real economic and political stake, fascinates as much as it worries. Young African people appear as an opportunity for development, but they are also often described by the authorities as rebellious, unstable, and volatile. One can then find a discourse of infantilization, of disempowerment which aims to justify the establishment of control structures and the ordering of the youth.

The question of political control of young people then appears central in a context where the youth, affected by many economic difficulties (training, access to employment, etc.) is increasingly leaving the countryside to try their luck in the urban centers. Consequently, in order to control a rapidly changing urban space, the Senegalese and Malian political elites are setting up disciplinary structures in order to control the youth. It is in this context that West African postcolonial authorities attempt to establish a national civic service. The initial objectives of these civic services are threefold: rural, political, and civic training during a two-year enrollment period to prepare the country's youth to become peasants able of leading their own villages and communities. However, the daily functioning of the civic service shows that it has been quickly diverted to provide a source of labor for the national construction rather than to educate the young generation of West Africa.

The Senegalese and Malian Experiences of Civic Service

Initially, in Senegal, the idea is to incorporate all young people not integrated into the army into the civic service. At the turn of the 1960s, the Senegalese authorities consider that nearly 34,000 young people are available.[40] But the government does not stop there. In a summary

---

[38] In capital letters in the report. ANS, 2G60/08, Ministère de la Jeunesse et des Sports du Sénégal, Discours de Mamadou Dia, around 1960.

[39] Yiriba Coulibaly (ed.), *Le Mali en marche* (Bamako: Édition du secrétariat d'État à l'information, 1962), 98.

[40] ANS, VP269, Service Civique, Premières options à prendre immédiatement, around 1960.

report of the work of a commission on unemployment, the Senegalese authorities propose to extend the conditions of recruitment for civic service, "not only to young people likely to be called up to the armed forces, but also to all those without proper work."[41] This comment perfectly sums up the spirit at work in the formulation of civic service: There is a twofold desire to supervise and control a significant part of the population, while at the same time fighting idleness by compelling all inactive young people to participate, in labor, to the national construction.

In Senegal, various attempts are being set up to mobilize the youth and involve them in national development through work. A first attempt is launched in 1959 with the setting up of youth volunteer camps (*chantiers de jeunes volontaires*) bringing together "young people aged 14 to 25 years old, in order to work on a voluntary basis to carry out a work of public interest, such as the construction of roads, schools, dispensaries, etc."[42] These *chantiers* are quickly reformulated into youth camps (*camps de jeunesse*) in January 1960. This new mobilization formula aims to "integrate into development actions, unemployed young people in cities and rural youth idle by the off-season in order to adapt them to production tasks."[43] We notice the change in vocabulary and objectives. While the 1959 formula, aimed at "young volunteers," encourages them to participate "voluntarily" in actions of public interest, the youth camp is aimed at populations considered inactive, who must be put to work in rural areas. Young people still have to do work of public interest: Planting trees and building gutters in Tambacounda, establishing local tracks or markets in Kédougou, for instance.[44]

The Senegalese civic service is then used as a labor pool and is diverted from its main objective, to integrate the youth into the national project. Many young people then desert the sites, the lack of supervision and resources helping. For example, in the Richard-Toll *camp de jeunesse* in the north of the country, the camp is described as "more of a burden than a help." This failure then prompted the

[41] ANS, VP302, Rapport de synthèse sur les travaux de la commission sur le chômage, 1959.
[42] UNESCO, *Sénégal. Plan d'un programme en faveur de l'éducation extrascolaire des jeunes* (Paris: UNESCO, 1969), 35.
[43] Ibid.
[44] ANS, 2G60/08, Ministère de la Jeunesse et des Sports, Camps de jeunesse, around 1960.

authorities to consider a new form of civic service to ensure a massive and more effective mobilization of young people. After the failure of the youth camps, a new formula is introduced in 1962 with the implementation of the *chantiers-écoles*. The main ambition of this new attempt is to combine the active participation in work of young recruits—called "pioneers"—with intellectual, physical, and civic training. The objective is to set up sites with a specific agricultural vocation and to train people to become future farmers who will be able to take the lead of the *chantier-école* that has become a village pilote after two to three years of training. This new formula reflects the major concern of the Senegalese authorities: to encourage the promotion of local areas while fighting against congestion in urban centers by encouraging the (re)settlement of hundreds of young people in the countryside.

It is in this context that the Senegalese army took the initiative to open its own *chantier-école* in 1964 in Savoigne in northern Senegal. The army calls for the recruitment of young men between the ages of 16 and 20, single, voluntary, and qualified for medical examinations, to take part in this project. The leitmotif of this new attempt was: "To become a useful citizen capable of ensuring your individual destiny."[45] About 150 pioneers were recruited and sent on 11 November 1964, to Savoigne, where 500 hectares were allocated to the army to set up the crop fields and build pioneer housing. Savoigne was then a small town, located 35 km north of Saint-Louis, a few minutes from the Mauritanian border. The Savoigne camp is supervised by a Senegalese army lieutenant and is divided into 3 sections of 50 recruits, each of whom is led by a sergeant. The young people, dressed in military uniform, are subject to a military schedule. A pioneer remembers being woken up every day at 6 a.m. to go water the plantations. Between 7 a.m. and 8 a.m., recruits jog before gathering in the camp's central square for a flag call. After breakfast, they are sent to the various sites until the end of the afternoon. Then comes the time of the study until nightfall when the pioneers receive general literacy training. Weekend permissions are granted to some sections.[46] The three pioneer sections are divided between public works and agricultural sites. In 1965, with the support of the Senegalese military engineer, the pioneers built a bridge crossing the Lampsar River,

---

[45] Anonyme, "L'Armée Sénégalaise recrute de jeunes pionniers pour le chantier école de Savoigne," *Dakar-Matin*, 24 October 1964.
[46] Interview with Malick Bâ, Savoigne, 24 January 2015.

more than 110 meters long. The pioneers also dig 3.5 km of canals, 3 wells, a health post, and participate with the engineers in the construction of the road linking Saint-Louis to Mauritania. A French agricultural engineer, Erwan Le Menn, is sent on the camp and trained pioneers in agricultural techniques and launched crop production. Production in 1965–1966 is good: 24.4 tonnes of Paddy rice, 4 tonnes of tomatoes, and several tonnes of potatoes. The pioneers also plant nearly 500 fruit trees, some of which still bear fruit in the village today.

After three years, the *chantier-école* was transformed into a cooperative village. Savoigne was one of the few successful civic service experiences in Senegal. Indeed, the Senegalese experience of civic service can be summed up as the story of "a great idea that has never been fully implemented,"[47] the ambitious youth mobilization program launched in the aftermath of independence having been reduced to a shagreen. The difficulties encountered in the establishment of civic service by the authorities highlight the many limitations—particularly budgetary and political—of a Senegalese government unable to organize on a large scale the mobilization of thousands of young people and to offer them opportunities after their civic service to integrate them into the country's economy.

In the neighboring Mali, a similar system is established in 1960 by Modibo Keita's government. The *service civique rural* is a central part of the program of building a socialist and self-sufficient Malian state. Young men of eighteen to twenty-one years old were called into a rural civic service that was to be considered equivalent to service in the army. The civic service was first enacted into law during the short-lived Mali Federation (1959–1960): "the Soudanese Republic [set up] a rural civic for young men recognized as fit for military service."[48] Two decrees describing methods of recruitment were then passed on October 29, 1960, right after the independence of 22 September 1960. The goal of the civic service was to: "give to all the youth of the Malian Republic a

---

[47] Alain Gillette, "Les services civiques de jeunesse dans le développement de l'Afrique rurale: nouvelles réflexions sur l'art de coiffer Saint-Pierre sans décoiffer Saint-Paul," *Cahiers de l'animation*, no. 18 (1977): 40.

[48] "Loi no. 60–15 A.L.-R.S. portant institution d'un Service civique rural," *Journal Officiel de la République Soudanaise*, 15 July 1960.

formation that will develop in them good citizenship, conscience and a sense of responsibility in the building fatherland."[49]

The youth was recruited into the civic service in order to learn modern agricultural methods. They receive lessons in literacy and become familiar with the values of the socialist state and the duties of citizens within that state.[50] The recruits are dressed in uniforms and worked together on state farms. Unlike Senegal, which has only recruited a few hundred recruits, Mali's civic service mobilized about 40,000 young people in the early 1960s, in highly controlled structures linked to the Single Party of Modibo Keita (US-RDA). Indeed, contrary to the government of Léopold Sédar Senghor and Mamadou Dia in Senegal, which advocates an *auto-gestionnaire* socialism, the Single Party in Mali was the lever for revolutionary development.[51] As in Senegal, the initial educational objectives of the civic service in Mali were also progressively diverted to the mobilization of young people as laborers for the mean of national construction. Desertions became more and more frequent and the numbers of recruits in the Malian civic service gradually declined.

THE MORE THINGS CHANGE, THE MORE THEY STAY THE SAME

Legislative Legacies

In analyzing the justification and the functioning of civic services in Senegal and Mali, it is difficult not to see a number of similarities with the *deuxième portion du contingent*. In Mali, the men in the civic service were often described either as farmers in uniform or as soldiers armed with shovel. This image echoes the one depicted by Léopold Sédar Senghor in 1947, deputy of Senegal at that time, in a letter sent to the Governor of AOF. He called the recruits of the *deuxième portion du contingent* "tirailleur-shovel" (*tirailleurs-la-pelle*) as opposed to the

---

[49] "Décret portant organisation du Service civique rural and décret portant mode de recrutement du Service civique rural," *Journal Officiel de la République du Mali*, 15 November 1960.

[50] Catherine Bogosian, "The 'Little Farming Soldiers': The Evolution of a Labor Army in Post-colonial Mali," *Mande Studies*, no. 5 (2003): 83–100.

[51] Oumar Diarrah Cheick, *Le Mali de Modibo Keita* (Paris: L'Harmattan, 1986).

tirailleurs of the first portion wearing a rifle.[52] He expressed furthermore emotion at the use of these recruits as forced laborers even though the 1946 Houphoüet-Boigny law was passed.

The legislation of the *deuxième portion du contingent* in AOF and the civic services in Senegal and Mali share some similarities. Article 3 of the initial draft law on civic service in Senegal stipulates that: "Persons subject to the civic service shall be kept in their homes at the disposal of the Government; the latter may prescribe their temporary employment for work of interest to the national economy."[53] The wording, than can also be found in the Malian legislation on the civic service, recalls the 1926 regulation that distinguished the first military portion and a second reserve portion, compelled to work on public work for 2 years. While the colonial authorities saw in the *deuxième portion* a stable and directly available labor pool for the "mise en valeur" of the colonies, the Senegalese authorities formulated the civic service as a means of massively mobilizing a segment of the population to participate economically and politically in national construction.

Senegalese and Malian authorities' willingness to set up a civic service on the territory embodied the central problem facing West African governments after their independence: How was it possible to mobilize the greatest number of people in order to meet the challenges of national development, in a country with a limited budget and limited capital? This legislative mimicry does not seem to escape the legal service of the French cooperation mission, which wondered in the early 1960s whether Senegalese civic service was really "a mode of civic education for the contingent or a convenient method of recruiting labor for public utility work?"[54] It is not unimaginable that politicians in newly independent Senegal and Mali looked to colonial legislation as templates for their own laws. As Catherine Bogosian argued for Mali, "though colonial laws

---

[52] ANS, K260(26), Lettre de Léopold Sédar Senghor au gouverneur général de l'AOF, 20 March 1947.

[53] Centre des archives diplomatiques de Nantes (CADN), Fond Ambassade de France à Dakar, 184PO/1, Dossier 326 Camp de pionniers de Savoigne, Projet de loi sur le Service Civique, around 1960.

[54] CADN, 184PO/1, Dossier 383 Service Civique, Note sur l'organisation du Service Civique au Sénégal par le service juridique de mission aide et coopération, 30 October 1962.

were problematic, they provided a starting point for resolving some basic logistical concerns at a time when Malian politicians were faced with creating their new government."[55]

Obligation, Civic Duty, and Memory

The concern over how to incorporate rural youth into of the colony or the state was voiced in two ways: The law establishing the *deuxième portion* first used a language of obligation of the colonial subjects to contribute to the general interest and the economic development of the colony. One can find the same language in the discourse on civic service, the new independent state calling for a mandatory participation of the youth in labor for the national construction. Furthermore, we find in the notion of civic service itself, as well as in the public discourses of the Malian and Senegalese authorities, the ideology of the moral duty, of the civic duty, already used under the colonial period to legitimize the mobilization of the populations for the "mise en valeur." For the French colonial authorities, the *deuxième portion du contingent* constituted a "collective social effort,"[56] a duty to work equivalent to other civic obligations such as the payment of taxes or military service. For postcolonial authorities, the civic obligation of participation was at the core of the political project of the newly independent countries for national construction.

It is also interesting to notice that as the recruits of the *deuxième portion* have played with the rhetoric of civic obligation to call for respect for their rights and dignity,[57] some participants in the civic service have done the same using the repertoire of mutual obligation and reciprocity when the working and living conditions imposed by the civic service exceeded the regulations put in place. The pioneers of Savoigne organized for instance a collective refusal of work in 1966 to protest on the postpone of the transformation of the *chantier-école* into a *village pilote*,

---

[55] Bogosian, "The 'Little Farming Soldiers'," 94.

[56] ANOM, 7affeco, Carton 31, Rapport du ministre des Colonies au président de la République, Exécution des travaux d'intérêt général en AOF par des travailleurs prélevés sur la deuxième portion du contingent indigène, 31 October 1926.

[57] Tiquet, "Enfermement ordinaire et éducation par le travail au Sénégal (1926–1950)," 29–40.

arguing that the terms of the initial agreement (liberation of the *chantier-école* after 2 years) were not respected.[58] Populations shared another legacy: a communal memory distaste for requisitioned labor in any form. Especially in the case of Mali where the *deuxième portion* was intensively used for the Office du Niger's work, Bogosian argues that "this dead weight that subtly but effectively hindered the civic service."[59] One might not forget that the *deuxième portion* ended in 1950 after twenty-three years of existence. Only ten years later, the civic service was born in newly independent West African countries.

In Mali, youth enlisted for the civic service were often called "farming asses," "little farming soldier," or people mocked them telling that they had been "given a belt and ordered to bend."[60] Such reaction implies that the men of the civic service were less honorable than regular soldier. Despite the very different natures of the two organizations, both the civic service and the *deuxième portion* were coercive by essence. The coercive aspect of these forms of mobilization combined with the lack of prestige of being part of a "second army," an army with shovel rather than with rifle, plays a central role in the distaste of the civic service both in Senegal and Mali. Populations remembered the decades of obligations and coercion under French colonial rule. Such memories lingered and shaped their interpretations of the demands made upon them by the new postcolonial authorities. Many people remembered the pain of the colonial years and the civic service, as a new obligatory form of participation in labor for the State, unpleasant reminders of colonial forced labor embodied by the *deuxième portion*.

The link was also made at a transnational level. In the 1960s, youth mobilization projects for national development in newly independent African countries received special attention from International Labor Organization (ILO) officials. In 1962 the annual report of the permanent Committee of Experts on the Application of Conventions and Recommendations (COE) proposes a general survey of the situation on the ground since the new Forced Labor Convention of 1957 was enacted. According to the report, a range of forms of forced and

---

[58] Romain Tiquet, "Service civique et développement au Sénégal. Une utopie au cœur des relations entre armée et pouvoir politique (1960–1968)," *Afrique Contemporaine*, no. 260 (2016): 45–59.

[59] Bogosian, "The 'Little Farming Soldiers'," 84.

[60] Ibid., 83.

compulsory labor outlawed by the Conventions of 1930 and 1957 had survived African countries' independence. The report listed many West African countries, including Mali and Senegal, whose methods of mobilization of labor were described as incompatible with forced labor conventions, especially regarding youth labor service.[61] Indeed, the ILO considered, under Article 1 of the 1957 Convention on the Abolition of Forced Labor, that the military recruitment of young people for the purpose of participating in labor in development was considered a form of forced labor. The reaction of West African countries, most of which had rightly ratified the 1957 Convention unlike the former colonial authority, France, was swift.[62] They reacted with virulence, feeling unfairly attacked of a "colonial" crime even though their entire discursive apparatus and policies were intended to be at odds with past colonial practices. As historian Daniel Maul argues:

> At first they vehemently defended the immense importance, in their view, of youth service for development. They had no time for the scruples of the COE, which, while recognizing the need of these countries to build up a qualified workforce and to tackle the problems of growing cities, youth unemployment and underemployment, still rated the danger of abuse intrinsic to systems based on coercion as more relevant than their potential benefits.[63]

Yet, they did not stop the mobilization of the youth for economic purpose for all, Senegalese official enacted a new law in 1968, generalizing the model of Savoigne military camp to the entire country.[64]

Conclusion

This chapter has highlighted two forms of mobilization and education through work in Senegal and Mali. The *deuxième portion du contingent* was conceived as a reservoir of labor for the "mise en valeur" of

---

[61] Daniel R. Maul, "The International Labor Organization and the Struggle Against Forced Labor from 1919 to the Present," *Labor History* 48, no. 4 (2007): 489.

[62] Senegal signed the convention in 1961 and Mali in 1962, France only in 1967.

[63] Maul, "The International Labor Organization," 490.

[64] Mamadou M. Diouf, *Stratégies de formation citoyenne et de préparation à une vie professionnelle: l'exemple du service civique national au Sénégal* (INSEPS, UCAD, 2002).

the colonies and justified, in an international context increasingly critical to the use of forced labor, as a means of education, within the framework of the "civilizing mission." After independence, the Senegalese and Malian civic services were conceived above all as means of education and training for young people but were finally diverted to put hundreds of young people to work as part of the national construction.

While the colonial authorities saw in the *deuxième portion* a stable and directly available labor pool for the "mise en valeur" of the colonies, the independent Senegalese and Malian authorities formulated the civic service as a means of massively mobilizing a segment of the population to participate economically and politically in national construction. Although it would be too simplistic to reduce the spirit of civic services to a direct colonial legacy, the emphasis on the second portion and youth education experiences in Senegal and Mali showed a number of similarities and allowed a broader reflection on the borrowings, inspirations, and legacies in projects, discourses and mentalities in colonial and postcolonial times in West Africa.

The French empire relied on the moral argument of the "civilizing mission" to justify the colonial conquest of African territories and the coercive forms of mobilization and employment of the population. With regard to the establishment of civic services in Senegal and Mali and certain similarities both in spirit and in practice with the *deuxième portion du contingent*, the postcolonial Senegalese and Malian elites also propose to be in a certain way "civilizing," no longer in the name of the "mise en valeur" but in the name of national development.[65]

---

[65] In this regard, John Lonsdale speaks of a "new civilising mission of 'development'" from postcolonial African State in the 1960s. See John Lonsdale, "Political Accountability in African History," in *Political Domination in Africa*, ed. by Chabal Patrick (Cambridge: Cambridge University Press, 1986), 153. See also, Romain Tiquet, "Le renouveau de la «mission civilisatrice»? Développement et mobilisation de la main-d'œuvre au Sénégal (années 1960)," *Relations Internationales*, no. 177 (2019): 73–84.

Bibliography

Ahlman, Jeffrey S. "A New Type of Citizen: Youth, Gender, and Generation in the Ghanaian Builders Brigade." *The Journal of African History* 53, no. 1 (2012): 87–105.

Bogosian, Catherine. *Forced Labor, Resistance and Memory: The deuxieme portion in the French Soudan, 1926–1950*. PhD diss., University of Pennsylvania, 2002.

———. "The 'Little Farming Soldiers': The Evolution of a Labor Army in Postcolonial Mali." *Mande Studies*, no. 5 (2003): 83–100.

Chapuis, Jean-Luc. *Les Mouvements de service civique en Afrique noire francophone: l'exemple centrafricain. Armée, jeunesse et développement*. MA diss., University Paris 1, 1972.

Cissé, Ben Mady. "L'Animation rurale base essentielle de tout développement. Où en est l'expérience sénégalaise?" *Afrique Documents* (1963): 115–128.

Conklin, Alice L. *A Mission to Civilize: The Republican Idea of Empire in France and West Africa, 1895–1930*. Stanford: Stanford University Press, 1997.

Cooper, Frederick. *Decolonization and African Society: The Labor Question in French and British Africa*. Cambridge: Cambridge University Press, 1996.

Coulibaly Chéibane, Alinon Koffi, and Dave Benoît. *L'Office du Niger en question*. Bamako: Les cahiers de Mandé Bukari no. 5, éditions Le Cauri d'Or, 2005.

Coulibaly, Yiriba, ed. *Le Mali en marche*. Bamako: Édition du secrétariat d'État à l'information, 1962.

D'Almeida-Topor, Catherine, ed. *Les jeunes en Afrique*. Paris: l'Harmattan, 1992.

De Boeck, Filip, and Alcinda Honwana, eds. *Makers and Breakers: Children and Youth in Postcolonial Africa*. Oxford/Dakar: J. Currey/Codesria, 2005.

Diarrah, Cheick Oumar. *Le Mali de Modibo Keita*. Paris: l'Harmattan, 1986.

Diouf, Mamadou. "Urban Youth and Senegalese Politics: Dakar 1988–1994." *Public Culture*, no. 8 (1996): 225–249.

———. *Stratégies de formation citoyenne et de préparation à une vie professionnelle: l'exemple du service civique national au Sénégal*. INSEPS: UCAD, 2002.

Echenberg, Myron, and Jean Filipovich. "African Military Labour and the Building of the 'Office du Niger' Installations, 1925–1950." *Journal of African History* 27, no. 3 (1986): 533–552.

Foucault, Michel. *Surveiller et punir: naissance de la prison*. Paris: Gallimard, 1975.

———. *Dits et écrits* (1984), T IV, "Des espaces autres." Paris: Gallimard, 1994.

Gary-Tounkara, Daouda. "Quand les migrants demandent la route, Modibo Keïta rétorque: 'retournez à la terre!': Les Baragnini et la désertion du 'chantier national' (1958–1968)." *Mande Studies*, no. 5 (2003): 49–64.

Gillette, Alain. "Les services civiques de jeunesse dans le développement de l'Afrique rurale: nouvelles réflexions sur l'art de coiffer Saint-Pierre sans décoiffer Saint-Paul." *Cahiers de l'animation*, no. 18 (1977): 31–40.

Lonsdale, John. "Political Accountability in African History." In *Political Domination in Africa*, edited by Patrick Chabal, 126–157. Cambridge: Cambridge University Press, 1986.

Maul, Daniel R. "The International Labor Organization and the Struggle Against Forced Labor from 1919 to the Present." *Labor History* 48, no. 4 (2007): 477–500.

Nedelec, Serge. *Jeunesses, sociétés et État au Mali au XXe siècle*. PhD diss., University Paris 7, 1994.

Nicolas, Claire. "Des corps connectés: les Ghana Young Pioneers, tête de proue de la mondialisation du nkrumahisme (1960–1966)." *Politique Africaine*, no. 147 (2017): 87–107.

Sarraut, Albert. *La mise en valeur des colonies françaises*. Paris: Payot et Cie, 1923.

Tiquet, Romain. "Service civique et développement au Sénégal. Une utopie au cœur des relations entre armée et pouvoir politique (1960–1968)." *Afrique Contemporaine*, no. 260 (2016): 45–59.

———. "Enfermement ordinaire et éducation par le travail au Sénégal (1926–1950)." *Vingtième Siècle. Revue d'Histoire* 140, no. 4 (2018): 29–40.

———. "Challenging Colonial Forced Labor? Resistance, Resilience, and Power in Senegal (1920s–1940s)." *Journal of International Labor and Working-Class History*, no. 93 (2018): 135–150.

———. "Encadrement de la 'jeunesse' et service civique national au Sénégal: l'expérience limitée de Savoigne (1960–1968)." In *Décolonisation et enjeux post-coloniaux de l'enfance et de la jeunesse (1945–1980)*, edited by Yves Denechère, 161–170. Bruxelles: Peter Lang, 2019.

———. "Le renouveau de la «mission civilisatrice»? Développement et mobilisation de la main-d'œuvre au Sénégal (années 1960)." *Relations Internationales*, no. 177 (2019): 73–84.

UNESCO. *Sénégal. Plan d'un programme en faveur de l'éducation extrascolaire des jeunes*. Paris: UNESCO, 1969.

Van Beusekom, Monica M. *Negotiating Development: African Farmers and Colonial Experts at the Office du Niger, 1920–1960*. Portsmouth: Heinemann, 2002.

4 EDUCATION THROUGH LABOR: FROM THE *DEUXIÈME PORTION DU ...* 105

Open Access This chapter is licensed under the terms of the Creative Commons Attribution 4.0 International License (http://creativecommons.org/licenses/by/4.0/), which permits use, sharing, adaptation, distribution and reproduction in any medium or format, as long as you give appropriate credit to the original author(s) and the source, provide a link to the Creative Commons license and indicate if changes were made.

The images or other third party material in this chapter are included in the chapter's Creative Commons license, unless indicated otherwise in a credit line to the material. If material is not included in the chapter's Creative Commons license and your intended use is not permitted by statutory regulation or exceeds the permitted use, you will need to obtain permission directly from the copyright holder.

PART II

Training Economic Actors

CHAPTER 5

Becoming a Good Farmer—Becoming a Good Farm Worker: On Colonial Educational Policies in Germany and German South-West Africa, Circa 1890 to 1918

Jakob Zollmann

Notions of difference dominated contemporary German discourses about African colonies under German rule since 1885. Otherness and conceptual othering informed writing about Africans but also affected those Germans who decided to live in the colonies (German South-West Africa [GSWA, present-day Namibia], German East Africa [GEA, present-day Tanzania], Cameroon, and Togo). The requirements these men (and soon also women) had to fulfil, it was postulated, were different

---

The author expresses his gratitude to Dag Henrichsen and Herbert Lewis for their critical comments.

J. Zollmann (✉)
WZB Berlin Social Science Center, Berlin, Germany
e-mail: jakob.zollmann@wzb.eu

© The Author(s) 2020
D. Matasci et al. (eds.), *Education and Development in Colonial and Postcolonial Africa*, Global Histories of Education,
https://doi.org/10.1007/978-3-030-27801-4_5

from what was necessary for a "successful" life in the metropole. In Germany, colonial pressure groups and the colonial administration were thus looking for the "ideal settler," who was in pursuit of better prospects than the overcrowded metropolis could offer. Yet the question for contemporaries was: What was to be expected from such an "ideal settler"? How should these men earn a living in Africa (or the few other German colonies on the Pacific Islands)? Agriculture was often seen as the most advisable and preferable undertaking for settlers. The reason for this was that it would allow men from all walks of life to develop their own homesteads, using their own two hands, in the "primitive" conditions of the colonies. But given the imaginary task to create not only a *Neu-Deutschland*, but a different, a "better Germany" overseas, free from the "vices of modernity," were those Germans arriving in the colonies prepared for their futures?[1] How and where were they supposed to gain the knowledge needed for their colonial ventures?[2] In short, questions of knowledge accumulation with regard to the colonies and "colonial education" for (future) economic actors were paramount to the entire German colonial project and the settlement schemes that served to justify associated public expense (on this issue, see Chapter 6 by Caterina Scalvedi and Chapter 7 by Michael A. Kozakowski, both in this book).

Taking the example of German South-West Africa and the education of (prospective) farmers for life in this colony, this chapter is an attempt to merge the sub-fields of German (colonial) agrarian history and the history of (colonial) education into one analytical field. Education, teaching, learning, and knowledge are elementary and interrelated terms of pedagogy, and the theory and practice of education, teaching, and learning by historical actors offers concrete insights into societal norms and historical ideas about the future.[3] This is particularly relevant for contemporary debates about the German colonies and their intended

---

[1] Birte Kundrus, *Moderne Imperialisten: Das Kaiserreich im Spiegel Seiner Kolonien* (Cologne: Böhlau, 2003), 43.

[2] On questions of "colonial knowledge," see Rebekka Habermas and Alexandra Przyrembel, *Von Käfern, Märkten und Menschen: Kolonialismus und Wissen in der Moderne* (Göttingen: V&R, 2013), 10.

[3] Theodor Schulze, "Erziehung und Lernen. Plädoyer für eine mathetische Erziehungswissenschaft," in *Erziehungsdiskurse*, ed. by Winfried Marotzki and Lothar Wigger (Bad Heilbrunn: Klinkhardt, 2008), 29–50, 37.

futures. Colonial activities by law makers, administrators, and—last but not least—settler communities were not only meant to "initiate the beginning of state formation,"[4] as argued in 1886 by the state secretary of justice Herrmann von Schelling; colonies were also meant to develop into future sources of national wealth.[5]

From the perspective of policy makers, colonial education, as one form of colonial activity by officials and missionaries, was thus a process that concerned both the colonizers *and* colonized in the colonies *and* the metropolis. Its aim was to contribute to an improved, economically viable future for the colonies (on this issue, see Chapter 1 of this book by Damiano Matasci). Typically, there was a generational aspect of transferring agrarian knowledge. In the case of agrarian knowledge to be applied successfully by settlers in the colonies, this generational aspect of knowledge transfer, however, differed from other educational efforts in schools and universities in the metropole. The knowledge about the colonies often had to be gained at almost the same time (during research excursions) as it was supposed to be already available for dissemination to future farmers and others in Germany and the colonies. Those teaching and those learning about the agricultural conditions in the colony understood that many questions remained unanswered for the time being. For many problems related to farming in the colonies, solutions still had to be found through continued research before being institutionally transformed into empirical knowledge and educational material. Further, farmers did not always accept as applicable research findings by academics. Complaints about the "amateurism [*Laientum*] of our farmers" in GSWA remained until the demise of the German colonial empire in 1914.[6]

---

[4] Stenographische Berichte des Reichstags, 6. Leg. Per., 2. Session, 1885/1886, vol. 1, session of 20.1.1886, 653.

[5] See Jakob Zollmann, "'Neither the State Nor the Individual Goes to the Colony in Order to Make a Bad Business': State and Private Enterprise in the Making of Commercial Law in the German Colonies, ca. 1884 to 1914," in *The Influence of Colonies on Commercial Law and Practice*, ed. by Serge Dauchy and Albrecht Cordes (Leiden: Brill, 2020).

[6] Bundesarchiv Berlin (BAB) N 2272/1, Bl. 28–30, Heydebreck to Schuckmann, 9 February 1914.

The necessity to contextualize knowledge and education is most evident[7] in the context of colonization. Therefore, this chapter will consider four points of interest: (1) how colonial enthusiasts and administrators perceived the necessity for improved tropical agricultural education given the setbacks farmers experienced in GSWA; (2) how knowledge related to tropical agriculture was institutionalized and administered; (3) how, in Germany, two schools for tropical agriculture were set up; and (4) how the debate on the "education" of the African workforce in GSWA contributed to the exclusion of this group from the most elementary forms of education.

Conditions and Development Plans for Farming in GSWA—The Necessity for Agricultural Education

In 1883—in German pre-colonial times—the Hamburg lawyer, tradesman, and self-stylized expert on Africa, Wilhelm Hübbe-Schleiden (1846–1916), defined "colonialization-policy and colonization-technique" as the "art of colonial culture work [*colonisatorische Kulturarbeit*]." "Extensive cultivation" of colonized territories was for him, in the interpretation of historian Dirk van Laak, "cultural education," because, as Hübbe-Schleiden argued: "Colonization in new territories is a repetition of our own cultural development."[8]

In GSWA, such attempts at "repetition" and "cultural education"[9] were hampered, however, by the main constraint faced by the agricultural sector—the lack of water. The territory "has the driest climate in Africa south of the Sahara" and thus "agricultural production has, for the most part, remained marginal."[10] Whereas, due to the growing urban markets in the region, neighboring South Africa, witnessed, in the words

---

[7] Carola Groppe, *Im deutschen Kaiserreich: Eine Bildungsgeschichte des Bürgertums 1871–1918* (Vienna: Böhlau, 2018), 5.

[8] Dirk van Laak, *Imperiale Infrastruktur: Deutsche Planungen für eine Erschließung Afrikas 1880–1960* (Paderborn: Schöningh, 2004), 62; quoting W. Hübbe-Schleiden, Colonisations-Politik und Colonisation-Technik (Hamburg, 1883), 3.

[9] On the colonial topos of the paternalistic "education" of "backward peoples," see Sebastian Conrad, *Globalisierung und Nation im deutschen Kaiserreich* (Munich: Beck, 2006), 55.

[10] Tony Emmett, *Popular Resistance and the Roots of Nationalism in Namibia, 1915–1966* (Basel: Schlettwein, 1999), 39.

of historian Colin Bundy, a "virtual 'explosion' of peasant activity in the 1870s,"[11] the more arid regions to the north remained untouched by this "explosion." Whereas south of the Orange (Gariep) River, peasants increased their output of meat and wool production, breeding levels of ostrich and drought animals (oxen), dairy products, grain, fruit, and vegetables, the thinly populated Great Namaqualand, as it was contemporarily called, remained most famous for its hunting grounds for hides, ostrich feathers (which dwindled), and livestock breeding (i.e., small stock). Further north, in Hereroland, for example, cattle were bred and elephants were hunted for their ivory.

Bearing in mind such challenging environmental conditions, starting in the 1880s, German colonial enthusiasts still envisioned grandiose settlement schemes for GSWA. Their financial viability and feasibility in the face of the arid realities of the country remained, however, dubious.[12] Given the extremely dry climate in GSWA, barely 1% of the territory was suitable for crop cultivation. However, at least large parts could be used for cattle, goat, and sheep breeding.[13] From pre-colonial times, and until the outbreak of the war in 1904, the export of cattle from Hereroland (a grassland and bushland zone in the center of the later German colony) to the industrialized zones of the Cape and the mining districts of the Rand proved lucrative and remained an important economic factor for the territory.[14] Up to the 1890s, the main export product remained, however, guano deposits from Cape Cross and other coastal areas—used mostly as a fertilizer in the wineries of the Cape region. Once deposits were depleted, hopes remained high that gold, copper, and other minerals would prove lucrative. However, apart from the copper mines of Otavi most of these plans came to nothing, with diamonds only being found in 1908. Promising investment options were thus limited and by the mid-1890s it became evident that very few individuals had come over

---

[11] Colin Bundy, *The Rise and Fall of the South African Peasantry* (London: Currey, 1979), 67.

[12] See Alvin Kienetz, *Nineteenth-Century South West Africa as a German Settlement Colony* (2 vols.), diss. phil. University of Minnesota, 1976.

[13] Markus Denzel, "Die wirtschaftliche Bilanz des deutschen Kolonialreiches," in *Die Deutschen und ihre Kolonien. Ein Überblick*, ed. by Horst Gründer and Hermann Hiery (Berlin: Bebra, 2017), 144–160, 148.

[14] Johann Rawlinson, *The Meat Industry of Namibia, 1835–1994* (Windhoek: Gamsberg, 1994).

from Germany, daring to invest their capital and labor in colonial land in order to raise cattle. The German colonial government tried to find some arable land and further territories suitable for extensive cattle farming by usurping land from the Africans. Yet, by the late 1890s, barely 1200 Germans lived in the colony, of which around 800 were soldiers or government officials.[15] Thus, in GSWA "farmers" of European origin barely numbered in the hundreds—many of them were not Germans, but Afrikaners arriving from the Cape or Transvaal.[16] This hesitation to settle in GSWA points to issues in the political economy of this colony that are in need of further explanation.

In the early days of formal German rule in GSWA, the indigenous population, mostly Ovaherero herders, continued to raise cattle successfully in order to amass wealth and status. "[F]rom the 1880s Herero were regarded as wealthy cattle-owners par excellence."[17] It is said that the cattle herds of the most important *ovahona* (big men), such as Maharero and Kambazembi, numbered at times 40,000 or even 70,000. Given Herero knowledge of water sources and grazing areas, it was inconceivable that new arrivals from Germany would be able to compete with the African cattle breeders, let alone "outfarm black peasants"—to borrow an expression from Colin Bundy.[18] The few who did try often failed miserably. They attempted to diversify their business into hunting and most of all itinerant trading in (European consumption) goods in exchange for cattle and hides.[19]

However, the economic and thus the political situation changed completely with the *rinderpest* epidemic of 1897/1898. The dangers of animal diseases in southern Africa, especially for horses and oxen, had been described early on by European travelers and scientists.[20] However, the

[15] Deutsche Kolonialgesellschaft, Kleiner Deutscher Kolonialatlas (Berlin: Reimer, 1899), remarks Map 5.

[16] Robbie Aitken, "Looking for Die Besten Boeren: The Normalisation of Afrikaner Settlement in German South West Africa, 1884–1914," *Journal of Southern African Studies* 33, no. 2 (2007): 343–360.

[17] Dag Henrichsen, *Herrschaft und Alltag im vorkolonialen Zentralnamibia. Das Herero- und Damaraland im 19. Jahrhundert* (Basel: BAB, 2011), 186, translation in Marion Wallace, *A History of Namibia* (London, 2011), 104.

[18] Bundy, *The Rise and Fall of the South African Peasantry*, 67.

[19] Matthias Häussler, *Der Genozid an den Herero* (Weilerswist: Velbrück, 2018), 47.

[20] See Hans Schinz, "Ein neuer Bauernstaat im Südwesten Afrika's," *Mitteilungen der Ostschweizerischen Geographisch-Commerciellen Gesellschaft in St. Gallen* (1886), 26–31, 27.

rinderpest had a hitherto unprecedented death toll. The German colonial army (*Schutztruppe*) helped to inoculate animals owned by German farmers or the government using a method developed on the spot by Robert Koch. About 80,000 cattle were rescued.[21] Ovaherero, on the other hand, were much harder hit because they lacked the ability to vaccinate. At the same time, Governor Leutwein continued with his policy of land confiscation from Africans, trying to free grazing ground for prospective German farmers through "agreements" with Herero chiefs about "German" and "Herero" land. Given the unattainable knowledge of Ovaherero herders about the raising of cattle, Leutwein was intent on actively reducing their herds. He justified this measure by invoking the necessity to protect "our farmers" from the economic power of the Ovaherero (through their expanding cattle herds); otherwise he foresaw "difficult imbroglios."[22] During the epidemic, some Herero families lost up to 90% of their herds. These disastrous losses forced them to sell their remaining cattle as well as land to the Germans in order to repay their "debts" to German traders.

In this context, it is relevant to recall that "in pre-colonial societies the land was owned communally and could therefore not be inherited, private property existed mainly in the form of livestock, especially cattle, goats, sheep, horses, donkeys."[23] The notion of private, vendible land titles (including water wells) was thus foreign to Herero and other groups. And yet the German colonial government continued to press for strict limits between communal (African) land and private (German) land acquired from Africans—cattle that had "trespassed" into German farming areas were confiscated. The political goal behind this willingly accepted impoverishment of the Herero was twofold: first, the creation of large swathes of land "free" to be "developed" by German settlers eager to start their own farms; and second, the creation of a class of wage-dependent African farmworkers. As long as Herero chiefs

---

[21] Myron Echenberg, "'Scientific Gold': Robert Koch and Africa, 1883–1906," in *Agency and Action in Colonial Africa*, ed. by C.P. Youé and T.J. Stapleton (London: Palgrave, 2001), 34–49; Giorgio Miescher, "Namibia's Red Line," *The History of a Veterinary and Settlement Border* (New York: Palgrave, 2012), 29.

[22] Cited in Helmut Bley, *Kolonialherrschaft und Sozialstruktur in Deutsch-Südwestafrika* (Hamburg: Leibnitz, 1968), 75, 82–85.

[23] Ellen Ndeshi Namhila, *"Little Research Value": African Estate Records and Colonial Gaps in a Post-colonial Archives* (Basel: BAB, 2017), 59.

controlled huge cattle herds and large territories, these German plans for a colonial future were impossible to attain. Therefore, the rinderpest epidemic was an important stepping stone toward the goal of a strong German farming community in GSWA. By 1902, Herero-owned cattle herds had diminished to about 46,000, down from about 100,000 in the early 1890s, and the number of cattle owned by Germans had risen to 44,000.[24] It was thus no wonder that Germans in GSWA believed that "the outbreak [of the rinderpest] had a positive impact on economic development."[25]

Given the hesitation of individual Germans to purchase land in GSWA, in the 1890s the German colonial administration resorted to selling concessions for large tracts of land in the colony to joint-stock companies—these were often financed by British money, which many in Germany deplored.[26] Consequently, in 1903 six companies owned around 38% of the territory of GSWA.[27] However, their land policies, aimed at selling farms to individual farmers, were poorly planned and executed. They barely served the overall aim of establishing a settler colony. The "first organized efforts to resettle Germans on the colonial frontier," having started in 1892, ended with a "string of failures and lawsuits and a dire tale of proletarianization."[28]

Other areas remained "crown land," owned by the government. Yet despite a growing number of Germans in GSWA (3000 in 1903) the development of a farming economy did not take off. Former governor (*Landeshauptmann*) Curt von François stated that GSWA is not "what it is supposed to be, an export market for Germany."[29] Nor were German farmers in GSWA exporting their produce to Germany. Whereas by "the

[24] Wolfgang Werner, *No One Will Become Rich: Economy and Society in the Herero Reserves in Namibia, 1915–1946* (Basel: Schlettwein, 1998), 44f.

[25] Miescher, *Namibia's Red Line*, 30.

[26] Friedrich Bruck, "Die Zukunft Deutsch-Südwestafrika," *Die Grenzboten* 1/1899 (59. Jg): 289–299; Curt von Francois, *Staat oder Gesellschaft in unseren Kolonien* (Berlin, 1901) (Soziale Streitfragen vol. X).

[27] Kundrus, *Moderne Imperialisten*, 47; see Horst Drechsler, *Südwestafrika unter deutscher Kolonialherrschaft. Die großen Land- und Minengesellschaften, 1885–1914* (Stuttgart: Steiner, 1996).

[28] John Phillip Short, *Magic Lantern Empire: Colonialism and Society in Germany* (Ithaca, NY: Cornell University Press, 2012), 71.

[29] Curt von Francois, "Unsere südwestafrikanische Kolonie," *Die Grenzboten* 56, no. 4 (1897): 67.

turn of the twentieth century, Britain's tropical African colonies had begun to undergo an 'export boom' in agricultural and mineral products,"[30] in 1899, a publication by the pressure group, German Colonial Society (*DKG*), listed very few export products of GSWA: "hides, horns, ostrich feathers, natural resin, tanning substances, guano, raw furs." GSWA's exports amounted to barely 1.2 million Reichsmark.[31] In fact, around 1900, most of the Europeans still lived "almost exclusively on the money ... that the military and officials bring into the [colony]," with most Germans in the colony working either directly or indirectly for the government.[32] The privileged land allocations to big land companies were repeatedly met with criticism.[33] With regard to German colonization, the geographer Friedrich Ratzel criticized, in his *Introduction to Heimatkunde*, that it had "benefitted only the freer activity of individuals or small groups, not the masses."[34]

After 1900, it became increasingly clear to the colonial administration in Berlin that the old Bismarckian idea that private money exclusively should stir colonial development had failed. Government measures taken to promote the economy in the colonies were half-hearted. However, the 1901 imperial budget for GSWA listed not only planned expenses for new buildings, roads, and the expansion of the harbor in Swakopmund, but also investments in wells and dams and other activities that aimed to improve agriculture and stock farming.[35] By engaging in such fiscal activity, the government aimed to respond to allegations that the colonial administrators had privileged land companies over ordinary settlers.[36] Despite such efforts, by 1904 the number of farmers from Germany had barely risen to 300.[37]

[30] Helen Tilley, *Africa as a Living Laboratory: Empire, Development, and the Problem of Scientific Knowledge, 1870–1950* (Chicago: University of Chicago Press, 2011), 124.

[31] Deutsche Kolonialgesellschaft, *Kleiner Deutscher Kolonialatlas* (Berlin: Reimer, 1899), remark Map 5.

[32] Francois, "Unsere südwestafrikanische Kolonie," 72.

[33] Friedrich Bruck, "Die Zukunft Deutsch-Südwestafrikas," *Die Grenzboten* 1, no. 59 (1899): 289–299, 298.

[34] Friedrich Ratzel, *Deutschland: Einführung in die Heimatkunde* (Leipzig: Grunow, 1898), 308.

[35] *Reichsgesetzblatt* (Berlin, 1901), 92.

[36] See Bley, *Kolonialherrschaft*, 110, 172.

[37] Berengar von Zastrow, "Farmwirtschaft," in *Die deutschen Kolonien in Wort und Bild*, ed. by Hans Zache (Berlin: Andermann, 1926), 163–169, 163.

Government plans for the settlement of farmers did not guarantee success either, some ended in disaster for the individuals involved—often former colonial soldiers. From the colonial government, they had received "crown land" very cheaply (3000–5000 hectares in the savanna areas in the central and northern part of GSWA, and up to 20,000 hectares in the arid south); but their business plans were underfinanced and many lacked specific knowledge and experience in agriculture. In addition, living conditions could worsen any time due to a lack of rain, transport, customers and thus turnover. An additional problem in this respect was a lack of workforce. In many cases relations between German farmers and their African workforces were characterized by poor payments, lack of food, and—at times—violence.[38] Given these underlying difficulties, if diseases struck herds or crops, farmers became bankrupt. For example, the 33-year-old W. Bandelow, who had served with the colonial military, the *Schutztruppe*, from 1893 to 1899 and then settled as a farmer near Rehoboth, had, after "many setbacks, loss of property and cattle diseases," merely 1 horse, 6 cows, and 20 goats. In 1903 he wrote to the colonial administration: "Since I cannot get on with this, I beg... to get me a position as a policeman somewhere."[39]

There were of course counterexamples of farmers having financial success due to their cattle sales. But in response to the difficulties that farmers complained about and given the overarching political goal to populate the colony with more German settlers in order to "make the country German," the government became more willing to grant loans for prospective farmers. Colonial administrators like the future governor Friedrich von Lindequist further developed plans to accelerate this population policy with the granting of smaller plots of farmland (a few hectares) to German settlers (*Kleinsiedler*) in the few parts of Hereroland where rain was more abundant, for example, near Okahandja or around the Waterberg. The *Kleinsiedler* were supposed to grow wheat, fruit, and vegetables for the few towns in the colony. Again, the experience and

---

[38] See Andreas Eckl, "Weiß oder Schwarz? Kolonialer Farmalltag in Deutsch-Südwestafrika," in *Die (koloniale) Begegnung: AfrikanerInnen in Deutschland und schwarze Deutsche*, ed. by Marianne Bechhaus-Gerst and Reinhard Klein-Arendt (Frankfurt/M.: P. Lang, 2003), 109–124; Jakob Zollmann, *Koloniale Herrschaft und ihre Grenzen: Die Kolonialpolizei in Deutsch-Südwestafrika* (Göttingen: V&R, 2010), 281–299.

[39] National Archives of Namibia (NAN) BWI 155, L 2 e, Bl.37, Protokoll W. Bandelow. DKdo Rehoboth, 9.1.1903; Bl. 36, BHpt Windhoek to DKdo Rehoboth, 19.1.1903.

knowledge of the Ovaherero was decisive here, since in the early 1890s Herero farmers had already had some success growing wheat, corn, and tobacco. Cereal cropping was part of their economic strategy of diversifying their income in times of falling cattle prices. However, in absolute terms the quantity of cereals produced remained limited.[40] It turned out that a colonial project like the *Kleinsiedlungen* (literally "small settlements"), aiming at the *mise en valeur* and the socioeconomic transformation of GSWA, could not transcend the bounds set by the climate and (colonial) economy. As horticulturalists, the German *Kleinsiedler*, as contemporary critics had warned, hardly had success in this attempt to meaningfully expand the production patterns of the colony. And even if they succeeded in their production, they had not enough customers in the vicinity to make their undertaking economically viable.[41]

If "cultural education" in the colony was the political goal, in an attempt to repeat the economic development of Germany, very little had been achieved. It was only in the aftermath of the wars against the Ovaherero and Nama (1904–1908) that the colonial administration started in earnest to implement its plans for a German farming community in the center of the colony. But even then, and despite state-funded subsidies for new farmers (around 500,000 Marks per year), "many farms, undercapitalised and in debt, were soon in a parlous economic state."[42] In Germany, the press ridiculed the "dream of settlement colonialism."[43]

In modern academic parlance, these administrative policies can rightfully be described as "social engineering,"[44] aimed at creating order, security, and economic viability in an agricultural zone that was still to be established in an environment perceived by the German settlers as dangerous and inimical. It turned out that Germans willing to work in GSWA had first to educate themselves about the conditions of its territories before attempts to develop the colony could be undertaken. The colonial government's increasing reliance on knowledge

---

[40] See Henrichsen, *Herrschaft und Alltag im vorkolonialen Zentralnamibia*, 184.

[41] Zastrow, "Farmwirtschaft," 165; see Kundrus, *Moderne Imperialisten*, 61–77.

[42] Wallace, *A History of Namibia*, 186.

[43] Short, *Magic Lantern Empire*, 71.

[44] See Carl Marklund, "Begriffsgeschicht and Übergriffsgeschichte in the History of Social Engineering," in *Die Ordnung der Moderne: Social Engineering im 20. Jahrhundert*, ed. by Thomas Etzemüller (Bielefeld: transcript, 2009), 199–222, 199.

about the colonies and "scientific" techniques to attain its goals grew out of the experiences of those having failed during the two decades following 1885.

Colonial Knowledge and Tropical Agriculture: A Research and Teaching Subject in Germany—An Administrative Task in GSWA

Knowledge about humans, animals, plants, geology, etc., that was specific to the colonies had always played an important role in the upkeep of colonial rule by European overlords. Since the days of the Portuguese "explorers" (self-declared) academic specialists had accompanied colonial administrators. They observed, took notes, compared, and produced texts about their findings. They were asked to do so in order to enable colonial officials and their troops to penetrate ever deeper into hitherto unknown territories, which were in the long run to be transformed into economically viable colonies. To this end, in the British colonies throughout the eighteenth and nineteenth centuries a number of publications were written on "tropical" agricultural questions.[45]

By the late nineteenth century, the buildup of a corpus of knowledge about tropical agriculture, mostly acquired through the experiences of settlers in the colonies, was part of the general development toward the "scientification of the colonial" (*Verwissenschaftlichung des Kolonialen*).[46] Near London, the botanical gardens at Kew collected plants from all over the globe. In Berlin, in 1891, the *Botanische Zentralstelle für die deutschen Kolonien* began to undertake research on the plants and seeds it received from the colonies. Government departments dedicated to agricultural services were set up in colonies around the world. Questions arose about the educational requirements of future staff at such departments. At the same time training, not only of (academic) specialists but also settlers eager to work in agriculture, was given greater attention by colonial administrators. In 1893, in Ceylon a "Superintendent of

---

[45] See George Porter, *The Tropical Agriculturist: A Practical Treatise* (London: Smith, 1833).

[46] Anne Kwaschik, *Der Griff nach dem Weltwissen: Zur Genealogie von Area Studies im 19. und 20. Jahrhundert* (Göttingen: V&R, 2018), 29.

the School of Agriculture" was appointed. In 1899, in Dominica in the Caribbean the title "agricultural instructor" was used for the first time.[47]

The establishment of institutions of tertiary education, specifically set up for men (and sometimes women) planning to work in the colonies, was on the agenda of colonial officials around 1900. British, French, German, Belgian, and Dutch administrations developed curricula, and Ph.D. and M.D. theses were written on "colonial subjects." Contemporaries were aware that such knowledge served as an "Instrument of Empire."[48] However, in the age of empire before World War I the "science of colonization" still had to prove, to contemporaries, its scientific character (*Wissenschaftlichkeit*). As historian Anne Kwaschik has shown, "colonial science" or *la colonistique*, *Kolonistik* did not yet have the status of a discipline among the other academic disciplines with a clear definition about the areas of knowledge covered and a canon on methods and questions. Rather, many disciplines from medicine, geography, ethnography, agriculture, and botany to theology, law, and economics participated in the academic discourses on colonialism and the colonies. On the other hand, promoters of the idea of colonization of foreign territories were adamant to prove that the *mise en valeur* of the colonies required "colonial sciences." Thus, *Wissenschaftlichkeit* as a methodical approach to the colonies was—most of all—a cultural code that granted legitimacy to colonial policies around the world.[49]

It has recently been argued that "German imperialists ranked amongst the most ardent advocates of the use of science and technology in the systematic development of the colonies, not least because of Germany's belatedness as an imperial power."[50] In view of this self-perceived "belatedness," German administrators eagerly attempted to, sooner rather than later, reach the same stage of colonial development as France and most

---

[47] G.B. Masefield, *A History of the Colonial Agricultural Service* (Oxford: Oxford University Press, 1972), 117, 132.

[48] Sir Charles Bruce, "Tropical Medicine as Instrument of Empire," *Journal of Tropical Medicine and Hygiene* 11 (1908): 334; but cf. Herbert Lewis, *In Defense of Anthropology: An Investigation of the Critique of Anthropology* (New Brunswick, NJ: Transaction Publishers, 2014), 99f.

[49] Kwaschik, *Der Griff nach dem Weltwissen*, 29, 31, 39.

[50] Robrecht Declerq, "Building Imperial Frontiers: Business, Science and Karakul Sheep Farming in (German) South-West Africa (1903–1939)," *Journal of Modern European History* 14 (2016): 54–77, 55.

of all Great Britain. The German willingness to learn from the "methods" and past and present experiences in foreign colonies, whether through reports or on-site visits, is most evident in German colonial files.[51] Given the lack of economic alternatives and the ideas by German colonial enthusiasts to develop colonies into agrarian anti-modern refuges, agriculture as a way of life and as a knowledge system always played an important part in these debates. This can also be seen in the "colonial programme" of the colonial secretary Bernhard Dernburg (in office from 1906 to 1910). In 1907, after the genocidal wars in GSWA that led to the decimation of the labor force and the financial disaster German colonialism had caused over the last 20 years, he aimed at putting a greater emphasis on the "rational" exploitation of the riches of the colonies. In his "colonial programme," he combined economic and civilizational narratives. The colonial goal was, he argued, the "utilization of the soil, its riches, of the flora and fauna and most of all of the people for the benefit of the economy of the colonizing nation." The latter in turn was obliged to the "counter-present [*Gegengabe*] of its higher culture, its moral ideas, its better methods."[52]

At the time the colonial secretary set these goals, the "utilization of the soil" was an accepted research and teaching subject in German universities. In German territories, literature on agriculture, horticulture, and silviculture was well established by the sixteenth century and fulfilled mostly practical requirements proprietors and managers had in terms of enhancing their returns from estates.[53] In 1863, one of the first German chairs of agriculture (Professor Julius Kühn) had been institutionalized at the University of Halle. Thirty years later, Ferdinand Wohltmann, a professor of agriculture in Bonn began his study excursions to the German colonies. Due to his publications he became recognized as Germany's leading expert on tropical agriculture. Wohltmann intended to impress upon his readers the "national importance" of research in (tropical) agricultural questions and was elected a member of the board of the

---

[51] See Ulrike Lindner, *Koloniale Begegnungen: Deutschland und Großbritannien als Imperialmächte in Afrika 1880–1914* (Frankfurt/M.: Campus, 2011); Dirk van Laak, "Kolonien als 'Laboratorien der Moderne'?" in *Das Kaiserreich transnational: Deutschland in der Welt 1871–1914*, ed. by Sebastian Conrad and Jürgen Osterhammel (Göttingen: V&R, 2004), 257–279, 257.

[52] Bernhard Dernburg, *Zielpunkte des deutschen Kolonialwesens* (Berlin: Mittler, 1907), 5.

[53] Gertrud Schröder-Lembke, *Studien zur Agrargeschichte* (Stuttgart: Lucius, 1977), 81.

Deutsche Kolonialgesellschaft in 1897. From 1900, he edited jointly with Otto Warburg (1859–1938) the journal *Der Tropenpflanzer*, which reported regularly on agricultural "progress" in all the German colonies.[54] Following his transfer to the University of Halle in 1905, Wohltmann took the opportunity to set up (in 1908) and head the "Halle colonial academy," with the purpose of supporting the colonial administration with its research and teaching in tropical agriculture.[55]

After 1900, the research topic of "tropical agriculture" developed into an academic subject taught at a number of German universities. Similar to "colonial geography," with its practical relevance for the "development" of Germany's colonial empire, "colonial and tropical agriculture" became a research topic for which qualification theses could be written, namely German *promotion* and *habilitation* qualifications. The agriculturalist Arthur Golf was one of the first German academics who, having defended in 1903 his dissertation on agricultural irrigation in North America,[56] specialized from the very beginning of his career in colonial agriculture. An academic pupil of Wohltmann, in 1907 he obtained his habilitation for colonial and tropical agriculture. Also in 1907, Golf traveled on the request of the colonial secretary to South Africa and GSWA to undertake research on the improvement of farming methods under arid conditions.[57] Similar to their British counterparts, German (agricultural) scientists saw "Africa as a living laboratory," as historian Hellen Tilley argues, examining African soils and plants with modern methods, but at the same time trying to give credit to local systems of knowledge, for example, by researching the pharmaceutical value of "plants of the Herero and Hottentotts."[58] Given the fact that there were few specialists in the field, in 1912 the University of Leipzig installed the first and only extraordinary chair of tropical and colonial agriculture.

[54] "Aus deutschen Kolonien," *Der Tropenpflanzer* (1901), 90f.; Otto Warburg, "Die wirtschaftliche Entwicklung unserer Schutzgebiete im Jahre 1903," *Der Tropenpflanzer* 8. Jg (1904), 14.

[55] Arthur Golf, *Zu Ferdinand Wohltmanns Gedächtnis* (Leipzig, 1919).

[56] Arthur Golf, *Untersuchungen über die natürlichen Grundlagen der nordamerikanischen Bewässerungswirtschaft*, Ph.D. diss., University of Halle, 1903.

[57] Arthur Golf, *Ackerbau in Deutsch-Südwestafrika: Das Trockenfarmen und seine Anwendung in D.S.W.A.* (Berlin: Süsserott, 1911) (Koloniale Abhandlungen no. 47/50).

[58] Tilley, *Africa as a Living Laboratory*, 127; NAN ZBU 1013 J.XIII. c. 1–2 Botanische Forschungen, Hellwig: Angaben von Eingeborenen über die Feldkost und Arzneipflanzen, June 1907.

Golf was, thanks to his mentor Ferdinand Wohltmann, successful in his bid for this position and became a professor in Leipzig. Golf's teaching before the war centered mostly on farming agriculture as he had experienced it in GSWA.

The authorities in GSWA were well aware of the opportunities "modern science" provided for the agricultural sector of the colony. Most of all the "traumatic experience of the rinderpest epidemic had triggered the improvement and professionalization of veterinary science and services."[59] It had become clear that even those men who had succeeded in becoming good farmers were helpless before the onslaught of a hitherto incurable disease. State invention for their protection seemed thus without alternative and came in addition to massive state investment in water drilling and dam building. In 1899 the governorate in Windhoek installed its own veterinary administration in addition to the departments of agriculture and land surveying.[60] In doing so, the German colonial administration was even ahead of its British counterparts in most British colonies and protectorates, where departments of agriculture were mostly institutionalized between 1902 and 1912.[61]

By 1911 the government's care for economic actors related to all forms of agriculture, which had developed into a sophisticated administration: seven sub-departments (*Referate*) were tasked with questions related to farming, veterinarian services, and water exploration.[62] The veterinary service in GSWA, for a long time headed by *Oberveterinär* Wilhelm Rickmann, consisted of 17 veterinarians. Furthermore, from 1898 the bacteriological institute in Gammams, near Windhoek, undertook research into the causes of animal diseases and means to prevent their spread. Also, the colonial police force, established in 1907 was tasked with not only controlling the trade in livestock but also, after receiving training, as economic actors in their own right. In addition to their duty to control and closely watch the African workforce, policemen

---

[59] Giorgio Miescher, "Facing Barbarians: A Narrative of Spatial Segregation in Namibia," *Journal of Southern African Studies* 38 (2012): 769–786, 774.

[60] "Referate des Gouvernements" (… Ref. VIII Veterinärwesen, Viehzucht (Rossarzt Rickmann); Ref. IX Landwirtschaft, Wasseranlagen, Meteorologie (Watermeyer); Ref. X Landvermessung. Landesaufnahme (Görgens)), "Decree of June 1899," reprinted in Windhoeker Anzeiger No. 29, 9.11.1899, 2.

[61] Masefield, *A History of the Colonial*, 33; Tilley, *Africa as a Living Laboratory*, 124.

[62] BAB R 1002/47, 20, 23, Geschäftsverteilungsplan Gouvernement, 2 June 1911.

were given basic veterinary education in order to be able to protect cattle from diseases by controlling animals and their movement. They were given specific legal competences by the governorate concerning quarantine; yet the "veterinary service was able to fulfil these goals [of animal health] only in part."[63] Nevertheless, by 1914, it is estimated that livestock numbered at least 1.2 million animals in farm areas (within the "police zone") of GSWA (mainly goats, cattle, and sheep).[64] In the words of historian Giorgio Miescher these veterinary projects need to be understood "as representations of state intervention and as specific examples of the modernization of agriculture and livestock farming. In both these instances, scientific arguments assumed increasing importance."[65]

"GERMANY HAS THE EDUCATION AND NOT THE COLONIES." THE *DEUTSCHE KOLONIALSCHULE FÜR LANDWIRTSCHAFT* AND THE COLONIAL WOMEN'S SCHOOL

Education (*Erziehung*) was a theme and a trope regularly applied in German colonial discourses. Early on in the debate the "necessity of a specific professional training of the colonial officials... generally already in the mother country" was perceived.[66] Given the recurring accusations that German (colonial) officials acted rather naively with regard to economic questions, in 1892 a member of the colonial council, an (economic) advisory body to the colonial department, suggested that Germany's colonial service should be based on commercial and agricultural training. The council, however, did not support this proposal.[67]

Founded in 1887, 2 years after the formal declaration of German sovereignty overseas, the Berlin "Seminar for Oriental Languages" (*Seminar für Orientalische Sprachen*) was most of all meant to improve the communication abilities of tradesmen and colonial administrators.[68]

[63] Miescher, *Namibia's Red Line*, 58, 86.
[64] Werner, "*No One Will Become Rich*," 63.
[65] Miescher, *Namibia's Red Line*, 200.
[66] Max Beneke, *Die Ausbildung der Kolonialbeamten* (Berlin: Heymann, 1894), v.
[67] B. v. König, "Die Beamten der deutschen Schutzgebiete, ihre Rechtsverhältnisse, Bezüge und Auswahl," *Jahrbuch der internationalen Vereinigung für vergleichende Rechtswissenschaft und Volkswirtschaftslehre* 8 (1905): 217–257, 251.
[68] Beneke, *Die Ausbildung der Kolonialbeamten*, 74; R. Ehrenberg, "Zur wirtschaftlichen Vorbildung höherer deutscher Kolonialbeamter," *Beiträge zur Kolonialpolitik und Kolonialwirtschaft* 1 (1899/1900): 97–98.

Following criticism from the colonial council and press, after 1893 the areas of meteorology, trade policy, "tropical hygiene," and "tropical agriculture" were added.[69]

Apart from this "department of Colonial studies," more and more universities all over Germany added subjects they considered to be of "colonial relevance" to their curricula. In 1908, the *Kolonialinstitut* was founded in Hamburg as a central academic institution for colonial questions.[70] However, as the bankruptcy of many farmers in GSWA illustrated, private individuals without academic qualification who were willing to set up businesses in the colonies needed specific knowledge too, not only capital. Already in the proto-colonial era, German businessmen dealing with agricultural products from Africa noted with remorse that in "Germany currently [1879] the number of people who know something about tropical plantations is still very small."[71]

But whereas the *Reich* administration chose to intervene in the training of colonial officials—also in light of reoccurring colonial scandals due to the ruthless behavior of colonial officials like Carl Peters in East Africa—improvement in the education of settlers was left to private initiative. It was only in 1898, thus more than 10 years after the founding of the *Seminar für Orientalische Sprachen*, that colonial enthusiasts around the Lutheran pastor Ernst Albert Fabarius (1859–1927), politicians of the conservative *Deutschnationale* party, merchants and industrialists especially from the Rhineland, and nobility the likes of Duke Johann Albrecht zu Mecklenburg (president of the DKG) came together in order to set up an institution that could alleviate the long-felt problem of the lack of preparation of German settlers. The group envisioned a school for prospective settlers, where essential and practical up-to-date agricultural knowledge about, and for, the German colonies (but also

---

[69] Karl Gareis, *Deutsches Kolonialrecht* (Giessen: Roth, 1902), 42; see Marc Grohmann, *Exotische Verfassung: Die Kompetenzen des Reichstags für die deutschen Kolonien in Gesetzgebung und Staatsrechtswissenschaft des Kaiserreichs (1884–1914)* (Tübingen: Mohr, 2001), 264; Stephan Besser, "Die Organisation des kolonialen Wissens," in *Mit Deutschland um die Welt: Eine Kulturgeschichte des Fremden in der Kolonialzeit*, ed. by Alexander Honold and Klaus R. Scherpe (Stuttgart: Metzler, 2004), 272–279, 274.

[70] Kwaschik, Der Griff nach dem Weltwissen, 70. See Jens Ruppenthal, *Kolonialismus als "Wissenschaft und Technik:" Das Hamburgische Kolonialinstitut 1908 bis 1919* (Stuttgart: Steiner, 2007).

[71] Wilhelm Hübbe-Schleiden, *Ethiopien, Studien über West-Afrika* (Hamburg: Friederichsen, 1879), 238.

other overseas territories) could be collected and disseminated. By creating colonial experts in their field, it would be possible to "save part of the time of apprenticeship overseas"—a time that hitherto cost dearly to those settlers who arrived in the colonies unprepared.[72] By this logic, it seemed more promising to obtain in Europe the education needed for the training of competent economic actors and thus for the development of colonial Africa.[73] Similar to the British case, German colonial enthusiasts believed in the "triumph of experts" and their "agrarian doctrines of development" for the colonies.[74]

In May 1898 the *Deutsche Kolonialschule für Landwirtschaft, Handel und Gewerbe Wilhelmshof* (DKS) in Witzenhausen (northern Hesse) was founded as a private enterprise (*GmbH*), but with the moral and continuing financial support of the colonial administration in Berlin. The DKS provided a concrete example for actors and institutions involved in shaping the link between education and "development" in German colonial Africa. This initiative was part of a "wave of foundations of [colonial] institutes in Europe" around 1900.[75] The school board, including the agriculturalist professor Wohltmann, viewed (colonial) agricultural education as a means not only to make the German colonies economically more viable through the application of "modern," "scientific" methods, but also as a means to spread the *kolonialer Gedanke* in Germany.[76]

Also, the DKS was a prime example of how international and imperial discourses on the agricultural *mise en valeur* of the colonies led to concrete attempts to copy best-practice examples from one colonial power to another. For the German case such transnational and inter-imperial entanglements have been investigated, most of all for the German cotton industry in Togo.[77] But the inter-imperial circulations of knowledge also

---

[72] Article "Witzenhausen," in *Deutsches Kolonial-Lexikon*, vol. III (Leipzig, 1920), 723f.

[73] Kwaschik, *Der Griff nach dem Weltwissen*, 70.

[74] Joseph Hodge, *Triumph of the Expert: Agrarian Doctrines of Developments and the Legacies of British Colonialism* (Athens: Ohio University Press, 2007).

[75] Kwaschik, *Der Griff nach dem Weltwissen*, 49; Jens Böhlke, *Zur Geschichte der Deutschen Kolonialschule in Witzenhausen: Aspekte ihres Entstehens und Wirkens* (Witzenhausen: Werratalverein, 1995), 96.

[76] Karsten Linne, *Von Witzenhausen in die Welt: Ausbildung und Arbeit von Tropenlandwirten 1898 bis 1971* (Göttingen: Wallstein, 2017), 25–35.

[77] Andrew Zimmerman, *Alabama in Africa: Booker T. Washington, the German Empire, and the Globalization of the New South* (Princeton: Princeton University Press, 2010).

concerned the history of education—both in and about Africa. Like the academic colonial institutions set up around 1900 in Germany, in a similar manner to the DKS, the German colonial "late-comers" were willing to look west and learn from the more seasoned colonial powers.[78] Fabarius considered as most relevant the British *Colonial college and training farms* in Harwich and the Dutch *Rijkslandbouwschool* (National Agricultural College), already established in 1876 in Wageningen.

In turn, it was seen by Germans with satisfaction that the "colonial school" in Nantes, France, was allegedly "modeled exactly after the plan of the German colonial school" in Witzenhausen.[79] The first edition of the DKS's own publication *Der deutsche Kulturpionier* (1900) quoted with pride an unnamed French newspaper that had characterized the DKS as "*l'institut colonial le plus complet!*"[80] In 1911, the British journalist Louis Hamilton, who worked in Berlin as an English teacher at the Seminar for Oriental Languages, commented: "the Colonial School of Witzenhausen … is in reality preeminently an agricultural college … What is evident is that in education of the better class of colonists Germany is ahead of all countries, as she always is in matters educational. If we Britishers, with our vast Empire, would only remember what our own opportunities for Colonial education are, we might begin to turn over a new leaf. … Germany has the education and not the Colonies; we have the Colonies and not the education."[81]

The DKS offered to educate and practically train future plantation officials, as well as farmers, livestock farmers, or wine and fruit farmers for the German colonies and other settlement areas in the (sub)tropics. For such settlements, the DKS welcomed German nationals aged between 17 and 27 years of age on training courses lasting between 2 and 3 years. Fabarius remained eager in emphasizing the "academic character" (*Hochschulcharakter*) of the DKS. There were, however, no formal secondary education requirements for admittance to the DKS. It was a

---

[78] See Jakob Zollmann, "German Colonial Law and Comparative Law, 1884–1919," in *Entanglements in Legal History: Conceptual Approaches*, ed. by Thomas Duve (Frankfurt/M.: MPI, 2014), 253–294.

[79] Article "Kolonialschulen," in *Meyers Großes Konversations-Lexikon*, vol. 11 (Leipzig, 1907), 290.

[80] "Ausländische Kolonialschulen," *Der deutsche Kulturpionier* 1, no. 1 (1900): 40.

[81] Cited in Böhlke, *Zur Geschichte der Deutschen Kolonialschule*, 95; see Besser, "Die Organisation," 274.

tenet of Fabarius to jointly consider practice and theory in the school's efforts to impart knowledge about (colonial) agriculture. This policy—Fabarius spoke of "colonial pedagogics"—resulted in an immense curriculum (laid out over 6 days a week from 7:15 a.m. to 6 p.m.) that all too often demanded too much of students. The subjects taught were grouped into "general," "agriculture," "tropical," "practical works," and "physical exercises,"[82] topics, thus:

The "course list" of the summer term 1900 included the following courses:

   I. General: 1. Ethnology, 2. History of Religion, 3. Organic Chemistry, 4. General Botany and Plant Physiology, 5. Practical Geology, 6. Veterinary Medicine, 7. Tropical Medicine, 8. Economics with special reference to the colonial economy.
  II. Agriculture: 1. Crop production, 2. Vegetables, Horticulture, and Viticulture, 3. Land Surveying, 4. Forestry, 5. Civil Engineering (bridge construction, road construction, irrigation and drainage).
 III. Tropical: 1. Planting and operating plantations, 2. Tropical fruits and vegetables, 3. Tropical domestic animals and steppe farming.
  IV. Practical work: 1. Forge, 2. Locksmithery, 3. Wagon construction, 4. Carpentry, 5. Timber framing [*Zimmerei*], 6. Saddlery, 7. Boatbuilding, 8. Fishing.
   V. Physical exercises: gymnastics and fencing, horse riding, shooting.
  VI. Participation in private lessons in foreign languages "is not compulsory for all students."[83]

In Witzenhausen, physical exercises and horse riding were perceived as an important part of the general education of future colonialists. In this respect, the curricula of the DKS were closer to those in British and French institutions than to their German academic counterparts in Berlin and Hamburg. The belief was widespread that virile and hardy characters were a prerequisite for a successful colonial career. And it was equally

[82] Böhlke, *Zur Geschichte der Deutschen Kolonialschule*, 81; Linne, *Von Witzenhausen*, 37.
[83] "Vorlesungs- und Unterrichtsverzeichnis für das Sommerhalbjahr 1900," *Der deutsche Kulturpionier* 1, no. 1 (1900): 1.

assumed that such characters were necessarily formed through (hard) exercise. Behind this emphasis on "character formation" and "corporeality" was, as historian Anne Kwaschik points out, more than the intention to secure the work capability of settlers. There was an anthropological dimension in the debates about the vocational training of (future) colonialists, which perceived the hardy man needed in the colonies as an "antitype to the modern urban-civilized man."[84] In the age of widespread criticism of civilization, the colonies were thus imagined as spaces that could—on an individual basis—help to renew, improve, and "rejuvenate" metropolitan societies.

Given the ideals connected to his institution, Fabarius, a towering figure and authoritarian character, was convinced that the German colonies required the "noblest, most reliable and best sons of our people." He expected that the sons of the "most competent classes of our nation, in particular [the sons] of agronomists, civil servants, doctors, merchants, and officers" would apply to join the DKS. Evidently, these demands stood in sharp contrast to the "image" widespread in Germany "of a debased settler population [in GSWA] prone to violence, alcoholism, and crime."[85] Apparently, according to tables giving an overview of the parents of DKS students, most were indeed from a middle-class background. The average age of admitted students was 19–20 years with some having already been conscripted to military service.[86] The school was organized in the spirit of a German cadet school. Fabarius required of his students a "German national attitude" (*deutsch nationale Gesinnung*) and applied a militaristic code of conduct for all students. Similar to what school children experienced in Wilhelminian schools[87] the strictest discipline was enforced with the aim to educate "self-discipline," a trait that was assumed necessary to farm in the colonies. Between 1898 and 1918 some 779 students joined the DKS, but only 60% of them received an official diploma from the school.[88]

Much to the chagrin of the directorate, by 1910 less than half the DKS graduates had settled in German colonies. The territory that

---

[84] Kwaschik, *Der Griff nach dem Weltwissen*, 86f.

[85] Short, *Magic Lantern Empire*, 71.

[86] Böhlke, *Zur Geschichte der Deutschen Kolonialschule*, 91f.

[87] See York-Gothart Mix, *Die Schulen der Nation: Bildungskritik in der Literatur der frühen Moderne* (Stuttgart: Metzler, 1995), 217f.

[88] Böhlke, *Zur Geschichte der Deutschen Kolonialschule*, 93.

welcomed the largest group of DKS graduates before World War I was GSWA (133), followed by GEA (88), Nigeria (32), Argentina and Canada (25 each), the United States (23), and German New Guinea (18). Thus, the majority did indeed settle in Africa, but Fabarius was concerned that education offered at the DKS served merely as a "cultural fertilizer" for other colonial powers.[89]

The education and work undertaken at the DKS was a strictly male affair. Women were not admitted. In 1907, however, plans were made in Witzenhausen to open a colonial women's school (*Kolonialfrauenschule*) as a partner institution in the neighborhood.[90] From the 1890s, colonial enthusiasts were convinced of the relevance of women in Germany's colonial endeavors. In their writings they created "the colonial women's question," which was to be solved by bringing more German women to the colonies. Over the last decades, historians have repeatedly shown how the colonial administration, colonial pressure groups like the DKG, as well as women's movements cooperated to settle more German women in the German colonies (most of all GSWA) and thereby assumed to protect and maintain the *Deutschtum* (Germandom) overseas. In the debates about women in the colonies, discourses on race, class, gender, feminism, nationalism, colonialism, and education partly merged, as the "right" women (but only those women, not members of the "lower classes") were imagined as *Kulturträgerinnen*, as bearers of (German) culture.[91] The goal of a more "civilised" environment on a private and public level, it was argued, would have remained unattainable without female support and female "abilities" to create, through their "domesticity," a German home with German (white) children; a German *Heimat*—and thus prevent "the German men" from "going native" by

---

[89] Map, Ausreiseziele 1899–1914, reproduced in Böhlke, *Zur Geschichte*, 90; Linne, *Von Witzenhausen*, 77, 79.

[90] Dörte Lerp, "Zwischen Bevölkerungspolitik und Frauenbildung, Die Kolonialfrauenschulen in Witzenhausen und Bad Weilbach," in *Frauen in den deutschen Kolonien*, ed. by Marianne Bechhaus-Gerst and Mechthild Leutner (Berlin: Links, 2009), 32–39, 32.

[91] Katharina Walgenbach, *"Die weiße Frau als Trägerin deutscher Kultur". Koloniale Diskurse über Geschlecht, "Rasse" und Klasse im Kaiserreich* (Frankfurt/M.: Campus, 2005); Krista O'Donnell, "Home, Nation, Empire: Domestic Germanness and Colonial Citizenship," in *The Heimat Abroad: The Boundaries of Germanness*, ed. by Krista O'Donnell, Renate Bridenthal, and Nancy Reagin (Ann Arbor: University of Michigan Press, 2005), 40–57; Kundrus, *Moderne Imperialisten*.

living with "native women," resulting in racial "degeneration." Such biopolitical argumentation about "mothers for the state" conformed to contemporary women's rights activists' parlance about "specific female qualities" or "motherly abilities." These were to be supported and provided for the greater good and in the interest of the nation—be it, for example, through better education of young women or the recognition of the societal relevance of motherhood.[92]

The colonial women's school in Witzenhausen was initiated by the DKG, the DKS, the *Deutsch-Evangelische Frauenbund*, the Association for Women's Education, the *Deutsche Frauenverein für Krankenpflege in den Kolonien*, and further individuals including Empress Auguste Victoria—their purpose being to convince more unmarried, *gebildete*, that is, women of bourgeois respectability, not only to go to the (German) colonies, but to seek special education before doing so. The school was supposed to prepare students for roles in the colonies as teachers, kindergarten teachers, and nurses, but primarily as farmers' wives, who were—apart from managing a "German" household (cooking, cleaning, childcare)—well versed in tasks such as gardening, carpentry, or poultry farming. Director Fabarius always remained involved in the development of curricula for the colonial women's school and was eager to make it more or less a dependency of "his" DKS.[93]

The first four female students enrolled in May 1908 on a 1-year course, but in 1910 the number had barely risen to 13. Initially, under the directorship of Helene von Falkenhausen (a teacher who had been a trader's/farmer's wife in GSWA[94]) and, from 1909, Anna von Zech, young women had to study, in addition to housekeeping, most of the courses their male colleagues at the DKS took, such as natural sciences, tropical agriculture, and health. Considering the very low enrollment numbers, Fabarius admitted that the offers made by the women's school seemed to be unattractive to young women. When Helene von Falkenhausen quit as director, her successor Anna von Zech, however, insisted on the overloaded curriculum, since only this would enable her students to acquire an education "which corresponds to that of the

---

[92] Short, *Magic Lantern*, 72f.; Sylvia Schraut, *Bürgerinnen im Kaiserreich: Biografie eines Lebensstils* (Stuttgart: Kohlhammer, 2013), 115.

[93] Lerp, "Zwischen Bevölkerungspolitik und Frauenbildung," 33f.

[94] Helene von Falkenhausen, *Ansiedler-Schicksale: Elf Jahre in Deutsch-Südwestafrika 1893–1904* (Berlin: Reimer, 1906).

young men." Considering wives as "comrades" of their husbands, von Zech aimed to enable her students to "deputize" (*vertreten*) for their (future) husbands in terms of running a farm. Thus, she wanted her students to be good "German" wives and good farmers at the same time. Such an understanding of *comaraderie* and equality between women and men in the colonies was, however, not the educational ideal of Fabarius. Continuing disputes with Fabarius alongside protests from female students against the overloaded curriculum, financial difficulties, and the very small number of students finally led, in August 1910, to the colonial women's school closing. A few months later, however, the same organizers of Witzenhausen attached a new colonial women's school to the already existing women's economic school in Bad Weilbach near Wiesbaden. Between 1911 and 1915 around 40 female students enrolled on the "colonial courses." It is known that five of them indeed migrated to GSWA or East Africa. It is also known that many settlers rejected the "well-educated," "bourgeois" women whom they deemed as too demanding and "less resilient" in comparison to lower class women from Germany. Given this dispute about the "right" women for the colonies and the prejudices against educated women, despite support from the DKG, the colonial women's school did not always succeed in finding graduates an appropriate position in GSWA or elsewhere.[95] However, male experts also experienced a bias of farmers in GSWA away from academic expertise. After one agricultural expert had traveled in GSWA he complained to a high-ranking administrator: "everyone comes to see me, except for the farmers. They know everything better ...."[96] This aversion of some settlers in GSWA against formal education became even more evident in respect to their African workforce.

EDUCATING AFRICANS AS WORKERS? WHY OR WHY NOT?

In his classic *Portrait du colonisé* (1957), the Tunisian sociologist Albert Memmi commences his chapter on the "mythical portrait of the colonized" with a consideration of the colonial image of the "often cited trait of laziness." This image of the "unbelievable laziness" of the colonized

---

[95] Lerp, "Zwischen Bevölkerungspolitik und Frauenbildung," 32, 36, 39. Jens Böhlke, *Zur Geschichte der Deutschen Kolonialschule*, 59–64.

[96] BAB N 2272/1, Bl. 28–30, Heydebreck an Schuckmann, 9.2.1914; see Linne, *Von Witzenhausen*, 78.

served several purposes; not least it "justifies the colonized's destitution." Memmi also rightfully pointed out that it "may seem that colonization would profit by employing experienced personnel [i.e., educated Europeans]. Nothing is less true"—for the simple reason that in the colonies it was more advantageous to employ the colonized than colonizers: "three or four can be taken for the price of one European," whereas the European would not "produce three or four times as much" as one colonized would.[97]

Even 50 years earlier, in German colonial discourses the "myth of the lazy native"[98] was omnipresent. For example, during the three German Colonial Congresses held in 1902, 1905, and 1910 "discussions of race and labor ... emphasized the need to educate the Negro to work."[99] One response of the colonial administration in GSWA to the widespread complaints about the insufficiency of the African workforce in general was a wide-ranging legal package. With three "native ordinances" (1907) dealing with control measures, passes, and work contracts for all Africans, the administration in Windhoek hoped "to transform the Africans into a landless proletariat, destroy their political organization and culture, and forcing them to work in a disciplined and orderly manner for white employers."[100] The ordinances, however, also speak of the German insight that African labor was irreplaceable for German employers—the colony could not be developed without them. In fact, in GSWA the "value" of "the native" was seen most of all as being his or her ability to work for the Germans. This was also the philosophy of long-term governor Theodor Leutwein. However, beginning with the Herero war and the demotion of Leutwein by his successor General Lothar von Trotha in 1904, the necessity of Africans in this colony was increasingly in doubt. Trotha "in contrast to Leutwein saw the indigenous workforce in the settler colony as replaceable."[101] Trotha did not believe in the viability of the colonial tenet—to adapt a book title—of "white farms,

---

[97] Albert Memmi, *The Colonizer and the Colonized* (Boston: Beacon Press, 1965), 79f.

[98] Syed H. Alatas, *The Myth of the Lazy Native* (London: Cass, 1977).

[99] Zimmerman, *Alabama in Africa*, 188. See Alexander Merensky, *Wie erzieht man am besten den Neger zur Plantagen-Arbeit?* (Berlin: Walther, 1886); Ulrike Schaper, *Koloniale Verhandlungen: Gerichtsbarkeit, Verwaltung und Herrschaft in Kamerun 1884–1916* (Frankfurt/M.: Campus, 2012), 367.

[100] Wallace, *A History of Namibia*, 184.

[101] Häussler, *Der Genozid an den Herero*, 47.

black labour."¹⁰² On his vision of a "white man's country," Trotha wrote in his diary: "but SWA is, or should be, the colony where the European can work himself."¹⁰³

Even though Trotha was for some time governor of GSWA, such comments, however, never meant that there was an official German policy that aimed at a sort of colonial rule without the colonized. Yet, it is evident from sources as well as comparisons with other colonies, that in GSWA debates about "native uplift" were, if not wholly absent, muted at best. For a number of African children (mostly mission), primary schools were opened that received small government subsidies.¹⁰⁴ Yet, illiteracy remained the norm for African children and youths. After 1907, with the end of the wars, civilizational discourses about "the natives" and their "improvement," "education," and "development" were rather transformed into debates about security. Administrators and settlers hoped for a more "docile" African populace that was "taught a lesson" by the Germans and was to be constantly reminded of its place on the lowest level of the colony's social ladder. Whereas in many African colonies, including GEA and Togo, administrators considered it "part of the state-building process" to encourage "the natives" to cultivate cash crops,¹⁰⁵ in GSWA Africans were imagined only as (farm) workers, not as independent (subsistence) agriculturalists. Still, given the relative economic insignificance of GSWA, administrators never grew tired of reminding settlers that the "native population"—through its capacity to work for the colonial economy—was the colony's most important asset. Therefore, following his genocidal warfare against the Ovaherero in 1904, Trotha was harshly criticized by other officials for having destroyed almost all the "properties" of GSWA: native workers and cattle, and thus he would "ruin" the colony.¹⁰⁶ Most of all, for employers Africans were—as Memmi had already emphasized—much cheaper than an imported German workforce.

---

¹⁰²Alan H. Jeeves and Jonathan Crush (eds.), *White Farms, Black Labor: The State of Agrarian Change in Southern Africa, 1910–1950* (Portsmouth: Heinemann, 1997).

¹⁰³Trotha diary entry of 1 July 1904, cited in Häussler, *Der Genozid an den Herero*, 47.

¹⁰⁴Jakob Zollmann, "Children of Empire: Childhood, Education and Space in German South West Africa, c. 1880–1915," *Journal of Namibian Studies* 17 (2015): 71–124.

¹⁰⁵Tilley, *Africa as a Living Laboratory*, 128.

¹⁰⁶Rohrbach, cited in Häussler, *Der Genozid an den Herero*, 219.

These employers most often fervently believed in the idea of racially inherent traits in blacks, and "education" in whatever form was seen by them as time consuming, disturbing, and creating the wrong sense of self-esteem among those Africans lucky enough to have experienced a school. Others, perversely, argued that they educated "their natives" by the whip, by teaching them "a lesson" in obedience. In the rare cases that the colonial administration, through policemen and judges, reacted to these violent excesses (very few farmers actually went to jail for flogging their workers), settlers complained angrily that the authorities dared to interfere with their "right" to "paternal chastisement." Arbitrariness, despotism, and violence against Africans was seen by many farmers "as an integral part of their white *Herrenanspruch*."[107] They rejected any state inference with what they conceived as their "education." After all, the journal *Kulturpionier* from Witzenhauses had declared "that every colonial employer is first of all an educator," teaching "natives" how to work.[108] Additionally, academics never grew tired of emphasizing that "the native must be treated like a child and a certain force is thus necessary."[109]

The very harsh treatment of African workers by some German farmers led farm workers regularly to the decision to flee their farms rather than endure further hardship. "These Africans living on the veld occasionally raided European farms, stealing cattle for food or slaughtering the animals in revenge."[110] Such events were used as self-fulfilling prophecies seemingly proving that "the native" was unwilling or even incapable of serious labor. How could Africans be compelled to work—especially for (settler) farmers? This question had, since the beginning of the abolition of slavery in the United States (1865) and Brazil (1888), a distinctive transatlantic dimension and German academics and farmers participated in this transnational debate alike.[111]

---

[107] Häussler, *Der Genozid an den Herero*, 52.

[108] "Die Völkerkunde und Kolonialwirtschaft," *Der deutsche Kulturpionier* 1, no. 3 (1900): 46f.

[109] Bernhard Dernburg, *Zielpunkte des deutschen Kolonialwesens* (Berlin: Mittler, 1907), 61 (Anlage 1 Bericht des Prof. Dr. Hahn und des Farmers Schlettwein in der Kommission für den Reichshaushalts-Etat am 12. Dezember 1906).

[110] Miescher, *Namibia's Red Line*, 63.

[111] Bradley Naranch, "Global Proletarians, Uncle Toms, and Native Savages: Popular German Race Science in the Emancipation Era," in *Germany and the Black Diaspora: Points of Contact, 1250–1914*, ed. by Mischa Honeck, Martin Klimke, and Anne Kuhlmann, 169–186, 171f.

Ferdinand Wohltmann pleaded: "Without a duty to work [for Africans] a development of culture ... is impossible."[112]

Vocational training and other educational policies for Africans differed widely between German colonies. In Cameroon, private companies, for example, construction firms, were prepared to send African apprentices for further instruction to Germany.[113] However, in comparison with German Togo and a number of British colonies, in GSWA, agricultural education and practical training for African children and young adults was not on the agenda of government institutions. One reason for this decision not to act was certainly the fact that, much to the surprise of German settlers and administrators, in "the years after 1907, Africans were also taking whatever opportunity they could find to regenerate the herds they had lost." Herero agricultural knowledge and their own forms of educating a new generation of pastoralists sufficed in establishing new cattle herds. "By 1913, Ovaherero owned more than 25 percent of the small stock in the colony, as well as more than twenty thousand head of large stock."[114] Thus, the German settlers had ample reason to fear competition and they "lobbied for protection from [it]."[115] Any sort of broader education would have further strengthened the position of the Africans. In German mission schools, however, the management of a school garden was at times part of the curriculum for African children.[116] Whereas in neighboring South Africa "agricultural education gained momentum" in the early 1900s, for example, in the Transkei, with

---

[112] "Die Beamten- und Arbeiterfrage in unseren Kolonien von Geh. Rat Prof. Dr. Wohltmann," in *Der deutsche Kulturpionier* 2, no. 3 (1901): 54. Cf. Christel Adick and Wolfgang Mehnert (eds.), *Deutsche Missions- und Kolonialpädagogik in Dokumenten. Eine kommentierte Quellensammlung aus den Afrikabeständen deutschsprachiger Archive 1884–1914* (Frankfurt/M: IKO, 2001), 337.

[113] Robbie Aitken, "Education and Migration: Cameroonian Schoolchildren and Apprentices in Germany, 1884–1914," in *Germany and the Black Diaspora*, ed. by Honeck, Klimke and Kuhlmannp, 213–230, 217f.

[114] Wallace, *A History of Namibia*, 184.

[115] Cynthia Cohen, "'The Natives Must First Become Good Workmen': Formal Educational Provisions in German South West and East Africa Compared," *Journal of Southern African Studies* 19 (1993): 115–134, 129.

[116] Adick, *Kolonialpädagogik*, 338.

"chiefs, headmen, and progressive [African] farmers ... actively engaged with the idea of 'scientific agriculture', [and] invested in machinery and better stock,"[117] in GSWA the political goals concerning the education of Africans remained bound by notions of obedience and unfree labor in the service of Germans.

This is a stark reminder that a history of education must also consider and analyze the reasons for an active denial of an education (and development) for certain groups enabling the profit of others.

BIBLIOGRAPHY

Adick, Christel, and Wolfgang Mehnert, eds. *Deutsche Missions- und Kolonialpädagogik in Dokumenten. Eine kommentierte Quellensammlung aus den Afrikabeständen deutschsprachiger Archive 1884–1914.* Frankfurt/M: IKO, 2001.

Aitken, Robbie. "Looking for Die Besten Boeren: The Normalisation of Afrikaner Settlement in German South West Africa, 1884–1914." *Journal of Southern African Studies* 33, no. 2 (2007): 343–360.

———. "Education and Migration: Cameroonian Schoolchildren and Apprentices in Germany, 1884–1914." In *Germany and the Black Diaspora: Points of Contact, 1250–1914*, edited by Mischa Honeck, Martin Klimke, and Anne Kuhlmann, 213–230. New York: Berghahn, 2013.

Alatas, Syed H. *The Myth of the Lazy Native.* London: Cass, 1977.

Bechhaus-Gerst, Marianne, and Reinhard Klein-Arendt, eds. *Die (koloniale) Begegnung: AfrikanerInnen in Deutschland und schwarze Deutsche.* Frankfurt/M.: P. Lang, 2004.

Besser, Stephan. "Die Organisation des kolonialen Wissens." In *Mit Deutschland um die Welt: Eine Kulturgeschichte des Fremden in der Kolonialzeit*, edited by Alexander Honold and Klaus R. Scherpe, 272–279. Stuttgart: Metzler, 2004.

Bley, Helmut. *Kolonialherrschaft und Sozialstruktur in Südwestafrika.* Hamburg: Leibnitz, 1968.

Böhlke, Jens. *Zur Geschichte der Deutschen Kolonialschule in Witzenhausen: Aspekte ihres Entstehens und Wirkens.* Witzenhausen: Werratalverein, 1995.

Bundy, Colin. *The Rise and Fall of the South African Peasantry.* London: Currey, 1979.

---

[117] Julia Tischler, "Education and the Agrarian Question in South Africa, c. 1900–40," *Journal of African History* 57 (2016): 251–270, 254f.; see Masefield, *History of Colonial Agricultural Service*, 117f.

Cohen, Cynthia. "'The Natives Must First Become Good Workmen': Formal Educational Provisions in German South West and East Africa Compared." *Journal of Southern African Studies* 19 (1993): 115–134.

Conrad, Sebastian. *Globalisierung und Nation im deutschen Kaiserreich*. Munich: Beck, 2006.

Declerq, Robrecht. "Building Imperial Frontiers: Business, Science and Karakul Sheep Farming in (German) South-West Africa (1903–1939)." *Journal of Modern European History* 14 (2016): 54–77.

Denzel, Markus. "Die wirtschaftliche Bilanz des deutschen Kolonialreiches." In *Die Deutschen und ihre Kolonien: Ein Überblick*, edited by Horst Gründer and Hermann Hiery, 144–160. Berlin: Bebra, 2017.

Echenberg, Myron. "'Scientific Gold': Robert Koch and Africa, 1883–1906." In *Agency and Action in Colonial Africa*, 34–49. London, 2001.

Eckl, Andreas. "'Weiß oder Schwarz?' Kolonialer Farmalltag in Deutsch-Südwestafrika." In *Die (koloniale) Begegnung: AfrikanerInnen in Deutschland und schwarze Deutsche*, edited by Marianne Bechhaus-Gerst and Reinhard Klein-Arendt, 109–124. Frankfurt/M.: P. Lang, 2003.

Emmett, Tony. *Popular Resistance and the Roots of Nationalism in Namibia, 1915–1966*. Basel: Schlettwein, 1999.

Grohmann, Marc. *Exotische Verfassung: Die Kompetenzen des Reichstags für die deutschen Kolonien in Gesetzgebung und Staatsrechtswissenschaft des Kaiserreichs (1884–1914)*. Tübingen: Mohr, 2001.

Groppe, Carola. *Im deutschen Kaiserreich: Eine Bildungsgeschichte des Bürgertums 1871–1918*. Vienna: Böhlau, 2018.

Habermas, Rebekka, and Alexandra Przyrembel. *Von Käfern, Märkten und Menschen: Kolonialismus und Wissen in der Moderne*. Göttingen: V&R, 2013.

Häussler, Matthias. *Der Genozid an den Herero*. Weilerswist: Velbrück, 2018.

Henrichsen, Dag. *Herrschaft und Alltag im vorkolonialen Zentralnamibia: Das Herero- und Damaraland im 19. Jahrhundert*. Basel: BAB, 2011.

Herbert, Lewis. *In Defense of Anthropology: An Investigation of the Critique of Anthropology*. New Brunswick, NJ: Transaction Publishers, 2014.

Hodge, Joseph. *Triumph of the Expert: Agrarian Doctrines of Developments and the Legacies of British Colonialism*. Athens: Ohio University Press, 2007.

Jeeves, Alan H., and Jonathan Crush, eds. *White Farms, Black Labor: The State of Agrarian Change in Southern Africa, 1910–1950*. Portsmouth: Heinemann, 1997.

Kienetz, Alvin. *Nineteenth-Century South West Africa as a German Settlement Colony* (2 vols.), diss. phil., University of Minnesota, 1976.

Kundrus, Birte. *Moderne Imperialiste: Das Kaiserreich im Spiegel seiner Kolonien*. Cologne: Böhlau, 2003.

Kwaschik, Anne. *Der Griff nach dem Weltwissen: Zur Genealogie von Area Studies im 19. und 20. Jahrhundert*. Göttingen: V&R, 2018.

Laak, Dirk van. *Imperiale Infrastruktur: Deutsche Planungen für Afrika*. Paderborn: Schöningh, 2004.

———. "Kolonien als 'Laboratorien der Moderne'?" In *Das Kaiserreich transnational: Deutschland in der Welt 1871–1914*, edited by Sebastian Conrad and Jürgen Osterhammel, 257–279. Göttingen: V&R, 2004.

Lerp, Dörte. "Zwischen Bevölkerungspolitik und Frauenbildung, Die Kolonialfrauenschulen in Witzenhausen und Bad Weilbach." In *Frauen in den deutschen Kolonien*, edited by Marianne Bechhaus-Gerst and Mechthild Leutner, 32–39. Berlin: Links, 2009.

Lindner, Ulrike. *Koloniale Begegnungen: Deutschland und Großbritannien als Imperialmächte in Afrika 1880–1914*. Frankfurt/M.: Campus, 2011.

Linne, Karsten. *Von Witzenhausen in die Welt: Ausbildung und Arbeit von Tropenlandwirten 1898 bis 1971*. Göttingen: Wallstein, 2017.

Marklund, Carl. "Begriffsgeschicht and Übergriffsgeschichte in the History of Social Engineering." In *Die Ordnung der Moderne: Social Engineering im 20. Jahrhundert*, edited by Thomas Etzemüller, 199–222. Bielefeld, 2009.

Masefield, G.B. *A History of the Colonial Agricultural Service*. Oxford: Oxford University Press, 1972.

Memmi, Albert. *The Colonizer and the Colonized*. Boston: Beacon Press, 1965.

Miescher, Giorgio. *Namibia's Red Line: The History of a Veterinary and Settlement Border*. New York: Palgrave, 2012.

———. "Facing Barbarians: A Narrative of Spatial Segregation in Namibia." *Journal of Southern African Studies* 38 (2012): 769–786.

Mix, York-Gothart. *Die Schulen der Nation: Bildungskritik in der Literatur der frühen Moderne*. Stuttgart: Metzler, 1995.

Namhila, Ellen Ndeshi. *"Little Research Value:" African Estate Records and Colonial Gaps in a Post-colonial Archives*. Basel: BAB, 2017.

Naranch, Bradley. "Global Proletarians, Uncle Toms, and Native Savages: Popular German Race Science in the Emancipation Era." In *Germany and the Black Diaspora: Points of Contact, 1250–1914*, edited by Mischa Honeck, Martin Klimke, and Anne Kuhlmann, 169–186. New York: Berghahn, 2013.

O'Donnell, Krista. "Home, Nation, Empire: Domestic Germanness and Colonial Citizenship." In *The Heimat Abroad: The Boundaries of Germanness*, edited by Krista O'Donnell, Renate Bridenthal, and Nancy Reagin, 40–57. Ann Arbor: University of Michigan Press, 2005.

Rawlinson, Johann. *The Meat Industry of Namibia, 1835–1994*. Windhoek: Gamsberg, 1994.

Ruppenthal, Jens. *Kolonialismus als "Wissenschaft und Technik:" Das Hamburgische Kolonialinstitut 1908 bis 1919*. Stuttgart: Steiner, 2007.

Schaper, Ulrike. *Koloniale Verhandlungen: Gerichtsbarkeit, Verwaltung und Herrschaft in Kamerun 1884–1916*. Frankfurt/M.: Campus, 2014.

Schraut, Sylvia. *Bürgerinnen im Kaiserreich: Biografie eines Lebensstils.* Stuttgart: Kohlhammer, 2013.

Schröder-Lembke, Gertrud. *Studien zur Agrargeschichte.* Stuttgart: Lucius, 1977.

Schulze, Theodor. "Erziehung und Lernen. Plädoyer für eine mathetische Erziehungswissenschaft." In *Erziehungsdiskurse,* edited by Winfried Marotzki and Lothar Wigger, 29–50. Bad Heilbrunn: Klinkhardt, 2008.

Short, John Phillip. *Magic Lantern Empire: Colonialism and Society in Germany.* Ithaca, NY: Cornell University Press, 2012.

Tilley, Helen. *Africa as a Living Laboratory: Empire, Development, and the Problem of Scientific Knowledge, 1870–1950.* Chicago: University of Chicago Press, 2011.

Tischler, Julia. "Education and the Agrarian Question in South Africa, c. 1900–1940." *Journal of African History* 57 (2016): 251–270.

Walgenbach, Katharina. *"Die weiße Frau als Trägerin deutscher Kultur:" Koloniale Diskurse über Geschlecht, "Rasse" und Klasse im Kaiserreich.* Frankfurt/M.: Campus, 2005.

Wallace, Marion. *A History of Namibia.* London: Hurst, 2011.

Werner, Wolfgang. *"No One Will Become Rich:" Economy and Society in the Herero Reserves in Namibia, 1915–1946.* Basel: BAB, 1998.

Zimmerman, Andrew. *Alabama in Africa: Booker T. Washington, the German Empire, and the Globalization of the New South.* Princeton: PUP, 2010.

Zollmann, Jakob. *Koloniale Herrschaft und ihre Grenzen: Die Kolonialpolizei in Deutsch-Südwestafrika.* Göttingen: V&R, 2010.

———. "German Colonial Law and Comparative Law, 1884–1919." In *Entanglements in Legal History: Conceptual Approaches,* edited by Thomas Duve, 253–294. Frankfurt/M.: MPI, 2014.

———. "Children of Empire: Childhood, Education and Space in German South West Africa, c. 1880–1915." *Journal of Namibian Studies* 17 (2015): 71–124.

———. "'Neither the State Nor the Individual Goes to the Colony in Order to Make a Bad Business:' State and Private Enterprise in the Making of Commercial Law in the German Colonies, ca. 1884 to 1914." In *The Influence of Colonies on Commercial Law and Practice,* edited by Serge Dauchy and Albrecht Cordes. Leiden: Brill, 2020.

Open Access This chapter is licensed under the terms of the Creative Commons Attribution 4.0 International License (http://creativecommons.org/licenses/by/4.0/), which permits use, sharing, adaptation, distribution and reproduction in any medium or format, as long as you give appropriate credit to the original author(s) and the source, provide a link to the Creative Commons license and indicate if changes were made.

The images or other third party material in this chapter are included in the chapter's Creative Commons license, unless indicated otherwise in a credit line to the material. If material is not included in the chapter's Creative Commons license and your intended use is not permitted by statutory regulation or exceeds the permitted use, you will need to obtain permission directly from the copyright holder.

CHAPTER 6

Cruce et Aratro: *Fascism, Missionary Schools, and Labor in 1920s Italian Somalia*

Caterina Scalvedi

Introduction

In May 1928, the Catholic missionary journal *La Consolata* opened with a piece titled "Cruce et Aratro." The anonymous author wrote that in Somalia "we [Italian missionaries] colonize only through the plow [*aratro*] and the cross [*cruce*], and by 'colonize' here we mean civilize." Earlier missionary work had proved such a strategy to be successful in the neighboring British colony of Kenya. For twenty-five years, the fathers had "civilized" men and women through nuns' "heroic charity" and increased "material wealth resulted from physical work." What the Italian missionaries had achieved for the British—the transformation of African subjects into Christians and workers—had to be achieved in Somalia.[1]

Scholarship on Italian colonialism in Somalia has addressed the study of developmentalist discourses and practices from both the colonial

[1] "Cruce et Aratro," May 1928, *La Consolata* (*LC*). All primary sources quoted in this paper are in Italian in the original; all translations from Italian into English are mine.

C. Scalvedi (✉)
University of Illinois at Chicago, Chicago, IL, USA
e-mail: cscalv2@uic.edu

© The Author(s) 2020
D. Matasci et al. (eds.), *Education and Development in Colonial and Postcolonial Africa*, Global Histories of Education,
https://doi.org/10.1007/978-3-030-27801-4_6

period (1908–1941) and the postwar UN trust mandate of Italian administration (1949–1960).[2] Historians have retraced how, with the arrival of the first fascist governor in the colony in 1923, the colonial state planned ambitious policies of agricultural and infrastructural expansion. Its goal was to prepare for the military conquest of neighboring Ethiopia, later achieved during the Second Italo-Ethiopian War in 1935–1936. It was thus no coincidence that in 1928 *La Consolata* depicted Somalia as "Italy's most promising colony."[3] Public and private investments aimed at the creation of a plantation system for crop export to Italy in the fertile southern regions of Somalia. Further, both private companies and the colonial state tried to resolve the shortage of workforce through coercive practices including native land expropriation, the promotion of forced marriages for the reproduction of labor, and the legalization of forced labor.[4] According to Annalisa Urbano, the development (*valorizzazione*) of Somalia was an evolving discourse that provided both a justification and a scope for the colonial venture. Colonial authorities legitimized forced labor recruitment as part of a modernizing strategy and "school of progress" for locals. Ultimately, she has shown, the investment in plantation agriculture and related decrease in the production

---

[2] Robert L. Hess, *Italian Colonialism in Somalia* (Chicago: University of Chicago Press, 1966); Michele Pandolfo, "La Somalia coloniale: una storia ai margini della memoria italiana," *Diacronie* 14, no. 2 (2013): 1–18; Gianluca Podestà, *Il mito dell'impero. Economia, politica e lavoro nelle colonie italiane dell'Africa orientale 1898–1941* (Turin: G. Giappichelli Editore, 2004), 199–225; Andrea Naletto, *Italiani in Somalia. Storia di un colonialismo straccione* (Padua: Cierre edizioni, 2011); Riccardo Tesolin, *Investire in colonia. Somalia italiana e Côte Française des Somalis 1920–1960* (M.A. diss., University of Bologna, 2018); Ercole Tuccimei, *La Banca d'Italia in Africa* (Bari: Laterza, 1999). On developmentalist planning in 1949–1960, see Antonio Maria Morone, "Politica e istruzione nella Somalia sotto tutela italiana," in *Colonia e Postcolonia come spazi diasporici*, ed. by Uoldelul Chelati Dirar et al. (Rome: Carocci, 2011), 75–92.

[3] "Cruce et Aratro," May 1928, *LC*.

[4] On labor in Italian Somalia, see Lee V. Cassanelli, "The End of Slavery and the 'Problem' of Farm Labor in Colonial Somalia," and Hassan O. Ahmed, "Sul primo decennio dell'era fascista in Somalia," both in *Proceedings of the Third International Congress of Somali Studies: History, Anthropology and Archaeology*, ed. by Annarita Puglielli and Francesco Antinucci (Rome: Pensiero Scientifico Editore, 1988), 269–282 and 291–297; Francesca Declich, "Italian Weddings and Memory of Trauma: Colonial Domestic Policy in Southern Somalia, 1910–1941," in *Marriage by Force? Contestation Over Consent and Coercion in Africa*, ed. by Annie Bunting et al. (Athens: Ohio University Press, 2016), 70–83; Angelo Del Boca, *Italiani, Brava Gente? Un mito duro a morire* (Vicenza: Neri Pozza, 2005).

for the local market made Somalia dependent on imports, which had a long-standing impact on postwar international programs for the development of the region.[5]

Colonial state, private businesses, credit institutes, and the exploited workforce are the protagonists of this historiography on "civilization through labor" in Italian Somalia. This essay's goal is to introduce two key actors that remain missing from the picture: the Catholic Church and education. I show that, as a result of fascist and Vatican converging agendas, missionaries occupied a leading role in the shaping of developmental discourses and practices in Italian Somalia. They did so by creating the colony's first school system and by making of labor the core of education. While highlighting the peculiarities of the *cruce et aratro* project as undertaken in Italian Somalia, I argue that it reflected broader trends both in religious and racial policy in Italian colonialism as well as in interwar educational and labor policies throughout Africa.[6]

In conducting this study, I relied on the archives of the Consolata Missions Institute (CMI) in Rome, Italy.[7] The Consolata Fathers directed all the Italian educational initiatives in the colony from 1924 to 1930,[8] leaving a rich set of primary sources including the correspondence with

---

[5] Annalisa Urbano, "A 'Grandiose Future for Italian Somalia': Colonial Developmentalist Discourse, Agricultural Planning, and Forced Labor (1900–1940)," *International Labor and Working-Class History* 92 (2017): 69–88.

[6] On the relationship between education and labor in colonial Africa, see two recent volumes: *Developing Africa: Concepts and Practices in Twentieth-Century Colonialism*, ed. by Joseph M. Hodge et al. (Manchester: Manchester University Press, 2014); *Empire and Education in Africa: The Shaping of a Comparative Perspective*, ed. by Peter Kallaway and Rebecca Swartz (New York: Peter Lang, 2016).

[7] Founded by Giuseppe Allamano in Turin (1901), the CMI was created to promote evangelization and education in Africa. In its first twenty-five years, the CMI sent missionaries also to the Kaffa region in southwestern Ethiopia, East British Africa (Kenya and Tanzania), and Mozambique. On the history of the Institute and its archives, see Alberto Sbacchi, "The Archives of the Consolata Mission and Italian Colonialism," in vol. I of *Fonti e problemi della politica coloniale italiana: atti del convegno Taormina-Messina, 23–29 ottobre 1989*, ed. by Carla Ghezzi (Rome: Ministero per i beni culturali e ambientali, Ufficio Centrale per i beni archivistici, 1997), 87–112.

[8] Two studies have provided surveys of Consolata missionary work in Italia Somalia: Bianca Maria Carcangiu, "I Missionari della Consolata nella Somalia italiana (1925–1930)," in *Studi mediterranei ed extraeuropei*, ed. by Vittorio Antonio Salvadorini (Pisa: Edistudio, 2002), 147–174; Daniele Natilli, "Le missioni cattoliche italiane all'estero: il caso della Consolata nella Somalia di Cesare Maria De Vecchi (1924–1928)," *A.S.E.I.*

fascist authorities, private letters, and self-reports. I have also consulted the official documentation produced by and stored at Italian and Vatican governmental institutions.[9] These sources provide insights into the quotidian life and administration of the colony.[10]

Church–State Reconciliation

In her book on Trinitarian missions in Italian Somalia (1903–1924), the historian Lucia Ceci shows how, up to the early 1920s, the Catholic presence in Somalia was very weak due to colonial authorities' anticlericalism and the missionaries' lack of both human and financial resources.[11] In 1904, the Congregation for the Propagation of the Faith founded the Vicariate of Benadir, comprising the Benadir coastal area under Italian protectorate to become the colony of Italian Somalia in 1908. The Congregation promoted abolitionism and assistance for freed slaves in a region where slavery was still widely practiced. Rulers supported the anti-slavery project but prevented missionaries from any activity of religious proselytism that could create tensions with the local Muslim society. The Trinitarians' duty was to provide for charity and to train locals

---

(7 November 2011), accessed February 28, 2019, https://www.asei.eu/it/2011/11/le-missioni-cattoliche-italiane-allestero-il-caso-della-consolata-nella-somalia-di-cesare-maria-de-vecchi-1924-1928/.

[9] All archives are in Rome, Italy: Archivio Centrale dello Stato. Ministero dell'Africa Italiana (ACS-MAI); Archivio dell'Istituto Missioni Consolata (AIMC); Archivio Storico Generale dei Frati Minori (AOFM); Archivio Storico Diplomatico del Ministero degli Affari Esteri. Ministero dell'Africa Italiana (ASDMAE-MAI) and Archivi di personalità. Guido Corni 1928–1931 (ASDMAE-Corni); Archivio Storico di Propaganda Fide (ASPF).

[10] Missionaries wrote about their routine and difficulties, published articles in the magazine of the Institute, *La Consolata*, and took pictures of everyday life, people, and landscapes. Photographs are located at the Archivio Fotografico Istituto Missioni Consolata (AFIMC) in Turin, Italy, and at the Fondi iconografici della Biblioteca di Storia Moderna e Contemporanea e del Museo centrale del Risorgimento di Roma (BSMC) in Rome, Italy.

[11] Lucia Ceci, *Il vessillo e la croce. Colonialismo, missioni cattoliche e islam in Somalia (1903–1924)* (Bologna: Il Mulino, 2006). According to the agreement between Trinitarians and the colonial rulers (July 1923), "missionaries commit themselves to abstain from any propaganda or interference [with religious beliefs and practices] as they respect the religious sentiment of students and pursue an exclusively civil mission towards the moral elevation and improvement [of students]" (Art. 2). See Carlo Riveri, "Convenzione con Trinitari sulle scuole," 9 July 1923, AIMC VIII 6,1.

as Italian language speaking skilled workers that one day could serve the labor needs of the Italian settler community. While Italian settlers paid for their children's school equipment, the colonial government entirely funded the local youth's education.[12] By 1923, Trinitarians had built three missionary stations in Mogadishu, Gelib, and Brava.[13]

Liberal authorities, in other words, encouraged the plow (*aratro*) but strictly prohibited the cross (*cruce*). Things would change with the arrival of the fascist governor Cesare Maria De Vecchi (1923–1928) and Consolata missionaries, Trinitarians' successors (1924–1930). On the one hand, De Vecchi pursued a resolute policy of direct rule through territorial expansion, native land expropriation, and increased Italian settlement. The consequent centralization of Italian rule and internal pacification of the colony paved the way for missionary activities. Not only missionaries could work under the colonial state's stronger protection, but the colonial state itself increasingly needed missionary work in the form of both the plow and the cross. De Vecchi launched infrastructure building projects as well as extended and intensified agricultural exploitation of newly acquired lands: the need for labor was high. Simultaneously, the Catholic settler population almost doubled in a few years (from 674 in 1921 to 1200 in 1929),[14] and the governor created a native army (*Corpo Zaptié*) whose members were to be granted with basic public services including Italian language teaching and healthcare. A fervent Catholic, De Vecchi announced that he aimed to intensify religious proselytizing, deploring previous governors' prohibitions.[15] Trinitarians, lacking funds and internally divided, abandoned Somalia a few weeks later.[16]

---

[12] Gabriele Perlo to Filippo Perlo, 13 November 1924, AIMC VIII 6,1.

[13] Prima relazione integrale inviata alla S.C. di Propaganda Fide sullo stato della Prefettura Apost. Della Somalia Italiana, AIMC VIII 6,1. See also *La partenza dei Missionari della Consolata per la Somalia Italiana*, 12 October 1924, insert of *LC*.

[14] Nicola Labanca, "Italiani d'Africa," in *Adua. Le ragioni di una sconfitta*, ed. by Angelo Del Boca (Bari: Laterza, 1998), 210. On the 1920s as decade of transition, see also Gian Paolo Calchi Novati, *L'Africa d'Italia. Una storia coloniale e postcoloniale* (Rome: Carocci, 2011), 188.

[15] De Vecchi removed the ban on proselytism soon after he landed in the colony. See Report by Alessandro Parenti to the Congregation for the Propagation of the Faith, 25 January 1924, AIMC VIII 6,1.

[16] Only a Trinitarian missionary, Alessandro Parenti, stayed in the colony and worked with Consolata missionaries. See the correspondence between Alessandro Parenti, Francesco Gamberutti, Gabriele and Filippo Perlo, 1924–1925, AIMC VIII 6,1.

In 1924, on the other hand, Consolata missionaries replaced Trinitarians as a result of an agreement between De Vecchi and the Congregation for the Propagation of Faith.[17] Evidence suggests that the Italian Ministry of the Colonies was closely following CMI's work in Africa and thinking about their possible replacement of Trinitarians since 1917. Italian authorities valued several factors. First, during the First World War missionaries had shown their devotion to Italy by sending letters of support for the military victories of the Italian army in the peninsula. Second, in British East Africa (Kenya), the mission had started medical activities and professional courses for the African youth. Through religious and commercial activities, Consolata missionaries had also penetrated in southwestern Ethiopia, a region the Italian government was interested in for a potential plan of expansion.[18] For these reasons, colonial authorities viewed the Consolata Fathers as champions of Italian loyalty and colonial agents professionally specialized in the vocational education of African subjects.[19]

Missionary work in Italian Somalia, however, was not only in the agenda of the Italian state. On the Vatican side, the work of Consolata missionaries was part of an ongoing missionary strategy plan set by Benedict XV and his successor Pius XI. In 1919 and 1926, the two Popes respectively published the apostolic letter *Maximum Illud* and the encyclical *Rerum Ecclesiae* exhorting evangelization among "pagan" people as a supranatural endeavor separated from national and imperial aims. The ultimate goal of missionaries, according to both documents, was the expansion of the kingdom of God, not an empire of man.[20]

---

[17] See "Azione della missione Cattolica nella Somalia Italiana – Trinitari scalzi," "Somalia Chiese e Missioni," "Missioni religiose in Somalia 'Consolata'," and "Somalia Vicariato Apostolico," in ASDMAE-MAI I 89/15; "Somalia Passaporti e Lasciapassare Passaporti per Missionari," in ASDMAE-MAI I 89/18.

[18] See correspondence in "Missioni cattoliche e culti 1914–1918," ASDMAE-MAI III 156.

[19] Ceci, *Il vessillo e la croce*, 222–223.

[20] The publication of both documents was strongly influenced by the ideas of Cardinal Willem Marinus van Rossum, prefect of the Congregation for the Propagation of the Faith (1918–1932). See Benedict XV, *Maximum Illud*, apostolic letter, November 30, 1919, Vatican Web site, accessed February 28, 2019, http://w2.vatican.va/content/benedict-xv/en/apost_letters/documents/hf_ben-xv_apl_19191130_maximum-illud.html; Pius XI, *Rerum Ecclesiae*, encyclical letter, February 28, 1926, Vatican website, accessed February 28, 2019, http://w2.vatican.va/content/pius-xi/en/encyclicals/documents/hf_p-xi_enc_28021926_rerum-ecclesiae.html. As part of the Holy See's evangelization

In fact, CMI adopted an explicitly pro-Italian attitude that seemed to contrast the encyclical's scope: *La Consolata* consistently praised Italy's colonial presence in Somalia as well as emphasized the "Italian" character of missionary teaching.[21] I found no evidence suggesting that CMI's posture played a role in either the choice or later replacement of Consolata missionaries by Vatican authorities—whereas it certainly influenced Italian authorities' active support of their work. Most likely, the Pope prioritized the good and cooperative relationship between the Catholic Church and the (highly nationalist) fascist state as a precondition to evangelization in Italian colonies, especially given that such a relationship came after a long season of Italian authorities' strong anticlericalism and diffidence toward Catholics.[22] In 1926, a journalist wrote:

> Vatican authorities are following with great interest the work of Consolata missionaries in Somalia, as their work is the first complete experiment the Pope has potentially created for the conversion of the Muslims... [The plan] could be explained as such: [missionaries should] first of all study Islamism deeply, the language, habits, the mentality of Muslim people, and then, through charity, address them directly, trying to earn their respect, then their love, eventually their soul.[23]

La Consolata depicted the apostolate as explicitly "experimental."[24] While the 1926 encyclical focused on evangelization in terms of preaching to the natives and building up native clergy and congregations, Consolata missionaries developed their own strategy as to fit best the reality of Italian

---

plan, in 1926 Pius XI also founded the Institute for Islamic Studies in Rome. *La Consolata* published several articles on *Rerum Ecclesiae*: "L'enciclica del Papa sulle Missioni," May, July, August, September, and October 1926, LC.

[21] See, for example, "Il solenne 'Te Deum' per il Governatore della Somalia," June 1927; "Luci di redenzione nella Somalia Italiana. I grandiosi avvenimenti religiosi e civili con l'avvento del Figlio del Re," May, June, July, August, November, and December 1928, LC.

[22] On Church–State relations in Italy in the 1920s, see Lucia Ceci, *The Vatican and Mussolini's Italy* (Leiden: Brill, 2016).

[23] Published in "Il nostro esperimento tra i musulmani," October 1926, LC.

[24] "Il nostro esperimento in Somalia," July 1926, and "Il nostro esperimento tra i musulmani," October 1926, LC.

Somalia, where there were no Christian natives. In 1925, Gabriele Perlo, new Apostolic Administrator of the Benadir Vicariate,[25] wrote:

> We are in a wholly Muslim fieldwork and can pursue our direct apostolate only among the Italians ... and a few Catholic Eritreans who have moved here as workers, as well as among mixed-race children [*meticci*] and orphans of whom we take care.[26]

"With Muslims," another missionary wrote in 1926, "it is necessary to pursue other strategies [than direct apostolate]: education, labor, and Christian charity."[27] Consolata missionaries thus distinguished between "direct" and "indirect" apostolate. Direct apostolate addressed the already Christian segment of the population as well as its socially least integrated segment (foundlings) and consisted of catechism. Indirect apostolate involved the Muslim population and consisted in showing how magnanimous missionaries were by providing Muslims with various charity activities, including education and job opportunities.

To sum up, both the fascist colonial state and the Catholic Church espoused the *cruce et aratro* project, though from different perspectives and with different aims. On the one hand, De Vecchi was interested in training programs for the native youth (*aratro*) and Catholic services (*cruce*) to meet the labor and religious needs respectively of the emergent settler community. On the other hand, with the Pope's support Consolata missionaries aimed at providing direct Christian teaching among Italian and Eritrean Christians (*cruce*) while surreptitiously (indirectly) showing that missionaries were benefactors to the native Muslims.

---

[25] Cesare Pecorari to Filippo Perlo, 20 August 1924; Nomina ad Amministratore Apostolico della Prefettura del Benadir. Both in AIMC VII 13.

[26] Relazione 1925, AIMC VIII 6,1. See also: Giovanni Ciravegna, "Dalla Somalia Italiana. Il Primo nostro lavoro: le scuole," July 1925, *LC*.

[27] Giovanni Ciravegna, "Dalla Somalia Italiana. La via da seguire," March 1926, *LC*. Scholars have explored how notions of agricultural labor and salvation were mutually connected within missionary evangelism, which in given cases contributed to the emergence of intensive cultivation prior to the formal establishment of colonial rule. See, for example, John L. and Jean Comaroff, "Cultivation, Colonialism, and Christianity," Chapter 3 of *Of Revelation and Revolution: Volume Two* (Chicago: University of Chicago Press, 1997), 119–165.

Charity and vocational education would give Muslims better opportunities in the job market (*aratro*). As a consequence of this close church–state collaboration, the Apostolic Vicariate of Benadir increased its religious and missionary power in accordance with the colony's territorial expansion.[28] Cross and plow, Italian and Vatican interests, colonial policy and missionary work went hand in hand for the first time in the history of Somalia.

In the years 1924 to 1930, missionaries considerably expanded the Catholic network from Mogadishu, Gelib, and Brava to Villabruzzi, Merca, Afgoi, Gelib, Genale, Baidoa, Vittorio d'Africa, and Hafun. With De Vecchi's support, they founded missionary residences, hospitals, shelters for the poor and the elderly, leproseries, orphanages, agricultural settlements, and churches, including a monumental cathedral in Mogadishu.[29] As *La Consolata* reported in July 1925, however, education was the very arena where missionaries could enact their "civilizing" plan with the same gradualism they had experimented in Kenya.[30]

---

[28] In 1927, the Vicariate was renamed Episcopal Prefecture of Somalia and Gabriele Perlo became the first bishop of Mogadishu. Both Somali Abyssinia and Jubaland, acquired by Italian Somalia in the 1920s but under the Vicariates of Djibouti and Zanzibar respectively, were annexed to the Prefecture so that the territories under Italian rule and those under the Prefecture would coincide. At first, only the governor was in favor of the expansion of the Vicariate to the rest of the colony, as he wanted the missionaries to found schools in the newly acquired territories. The CMI headquarters were contrary to the annexation of Jubaland to the Vicariate due to the lack of personnel and resources. See Francesco Gamberutti to Willem Marinus van Rossum, 1 January 1926, ASPF, Rubrica 39/10 N. S., Vol. 922, 4; Elevazione alla dignità episcopale e nomina a Vicario di Mogadiscio, AIMC VII 13. The Congregation for the Propagation of the Faith selected Gabriele Perlo as he had a very good relationship with the Italian authorities and by 1927 had already practiced a few years of apostolate in Somalia. See ASPF, Rubrica 39/10 N. S., Vol. 922, 56–73.

[29] Twenty-five male missionaries, including a few non-ordained, moved to Somalia, followed by more than thirty nuns of the female branch of CMI. See the list of missionaries in Padri della Prefettura Somalia, AIMC VIII 6,2, and Francesco Gamberutti, "L'operato dei missionari della Consolata nella Somalia Italiana," *Atti del IV Congresso Nazionale della Società Antischiavista d'Italia*, 1926.

[30] Ciravegna, "Dalla Somalia Italiana. Il Primo nostro lavoro: le scuole."

The Shaping of Colonial Education Under De Vecchi (1923–28)

In the 1920s, missionary work was officially regulated through a series of agreements signed by missionaries and governors. These negotiations fostered the creation, shaping, and progressive consolidation of Italian language schools in Somalia. Was there continuity between liberal and fascist approaches to colonial education? What were the prevailing pedagogies of the colonial state in Somalia? Can we trace trends and change over time during the first decade of fascist rule?

Italian Somalia's colonial school system—entirely controlled by missionaries—was born fifteen years after its official foundation as a colony in 1908. In July 1923, liberal authorities signed a two-year agreement on education with Trinitarian missionaries. The government would officially appoint missionaries to teach only the indigenous youth.[31] The goal was to put an "experiment" in place, through which colonial authorities could "gradually find the final shape colonial schools will have to assume." Missionaries had to have earned a teaching license in the metropole but could be assisted by a non-licensed father with some missionary experience in Somalia. The government would provide for all the school materials and general expenses, as well as pay 3000 rupees per year to the mission. Classes had to be divided according to the "traditional division of the population" and "pedagogical exigencies as established by the government." As mentioned, any religious propaganda was strictly prohibited. School subjects included morals and civics, reading, writing, math, calligraphy, geography, and history of Italy and its colonies, drawing and practical arts. The detailed description of morals and civics teaching content is revealing in that it put great emphasis on the convenience of colonial rule and settled life (as opposed to vagrancy) as well as the division between Italian citizens and colonial subjects:

> Morals and civics: respect of the elderly, women, disadvantaged, etc. *Every man needs the other men – Advantages of civil life – Concept of residence – Respect of public goods (property of all, result of common labor)* – Goodness towards animals – Economy – *Italian citizens and colonial subjects.*

---

[31] I employ the terms Italo-Somali, *meticci*, indigenous, assimilated and Somali not as categories reflecting reality, but to refer to the racial categories used by Italian settlers in the 1920s.

The state, the Residence is for everybody's convenience. Duties towards the Residence. Good use of time. Benevolence and solidarity. Not to do justice on your own. Concept of the state.[32]

Such an insistence on settled and civil life was not a mere matter of public order for De Vecchi. Lee Cassanelli's scholarship explains how vagrancy resulted from freed slaves' escape from colonial plantations and infrastructure building sites due to harsh working conditions. The colonial state considered it a prominent problem to contribute to the scarcity of available labor.[33] By teaching the local youth not to leave the settler community, missionaries would encourage them to be reliable and loyal workers in the future.

In February 1924, after only six months, the agreement was changed and re-signed by both parties. With De Vecchi, fascism arrived in the colony and the anti-clerical liberal leadership left Somalia. First, the ban over evangelization was removed. Missionaries were appointed to open morning elementary schools for European children and evening (after-work) elementary schools for indigenous adults, with preference for those working for the colonial government. The curriculum for indigenous students was the same as that attached to the previous agreement, with no mention of the subjects to be taught to Europeans. Also, while missionaries teaching the indigenous could be assisted by non-licensed evangelists, as established by the former contract, in the elementary schools for Europeans all instructors had to have earned a teaching license in the metropole. The funds provided by the government increased to 4500 rupees per year.[34]

After another ten months, in December 1924, the agreement was replaced with a new contract, this time between De Vecchi and Consolata missionaries. Elementary schools would provide day classes

---

[32] Carlo Riveri, "Convenzione con Trinitari sulle scuole," 9 July 1923, AIMC VIII 6,1. Italics added.

[33] On harsh working conditions and vagrancy, see Cassanelli, "The End of Slavery."

[34] Cesare Maria De Vecchi, "Decreto di approvazione convenzione con Trinitari sulle scuole," 22 February 1924, AIMC VIII 6,1. Consolata missionary activity was funded by the CMI, the Congregation for the Propagation of the Faith and other missionary or charity initiatives (including the Società antischiavista d'Italia), local alms, earnings from sales at the arts and crafts laboratories, and, above all, the Italian colonial government. See Informatio, 1927, ASPF, Rubrica 39/10 N. S., Vol. 922, 84–94.

to, respectively, European and indigenous with assimilated children.[35] The assimilated now appeared in the school hierarchy together with indigenous students. Regarding the teaching contents, classes would "follow the Italian national curriculum by and large with appropriate accommodations according to the students' age" and, as for evening classes, to the "practical aim" of those. Each father could be assisted by two nuns who were not required to have earned a diploma but only to be "expert at teaching." In addition to elementary schools, the mission would start vocational programs and a nursery school for both "mixed-race" foundlings (*meticci*) and Somali orphans, whose admission and religious education would be established by the government. The curriculum of vocational schools included woodwork, cabinet making, metalwork, and tinwork. Public funds remained at 4500 rupees per year, an amount that would increase over time had the governmental budget grown and "the school system been better organized [by missionaries]."[36]

In comparison with earlier prescriptions involving liberal authorities and Trinitarians, De Vecchi and Consolata missionaries negotiated several changes involving curriculum, funding, religious instruction, new categories of pupils (assimilated, *meticci*), qualification of instructors and the opening of vocational and nursery schools. Primary schooling was expanding (see Table 6.1) and provided assimilationist teaching (national curriculum, religious proselytism). Missionaries imported textbooks from Italy: teaching materials were national, not colonial.[37] Yet, classes were increasingly segregated in accordance with racial categories. The appearance of vocational schooling and the "practical" character of native elementary education confirmed that, like for liberal authorities, the primary aim of missionary teaching among the native youth was to train skilled laborers and by doing so resolve the labor question in Italian Somalia.

---

[35] "Assimilated" was the category the colonial authorities used for that segment of the population that was neither Italian nor African. "Assimilated" subjects did not have the Italian citizenship, but, in Italian colonies, were under the same legislation as the Italians—as opposed to colonial subjects, who were under "indigenous" law. See Bat-Zion Eraqi Klorman, "Yemen, Aden and Ethiopia: Jewish Emigration and Italian Colonialism," *Journal of the Royal Asiatic Society* 19, no. 4 (October 2009): 415–426.

[36] Agreement between Cesare Maria De Vecchi and Gabriele Perlo, 7 December 1924, AIMC VIII 6,1.

[37] Ciravegna, "Dalla Somalia Italiana. Il Primo nostro lavoro: le scuole."

Table 6.1 School Enrolment in Italian Somalia, 1924–1940[a]

School year	Native students	Italian students
1924–25	326	0
1925–26	667	6
1926–27	995	15
1927–28	1806	28
1928–29	2456	37
1929–30	1290	60
1930–31	1683	65
1931–32	1131	80
1932–33	1793	91
1933–34	1991	90
1934–35	1115	92
1935–36	1593	107
1936–37	1714	100
1937–38	2005	140
1938–39	No data	No data
1939–40	2010	249
1940–41	1158	276

[a]Le scuole della Somalia, ASDMAE-MAI III 36 3. I found the same statistics for the years 1922–1932 in Cesare Maria De Vecchi, *Orizzonti d'Impero. Cinque anni in Somalia* (Mondadori: Milan, 1935), 350.

Expansion, centralization, and a combination of assimilation and segregation marked the emergence of the first school system in the colony.

Private letters and reports by Consolata missionaries illustrate how the *cruce et aratro* project and its legalization translated into everyday life. I focus on the years 1924–1928 (when the December 1924 agreement was in place) and proceed in accordance with school orders: nursery school, elementary, and post-elementary education.

In 1925, Consolata missionaries established an orphanage and nursery school for foundlings in Mogadishu. Their purpose was to provide charity to the socially marginal segment of the urban population and consequently "pacifically penetrate in" and "establish a direct contact with" local communities.[38] Unable to propagandize their faith among Muslim families, missionaries turned to that segment of Somali society that occupied a liminal position: foundlings. The orphanage was thus a tool for

[38] Giovanni Ciravegna, "Dalla Somalia Italiana. L'asilo infantile di Mogadiscio," November 1926, *LC*.

missionaries and De Vecchi to self-fashion themselves as benefactors and practice evangelization. On Christmas 1926, forty *meticci* were publicly baptized. Abandoned by their Italian fathers, they were raised by their Somali Muslim mothers. Missionaries intended to baptize twenty Somali orphans too but De Vecchi asked them to postpone their conversion. He believed that public baptisms of orphans from Muslim families could find the dissent of the Muslim community. It was a critical moment for the internal stability of the colony as the Italian Army was occupying its Northern borderland and tension was high. Eventually, missionaries baptized only the forty *meticci*.[39] The twenty Somali orphans whose baptism had been denied by the governor were baptized two months later, in February 1927, after the Italian Army had completed the occupation of the Northern borderland. Another forty Somali orphans and five *meticci* were baptized in 1928.[40] One of them was baptized in Italy, when missionaries organized a school trip to the metropole.[41] However, in 1929 a nun recounted that she had secretly baptized a Somali child *in periculo mortis*: secret deathbed baptisms remained the norm throughout the 1920s (see Table 6.2).[42]

Sources do not provide enough information on the way children felt about conversion. Certainly, some form of coercion took place. In 1927, Gabriele Perlo wrote in a letter to a donor that Muslim mothers of *meticci* were forced by the governor to enroll their children in the missionary nursery school, as they were "reluctant" and "diffident" and would never do it spontaneously.[43] Another report says that in March 1928 thirty-four Somali orphans were baptized, which constituted a "success" given that prior to that event "many of them had repeatedly refused to be baptized."[44] Similarly, four documents from July to August 1928

---

[39] Cronistoria della Prefettura Apostolica della Somalia Italiana, 24 December 1926, AIMC VIII 6,2.

[40] Ibid., 11 March 1928.

[41] "Festa di fede a Revigliasco per il battesimo d'un moretto somalo," November 1928, *LC*.

[42] "Dal Vicariato di Mogadiscio," April 1929, *LC*. Another nun wrote about practicing secret baptisms in Suor Adele, "Il primo fiore sulla brulla duna," August 1927, *LC*. See also Relazione ordinaria dell'anno 1929, AIMC VIII 6,1: "We baptize dying babies while pretending we are curing them."

[43] Gabriele Perlo to Contessa, 5 February 1927, AIMC VII 13.

[44] Cronistoria della Prefettura Apostolica della Somalia Italiana, AIMC VIII 6,2.

Table 6.2 Baptisms in Italian Somalia, 1925–1929[a]

Year	Secret deathbed baptisms of Somali children in periculo mortis	Somali orphans	Meticci
1925	12	0	
1926	23	40	
1927	32	21	
1928	25	43 or 44	5
1929	84	0	12

[a]I compiled this chronological list of baptisms administrated in Italian Somalia (excluding baptisms of children from Christian families) by looking at *Prospectus Missionis* (an annual report sent by missionaries to the Congregation for the Propagation of Faith) and private missionary correspondence.

reported that two Muslim mothers implored the governor to have their respective children back from the missionary schools.[45] These passages suggest that foundlings went to schools as a result of a coercive assimilation and evangelization policy.

The number of baptisms remained small. By 1929, five years after their arrival in the colony, missionaries had publicly baptized less than 150 people. The impact of missionary activity on Muslim communities was overall negligible, as the few baptisms involved a small, marginalized segment of the population. Yet, while Trinitarians struggled with the official ban over evangelization, Consolata missionaries, supported by the governor and the Holy See, tested a new strategy that allowed for the first appearance of Christianity in the colonial society. Overall, thus, the "civilization through the cross" undertaken by missionaries proved to be successful if compared to the liberal period.[46]

While legislation on proselytism corresponded to practice, this was not the case of racial segregation in elementary education. According

[45] Nicola Crocesi to Guido Corni, 3 September 1928, ASDMAE-Corni 1.

[46] Recent scholarship suggests that in the mid-1920s fascist authorities similarly collaborated with the Catholic Church in colonial expansion in Libya. See Eileen Ryan, *Religion as Resistance: Negotiating Authority in Italian Libya* (New York: Oxford University Press, 2018). In Eritrea, Catholic missionaries constituted only a portion of missionaries (the Protestant network was even more extended than the Catholic), and the local Orthodox Church was majoritarian: there was no colonial state church as it was the case in Somalia. See Cesare Marongiu Bonaiuti, *Politica e religioni nel colonialismo italiano (1882–1941)* (Milan: Giuffrè Editore, 1982), 426; Uoldelul Chelati Dirar, "Le religioni nella politica coloniale italiana," *Africa e Mediterraneo* 1 (1996): 9–14.

to the 1924 Agreement, missionaries had to divide Italian from *meticci* and indigenous children. Yet, archival documents reveal that in Afgoi in 1925 Italian and indigenous students attended the same class,[47] and in Brava, there was a school for white and *meticci* separated from a school for Muslims.[48] In Mogadishu, in 1928 European and Italo-Somali students were in the same class.[49] Also, in 1928 in Merca there was a school for Indians and in Baidoa one for both Eritrean and Somali members of the African section of the Italian colonial army.[50] Classes for Indians and African soldiers, as well as the "mixing" of *meticci*, Italian and indigenous children did not reflect what the 1924 Agreement established. Reality reflected the overall process of slow adaptation and improvisation of missionaries to the life of the colony.

After elementary education, settlers' children went to middle school in Eritrea or Italy or were tutored privately by missionaries (the first middle school in Mogadishu was founded in 1932). Missionaries also opened a Latin class in Mogadishu in 1925 to allow Italian pupils to pursue their studies after elementary school, though no agreement formally mentioned Latin or in general education for Europeans after elementary schools.[51] Improvisation, accommodation, and fortuity once again prevailed over prescription.

Missionaries often complained that available workers in Somalia were very hard to find. In the building of the cathedral in Mogadishu, they employed skilled free workers from Italy or local conscript laborers. They often lamented high life expenses, the absence of a printing house as well as affordable clothes and bread.[52] The "indigenous" youth educated by missionaries would have provided for cheap skilled workforce.

---

[47] Gabriele Perlo to Filippo Perlo, 25 December 1925, AIMC VIII 6,1.

[48] Prima relazione integrale inviata alla S.C. di PF sullo stato della Prefettura Apostolica della Somalia Italiana, 1925, AIMC VIII 6,1.

[49] Giovanni Gaudissard, "Situazione scolastica nella Somalia italiana sotto i missionari della Consolata (1924–1930)," 3 August 1938, AIMC VIII 6,2.

[50] Ibid. The mention of "Indians" is not surprising as, since the Middle Ages, the Indian Ocean had been a much interconnected place, with many Indian merchants living along the East African coastline. See *Trade, Circulation and Flow in the Indian Ocean World*, ed. by Michael N. Pearson (Houndmills: Palgrave Macmillan, 2015).

[51] Gabriele Perlo to Filippo Perlo, 25 December 1925, AIMC VIII 6,1.

[52] For example: Gabriele Perlo to Filippo Perlo, 13 November 1924, AIMC VIII 6,1.

Fig. 6.1 A class for metalworkers (Mogadishu, 1928?) (Courtesy of AFIMC)

Thus, while elementary education was the same for all students, secondary education was divided into two different paths for Italians and Africans.

In 1925, *La Consolata* reported that native education aimed to "prepare the Somali to replace the Eritreans in the colonial office."[53] As the Italian language school system had just been established in Somalia, there were not many locals speaking Italian or trained to work for colonial offices. As a result, colonial offices hired Eritreans, who spoke Italian because they had attended Italian schools in Eritrea.[54] For settlers, it was more convenient to employ local workers as clerks, interpreters, and skilled labor in the colonies than importing Italian labor from the metropole. It would have been even more convenient to hire Somali people, as they knew the local language,

---

[53] Ciravegna, "Dalla Somalia Italiana. Il Primo nostro lavoro: le scuole."

[54] An Italian school system had been institutionalized in Eritrea in the previous decades. Christine Smith-Simonsen, "The Beginnings of Western Education in Eritrea," *Eritrean Studies Review* 5, no. 1 (2007): 259–309.

Fig. 6.2 A sewing class (Mogadishu, 1928?) (Courtesy of AFIMC)

and Eritrea could not provide for further workers as it was itself experiencing a high demand for labor.[55] In Mogadishu, missionaries opened a male school of arts and crafts for woodworkers, smiths, printers, mechanics, and shoemakers, as well as a female school for sewing and domestic work (Figs. 6.1, 6.2, 6.3, and 6.4).[56] In 1927, the two schools had started, respectively, a printing house, a bookbinder, a bakery, and a textile factory.[57] Educational opportunities mirrored the labor needs of missionaries and the

---

[55] Stefano Bellucci and Massimo Zaccaria, "Wage Labor and Mobility in Colonial Eritrea, 1880s to 1920s," *International Labor and Working-Class History* 86 (2014): 89–106. On the labor question and employment of local workers in colonial settings, see *Intermediaries, Interpreters, and Clerks: African Employees in the Making of Colonial Africa*, ed. by Benjamin N. Lawrance et al. (Madison: The University of Wisconsin Press, 2006).

[56] Relazione 1925, AIMC VIII 6,1. On arts and crafts teaching, see also Giovanni Ciravegna, "Dalla Somalia Italiana: La Scuola di Arti e Mestieri a Mogadiscio," June 1927, and Alberto Gandino, "Dal vicariato di Mogadiscio il lebbrosario di Gelib sul Giuba," May 1929, both in *LC*.

[57] Gabriele Perlo to Filippo Perlo, 3 October 1927, AIMC VIII 6,1.

Fig. 6.3 A class for woodworkers (Mogadishu, 1928?) (Courtesy of AFIMC)

Fig. 6.4 A class for printers (Mogadishu, 1928?) (Courtesy of AFIMC)

settler community as a whole. In this regard, in 1935 a Consolata missionary wrote about orphans that had attended missionary schools in the 1920s:

> Nowadays, they work at the building site and the printing house, they are metal workers, drivers, civil clerks, and start founding Christian families.[58]

Private letters reveal that De Vecchi always agreed on missionary teaching strategies except once. In 1925 and 1926, Gabriele Perlo was rebuked by the mission's headquarters because he did not prohibit his fellow missionaries to smoke in public. The governor believed that such behavior undermined the image of religious men in front of both the Italian community living in the colony and the students attending missionary schools.[59] Smoking was a bad habit that compromised the "holy" posture of missionaries. The reproach was probably ignored. In January 1927, a missionary published an article in *La Consolata* in which he described his work in the colony. "I will gladly tell you about my savages," he addressed the readers "[they are like] raw materials that missionaries aim to shape … to Europeanize, to make them put a cigarette in their mouth," and "to Christianize."[60] According to the missionary, the aim of missionary education was to "Europeanize" their pupils by making them smokers and Christians. While the governor agreed on the latter, he was certainly skeptical toward the former.

Missionaries significantly contributed to non-educational activities as well. In 1924, De Vecchi assigned them a 99-year agricultural concession of four-hundred hectares in the fertile Southern region of the colony for an annual rent in rupees.[61] CMI could increase funds for education and other missionary activities through agricultural work.[62] In this respect, I found five depositions from July 1929 that document missionaries' abusive practices toward agricultural workers. Interviewees were all local workers that had escaped from plantations and, with the help of police-appointed translators, had officially accused missionaries of providing very little money and food, as well as beating and threatening them with

---

[58] "Storia della Missione," December 1935, *Somalia Cristiana*.
[59] Filippo Perlo to Gabriele Perlo, 3 August 1925 and 6 January 1926, AIMC VIII 6,3.
[60] "Colloqui missionari," January 1927, *LC*.
[61] Cesare Maria De Vecchi, Decreto 4181, 17 January 1925, AIMC VIII 6,1.
[62] Gabriele Perlo to Filippo Perlo, 13 December 1924, AIMC VIII 6,1.

death if they had stopped working.[63] The fathers' abuses most probably reflected the overall behavior of the Italian settler community toward local workers[64]; they did not actively oppose but rather took advantage of the well-spread coercive practices of labor recruitment and exploitation.

Missionaries also had a role in the policy of morals in Mogadishu. According to an official report on "indigenous prostitution" documented sometime between 1928 and 1931, Gabriele Perlo joined De Vecchi's wife in the active opposition to the institution of regulated brothels (*case di tolleranza*).[65] Through both educational and non-educational activities the fathers occupied a leading role within the settler community. While liberals considered the Catholic Church as an old, superstitious body, in the 1920s De Vecchi appointed missionaries as agents of modernization in the development of Somalia.

TOWARDS ADAPTED EDUCATION, 1930S

The December 1924 contract was revised in June 1928.[66] The new governor Guido Corni (1928–1931), De Vecchi's successor, requested Consolata missionaries to provide for at least twenty-five instructors and follow the teaching plan indicated by the colonial government (but not attached to the agreement). The governmental check was increased from 10,400 to 22,600 lire per month[67] and missionary elementary schools were proclaimed "state governmental schools."[68] In continuity with De Vecchi's policy, Corni encouraged the progressive expansion and centralization of colonial education by increasing funds and making missionary

---

[63] See correspondence and interviews from 1929 in the file "Missioni Consolata. Lettere Vescovo Perlo," ASDMAE-Corni 1.

[64] Cassanelli, "The End of Slavery."

[65] Prostituzione Indigena, ASDMAE-Corni 1 2/3.

[66] Agreement between Giovanni Pellettieri and Gabriele Perlo, 1 June 1928, ACS-MAI 160.

[67] In 1925, the Italian lira had replaced the local rupee with a ratio 1:8. On this topic, see Tuccimei, *La Banca d'Italia in Africa*, 149–151.

[68] Guido Corni to Benito Mussolini, 1 July 1929, ACS-MAI 160; for the increase of the funds, see Pietro Gaveglio to Guido Corni, Promemoria sull'istruzione, 30 September 1928, ASDMAE-Corni 1 2/8.

schools officially public. In opposition to De Vecchi, though, Corni proposed a shift from assimilationist to adapted teaching. He wrote that he was contrary to the Christian evangelization of native students,[69] and that his government would have paid greater attention to native schooling and particularly to both vocational and Arabic language teaching.[70] After 1928, missionaries had to follow not the national, but the colonial curriculum. Further, the lack of any curriculum attached to the agreement allowed the government to change it at any given time. In 1930, both Italian and Vatican authorities commanded Consolata Fathers to leave the colony due to some unspecified scandal within the mission. The Congregation for the Propagation of the Faith replaced them with Capuchin missionaries, while Consolata nuns continued working as nurses and teachers in Somalia.[71]

Such a new policy of curriculum adaptation did indeed proceed in the early 1930s, as shown, for example, by the publication in 1933 of the "First Italian Language Book for the Somali" (*Primo libro di italiano per somali*). The author, a Capuchin missionary, included language exercises on the greatness of Italy, but also on "Allah," as well as images of mosques and local flora and fauna. The mention of Allah would have been unthinkable in the 1920s, when Consolata missionaries and De Vecchi pushed for Christian teaching in the curriculum. One of the textbook readings, titled "Story of a gazelle" (*Storia di una gazzella*), told how a female gazelle, after losing her husband to hunters, wandered around in search for her friends. When she came across a village, she decided not to stop and went on wandering until a lion killed her. The story ended with a short explanation:

---

[69] Correspondence between Guido Corni and Nicola Crocesi, 25, 27, and 28 August 1928, 3 September 1928, ASDMAE-Corni 1 10/3.

[70] Guido Corni, Rapporto sull'opera di governo svolta dal 23 luglio al 30 settembre 1928, ASDMAE-Corni 1.

[71] Neither Italian nor Vatican sources mention the actual scandal and the reasons why the Congregation sent Capuchins to Italian Somalia. A few letters refer to the promiscuous relations between Consolata nuns and fathers, while others to fathers' venal attitude and conflict of interest with respect to the mission-assigned agricultural concession. A 1930-dated entry of De Vecchi's posthumously published diary confirms the latter hypothesis. See AIMC VIII 6,1 and 6,3; ASPF, Rubrica 39/10 N. S., Vol. 1034; Cesare Maria De Vecchi, *Tra papa, duce e re: il conflitto tra Chiesa cattolica e Stato fascista nel diario 1930–1931 del primo ambasciatore del Regno d'Italia presso la Santa Sede*, ed. by Sandro Setta (Rome: Jouvence, 1998), April 14, 1930, 138.

Teaching: we must stay united and loyal to our family, people, laws; because those who want to go vagabond in the world always ... suffer starvation, meet serious risks and, like the gazelle, end up being eaten by lions, meaning by the arrogant.[72]

The main purpose of the gazelle's story was to alert children against vagrancy and prevent them from escaping their fate as loyal subjects and productive workers under the Italians. As under liberal rule, Corni discouraged (but never prohibited) the cross and highlighted the plow. Differentiation also reflected the up-bringing of *meticci*. While Consolata missionaries and De Vecchi pursued assimilationist teaching among them in the 1920s, Capuchin missionaries wrote in 1930:

> For the spiritual formation of *meticci*, so far educated according to a teaching strategy that is not conform with their origin and future, I have disposed that the director of studies provides life regulations better fitting their social position, so that later in life they will be able to earn honestly while preserving their Catholic faith.[73]

The colonial state opened a middle school and a high school for Italians in Mogadishu respectively in 1932 and 1937. The only educational option for non-Italians remained mission-run vocational education, lasting until the establishment of a middle school for Somalis in 1950.[74] To retrace the social and economic repercussions of the 1928 Agreement and the overall policy of curriculum adaptation remains a research perspective worth exploring in the future.[75]

---

[72] Daniele Gorlani, *Primo libro di italiano per somali* (Mogadishu: Regia Stamperia della Colonia, 1933), 104.

[73] ASPF, Rubrica 39/10 N.S., Vol. 1034, 375–376.

[74] Le scuole della Somalia, ASDMAE-MAI III 36, 3.

[75] At this stage of the research, I have not been able to examine the local reception and impact of the 1928 Agreement and subsequent changes in missionary teaching due to the scarce and fragmentary nature of the 1930s' first-hand accounts by Capuchins. While I have not yet found the documentation produced by in-loco fathers, I could get access to the official correspondence of Capuchins' headquarters, which confirms the fathers' departure for Somalia. See AOFM SM/152-1 and SM/152-2.

Conclusion

Corni's shift from assimilationist to adapted curriculum is not surprising if placed in the broader context of racial thinking and religious policy in 1930s Italian colonialism. By then, a more rigid and biologically based racial hierarchy emerged throughout the empire, which had an impact on colonial discourse, prescription, and practice. In this respect, the treatment of "mixed-race" children is exemplary. In 1933, a law established that *meticci* received full Italian citizenship when they were not officially recognized by their fathers, who were to blame for that; after 1935, the fascist regime established a rigid colonial hierarchy based on biological racism and the purity of race. According to a 1940 law, the *meticci* were colonial subjects and could not receive Italian citizenship given their African heritage. Historians have interpreted such shift as a product of the climate of suspicion and state surveillance brought about by the Second Italo-Ethiopian War, where fascist Italy was diplomatically isolated and employed racial differentiation as a tool of governance in the Horn of Africa.[76] The matter goes beyond this essay's research goals, but it is still important to locate the transition from assimilationist to adapted curriculum in Italian Somalia within an imperial transition toward racial legislation and segregation. Further, in the 1930s Mussolini launched a pro-Muslim and pro-Arab policy in order to find military and economic partners in the Middle East and to pacify anti-colonial unrest in Muslim-majoritarian Libya. This policy culminated in the late 1930s, when, after the incorporation of Ethiopia, about nine million Muslims were under Italian rule. Not only did fascist propagandistic publications circulated in the Arab world as never before, but in 1937 Mussolini self-proclaimed himself "protector of Islam" in Tripoli. I suggest that apparently opposite trends in colonial and foreign politics converged in the integration of Islamic elements into missionary teaching. While the emergence of racial law resulted in the increase of curriculum differentiation, Mussolini's simultaneous

---

[76] Giulia Barrera, "Patrilinearity, Race, and Identity: The Upbringing of Italo-Eritreans During Italian Colonialism," in *Italian Colonialism*, ed. by Ruth Ben-Ghiat and Mia Fuller (New York: Palgrave Macmillan, 2005), 97–108. See also Gianluca Gabrielli, "Un aspetto della politica razzista nell'Impero: il«problema dei meticci»," *Passato e presente* XV, no. 41 (1997): 77–105; Barbara Sòrgoni, *Parole e corpi. Antropologia, discorso giuridico e politiche sessuali interraziali nella colonia Eritrea (1890–1941)* (Naples: Liguori, 1998).

pro-Arab policy allowed for the teaching of Islam among Muslim students.[77]

The history of missionary education in Italian Somalia during the first decade of fascist rule is overall not surprising either when placed in the history of global education and European colonialism. As explained by the editors in the general introduction to this volume, historians have recently shown how the inter-war period constituted a transitional phase in the "civilizing mission" discourse and practice. As the League of Nations proclaimed the "well-being and development of peoples" a "sacred trust of civilization," both British and French officials increasingly justified their policies as aimed toward native development and consequent rise in native life standards.[78] Published in 1922 and 1925, two inter-colonial reports on the state of native education in sub-Saharan Africa inaugurated a debate on colonial rule and mission.[79] The emergent model of native education—adapted education—fused developmentalist theories with practices that had been experimented with the education of African Americans in the United States in the previous decades.[80] Further, historians have highlighted how the 1919 peace treaty revising the General Acts of Berlin and Brussels established that, while native labor should be free and paid, compulsory labor could be imposed for public works that were in the general interest. Notions of "civilization through labor" and "redemptive labor" were internationally legitimized and increasingly pervaded British, French, and Portuguese

[77] On Islam in Italian colonial and foreign policy, see Nir Arielli, *Fascist Italy and the Middle East, 1933–1940* (New York: Palgrave Macmillan, 2010); Federico Cresti, "Per uno studio delle 'Elites' politiche nella Libia indipendente: la formazione scolastica (1912–1942)," *Studi Storici* 41, no. 1 (2000): 121–158; Renzo De Felice, *Il Fascismo e l'Oriente. Arabi, Ebrei e Indiani nella politica di Mussolini* (Bologna: Il Mulino, 1988); Francesca Di Pasquale, "La scuola di arti e mestieri di Tripoli in epoca coloniale (1911–1938)," *Africa* LXII, no. 3 (2007): 299–428; John Wright, "Mussolini, Libya, and the Sword of Islam," in *Italian Colonialism*, ed. by Ruth Ben-Ghiat and Mia Fuller (New York: Palgrave Macmillan, 2005), 121–130.

[78] Hodge et al., Introduction of *Developing Africa*, 1–34.

[79] Neither reports covered Italian Somalia. Thomas Jesse Jones, *Education in Africa: A Study of West, South and Equatorial Africa, by the African Education Commission* (New York: Phelps-Stokes Fund, 1922); Id., *Education in East Africa; a Study of East, Central and South Africa by the Second African Education Commission Under the Auspices of the Phelps-Stokes Fund, in Cooperation with the International Education Board* (New York: Phelps-Stokes Fund, 1925).

[80] Kallaway and Swartz, Introduction of *Empire and Education in Africa*, 1–28.

plans of "civilizing mission" or "development" for future political emancipation of African lands and peoples.[81]

The *cruce et aratro* project, I ultimately argue, belongs to this history. In the inter-war Italian Somalia context, the search for labor was the very motor of public-school building and reflected worldwide practices of native education. Moreover, fascist colonial authorities in the late 1920s and early 1930s placed a greater emphasis on education and promoted a shift toward adapted curriculum. In terms of structure, aims, teaching contents, and actors, the *cruce et aratro* project was not unique. This essay has illustrated how it came into being as a result of the convergence of church and state agendas in a peculiar colonial context, and to what extent prescription and practice corresponded and changed in the first years of fascist rule. Further scholarship awaits on how international debates and politics informed fascist educational policy and practice in Italian colonies.

Acknowledgements I am grateful to the Consolata Missions Institute archivists Carmen and Luigi, in Rome and Turin respectively, for their kind willingness to share materials with me in person or from afar. I would also like to thank the editors of the present volume, audiences in Chicago, Bologna, and Leuven, as well as Ismael Biyashev, Luigi Cajani, Kirk Hoppe, Lynn Hudson, and Filippo Petricca for their intellectual support and inspiring feedback on this and earlier versions of the chapter.

Bibliography

Ahmed, Hassan O. "Sul primo decennio dell'era fascista in Somalia." In *Proceedings of the Third International Congress of Somali Studies*, edited by Annarita Puglielli and Francesco Antinucci, 291–297. Rome: Pensiero Scientifico, 1988.

Arielli, Nir. *Fascist Italy and the Middle East, 1933–1940*. New York: Palgrave Macmillan, 2010.

Bandeira Jéronimo, Miguel. *The 'Civilising Mission' of Portuguese Colonialism, 1870–1930*. Houndmills: Palgrave Macmillan, 2015.

Barrera, Giulia. "Patrilinearity, Race, and Identity: The Upbringing of Italo-Eritreans During Italian Colonialism." In *Italian colonialism*, edited by Ruth Ben-Ghiat and Mia Fuller, 97–108. New York: Palgrave Macmillan, 2005.

---

[81] Miguel Bandeira Jéronimo, *The 'Civilising Mission' of Portuguese Colonialism, 1870–1930* (Houndmills: Palgrave Macmillan, 2015).

Bellucci, Stefano, and Massimo Zaccaria. "Wage Labor and Mobility in Colonial Eritrea, 1880s to 1920s." *International Labor and Working-Class History* 86 (2014): 89–106.

Benedict XV. *Maximum Illud*. Apostolic letter, November 30, 1919. Vatican website, accessed 28 February 2019. http://w2.vatican.va/content/benedict-xv/en/apost_letters/documents/hf_ben-xv_apl_19191130_maximum-illud.html.

Calchi Novati, Gian Paolo. *L'Africa d'Italia. Una storia coloniale e postcoloniale*. Rome: Carocci, 2011.

Carcangiu, Bianca Maria. "I Missionari della Consolata nella Somalia italiana (1925–1930)." In *Studi mediterranei ed extraeuropei*, edited by Vittorio Antonio Salvadorini, 147–174. Pisa: Edistudio, 2002.

Cassanelli, Lee V. "The End of Slavery and the «Problem» of Farm Labor in Colonial Somalia." In *Proceedings of the Third International Congress of Somali Studies. History, Anthropology and Archaeology*, edited by Annarita Puglielli and Francesco Antinucci, 269–282. Rome: Pensiero Scientifico, 1988.

Ceci, Lucia. *Il vessillo e la croce. Colonialismo, missioni cattoliche e islam in Somalia (1903–1924)*. Bologna: Il Mulino, 2006.

———. *The Vatican and Mussolini's Italy*. Leiden: Brill, 2016.

Chelati Dirar, Uoldelul. "Le religioni nella politica coloniale italiana." *Africa e Mediterraneo* 1 (1996): 9–14.

Cresti, Federico. "Per uno studio delle 'Elites' politiche nella Libia indipendente; la formazione scolastica (1912–1942)." *Studi Storici* 41, no. 1 (2000): 121–158.

Comaroff, John L., and Jean. *Of Revelation and Revolution: Volume Two*. Chicago: Chicago University Press, 1997.

De Felice, Renzo. *Il Fascismo e l'Oriente. Arabi, Ebrei e Indiani nella politica di Mussolini*. Bologna: Il Mulino, 1988.

De Vecchi, Cesare Maria. *Orizzonti d'Impero. Cinque anni in Somalia*. Milan: Mondadori, 1935.

———. *Tra papa, duce e re: il conflitto tra Chiesa cattolica e Stato fascista nel diario 1930–1931 del primo ambasciatore del Regno d'Italia presso la Santa Sede*, edited by Sandro Setta. Rome: Jouvence, 1998.

Declich, Francesca. "Italian Weddings and Memory of Trauma: Colonial Domestic Policy in Southern Somalia, 1910–1941." In *Marriage by Force? Contestation over Consent and Coercion in Africa*, edited by Annie Bunting et al., 70–83. Athens: Ohio University Press, 2016.

Del Boca, Angelo. *Italiani Brava Gente? Un mito duro a morire*. Venice: Neri Pozza, 2005.

Di Pasquale, Francesca. "La scuola di arti e mestieri di Tripoli in epoca coloniale (1911–1938)." *Africa* LXII, no. 3 (2007): 299–428.

Eraqi Klorman, Bat-Zion. "Yemen, Aden and Ethiopia: Jewish Emigration and Italian Colonialism." *Journal of the Royal Asiatic Society* 19, no. 4 (2009): 415–426.

Gabrielli, Gianluca. "Un aspetto della politica razzista nell'Impero: il «problema dei meticci»." *Passato e presente* XV, no. 41 (1997): 77–105.

Gorlani, Daniele. *Primo libro di italiano per somali*. Mogadishu: Regia Stamperia della Colonia, 1933.

Hess, Robert L. *Italian Colonialism in Somalia*. Chicago: The University of Chicago Press, 1966.

Hodge, Joseph M., et al., ed. *Developing Africa: Concepts and Practices in Twentieth-Century Colonialism*. Manchester: Manchester University Press, 2014.

Jones, Thomas Jesse. *Education in Africa: A Study of West, South and Equatorial Africa, by the African Education Commission*. New York: Phelps-Stokes Fund, 1922.

———. *Education in Africa; a study of East, Central and South Africa by the Second African Education Commission Under the Auspices of the Phelps-Stokes Fund, in Cooperation with the International Education Board*. New York: Phelps-Stokes Fund, 1925.

Kallaway, Peter, and Rebecca Swartz, eds. *Empire and Education in Africa: The Shaping of a Comparative Perspective*. New York: Peter Lang, 2016.

Labanca, Nicola. "Italiani d'Africa." In *Adua. Le ragioni di una sconfitta*, edited by Angelo Del Boca, 193–230. Bari: Laterza, 1998.

Lawrance, Benjamin N., et al., eds. *Intermediaries, Interpreters, and Clerks: African Employees in the Making of Colonial Africa*. Madison: The University of Wisconsin Press, 2006.

Marongiu Bonaiuti, Cesare. *Politica e religioni nel colonialismo italiano (1882–1941)*. Milan: Giuffrè Editore, 1982.

Morone, Antonio. "Politica e istruzione nella Somalia sotto tutela italiana." In *Colonia e Postcolonia come spazi diasporici*, edited by Uoldelul Chelati Dirar et al., 75–92. Rome: Carocci, 2011.

Naletto, Andrea. *Italiani in Somalia. Storia di un colonialismo straccione*. Padua: Cierre edizioni, 2001.

Natilli, Daniele. "Le missioni cattoliche italiane all'estero: il caso della Consolata nella Somalia di Cesare Maria De Vecchi (1924–1928)." *A.S.E.I.* (7 November 2011), accessed 28 February 2019, https://www.asei.eu/it/2011/11/le-missioni-cattoliche-italiane-allestero-il-caso-della-consolata-nella-somalia-di-cesare-maria-de-vecchi-1924-1928/.

Pandolfo, Michele. "La Somalia coloniale: una storia ai margini della memoria italiana." *Diacronie* 14, no. 2 (2013): 1–18.

Pearson, Michael N., ed. *Trade, Circulation and Flow in the Indian Ocean World*. Houndmills: Palgrave Macmillan, 2015.

6 CRUCE ET ARATRO: *FASCISM, MISSIONARY SCHOOLS, AND LABOR ...* 171

Pius XI. *Rerum Ecclesiae.* Encyclical Letter, 28 February 1926. Vatican website, accessed 28 February 2019, http://w2.vatican.va/content/pius-xi/en/encyclicals/documents/hf_p-xi_enc_28021926_rerum-ecclesiae.html.

Podestà, Gianluca. *Il mito dell'impero. Economia, politica e lavoro nelle colonie italiane dell'Africa orientale 1898–1941.* Turin: G. Giappicchelli Editore, 2004.

Ryan, Eileen. *Religion as Resistance: Negotiating Authority in Italian Libya.* New York: Oxford University Press, 2018.

Sbacchi, Alberto. "The Archives of the Consolata Mission and Italian Colonialism." In vol. I of *Fonti e problemi della politica coloniale italiana: atti del convegno Taormina-Messina, 23–29 ottobre 1989*, edited by Carla Ghezzi, 87–112. Rome: Ministero per i beni culturali e ambientali, Ufficio Centrale per i beni archivistici, 1997.

Smith-Simonsen, Christine. "The Beginnings of Western Education in Eritrea," *Eritrean Studies Review* 5, no. 1 (2007): 259–309.

Sòrgoni, Barbara. *Parole e corpi. Antropologia, discorso giuridico e politiche sessuali interraziali nella colonia Eritrea (1890–1941).* Naples: Liguori, 1998.

Tesolin, Riccardo. *Investire in colonia. Somalia italiana e Côte Française des Somalis 1920–1960.* M.A. thesis, University of Bologna, 2018.

Tuccimei, Ercole. *La Banca d'Italia in Africa.* Bari: Laterza, 1999.

Urbano, Annalisa. "A 'Grandiose Future for Italian Somalia': Colonial Developmentalist Discourse, Agricultural Planning, and Forced Labor (1900–1940)." *International Labor and Working-Class History* 92 (2017): 69–88.

Wright, John. "Mussolini, Libya, and the Sword of Islam." In *Italian Colonialism*, edited by Ruth Ben-Ghiat and Mia Fuller, 121–130. New York: Palgrave Macmillan, 2005.

Open Access This chapter is licensed under the terms of the Creative Commons Attribution 4.0 International License (http://creativecommons.org/licenses/by/4.0/), which permits use, sharing, adaptation, distribution and reproduction in any medium or format, as long as you give appropriate credit to the original author(s) and the source, provide a link to the Creative Commons license and indicate if changes were made.

The images or other third party material in this chapter are included in the chapter's Creative Commons license, unless indicated otherwise in a credit line to the material. If material is not included in the chapter's Creative Commons license and your intended use is not permitted by statutory regulation or exceeds the permitted use, you will need to obtain permission directly from the copyright holder.

CHAPTER 7

Becoming Workers of Greater France: Vocational Education in Colonial Morocco, 1912–1939

Michael A. Kozakowski

For two days in December of 1925, the teachers, school directors, and administrators of French Morocco gathered in Rabat to discuss the future of colonial education. Under the leadership of Georges Hardy, director-general of public education, fine arts, and antiquities in Morocco, they met in the *Institut des Hautes études marocaines*. The building's architecture reflected their ambition: to acknowledge Moroccan shapes and patterns, but to construct a modern and practical edifice.[1] Hardy was emphatic: "agreement has been established around a catchphrase: 'The education of indigenes will be vocational or it will not be.'"[2]

---

[1] Gwendolyn Wright, *The Politics of Design in French Colonial Urbanism* (Chicago: University of Chicago Press, 1991), 123.

[2] Georges Hardy, "Du souq à l'usine: Congrès de l'Enseignement Professionnel Indigène," *Bulletin de l'enseignement public du Maroc*, no. 72 (February 1926): 2.

M. A. Kozakowski (✉)
Keele University, Newcastle, UK
e-mail: m.a.kozakowski@keele.ac.uk

© The Author(s) 2020
D. Matasci et al. (eds.), *Education and Development in Colonial and Postcolonial Africa*, Global Histories of Education,
https://doi.org/10.1007/978-3-030-27801-4_7

Such a catchphrase summed up the theme of the appropriately entitled, Conference on Indigenous Vocational Education.

Yet there was more to such an agenda, Hardy noted, than a simple phrase, "because it is the fate of simple expressions to be incomplete."[3] In addition to the complexity of vocational reforms for the indigenous population, to whom Hardy referred in the conference, there was an equally complex and far-reaching series of reforms targeting the protectorate's French and foreign European populations. Indeed, vocational education was nothing less than a policy by which he and other French colonial administrators intended to build the educational, economic, social, and racial future of Morocco. A multifaceted, vocational emphasis, implemented through interlocking initiatives and across a variety of Moroccan school types (themselves differentiated by intersecting categories of class, gender, race, and urbanization), promoted a form of "adapted modernity" that aimed to promote modernization and incremental development without social disruption (see Chapter 1 by Damiano Matasci in this book).

For Hardy and other administrators, adopting a policy of vocational education in the interwar period meant implementing three interrelated reforms. First and most prominently, it meant establishing a system of vocational and technical schools [*l'école professionnelle*, or later, *l'école d'apprentissage*, as well as the *école technique*]. It also included efforts to make other schools more career-oriented, for example, by teaching drawing, agriculture, applied mathematics, and for girls, home economics. Finally, it meant creating institutions and methodologies to provide vocational guidance [*orientation professionnelle*, or as it is referred to in contemporary France, *orientation scolaire et professionnelle*]—a process to direct students to the right career and the appropriate training based on individual aptitude and social need.

Vocational education in all three of its forms represented a shift in thinking about the purpose of education, producing not just loyal subjects or intelligent humans, but *workers* of an industrializing "Greater France" [*la plus grande France*]. For interwar promoters like Albert Sarraut, "Greater France" evoked a vision of "100 million Frenchmen" between the metropole and colonies, not necessarily equal, but united in

---

[3] Ibid., 2.

increasing the security and prosperity of France.[4] In this context, vocational education promised to "rationally" and "efficiently" develop the human resources of Morocco so as to increase its economic productivity and ties to France in this strategy of *mise en valeur* (for other case studies, see Chapter 4 by Romain Tiquet and Chapter 6 by Caterina Scalvedi in this book).[5] At the same time, a proper vocational education would allegedly mitigate the dangers of new social aspirations and resulting conflicts that both economic development and education could produce.[6] As such, vocational education institutionalized and reinforced notions of class, race, religion, and gender through separate school systems and differentiated implementation of vocational reforms.

The increasingly broad literature on colonial education (often synonymous with the education of indigenous peoples) frequently points to vocational and "adapted" characteristics of education for indigenous peoples as a defining trait of "colonial" education.[7] This chapter agrees that one of the defining traits of Moroccan education in the French protectorate during the interwar, colonial period was that it indeed had a strong vocational imprint and orientation. However, this vocational focus was characteristic of many types of schools and different

---

[4] Martin Thomas, "Albert Sarraut, French Colonial Development, and the Communist Threat, 1919–1930," *Journal of Modern History* 77, no. 343 (December 2005): 917; Josep M. Fradera, "La *Plus Grande France*: el ciudadano y su negación en la República imperial," in *La nación imperial*, vol. 2 (Barcelona: Edhasa, 2015), 973.

[5] Gilbert Rist, *The History of Development: From Western Origins to Global Faith*, trans. Patrick Camiller (London: Zed Books, 2010), 48–52; Frederick Cooper, *Decolonization and African Society: The Labor Question in French and British Africa* (Cambridge: Cambridge University Press, 2010), 32, 71; Alice Conklin, *A Mission to Civilize: The Republican Idea of Empire in France and West Africa, 1895–1930* (Stanford: Stanford University Press, 1997), 212.

[6] Spencer D. Segalla, *The Moroccan Soul: French Education, Colonial Ethnology, and Muslim Resistance, 1912–1956* (Lincoln: University of Nebraska, 2009), 151–152; Conklin, *Mission to Civilize*, 70–79.

[7] Segalla, *Moroccan Soul*, 155; Mohamed Benchekroun, *L'éducation et l'enseignement au Maroc à travers les documents français et espagnols, 1912–1956: essai de bibliographie critique* (Rabat: [s.n.], 1985); Elsie Rockwell, "Tracing Assimilation and Adaptation Through School Exercise Books from Afrique Occidentale Française in the Early Twentieth Century," in *Empire and Education in Africa*, ed. by Peter Kallaway and Rebecca Swartz (New York: Peter Lang, 2016), 235; Sybille Kuster, "'Book Learning' Versus 'Adapted Education': The Impact of Phelps-Stokesism on Colonial Education Systems in Central Africa in the Interwar Period," *Paedagogica Historica* 43, no. 1 (2007): 79.

groups of students in interwar Morocco, including indigenous Muslims, indigenous Jews, who occupied a liminal position in French North Africa and were viewed as neither fully "native" nor fully "European," as well as European settlers.

This finding points to the inadequacies of viewing colonial education as exclusively—or even primarily—as indigenous education. For example in 1936, "Muslim" education received less than 22% of the educational budget. French and foreign students comprised half of the student population (in both vocational and non-vocational schools), and indigenous students with Muslim and Jewish juridical status split the remaining half. This was despite the fact that 94% of the total population was Muslim, 2.5% were indigenous Jews, and the remaining 3% were French and foreign.[8] Just as education in the protectorate was often targeted at non-Muslim youth, this chapter finds that much of the vocational inflection of this school system was aimed at—and was more successful in attracting students from—European and indigenous Jewish communities. Across all communities, vocational reforms left a greater mark on the philosophy, rhetoric, and ambition of education than on student outcomes. However, insofar as students benefited from vocational education, they tended to be European and indigenous Jewish (on this issue, see Chapter 5 by Jakob Zollmann in this book).

Viewing vocational training as a project responding to European and governmental elites' ambitions and fears, and targeting just as much European and Jewish as Muslim students, helps make sense of two puzzles. The first is how vocational training could be imagined as promoting modernization—strongly associated with social disruption—while preserving social stability. It was not just that vocational training was imagined as a less disruptive path to modernity; it was also imagined that a modern workforce could be created for the protectorate while leaving much of the population in situ (and uneducated). Second, administrators acknowledged by the mid-1920s that they had failed to attract Muslim students to vocational training or provide a credible path to jobs after graduation. Nonetheless, vocational training continued to be a cornerstone of interwar education in French Morocco and an inspiration for both subsequent decades and parts of Morocco not directly controlled by the French. Simply put, vocational education could

---

[8]Yvette Katan, "L'école, instrument de la modernisation sous le protectorat français au Maroc?" *Mediterrán tanulmányok* 5 (1993): 110–112.

continue, despite largely failing Muslim students, because it was not just designed with them in mind, and protectorate officials were unwilling to countenance or fund mass, general education until very late in the protectorate.

None of this is to minimize the fact that vocational training was highly racialized in its conceptions, reflected essentializing (and demeaning) assumptions about students' psychological and physical capabilities, and was highly unequal in both its quality and in the opportunities it provided. It was all of these things, as demonstrated in the first section, which focuses on protectorate politics, developmental ambitions, and their impact on Muslim schools in particular. Yet only through an examination of other communities, schools, and vocational programs outside of schools (in the second section), does one gain an appreciation for the broader ambitions of vocational reforms. In no small part because of this broader ambition and target audience, the very real and visible failures of vocational education, particularly in attracting Muslim students and securing them jobs (as shown in the third section), did not stop the continuation and even expansion of vocational education (as shown in the final section).

The Politics of Muslim Vocational Education

Vocational training was an integral part of the French educational system in Morocco from nearly the beginning of the protectorate in 1912. This marked a departure from earlier educational traditions, whereby indigenous Koranic schools had focused on teaching literacy and religion, with higher education positioning students for careers in government, law, and religion. In contrast, both manual trades and occupations like commerce were typically learned through apprenticeships and other direct training in the workplace, either after or instead of the years of Koranic education. World War I had delayed the implementation and expansion of French educational policies due to its disruptive effects on priorities, economic resources, students, and personnel. However, already in 1917, the Directorate of Education had converted a handful of urban schools for Muslims to vocational schools. That same year, the Industrial and Commercial School was opened in Casablanca. A private association, the Association of Commerce, Industry, and Agriculture (ACIA), which advocated for apprenticeships, also created night classes in trades and in French, open to members of all religions and backgrounds. When

Resident General Marshall Lyautey invited Georges Hardy to become the second director-general of education in 1920, in the renamed Directorate of Public Education, Fine Arts, and Antiquities (DIP), a position he would retain until 1926, Hardy inherited a school system still in its formative years. With the support of Lyautey, he was to endow it with its vocational character and attention to ethnicity and class. These hallmarks were to be continued by his successors until World War II.[9]

While Hardy is infamous for his highly racialized views of indigenous students' psychology, which fit well with Lyautey's avowedly "associationalist" policies,[10] one of Hardy's core objectives was to imbue this still nascent educational system with a strong vocational philosophy. Almost as soon as he took over the reins of the department of public education, the number of articles about vocational education appearing in the department's monthly bulletin, the *Bulletin de l'enseignement public du Maroc*, increased dramatically. Bringing together his experiences in French West Africa, the examples of education in Algeria and Tunisia, and trends in the metropole, Hardy viewed traditional French education as ill-suited to the needs of colonial students. Instead, he believed they required what is frequently termed an "adapted education," a philosophy that gained increasing prominence in Francophone and Anglophone African education in the 1920s, not least due to the work of the Phelps Stokes commission.[11] Largely speaking, his vision was compatible with that of Lyautey. While Lyautey was particularly interested in forging close bonds with the Moroccan elite, resulting in specially designated

---

[9] Lucien Paye, *Introduction et évolution de l'enseignement moderne au Maroc* (Paris: [s.n.], 1957); Segalla, *Moroccan Soul*, 35; Louis Brunot, "Histoire de l'enseignement des indigènes musulmans," in *Premiers Conseils* (Rabat: Ecole du Livre, 1934), 137, 138, 151; Georges Hardy, *L'âme marocaine d'après la littérature française* (Paris: É. Larose, 1926); Georges Hardy and Louis Brunot, *L'enfant marocain: Essai d'ethnographie scolaire* (Paris: E. Larose, 1925).

[10] Segalla, *Moroccan Soul*; Mohammed Rachid Belhaj Saif, "La politique scolaire du protectorat français au Maroc, 1912–1940," Thèse État, Université René Descartes Paris V, 1994.

[11] Kuster, "'Book Learning' Versus 'Adapted Education'," 83; Udo Bude, "The Adaptation Concept in British Colonial Education," *Comparative Education* 19, no. 3 (1983): 341–355; Pascale Barthélémy, Emmanuelle Picard, and Rebecca Rogers (eds.), "L'enseignement dans l'empire colonial français (XIXe-XXe siècles)," *Histoire de l'éducation* 128 (2010); Laurent Manière, "La politique française pour l'adaptation de l'enseignement en Afrique après les indépendances (1958–1964)," *Histoire de l'éducation*, no. 128 (2010): 163–190.

schools for sons of Moroccan elites, he also placed a high emphasis on basic, general education and the French language for indigenous students of humbler backgrounds.[12] European economic elites, however, tended to distrust education for Muslim students (and the aspirations they feared would accompany such an education), preferring to train any workers they needed through on-site apprenticeships. Beyond arguments about economic productivity, critics of "general education" feared that it would give students "useless knowledge" and more worryingly, "overly excite them," to use contemporary euphemisms, to protest, to rebel (as in the Spanish protectorate during the Rif War), or to strike (as in 1918 and 1919).

These differing objectives by different stakeholders resulted in a highly fragmented school system. In theory, education was "open to children of all nationalities and to all religions."[13] In practice, it had limited resources, limited appeal, and uneven enrollment. Lyautey adopted an explicitly "associationalist," rather than "assimilationist" educational policy, in which Moroccan subjects' local identities were reinforced, even as they were taught to participate in the French-dominated life of the protectorate.[14] Thus, there were separate school systems for "Europeans," "Muslims," and "Jews," as administrators most commonly divided the population. Schools were further segregated according to gender, and in practice, on the basis of class. While there were designated "Berber" schools in several rural areas, the construct of an Arab/Berber divide played a relatively minimal role in educational policy, in contrast, for example, to the poorly received "Berber Dahir" of 1930, assigning Berbers a distinct juridical status.[15] Nonetheless, the result of all these

---

[12] Segalla, *Moroccan Soul*, 154–155.

[13] Gaston Loth, "Règlement scolaire," *Bulletin de l'enseignement public du Maroc*, no. 1 (June 1914): 1.

[14] Louis Brunot, "L'action colonial et les mentalités indigènes," in *Premiers conseils* (Rabat: Ecole du Livre, 1934), 154; Raymond F. Betts, *Assimilation and Association in French Colonial Theory, 1890–1914* (New York: Columbia University Press, 1961); Belhaj Saif, *La politique scolaire*; Yvonne Knibiehler, "L'enseignement au Maroc pendant le protectorat (1912–1956): Les 'fils de notables'," *Revue d'histoire moderne et contemporaine* 41, no. 3 (July–September 1994): 489.

[15] Patricia Lorcin, *Imperial Identities: Stereotyping, Prejudice, and Race in Colonial Algeria* (London: I.B. Tauris, 1995); Fanny Colonna, *Instituteurs algériens, 1883–1939*, Travaux et recherches de science politique, no. 36 (Paris: Presses de la Fondation nationale des sciences politiques, 1975).

perceived differences was a variety of school types. For example in 1930, the Muslim population of Morocco was served by 15 schools for girls, 36 rural primary schools (of which 18 were designated as serving the Berber population), 25 urban primary schools, 14 schools of apprenticeship, six schools for the sons of notables, one regional Berber secondary school, and two Muslim secondary schools. All secondary schools, notably, were designated as a *collège*, and not the more advanced *lycée*, which would prepare students for the *baccalauréat* and entrance to universities.[16]

In theory, the Muslim vocational schools were designed to be secondary schools. In practice, in the early 1920s, the primary and vocational schools operated on parallel tracks for similarly aged pupils, rather than in subsequent order. Another compromise was that both primary and vocational schools tended to incorporate elements of both general and vocational education. Particularly in the latter half of the 1920s, the urban primary schools and rural schools cultivated those subjects, skills, and mindsets administrators imagined would increase economic productivity and a vocational orientation. Thus, primary school students received an hour and a half of daily "pre-apprenticeship" training to practice their manual dexterity, to familiarize them with basic tools, and to pique their interest in manual trades. In rural schools, as well as in many urban schools, the curriculum reflected the central role of agriculture in the Moroccan economy. For example, students were taught the vocabulary and basic principles of agriculture in *leçons de langage* and *leçons de choses*. These schools were also equipped with school gardens in which students worked, and often a school cooperative [*mutuelle*] in which products were sold. In these efforts, administrators sought a balance between the agricultural practices used by students' families and the practices used by the European settlers, who often had larger plots, grew different crops, or used more capital-intensive techniques. Rather than reinforcing old practices or potentially "disorienting" students, administrators sought to instruct students about "improved agriculture" that avoided both extremes.[17] Yet these compromises pleased few. For example, pupils

[16]Brunot, "Histoire," 145, 151.

[17]Louis Brunot, "Circulaire aux directeurs des écoles rurales et des écoles urbaines donnant un enseignement agricole," in *Premiers conseils* (Rabat: Ecole du Livre, 1934), 188.

often complained about the gardens, seeing them as demeaning and an excuse to extract cheap labor.[18]

The explicitly designated Muslim vocational schools—and the compromises on which they were founded—also struggled to gain support from pupils, their families, and the business community. These dedicated vocational schools [*l'école professionnelle*], or later, "schools of apprenticeship" [*écoles d'apprentissage*], provided more specialized training in the manual trades. Both the physical plant of the vocational school and its curriculum reflected its dual mandate (another compromise) to provide an education in both "general culture" [*culture générale*] and in a trade [*métier*]. General culture was taught in the classroom, whereas the trades were learned in school workshops, where students served apprenticeships. As a further compromise between partisans of these two different types of education, the lessons in the classroom were tailored to their potential application in the workshop, for example, by emphasizing the relevant technical vocabulary.[19] Directors of vocational schools saw their mission as creating the workers necessary for a modern economy, for "today's jobs demand, in effect, specialist workers," as one director wrote.[20] However, they generally realized that traditional (non-school) apprenticeships more than adequately taught manual skills. What Moroccan (and European) apprentices needed to be competitive in a European-dominated workplace, they argued, were the basics of French, math, drawing, and introductions to the organization and method of European work. Through specialization, vocational schools promised to transform the masses of laborers [*main-d'ouevre*] into skilled or semiskilled workers [*ouvriers*]. There was, admittedly, some disagreement about the degree of this specialization to be taught in school. For example, the director of Muslim education, Louis Brunot, felt that it was the role of vocational education to create semi-skilled workers, who would acquire the rest of their skills in their place of employment. In contrast, a Casablanca educator, Martial Lisard, felt that a worker who did not learn a trade remained only a "half-worker" [*demi-ouvrier*], in a derogatory

[18] Segalla, *Moroccan Soul*, 166.

[19] Mauguière et Achille, "Le problème de la culture générale," *Bulletin de l'enseignement public du Maroc*, no. 72 (February 1926): 31–34.

[20] M. Lisard, "L'orientation professionnelle au Maroc: Organisation et fonctionnement du Bureau d'Orientation professionnelle de Casablanca (Année 1927–1928)," *Bulletin de l'enseignement public du Maroc*, no. 93 (January 1929): 18.

sense. Yet most educators agreed that some degree of labor specialization was necessary, and that it required external coordination for this specialization, perhaps by the state.[21]

The types of trades that students learned in vocational schools varied by institution. Most of the approximately fifteen Muslim vocational schools for boys in operation at the end of 1925 prepared students for "trades such as are practiced in Europe with modern tools and processes," mostly involving wood and iron.[22] Many of these students learned relatively common jobs like carpentry or mechanics, but with specialized training and exposure to the latest techniques if facilities and trained overseers allowed (and neither was to be taken for granted). In a few schools, there were also electrified workshops. A minority of vocational schools were oriented toward Moroccan arts: as of the mid-1920s, two schools for boys taught cabinet-making, an additional two taught leatherwork and bookbinding, and one taught leather embroidery and woodworking. Furthermore, the five vocational schools for Muslim girls taught pupils to weave carpets and mats.[23]

These vocational schools for girls served the dual function of creating "traditional" art and providing women with a basic education that could overcome the objections of some religious conservatives. For Hardy, instruction in indigenous art served also as a means of preserving and restoring the originality of Moroccan art. These efforts meant producing luxurious, "authentic" Moroccan art to rescue it from its supposed corruptions by European techniques, motifs, and cost-cutting, even if tourists might not be able to appreciate or afford it.[24] More broadly, his and Lyautey's "preservation" policies positioned the French as defenders of Islam, of Moroccan culture, and of social stability. This was a calculated move to win the support of local elites and to minimize the likelihood of revolt, while simultaneously stimulating the economy through tourism.[25] Hardy's department, which oversaw public education, fine arts, and antiquities, assisted with all these requirements. In 1920, the

---

[21] Lisard, "L'orientation professionnelle," 18; Brunot, "Histoire," 143.

[22] Roger Gaudefroy-Demombynes, *L'œuvre française en matière d'enseignement au Maroc* (Paris: P. Geuthner, 1928), 89.

[23] Ibid., 89, n. 2.

[24] Baldoui, Hainaut, and Le Gozler, "Les écoles professionnelles et l'art indigène," *Bulletin de l'enseignement public du Maroc*, no. 72 (February 1926): 60, 62.

[25] Wright, *Politics of Design*, 89–90.

DIP's Service des arts had assumed control of training in handicrafts before integrating this training into vocational and urban schools two years later.[26] Thus, while part of Hardy's directorate preserved historic sites, its vocational schools trained workers to produce carpets, leather goods, embroideries, and small wooden objects with inlay for purchase. It was but one of several examples where Lyautey and Hardy mobilized their conceptions about ethnographic difference and the "authentically Moroccan"—whether expressed in art, architecture, or personhood—to promote economic development.

State-run schools so explicitly oriented to the needs of the economy represented a shift in how French colonial and metropolitan administrators thought about education. While elite technical schools had existed in France for some decades, vocational schools and the regulation and "scholarization" of apprenticeships were expanded during the first half of the twentieth century. In addition to an increased average time children spent in state schools, raising the question of what to with them in school, there was an increasing sense among French policymakers before and immediately after World War I that the country needed to increase its economic output to counter the threat of Germany to national security. This insecurity was coupled with a recognition that modern industries like metallurgy required skilled workers in narrow, specialized jobs. These were jobs for which traditional apprenticeships, general schools, or even on-the-job training appeared inadequate. Consequently, early twentieth-century French governments looked to increase collaboration with industry, standardize technical training, expand access to vocational schools, and even in non-vocational schools, make a clearer connection between pupils' education and their future jobs as workers. The new role of public education, as one teacher at the School for Industry and Commerce in Casablanca envisioned, would be "to prepare the citizen and the producer."[27]

In this particular form of linking the development of individual productivity to the productivity of the country, vocational education fit within a new, if still embryonic, vision of economic development. The French phrase increasingly heard during the period of roughly 1890 to 1950, particularly in the colonies, was *"mise en valeur,"* which

[26] Segalla, *Moroccan Soul*, 160.

[27] Jacquemet, "L'école primaire et l'orientation professionnelle," *Bulletin de l'enseignement public du Maroc*, no. 58 (April 1924): 267.

has a sense of "putting to productive use," "increasing the value," or "developing."[28] More than just ensuring that schools were producing physically fit and specialized workers, vocational education was also intended to create specific types of modern, manual workers with a scientific outlook corresponding to the needs of the evolving colonial economy. Whereas French public education had always been designed to transmit the moral *values* of hard and honest work, the reformed school would also teach the *skills* of industry and *develop* the productive capacity of its pupils. As one pair of presenters reported to the Conference on Indigenous Vocational Education, Morocco was undergoing drastic economic and social change, and vocational education was designed to facilitate a skilled workforce for this modern, "European" economy.[29] In this new economy, these educators specifically promoted industry and manual trades, rather than purely intellectual professions.[30] It was not that administrators did not want skilled bureaucrats or white-collar workers. Rather, they realized that the supply of such jobs was limited, that they could attract applicants without government support on account of their pay and easy working conditions, and believed that they did not directly boost production.

In this context, a vocational education with sensitivity to ethnicity and class and producing more industrious and specialized labor combined the promise of increased productivity and economic development while minimizing challenges to French authority. One perceived risk that contemporary commentators on education feared was the threat that a Moroccan "proletariat" might emerge, in the words of Gaudefroy-Demombynes.[31] To navigate the perilous "passage from 'the souk to the factory,'" as he and Hardy referred to it, a rigorous policy response was needed. Like his contemporaries, Hardy emphasized the need for specialization, regulation, and productivity at the

---

[28] Belhaj Saif, *La politique scolaire*, 53–74; Rist, *History of Development*; Corinna Unger, *International Development: A Postwar History* (London: Bloomsbury, 2018).

[29] Morisson and Montel, "Le recrutement des élèves et la fréquentation," *Bulletin de l'enseignement public du Maroc*, no. 72 (February 1926): 20–21.

[30] Louis Brunot, "Certificat d'études primaires et apprentissage," in *Premiers conseils* (Rabat: Ecole du Livre, 1934), 203.

[31] Gaudefroy-Demombynes, *L'œuvre française*, 102–103.

same time as the need to keep students rooted in social structures, lest they become declassed or uprooted.[32]

The social stability that vocational education promised both increased productivity and maintained students "where they belonged," that is, in their appropriate family, occupational, class, and ethnographic settings. Hardy and other educators were well aware—and to an extent regretted—that vocational education reinforced class divisions. They lamented, for example, that poor European families often had to send their children into the workforce as soon as possible, rather than pursue further education, and that the indigenous Moroccan elite families embraced a system that sent poor children to manual trades while preparing their own for administrative careers. Acceptance of class division was the norm in educational policy, not least because education officials were skeptical of the ability of education to change class structures. They were also more afraid of social instability than desirous of social mobility.[33] Thus, rather than making an effort to counteract class division to "democratize a society," administrators, as Inspector Paul Marty bluntly put it, "consider men and things such as they are…The child of a given social milieu should receive an education that is adapted to that milieu, that will maintain him there, and will render him more able to fulfill his social role, however humble it may be."[34] In accepting that class was going to be reproduced in the school system, administrators instead focused on ensuring that sufficient numbers entered the manual or "productive" trades, and that those who did would receive rigorous and specialized training.[35]

Vocational Education Beyond the Indigenous Classroom

Specialization and economic development were likewise the objectives of vocational schools and programs designed for non-Muslim students. The DIP, Alliance israélite universelle, and Comité israélite pour l'orientation professionnelle worked together to create a Jewish school of apprenticeship in Casablanca, whose curriculum emphasized wood and iron work,

---

[32] Hardy, "Du Souq," 3.
[33] Lisard, "L'orientation professionnelle," 19; Hardy, "Du Souq," 3.
[34] Paul Marty, *Le Maroc de demain* (Paris: Comité de l'Afrique française, 1925), 142.
[35] Lisard, "L'orientation professionnelle," 16–18.

design, technology, French, and math. These associations also strove to encourage vocations in industry and agriculture. The "European" school of apprenticeship in Rabat had 24 Muslim and 63 non-Muslim students in 1930. Both Rabat and Casablanca hosted schools where European girls aged 12–16 learned home economics (*école ménagère*). Yet much of the vocational orientation for European and Jewish students was for boys and took place either at the level of the curriculum, for example, in so-called complementary courses (*cours complémentaires*), or through specialized, technical schools.[36]

The specialized *technical* schools—rather than vocational and apprenticeship schools (*l'école professionnelle* or *l'école d'apprentissage*)—taught more technologically advanced jobs and tended to cater to European students, though they were open to indigenous Jews and Muslims, as well. The most famous institution was the Industrial and Commercial School in Casablanca [*l'Ecole industrielle et commerciale*], which opened in 1917 to all religions and nationalities. It trained technicians and managers in electricity, public works, agriculture, and administration. By 1928, it trained approximately 400 students, including those completing apprenticeships, further education, preparatory classes, preparation for university, and professional certificates.[37] An elementary school dedicated to maritime industries opened in 1931 in Casablanca. There was also a specialized school for agriculture in Fez. By 1934, vocational and technical schools offered training in electricity, zinc-plumbing, locksmithing, and car repairs, while agricultural mechanics and automobile bodywork were under consideration.[38]

In addition to promoting modern industries and techniques in general, vocational education also targeted export industries. A school was established at Kourigha in 1924 under the patronage of the Office des Phosphates. Phosphates were and remain to this day a principal export from Morocco. In Kourigha, students learned wood and iron work, and plans were afoot in 1925 to expand teaching to include mining and electricity, all with the aim of creating skilled workers for the phosphate

---

[36] Morocco, Direction Générale de l'instruction publique, des beaux-arts et des antiquités (DIP), *Historique, 1912–1930* (Rabat: Imprimerie de l'École du livre, 1930), 41, 46.

[37] Morocco, DIP, *Historique*, 31–33.

[38] Brunot, "Histoire," 143.

industry.³⁹ While the school might have represented an extreme example, the linkages between trade and education were clearly on the mind of Henri Velu, who justified the teaching of agricultural science in the elementary school due to the fact that, apart from phosphates, most export earnings from Morocco were agricultural.⁴⁰

Yet a vocational emphasis to education was not simply a matter of creating dedicated schools, nor simply a preoccupation toward one group of students. In order for the nation's members to put their state-provided education to productive use, all students had to be made aware of the path between school and career. When Hardy's successor, Jean Gotteland, lamented in 1932 of the "disquieting" "number of young boys and young girls who pursue here their [secondary] studies… without having any idea of the use that they will be able to make of their knowledge…," the students he had in mind were Europeans, although he feared that in time Moroccan Muslims and Jews would follow their example.⁴¹ The solution, pursued in most major Moroccan cities since the mid-1920s, was to create a system for students to learn about which profession they would be suited for, the potentials and limitations of such a profession, and how to best prepare for such a career, including what type of further education (if any) was most appropriate.⁴²

When established in places like Casablanca, the offices for vocational guidance [*Bureaux d'orientation professionnelle*] pursued activities that were typical for such offices in Europe. For example, they interviewed local leaders of industry to create brochures that they would distribute to students about the working conditions and prospects for common jobs. They charged teachers and school physicians with creating card files [*fiches*] for every student with information about the student's scholastic, moral, physical, and psychological aptitudes. Finally, they counseled students based on their aptitudes and interests, and when possible placed

---

³⁹ Gaudefroy-Demombynes, *L'œuvre française*, 91; Congrès de l'Enseignement Professionnel Indigène [Rabat 1925], "Situation des écoles d'apprentissage d'indigènes actuellement existantes," *Bulletin de l'enseignement public du Maroc*, no. 72 (February 1926): 86–88.

⁴⁰ H. Velu, "L'enseignement agricole élémentaire," *Bulletin de l'enseignement public du Maroc*, no. 89 (May 1928): 156–161.

⁴¹ Jean Gotteland and Mlle Alphandery, "A propos d'Orientation professionnelle," *Bulletin de l'enseignement public du Maroc* (November–December 1932): 449.

⁴² Morisson and Montel, "Le recrutement," 23.

them directly in apprenticeships. For example, during the 1927–1928 academic year, fifty-nine European students and families sought counseling in the Casablanca office. Of these, seven students were reportedly dissuaded from their choice of profession due to adverse economic conditions. Another seven with medical counterindications were directed to corrective medical care and to more appropriate trades. Five students were redirected because of their academic deficiencies, three were helped to make a decision, and thirty-seven were "permitted" by the office to exercise their choice of job. In fact, the vocational guidance office had no legal authority, so whether any of the students actually complied with the recommendations is unclear.[43]

Vocational guidance aimed to "scientifically" track students to the most appropriate and specialized careers, ensuring maximum efficient use of every laborer. Specialization was a hallmark of industrializing society and, as such, had been a secular trend for many decades. However during World War I and through the 1920s, French businessmen and policymakers looked to deliberately promote specialization by adopting "American" techniques, often associated with "Taylorism," such as time-motion studies, specialization of tasks, the determination of the optimal way to perform every step of a task, the recruitment of the right worker for a very specific job, and the restructuring of wages to reward increased output.[44] A key educator involved in the vocational guidance movement in Casablanca, Martial Lisard, expressed this ambition in his claim that, "social life rests on a just equilibrium of diverse activities, rationally coordinated in view of the common good,"[45] while others lauded vocational orientation as a "powerful factor of social peace."[46] While vocational guidance did not derive strictly from Taylorism, the two movements were mutually supportive. Both movements sought to recruit the "right man for the right job," to increase specialization and mastery of tasks (for vocational guidance, through apprenticeships), and to "rationalize"

---

[43] Lisard, "L'orientation professionnelle," 22–23; Edouard Gauthier, "L'orientation professionnelle," *Revue Internationale du Travail* 5, no. 5 (May 1922): 759–773.

[44] Elisa Camiscioli, *Reproducing the French Race* (Durham, NC: Duke, 2009), 51–74; Charles S. Maier, *In Search of Stability: Explorations in Historical Political Economy* (Cambridge: Cambridge University Press, 1987), 19–69.

[45] Lisard, "L'orientation professionnelle," 13.

[46] Gauthier, "L'orientation professionnelle," 761.

the workforce, for example, by directing students away from trades with a surplus of labor and toward other careers.

Ideally, individuals would benefit by pursuing a career that was interesting, practical, and financially rewarding. At the same time, society would benefit through increased specialization, the elimination of "waste," improved health, and the encouragement of students to pursue the most productive jobs. For example, the "scientific tracking" of students to the jobs they were physically suited for—facilitated by medical record cards completed by school physicians—promised to protect the individual and corporate health of the workforce.[47] Vocational counselors routinely directed students away from careers that they were not fit for, fearing that inappropriate placement would result in "bodily fatigue, as much as that of intellectual tension."[48] Some of this focus on medicine was clearly designed to give the vocational guidance movement the respectability of "science" as it directed individuals to particular jobs.[49] However, it was also part of a broader movement that thought about bodily health as a link between individual and collective health, the availability of future soldiers, and the productivity of future workers.

The Limits of Vocational Training

Although vocational thinking had a deep imprint on educational philosophy and curriculum, both within and beyond schools, themselves, several factors limited its impact on students, and particularly on Muslim students. In part, vocational training in interwar French Morocco was limited by the scope of public education, more generally. The number of students enrolled in Moroccan schools increased steadily from year to year, but from a low base. Enrollment was proportionally higher among the European population, while the total number of indigenous students enrolled in school was extremely modest—less than 10,000 in 1929 and less than 16,000 in 1933. Out of this population, the number of

---

[47] Gotteland and Alphandery, "A propos," 449; Montel and Morrison, "Le recrutement," 24; Lisard, "L'orientation professionnelle," 15; Gauthier, "L'orientation professionnelle," 759–773.

[48] Gauthier, "L'orientation professionnelle," 761–762.

[49] Mary Louise Roberts, *Civilization Without Sexes: Reconstructing Gender in Postwar France, 1917–1927*. Women in Culture and Society (Chicago: University of Chicago Press, 1994), 190–191.

apprentices in the French-controlled system varied greatly from year to year: down to 500 apprentices in 1930 from highs in the mid-1920s, then returning to 1155 apprentices in 1933.[50] Other programs like vocational guidance efforts, pre-apprenticeship classes, and school gardens increased the impact of vocational orientation outside the formal vocational schools, but it was still a minority of school-age children who attended school in interwar Morocco and a minority of those who attended explicitly vocational programs.

Part of the dynamic was that families shied away from vocational schools and programs. Muslim parents, it was lamented, "cannot conceive that a trade is taught in a school…One puts a child in school so that he is not a worker like his father. If, on the contrary, the parents really want to teach their son a trade, they prefer to entrust him to an artisan of the souk."[51] Preference for an "intellectual" education was also prevalent, if less commented upon, among other ethnic groups. Even if parents wanted to send their students to vocational school, the high cost of living and the availability of jobs that did not require prior training drove youth and their families toward immediate employment, rather than the possibility of higher earnings in a more distant future.[52]

When students did enroll in vocational schools, they did not always stay for long or have better career opportunities. The average student during the mid-1920s spent a few weeks or months at a vocational school, rather than the minimum of three years that one was said to need to learn a profession.[53] Instead, students often left as soon as they could find a job, even though this generally meant lower, if more immediate, salaries. Moreover, the training provided in vocational school did not provide a guaranteed return on investment. A lively debate at the time considered whether specialized schools actually depressed wages in the professions they taught by producing a surfeit of workers. While statistics are imprecise, the evidence suggests that graduates were most likely to find jobs in coastal cities with a strong European commercial presence, such as Rabat-Salé, Tangier, Casablanca, and Mazagan (El-Jadida), whereas students in inland cities most associated with

---

[50] Brunot, "Histoire de l'enseignement," 142.
[51] Morisson and Montel, "Le recrutement," 19.
[52] Lisard, "L'orientation professionnelle," 17–18.
[53] Gaudefroy-Demombynes, *L'œuvre française*, 94.

traditional Moroccan society, such as Fez or Marrakech, or who studied indigenous art in places like Oujda or Mogador, had difficulty finding jobs.[54] Moreover, many employers refused to take apprentices, preferring to teach most workers on the job and to bring a handful of skilled workers from France if their needs were not met locally.[55] The effect on students in Muslim vocational schools was pronounced. According to the (admittedly imprecise) statistics reported in the 1925 Conference on Indigenous Vocational Education, only half of students leaving such schools found or chose work in the trade that they had learned.[56]

Surveys of students' career choices demonstrate that these failures of vocational education for Muslim students, coupled with greater access for indigenous Jewish and European students, led to very different expectations about careers when students left school. For three years between 1924 and 1926, the *Bulletin de l'enseignement public* published the results of surveys about students' vocational choices. At the request of Hardy, the oldest students in every school—i.e., those who were old enough to enter the workforce, rather than those who had obtained a certain level of schooling—were asked to respond to two questions: what profession they intended to practice upon leaving school, and the reasons for that choice. The survey had multiple limitations, as Hardy himself freely admitted, including the impossibility of knowing whether the responses reflect students' dreams, intentions, or even attempts to give the "right" or "wrong" response.[57]

Nonetheless, an analysis of the 1926 survey reveals that European primary school students were approximately twice as willing as their counterparts in Muslim schools to embrace manual jobs. It is possible that this result reflected less the impact of education than the fact that enrollment in European schools reflected a broader and more representative spectrum of society than Muslim schools. However, in both communities, there were pronounced class differences. For example, Muslim students in primary schools were approximately six times more likely to declare an intention for manual, non-agricultural jobs than those students attending the elite *écoles des fils de notables*. A similar, if less

[54] Congrès de l'Enseignement, "Situation des écoles," 76–93.
[55] Segalla, *Moroccan Soul*, 157.
[56] Lisard, "L'orientation professionnelle," 17.
[57] Georges Hardy, "Les vocations de nos élèves," *Bulletin de l'enseignement public du Maroc* (April 1924): 211.

pronounced trend, is clear among the European community, where *lycée* students also eschewed manual professions.[58]

While many students wished to assume white-collar jobs, there were distinct differences in preference, based on background. No less than 44% of Jewish primary school students wished to assume jobs in commerce in 1926, mostly as shopkeepers but also as bookkeepers and bankers. Only a handful of Jewish students planned to enter public administration, which reflected both their political disadvantage and their limited opportunities for secondary education. In contrast, Muslim students preferred administration over commerce, and both over manual trades.[59] This preference was troubling for Hardy. Left to their own devices, he complained, the young Muslim bourgeoisie would all become petty bureaucrats. Although some indigenous administrators were necessary, the educational system should ensure that there were not too many aspiring bureaucrats and that only well-formed and well-chosen bureaucrats were hired. Finally, although European students also found public employment attractive, students in the prestigious lycées aspired to exercise more specialized and potentially more lucrative roles in an increasingly sophisticated economy as officers, civil engineers, teachers [*professeurs*, rather than *instituteurs*], doctors (of various specialties), and lawyers, rather than as junior civil servants.[60]

Among manual jobs, European students also best seemed positioned to take advantage of Morocco's economic growth. European students showed an appreciable interest in construction, which was something of a growth industry due to the influx of European immigrants who were housed in newly built sections of cities and due to public infrastructure projects. They expressed even more interest in mechanics, electricity, and engineering. In total, some 43% of European primary school students wished to work with metals, electricity, construction, or engineering. In contrast, virtually no Muslim students in the elite primary or secondary school systems were interested in such trades. The only Muslim school population to express interest in manual jobs, those attending primary

---

[58] Georges Hardy, "Les vocations de nos élèves," *Bulletin de l'enseignement public du Maroc* (May–June–July 1926): 82–144.

[59] Ibid.

[60] Hardy, "Du Souq," 14–16.

schools, wished to work almost exclusively with wood as carpenters, joiners, or cabinetmakers (and again, at a lower rate than their European peers). Although vocational educators insisted on high-quality work and introduced more mechanized and electrified techniques into these trades, woodworking was considered less industrialized or "modern" than the metalworking, mechanics, and electricity that attracted European students. In short, students' job preferences closely reflected conceptions of modernity and the racialized hierarchies of the protectorate, more broadly, with the most industrial, technical, and "modern" trades attracting primarily European students, followed by indigenous Jews.

For all the shortcomings of vocational education program as implemented in Morocco, and despite its mission to preserve class and racial hierarchies, it did offer a modicum of social mobility. For example, within the European community, there was evidence that vocational education—and education more generally—fulfilled the aspirations of upward social mobility of Spaniards in French Morocco, who often hailed from the least economically and educationally regions of Spain.[61] Among the indigenous Moroccan population, as was the case in France, pupils in vocational schools were often orphans, the sons of artisans whose trades faced an uncertain or declining future, or the sons of the petite bourgeoisie (who themselves often faced acute economic uncertainty).[62] While these social origins may not have impressed contemporaries, it suggests that the students from all religions and backgrounds who accepted vocational education nonetheless saw it as a chance, however uncertain, of acquiring skills and providing either an improvement over their current socioeconomic situation or a hedge to preserve that status.

Ineffective Reforms and Expansion

The very real challenges of vocational education, particularly for indigenous Muslim students, inspired heated discussion in the 1925 Conference on Indigenous Vocational Education and led to change. As a result of the 1925 conference, a series of reforms doubled stipends for students in vocational schools, and administrators strove to

[61] J. Vedel, "Les élèves espagnols des écoles du Maroc," *Bulletin de l'enseignement public du Maroc*, no. 56 (February 1924): 141–147.
[62] Morisson and Montel, "Le recrutement," 20.

provide better connections between schooling and jobs. Given the lack of employer interest, however, these efforts came to little fruition. In practice, after 1926, there was a greater convergence between vocational and non-vocational schools for Muslims. Vocational schools placed an increased emphasis on general education, especially French and math. Meanwhile, five out of sixteen vocational schools were officially converted to primary schools.[63]

Nonetheless, vocational training continued to leave its mark on education in Morocco. While some scholars have seen a decreased focus on vocational training after 1926, particularly under Hardy's successor, Gotteland, who took his post that year,[64] vocational education neither disappeared nor lost its importance (or resolved its challenges, for that matter). Gotteland was skeptical of vocational training's potential (and desirability) to modernize the country. However, there is little evidence that teachers, pupils, and their families—many of whom had long been aware of the system's shortcoming, substantially altered their perceptions. Rather, demand continued to increase for vocational training. Despite the conversion of five vocational schools to urban schools in 1926, the rebranding of vocational schools and opening of new locations meant that by 1930, there were 14 so-called schools of apprenticeship, nearly the same as before.[65] Furthermore, from hardly 500 students enrolled in Muslim vocational schools around 1930, the total increased to about 1200 Muslim students in 1935.[66]

Part of this countervailing dynamic was that demand for vocational schools increased, even as administrators began to acknowledge the challenges. Starting around 1926, the cumulative effect of a decade of economic changes brought about by the establishment of the protectorate and increased global trade, disrupting traditional handicrafts and leading to the loss of land, began to boost enrollment in Muslim schools. A majority of the pupils were the sons of the unskilled and landless. Families in traditional handicrafts and light industries often saw little benefit to the French-run schools, while elite families benefited from a separate school system. Many Moroccan families remained skeptical of the vocational

---

[63] Segalla, *Moroccan Soul*, 164.
[64] Ibid., 172–174.
[65] Brunot, "Histoire," 145, 151.
[66] Morocco, DIP, *Historique*, 60; Segalla, *Moroccan Soul*, 174.

schools. However, limited budgets, and limited places for Muslim students in the state school system—far short of anything approaching universal, or even widespread, education—meant that vocational schools were one of the few opportunities to receive a formal education. By way of example, when France was invaded in 1940, less than 3% of Moroccan children had spots in French-run schools, and demand for education exceeded supply.[67]

Moreover, despite its numerous shortcomings—well acknowledged at the time—vocational education had an impact beyond the boundaries of the interwar French protectorate. For example, the "indigenous" vocational school in the international city of Tangier, whose students in 1925 included 22 Muslims, 30 Jews, and 10 Spaniards [sic], had a strong French influence.[68] In the 1920s, the Alliance israélite universelle and Comité israélite pour l'orientation professionnelle, with the assistance of the DIP in the French sector, created workshops for sewing and embroidery in poor Jewish neighborhoods across Morocco, including Casablanca and Mogador (Essaouira) in the French protectorate, the international city of Tangier, and the capital of the Spanish protectorate, Tétouan.[69]

In the Spanish sector, authorities had long looked to French vocational reforms to inform their even more modest public education system. Spanish vocational education was by no means a slavish copy of a French model, having its own, local history and own tradition of participation in a broader international movement. Nonetheless, French efforts in Morocco were well known to Spanish school inspectors and other authorities, who approvingly quoted, for example, Paul Marty's claim that colonial education should not attempt to increase social mobility but train students for the position they were born into.[70] The roots of vocational education in the Spanish zone date to 1923, but it was not until the last years that the Second Republic exercised control over Morocco (1931–1936) that authorities slowly began to add workshops to primary schools.[71]

---

[67] Robin Bidwell, *Morocco Under Colonial Rule* (New York: Routledge, 1973), 253.

[68] Congrès de l'Enseignement, "Situation des écoles," 77.

[69] Morocco, DIP, *Historique*, 46.

[70] Luis Bello, *Viaje por las escuelas de España*, vol. 4 (Madrid: Magisterio español, 1926), 183–184.

[71] Federico Castro Morales and Alberto Darias Príncipe, *Al-Andalus: una identidad compartida: arte, ideología y enseñanza en el protectorado español en Marruecos* (Madrid: Universidad Carlos III de Madrid, 1999), 167–171.

Franco's seizure of power in Morocco in 1936 ushered in a shift in policy and official rhetoric that further favored vocational education. In 1937, Nationalist authorities launched plans to create Muslim vocational schools [*escuelas profesionales musulmanas*]. Like the vocational schools of the French sector, they were designed to give students with a preexisting basic education a combination of general knowledge, theoretical knowledge, and practice in given trades. As clarified in the regulations of 1942, these schools, now known as Moroccan schools of vocational orientation [*escuelas marroquíes de orientación profesional*], offered instruction in four trades: carpentry, leather embossing, printing and bookbinding, and mechanics and electricity.[72] Under Franco, Moroccan education emphasized racial and class separation in the pursuit of utilitarian ends. A reordering of the colonial education ministry and name changes in schools in the late 1930s reflected strict separation between Spanish and Moroccan education. The new high commissioner, Juan Beigbeder, stressed to teachers that the mission of the schools was vocational and/or practical, not intellectual or universalist, derogatory values associated with the Republic. Like Hardy before them, educators proudly proclaimed the motto of "school for life" [*la escuela para la vida*]. Yet under Franco, the rhetoric became even less equivocal about the segregational aims of their policy, explicitly attempting to freeze Moroccans in their religious, class, and rural settings, echoing important themes for Franco on the mainland.[73]

The Vichy regime in France implemented similar intensifications in vocational education policy. Senior Vichy officials strongly promoted manual labor as a moral good and vocational education as a means of regulating and civically molding youth. Despite insufficient budgets, the number of vocational schools and guidance centers increased, and the latter directed students more unswervingly toward the manual trades. Commercial and industrial schools [*écoles pratiques de commerce et d'industrie*] were renamed *collèges techniques*, conferring on them greater prestige by suggesting their equivalence with the schools that fed into academic *lycées*. Furthermore, officials mandated minimum salaries for apprentices. Meanwhile, even schools not specially designated as vocational schools consolidated the place of manual work in the curriculum.

---

[72] Valderrama, *Estado actual* and Ibid., *Historia de la acción cultural de España en Marruecos, 1912–1956*, 2 vols. (Tetuán, Morocco: Editora Marroquí, 1956).

[73] Ibid., 9, 15, 43, 63, 64.

For example in 1942, the curriculum for Muslim rural schools dedicated 5 out of 30 hours a week for the youngest pupils to agriculture—a figure growing to 11.5 hours per week (out of 35) in the final two years, with most of the remaining time dedicated to Arabic, French, math, and writing.[74] All of these measures were calculated to increase the prestige of manual labor and to expand its purview. Under the mantra of "work, family, country" [*travail, famille, patrie*], Vichy policymakers sought to reinforce social stability and freeze individuals in the positions into which they were born.

When the Fourth Republic built on Vichy foundations after 1945 and expanded vocational education, the impetus was not the preservation of social position and the dissolution of class conflict through hierarchical and corporatist harmony, as Vichy officials had hoped, but at least in theory, increased social mobility. In France, the postwar education reforms beneficial to vocational education, such as the creation of the *baccalauréat technique* and *l'école unique*, were embraced just as much for their egalitarian spirit and the prospect of social mobility through the prestige of education. Morocco in the late 1940s through independence in 1956 followed a similar trajectory, with the introduction of a *baccalauréat technique* and greater access to formalized degrees or certificates for trades and professions. However, the increasing prestige of vocational education and the manual trades was insufficient to counter demands for easier access to the more theoretically oriented *lycées*, to higher positions within the government, and for greater power for organized labor.

Moreover, vocational training continued to primarily attract and benefit European and indigenous Jewish students. European students and Moroccan Jews disproportionately attended—and completed—technical and vocational education. Even in absolute terms, Muslim students comprised a minority of those who completed technical, vocational, and professional certificates, even in the postwar period when Muslim school enrollment steadily increased. It is perhaps unsurprising that the most prestigious technical, vocational, and professional qualifications, specifically, the *baccalauréat technique*, went exclusively to non-indigenous students in 1950 (with the exception of one Moroccan Jew), as did a disproportionate number of recipients of a *brevet* or *CAP* (*certificat d'aptitude professionnel*). In contrast, the only certificate with a majority of

[74] Katan, *L'école*, 119.

Muslim recipients was the more humble, *certificat d'apprentissage*. What is more surprising is that European and Jewish students comprised four-fifths of all recipients of technical, vocational, and professional qualifications. For example, in 1950, 451 French and foreign (almost entirely all European) students received professional, vocational, and technical degrees and certificates (74% of the total). In comparison, there were 122 Muslim students (20% of the total) and 38 Jewish students (6% of the total). This was despite the fact that Moroccan Jews comprised 1.6% of the total population and French and foreigners 3.8% of the population, and despite the fact that Muslim students finally comprised a small majority of the secondary school population in the postwar period, up significantly from the 1920s.[75] Roughly speaking (as the proportional representation of each group in the total population does not correspond precisely to their proportional representation in the school-age population, and bearing in mind that successful completion does not correspond to enrollment), Moroccan Jewish students were approximately four times more likely to complete vocational education than the size of the population would suggest, French and foreign students were almost twenty times more likely to complete vocational education, and *Muslim students were nearly five times less likely to complete vocational education* than the size of the population would suggest.

Conclusion

French vocational education policy in Morocco undeniably failed to meet the needs and aspirations of many of its inhabitants during the interwar period. In many places and for many groups, the interwar expansion of education, scholarization of vocational training, and adaptation to the supposed needs of different pupils was repeatedly marked with disappointments: underwhelming interest among prospective pupils and their families, limited employer engagement and job placement, and constant suspicion that vocational tracks would reinforce disadvantage, rather than provide social mobility. Certainly, the "ethnological discourse and doctrine" of Georges Hardy and Louis Brunot, which dominated the "political and intellectual culture of the colonial educational system [and] blinded the colonizers to the economic and cultural agendas of

---

[75] Calculated from Katan, *L'école*, 111, 114.

Moroccan Muslims..." contributed greatly to this, as previously scholars have acknowledged.[76]

Yet, viewing interwar Moroccan education as not just colonial education—in the customary sense of education for the colonized—has the potential to reveal both its international contours—situated as it was in a global movement to increase vocational training and vocational orientation—and its non-Muslim beneficiaries. As the vocational surveys, certificate recipients, and qualitative reports suggest, European and indigenous Jewish students school leavers were more likely to consciously embrace manual and industrial careers than Muslim school leavers. Students in European schools were encouraged to and did in fact embrace fields like mechanics or engineering that required strong specialization and familiarity with modern machines and techniques. These students were more likely than students in Muslim schools to receive an education in manual trades during or after public schooling, perhaps through an apprenticeship with a European-controlled firm arranged through a local office for vocational guidance. While Muslims were also encouraged to adopt "European jobs" in vocational schools, the trades they learned were often in less capital-intensive fields like woodworking, even if students were instructed in modern techniques. Moreover, Muslim students and families in the public education system generally preferred bureaucratic jobs.

In contrast, indigenous Jewish students were highly shaped by vocational education policies. The Alliance Israélite Universelle had a long history of promoting manual trades. This strategy grew out of a French discourse that sought to "redeem" Jews from the perceived dangers of work in the service sector, either because they regarded such tertiary sector work as non-productive or to counterstereotypes. Moreover in Morocco, Jews were at a disadvantage in hiring for the sultan's government, both before and after the establishment of the protectorate. They also faced discrimination in the traditional, Muslim-dominated apprenticeship system.[77] Thus, a disproportionate number of Jewish students, facing discrimination and with limited job prospects with a normal school degree, enrolled in vocational schools as a means of attaining social mobility unavailable through other routes.

[76] Segalla, *Moroccan Soul*, 154.

[77] Saisset, "Le rôle de l'école dans les échanges franco-marocains," *Bulletin de l'enseignement public du Maroc*, no. 78 (January 1927): 21.

Looking at the broader population of students in the Moroccan educational system, this social mobility was limited and not always the most common outcome. However, substantial upward social mobility was not typically the goal of providers of vocationally inflected education. Vocational training—and broader efforts, such as vocational orientation to match students with careers—generally maintained racial, religious, gender, and class hierarchies. This was consistent with the goal to preserve social stability, rather than simply a failure to achieve goals, even if some of the vocational schools and curricula failed to fulfill the aspirations of their students and teachers. It was not that vocational education—or colonial education, more broadly—was designed to fail the indigenous population; rather, it was only partially designed with the indigenous population in mind. Thus, the growing Moroccan economy, which became more closely integrated in the metropolitan and global economy, could for many years rely on colonial education, including vocational education, to provide skilled workers, even as the same educational system left many indigenous Moroccan children unschooled, segregated, and underskilled to participate in the emerging economy. Yet the rejection of many Muslim families (certainly more privileged Muslim families) of vocational education, and more crucially, the shortcomings of vocational education for Muslim students, reinforced European domination of—and to a limited and unequal extent, Moroccan Jewish participation in—the so-called modern economic sector, and its industry, commerce, and exports.

Bibliography

Baldoui, Hainaut, and Le Gozler. "Les écoles professionnelles et l'art indigène." *Bulletin de l'enseignement public du Maroc*, no. 72 (February 1926): 60–63.

Barthélemy, Pascale, Emmanuelle Picard, and Rebecca Rogers, eds. "L'enseignement dans l'empire colonial français (XIXe-XXe siècles)." *Histoire de l'éducation* 128 (2010).

Belhaj Saif, Mohammed Rachid. "La politique scolaire du protectorat français au Maroc, 1912-1940." Thèse État, Université René Descartes Paris V, 1994.

Bello, Luis. *Viaje por las escuelas de España*, vol. 4. Madrid: Magisterio español, 1926.

Benchekroun, Mohamed b. A. *L'éducation et l'enseignement au Maroc à travers les documents français et espagnols,1912–1956: essai de bibliographie critique*. Rabat: [s.n.], 1985.

Betts, Raymond F. *Assimilation and Association in French Colonial Theory, 1890–1914*. New York: Columbia University Press, 1961.

Bidwell, Robin. *Morocco Under Colonial Rule*. New York: Routledge, 1973.
Brunot, Louis. "Certificat d'études primaires et apprentissage." In *Premiers conseils*, 203–204. Rabat: Ecole du Livre, 1934.
———. "Circulaire aux directeurs des écoles rurales et des écoles urbaines donnant un enseignement agricole." In *Premiers conseils*, 183–186. Rabat: Ecole du Livre, 1934.
———. "Comment pensent nos élèves marocains." In *Premiers conseils*, 175–182. Rabat: Ecole du Livre, 1934.
———. "Histoire de l'enseignement des indigènes musulmans." In *Premiers conseils*, 131–151. Rabat: Ecole du Livre, 1934.
———. "L'action colonial et les mentalités indigènes." In *Premiers conseils*, 153–164. Rabat: Ecole du livre, 1934.
Bude, Udo. "The Adaptation Concept in British Colonial Education." *Comparative Education* 19, no. 3 (1983): 341–355.
Camiscioli, Elisa. *Reproducing the French Race*. Durham, NC: Duke, 2009.
Castro Morales, Federico, and Alberto Darias Príncipe. *Al-Andalus: una identidad compartida: arte, ideología y enseñanza en el protectorado español en Marruecos*. Madrid: Universidad Carlos III de Madrid, 1999.
Charlot, Bernard, and Madeleine Figeat. *Histoire de la formation des ouvriers, 1789–1984*. Collection Voies de l'histoire. Paris: Minerve, 1985.
Colonna, Fanny. *Instituteurs algériens, 1883–1939*. Travaux et recherches de science politique, no 36. Paris: Presses de la Fondation nationale des sciences politiques, 1975.
Congrès de l'Enseignement Professionnel Indigène [Rabat 1925]. "Situation des écoles d'apprentissage d'indigènes actuellement existantes." *Bulletin de l'enseignement public du Maroc*, no. 72 (February 1926): 76–93.
Conklin, Alice. *A Mission to Civilize: The Republican Idea of Empire in France and West Africa, 1895–1930*. Stanford: Stanford University Press, 1997.
Cooper, Frederick. *Decolonization and African Society: The Labor Question in French and British Africa*. Cambridge: Cambridge University Press, 2010.
Crubellier, Maurice. *L'école Républicaine 1870–1940: Esquisse d'une histoire culturelle*. Paris: Editions Christian, 1993.
Danvers, Francis, and Michel Huteau. *Le conseil en orientation en France de 1914 à nos jours*. Issy-les-Moulineaux, France: Editions EAP, 1988.
Fradera, Josep M. "La *Plus Grande France*: el ciudadano y su negación en la República imperial." In *La nación imperial*, vol. 2, 973–1053. Barcelona: Edhasa, 2015.
Gaudefroy-Demombynes, Roger. *L'œuvre française en matière d'enseignement au Maroc*. Paris: Librairie orientaliste P. Geuthner, 1928.
Gauthier, Edouard. "L'orientation professionnelle." *Revue Internationale du Travail* 5, no. 5 (May 1922): 759–773.

Gotteland, Jean, and Mlle Alphandery. "A propos d'Orientation professionnelle." *Bulletin de l'enseignement public du Maroc* (November–December 1932): 449–454.

Hardy, Georges. "Du souq à l'usine: Congrès de l'Enseignement Professionnel Indigène." *Bulletin de l'enseignement public du Maroc*, no. 72 (February 1926): 1–18.

———. *L'âme marocaine d'après la littérature française*. Paris: É. Larose, 1926.

———. "Les vocations de nos élèves." *Bulletin de l'enseignement public du Maroc* [series] (April 1924): 211–266; (May 1925): 255–313; (May–June–July 1926): 82–144.

Hardy, Georges, and Louis Brunot. *L'enfant marocain: Essai d'etnographie scolaire*. Paris: E. Larose, 1925.

Jacquemet. "L'école primaire et l'orientation professionnelle." *Bulletin de l'enseignement public du Maroc*, no. 58 (April 1924): 267–272.

Katan, Yvette. "L'école, instrument de la modernisation sous le protectorat français au Maroc?" *Mediterrán tanulmányok* 5 (1993): 99–119.

Knibiehler, Yvonne. "L'enseignement au Maroc pendant le protectorat (1912–1956): Les 'fils de notables'." *Revue d'histoire moderne et contemporaine* 41, no. 3 (July–September 1994): 489–498.

Kuster, Sybille. "'Book Learning' versus 'Adapted Education': The Impact of Phelps-Stokesism on Colonial Education Systems in Central Africa in the Interwar Period." *Paedagogica Historica* 43, no. 1 (2007): 79–97.

Lisard, M. "L'orientation professionnelle au Maroc: Organisation et fonctionnement du Bureau d'Orientation professionnelle de Casablanca (Année 1927–1928)." *Bulletin de l'enseignement public du Maroc*, no. 93 (January 1929): 13–27.

Lorcin, Patricia M. E. *Imperial Identities: Stereotyping, Prejudice and Race in Colonial Algeria*. Society and Culture in the Modern Middle East. London: I.B. Tauris, 1995.

Loth, Gaston. "Règlement scolaire," *Bulletin de l'enseignement public du Maroc*, no. 1 (June 1914): 1.

Maier, Charles S. *In Search of Stability: Explorations in Historical Political Economy*. Cambridge: Cambridge University Press, 1987.

Manière, Laurent. "La politique française pour l'adaptation de l'enseignement en Afrique après les indépendances (1958–1964)." *Histoire de l'éducation*, no. 128 (2010): 163–190.

Marty, Paul. *Le Maroc de demain*. Paris: Comité de l'Afrique française, 1925.

Mauguière et Achille. "Le problème de la culture générale." *Bulletin de l'enseignement public du aroc*, no. 72 (February 1926): 31–34.

Morisson and Montel. "Le recrutement des élèves et la fréquentation." *Bulletin de l'enseignement public du Maroc*, no. 72 (February 1926): 19–30.

Morocco. Direction Générale de l'instruction publique, des beaux-arts et des antiquités (DIP). *Historique, 1912–1930*. Rabat: Imprimerie de l'École du livre, 1930.

Paye, Lucien. *Introduction et évolution de l'enseignement moderne au Maroc.* Paris: [s.n.], 1957.
Pelpel, Patrice, and Vincent Troger. *Histoire de l'enseignement technique.* Pédagogies pour demain. Paris: Hachette Education, 1993.
Rist, Gilbert. *The History of Development: From Western Origins to Global Faith.* Translated by Patrick Camiller. London: Zed Books, 2010.
Roberts, Mary Louise. *Civilization Without Sexes: Reconstructing Gender in Postwar France, 1917–1927.* Series Women in Culture and Society. Chicago: University of Chicago Press, 1994.
Rockwell, Elsie. "Tracing Assimilation and Adaptation through School Exercise Books from Afrique Occidentale Française in the Early Twentieth Century." In *Empire and Education in Africa,* edited by Peter Kallaway and Rebecca Swartz, 235–270. New York: Peter Lang, 2016.
Rodríguez, José María. "Labor pedagógico-cultural de los franciscanos en Marruecos." In *Segunda serie de trabajos leídos en la Semana de misiología de Barcelona* (29 de junio a 6 de julio de 1930). Barcelona: Escuela Tipográfica Salesiana, 1930.
Saisset. "Le rôle de l'école dans les échanges franco-marocains." *Bulletin de l'enseignement public du Maroc,* no. 78 (January 1927): 12–27.
Segalla, Spencer D. *The Moroccan Soul: French Education, Colonial Ethnology, and Muslim Resistance, 1912–1956.* Lincoln: University of Nebraska, 2009.
Thomas, Martin. "Albert Sarraut, French Colonial Development, and the Communist Threat, 1919–1930." *Journal of Modern History* 77, no. 343 (December 2005): 917–955.
Tselikas, Effy, and Lina Hayoun. *Les lycées français du soleil: Creusets cosmopolites du Maroc, de l'Algérie et de la Tunisie.* Mémoires, no. 99. Paris: Autrement, 2004.
Unger, Corinna R. *International Development: A Postwar History.* London: Bloomsbury, 2018.
Valderrama Martinez, Fernando. *Estado actual de la enseñanza marroquí.* Ceuta: Imperio, 1939.
———. *Historia de la acción cultural de España en Marruecos, 1912–1956,* 2 vols. Tetuán, Morocco: Editora Marroquí, 1956.
Vedel, J. "Les élèves espagnols des écoles du Maroc." *Bulletin de l'enseignement public du Maroc,* no. 56 (February 1924): 141–147.
Velu, H. "L'enseignement agricole élémentaire." *Bulletin de l'enseignement public du Maroc,* no. 89 (May 1928): 156–161.
Wright, Gwendolyn. *The Politics of Design in French Colonial Urbanism.* Chicago: University of Chicago Press, 1991.

Open Access This chapter is licensed under the terms of the Creative Commons Attribution 4.0 International License (http://creativecommons.org/licenses/by/4.0/), which permits use, sharing, adaptation, distribution and reproduction in any medium or format, as long as you give appropriate credit to the original author(s) and the source, provide a link to the Creative Commons license and indicate if changes were made.

The images or other third party material in this chapter are included in the chapter's Creative Commons license, unless indicated otherwise in a credit line to the material. If material is not included in the chapter's Creative Commons license and your intended use is not permitted by statutory regulation or exceeds the permitted use, you will need to obtain permission directly from the copyright holder.

CHAPTER 8

Engineering Socialism: The Faculty of Engineering at the University of Dar es Salaam (Tanzania) in the 1970s and 1980s

Eric Burton

In the age of decolonization after World War II, African political leaders emphasized the need to train their own citizens as engineers in order to implement large-scale infrastructural projects, foster industrialization, and man management posts in the expanding machinery of state

---

Research was supported by a scholarship (*Abschlussstipendium*) from the University of Vienna. Research has been funded by the Austrian Science Fund (FWF) within the framework of the research project "Personal cooperation in 'development aid' and 'socialist aid' in the context of system competition" (P-25949-G16).

E. Burton (✉)
University of Innsbruck, Innsbruck, Austria
e-mail: eric.burton@uibk.ac.at

bureaucracy and parastatal enterprises.[1] More than any other field and in agreement with contemporary theories of "manpower development," investment into engineering education was seen as key to economic growth.[2] As explained by the editors in the general introduction to this volume, the efforts of postcolonial governments to produce national academic elites—including engineers as well as doctors, agricultural experts, or lawyers—boiled down to two strategies: the first was to establish training institutions within the country and the second fostering training abroad, often at overseas universities. Shopping around the world for funds to implement this double strategy, these endeavors became entangled with the cultural and technical offensives of Cold War competition, the fault lines of which these governments had to navigate skilfully (on this issue, see Chapter 11 by Alexandra Piepiorka in this book).[3]

Tanzania was among the postcolonial states that were most successful in diversifying their aid relations following independence. By the mid-1960s, Tanzanian engineering students could be found not only in the UK and the United States, but also in the Soviet Union, Ethiopia, India, or the two German states, though the largest group was being trained in Kenya as part of an East African cooperation arrangement in the university sector.[4] By that time, Tanzania was embarking on a

---

[1] Valeska Huber, "Planning Education and Manpower in the Middle East, 1950s–60s," *Journal of Contemporary History* 52, no. 1 (2017): 95–117.

[2] Osman L. El-Sayed, Juan Lucena, and Gary L. Downey, "Engineering and Engineering Education in Egypt," *IEEE Technology and Society* 25, no. 2 (2006): 17–24; Andrés Valderrama, Juan Camargo, Idelman Mejía, Antonio Mejía, Ernesto Lleras, and Antonio García, "Engineering Education and the Identities of Engineers in Colombia, 1887–1972," *Technology and Culture* 50, no. 4 (2009): 811–838.

[3] Constantin Katsakioris, "Creating a Socialist Intelligentsia: Soviet Educational Aid and Its Impact on Africa (1960–1991)," *Cahiers d'Études Africaines* LVII, no. 2 (2017): 259–887.

[4] Eric Burton, "Navigating Global Socialism: Tanzanian Students in and Beyond East Germany," *Cold War History* 19, no. 1 (2019): 63–83; Eric Burton, "African Manpower Development During the Global Cold War: The Case of Tanzanian Students in the Two German States," in *Africa Research in Austria: Approaches and Perspectives*, ed. by Andreas Exenberger and Ulrich Pallua (Innsbruck: Innsbruck University Press, 2016), 101–134. In the 1960s, the three university colleges of Kampala, Nairobi, and Dar es Salaam together constituted the University of East Africa. While regional cooperation in terms of higher education (e.g., sending of students to neighboring territories) was in some ways a continuation of British colonial policies, the postcolonial governments of Tanzania, Kenya and Uganda acknowledged in a 1967 agreement that this would only be a temporal measure.

socialist project of development under the name of *ujamaa*, a variety of the African socialisms that took shape across the continent in the course of the 1960s. In contrast to African socialisms in Ghana, Kenya, Mali, Guinea, or Senegal, *ujamaa* had a life span of almost three decades. Formulated by the country's first prime minister and long-term president Julius Nyerere in 1962 and further shaped by him and other members of the ruling party, *ujamaa* was the one-party state's guiding ideology from 1967 until it was gradually dismantled in the wake of the economic crisis and structural adjustment policies of the 1980s. Important transformative policies after 1967 were the comprehensive nationalization of industries and the largest resettlement initiative in postcolonial Africa in a (largely failed) effort to create rural development villages with communal production. However, as Priya Lal has noted, *ujamaa* cannot be reduced to a single principle as it was contradictory both in theory and in practice.[5]

This was particularly visible in the educational sector where technocratic and politicized, egalitarian and elitist understandings of education coexisted. On the one hand, the state was successful in making primary education available to the whole population. This was accompanied by a drive to reeducate academics to identify with the state's development project and serve, rather than rule, the masses. On the other hand, the pyramidal system of education in which a tiny minority gained access to high-ranking positions through secondary school education and university degrees continued to exist, as did technocratic attitudes and careerism.[6]

These tensions between elite-building through education and egalitarianism also informed visions and encounters at the Faculty of Engineering at the University of Dar es Salaam which was officially opened in 1973. Much against the University of Dar es Salaam's image of being a hotbed of revolutionary fervor and leftist radicalism, discussions and practices at the faculty were dominated by technocratic considerations of manpower planning and questions of economic viability.

---

[5] Priya Lal, *African Socialism in Postcolonial Tanzania: Between the Village and the World* (Cambridge: Cambridge University Press, 2015).

[6] Lene Buchert, *Education in the Development of Tanzania, 1919–90* (London: James Currey, 1994), 93–122; Andreas Eckert, *Herrschen und Verwalten: Afrikanische Bürokraten, staatliche Ordnung und Politik in Tanzania, 1920–1970* (München: Oldenbourg, 2007), 251–252.

To some extent, this might not seem surprising. In Western, Eastern European, and postcolonial countries alike, the engineering profession has been closely linked to projects of modernization, industrialization, and development. Studies on different countries at different times in the twentieth century have suggested that members of the engineering profession often held technocratic attitudes (sometimes camouflaged as an "apolitical" stand) and represented a peculiar kind of "reactionary modernism" which allowed them to become thriving elites in regimes of different ideological colors.[7]

In the literature on state-socialist countries more specifically, engineers have been represented as being at the heart of the tension between economic and social goals.[8] One of the central contradictions of socialist development strategies in the twentieth century was that they relied on elites and elite education to produce a technical intelligentsia while trying to abolish elitism at the same time. On the one hand, "experts" were needed to devise plans, to allocate resources efficiently and to administer state institutions. On the other hand, tertiary education reproduced inequalities, fueled processes of stratification, undermined efforts to level cultural, and socioeconomic hierarchies and produced a cultural elite that challenged the political elite's authority. As Joel Andreas notes for the case of Beijing's "Red Engineers" from Tsinghua University in Maoist China, students' technocratic visions and their self-image as industrializing avant-garde sharply contradicted the party's efforts to abolish class distinctions. Especially during the Cultural Revolution, but also in the following decades, Tsinghua campus represented "the epicentre of conflicts surrounding the emergence of a new class of technocratic officials."[9] But in China, both the institution and the professional group had already existed before the revolution, while in Tanzania, the Faculty of

---

[7] Yiannis Antoniou, Michalis Assimakopoulos, and Konstantinos Chatzis, "The National Identity of Inter-war Greek Engineers: Elitism, Rationalization, Technocracy, and Reactionary Modernism," *History and Technology* 23, no. 3 (2007): 241–261; Dolores L. Augustine, *Red Prometheus: Engineering and Dictatorship in East Germany, 1945–1990* (Cambridge, MA: MIT Press, 2007), 22.

[8] The classic article on the supposed dichotomy of being "Red" and being "expert" and efforts to produce a new cohort of engineers being both is Sheila Fitzpatrick, "Stalin and the Making of a New Elite," *Slavic Review* 38, no. 3 (1979): 377–402.

[9] Joel Andreas, *Rise of the Red Engineers: The Cultural Revolution and the Origins of China's New Class* (Stanford: Stanford University Press, 2009), vi.

Engineering only emerged as the *ujamaa* experiment had already taken off and was showing its first signs of exhaustion and contradictions.

This chapter asks for the emergence and place of academic engineering education in socialist Tanzania, showing how it evolved amidst domestic and international struggles and alliances between different groups. The faculty is an excellent place to reveal the intersections of national tertiary education on the one hand with global practices of development politics and aid work on the other. The focus on a concrete arena allows us to see how donors and non-national staff shaped the agendas and practices, especially as far as the mentioned fault line between elitism and egalitarianism was concerned.[10] The faculty is a concrete "arena" in which actors of different generational, national, ideological, and class backgrounds struggled over the meaning of the engineering profession and the allocation of resources.[11] These struggles involved students as well as lecturers, academics, and politicians, Tanzanians and expatriates, all of whom used particular kinds of strategies to strengthen their positions and defend their interests. I argue that transnational alliances of Tanzanian and expatriate engineers, with the backing of resource-delivering donor institutions, pushed for a special status of the faculty that was at odds with *ujamaa* policies. As a result, the faculty spearheaded the economization at the university as part of a broader shift toward technocracy and economization. Based on archival research in Germany and Tanzania as well as oral history interviews, this contribution combines the global history of development with methods from historical anthropology to analyze global trajectories, circulating concepts, and rivalries through concrete interactions, tensions, and inequalities on the ground.

The first part of this contribution sketches the emergence of academic engineering education in Tanzania. The second part sheds light on official strategies to produce a socialist intelligentsia, while the third

---

[10] Concerning the theory of strategic groups see Hans-Dieter Evers, "Globale Macht: Zur Theorie strategischer Gruppen," Working Paper No. 322, Sociology of Development Research Centre Universität Bielefeld, Bielefeld, 1999.

[11] On this concept, see Thomas Bierschenk, "Development Projects as Arenas of Negotiation for Strategic Groups: A Case Study from Bénin," *Sociologia Ruralis* 28, nos. 2–3 (1988): 146–160; Kate Crehan and Achim von Oppen, "Understandings of 'Development': An Arena of Struggle: The Story of a Development Project in Zambia," *Sociologia Ruralis* 28, nos. 2–3 (1988): 113–145.

part shows how nationalist and neo-Marxist critiques of the faculty coexisted with an elitist and technocratic view of the engineering profession among students. The fourth part details how faculty leadership and Western donors, seeking a response to the social effects of the economic crisis unfolding in the late 1970s and 1980s, repeatedly undermined key educational policies the government had devised to produce *ujamaa*-minded academics. The chapter concludes by pointing to takeaways of this case study for the global history of education and development.

THE INTERNATIONAL ROOTS OF TANZANIA'S NATIONAL ENGINEERING EDUCATION

The establishment of the Faculty of Engineering at the University of Dar es Salaam was the outcome of a crossing between Tanzania's aspirations of national development with the global competition for prestige in development and technology. As an institution, it was not a legacy of colonialism. The British had invested little into the educational sector of Tanganyika (which became the United Republic of Tanzania after the union with Zanzibar in 1964), a territory they had taken over from the Germans as a League of Nations mandate after World War I and continued to rule as a UN trust territory after World War II. There was no university education offered within the territory and only few secondary school graduates were available to be sent to attend university colleges at Makerere in neighboring Uganda or overseas. Among them was the country's first president and architect of *ujamaa*, Julius Nyerere, who ruled Tanzania until 1985. He studied first in Uganda and then, as one of the first Tanganyikans, at Edinburgh University in the UK.

Engineering education offered to Africans in Tanganyika prior to independence was of a non-academic level, which barred the graduates from entering higher positions. Two years before independence, in 1959, six students of engineering at the Principal Technical Institute in Dar es Salaam sent a letter of resignation to the Public Works Department. Despite broad popular support for the nationalist Tanganyika African National Union (TANU), it was still unclear when and how independence would be achieved. In their letter, the six students stated that they were not willing to invest any more time and efforts into an education that was of a standard much lower than that of Kampala's Engineering School in neighboring Uganda. They complained that the government had not only downgraded the course (from Engineering to Junior Engineering), but had also reduced starting salaries for the position its graduates were to fill. With the prestige of the certificate crumbling and career and economic opportunities further diminished, the students were not ready "to be trained in such a way that we only provide cheap labour to the Engineers," all of whom were non-Africans at the time.[12]

The reasons the students gave for their resignation were about career expectations which were inevitably politically and racially charged as they implicitly or explicitly challenged the racialized hierarchies of colonial rule. Governor Turnbull estimated in the same year the students had resigned, in 1959, that the territory would remain dependent for twenty years to come, as only then would there be a "sufficient number of Africans of experience, ability and integrity to fill posts in the public service, and in commerce and industry."[13] To speed up the process, TANU had pushed for higher investments into education in the late 1950s and began sourcing and allocating scholarships for training wherever it was offered, including the United States, Liberia, Ethiopia, West Germany, India, Pakistan, and other countries.[14]

Despite these efforts, there was only one African among 84 civil engineers in the country one year after independence in 1962 (according to other sources, there were two).[15] With the economy and state apparatus projected to grow, more engineers were urgently needed for the planning, implementation, and administration of both industrial and agricultural projects. The University College of Dar es Salaam, which was established as a part of the University of East Africa eight weeks before independence with a Law Faculty in 1961, did not offer technical courses. Instead, engineering students were sent to Nairobi—an arrangement that produced the first real generation of Tanzanian engineers, but

---

[12] Chama cha Mapinduzi Party Archives (henceforth: CCMA), Dodoma, NP/003, Students of Principal Technical Institute to Director of Public Works Department, Dar es Salaam, 13 February 1959.

[13] Turnbull cited in Sebastian Edwards, *Toxic Aid: Economic Collapse and Recovery in Tanzania* (Oxford: Oxford University Press, 2014), 66.

[14] See, for instance, CCMA, 53—Mikutano ya Halmashauri Kuu, Memorandum of meeting of TANU Halmashauri Kuu [Executive Committee], 1 May 1958, p. 2.

[15] John Iliffe, *A Modern History of Tanganyika* (Cambridge: Cambridge University Press, 1979), 573.

was soon found to be inadequate, especially as Kenya's capitalist course and Tanzania's socialist path were increasingly at loggerheads. In 1970, all three East African university colleges became national, full-fledged independent universities, a step that was widely celebrated as a major achievement and milestone in the nationalist *zeitgeist* of the time as expressed by Pius Msekwa, the TANU functionary Nyerere had posted to oversee the restructuring of the university as its vice-chancellor:

> The establishment of a University in a country is clearly a sign of growth and maturity, and that, I know, is how the people of Tanzania view the establishment of the University of Dar es Salaam. It means that our nation has now reached a stage where it can produce its high-level manpower in circumstances and under conditions wholly decided, and guided, by the National Ethic.[16]

The "National Ethic" Msekwa talked about was Tanzania's brand of socialism, *ujamaa*. Socialism had been in the air in Tanzania since the early 1960s, but it was the 1967 Arusha Declaration that firmly put the state on a socialist path and made *ujamaa* the ideological basis of its development efforts. Like many other projects in Tanzania, the emergence of the Faculty of Engineering was part of a contradictory strategy of achieving self-reliance by attracting foreign aid. In 1969, Tanzania's leadership called in an international working group under the leadership of the Soviet professor S. A. Shumovsko which produced a study that recommended the establishment of a full technical faculty. A large project of this kind necessitated resources to an extent which only few countries in the world were, at the time, able and potentially willing to provide. With the Shumovsko study in hand, the government approached the Soviet Union for support but soon dropped the negotiations because the financial terms offered (loan repayment within a fairly short period of twelve years) were considered unattractive. West Germany, which was just embarking on re-establishing closer ties with Tanzania after a diplomatic crisis in the mid-1960s under the new social-democratic chancellor Willy Brandt, a friend of Nyerere, assured full financial and personal support for the project under more

---

[16] Appendix E, Vice-Chancellor's Speech for the Inauguration Ceremony 29 August 1970, in University of Dar es Salaam (henceforth: UDSM), *A Report on the Activities of the University of Dar es Salaam for the Year 1970–71*, Dar es Salaam 1971, p. 265.

favorable terms.¹⁷ As the West Germany ambassador proudly reported from Dar es Salaam, Nyerere had explicitly said that the Federal Republic was his preferred donor for the engineering faculty because of its financial power and the excellent reputation of German technology.¹⁸

For West Germany, the faculty was an opportunity to gain international prestige, flex its economic muscle and export its own industrial standards and technologies to countries in the periphery. It had already, successfully if not without frictions, assisted in the establishment of technical faculties in India and Cairo. Some of the leading personnel and blueprints from these projects were then transferred to Dar es Salaam. West Germany also supported technical education on a lower level as well as the parastatal engineering company and was thus involved in the whole "pyramid" of technical education. The faculty in Tanzania became a showpiece of West German technical aid and was the most important West German project in Africa's tertiary sector. However, given the need for long-term support to make operations viable, Tanzania and West Germany agreed to approach other donors to diversify the aid structure and personal makeup of the faculty. Switzerland (from 1974 onward), Norway (1979), the Netherlands (1980), UN agencies and other donors agreed to provide support but did not effectively check West German dominance in terms of providing resources.

The university was supposed to aim at servicing "the needs of a developing socialist Tanzania," as Nyerere proclaimed in 1970.¹⁹ In practice that meant, first and foremost, the production of "manpower." Each year, the university had to train a certain number of graduates who were then to man vacant positions in parastatal companies and state bureaucracy. The engineers were to subscribe to the objectives of *ujamaa*. Nyerere and other politicians had felt the need to create a socialist-minded intelligentsia especially following the 1966 National Service Crisis when university students had clearly staged their elitist aspirations in a protest against compulsory government service for reduced pay after

---

[17] United Republic of Tanzania (henceforth: URT), *Annual Manpower Report to the President 1969*, Dar es Salaam 1970, pp. 18–19.

[18] BArch Koblenz, B 102/86803, FRG-Rep to Foreign Office, Dar es Salaam, 2 October 1969.

[19] Julius Nyerere, Inauguration Speech as Chancellor at the University of Dar es Salaam (29 August 1970), in UDSM, *Report on the Activities 1970–71*, 254.

graduation.[20] In 1967, Nyerere published a pamphlet on *Education for self-reliance* which was at odds with the economy-centered tenets of manpower planning and formed the basis of Tanzania's educational policies for the next fifteen or so years.[21] The tensions between a developmentalist-cum-egalitarian ideology and pragmatic considerations gave birth to policies and practices that performed an uneasy dance between elitism, egalitarianism and the maintenance of the one-party state's authority.

Socializing Engineers: Protests and Transnational Technocracy

To understand the specificity of the faculty's role, one must first understand the opportunity structures for careers and social mobility during *ujamaa*. The one-party state in Tanzania radically cut opportunities for economic accumulation and initiated experiments that aimed at the leveling (or at least re-framing) of both material and cultural hierarchies.[22] Not all of the state interventions into the education and careers of academics were at odds with technocratic and meritocratic principles, but some clearly were. Four measures stand out for their political relevance and the impact they had on educational and career trajectories, making Tanzania a very distinct habitat for the intelligentsia: bonding, the leadership code, the Musoma Resolution, and political education. All of these should ensure that engineers and other academics were both experts and socialists, both educated elites and servants of the masses in a spirit of egalitarianism.

The first measure was the bonding of all government-sponsored university graduates to state service. Graduates were legally required to offer their services for official institutions for five years after graduation. This procedure had been usual practice in the British colonial system, where beneficiaries of government scholarships were automatically employed by state institutions after graduation. When the postcolonial

---

[20] Andrew M. Ivaska, "Of Students, 'Nizers,' and a Struggle Over Youth: Tanzania's 1966 National Service Crisis," *Africa Today* 51, no. 3 (2005): 83–107.

[21] Buchert, *Education in the Development*, 93–94.

[22] On the East German case cf. Ingrid Miethe, *Bildung und soziale Ungleichheit in der DDR: Möglichkeiten und Grenzen einer gegenprivilegierenden Bildungspolitik* (Opladen: Barbara Budrich, 2007).

state had secured control over most bursaries both from national and international sources, this practice was continued. For the buildup of the Faculty of Engineering in the 1970s, bonding was crucial as most engineers gravitated toward the private and parastatal industries which offered better economic prospects and career opportunities, including comprehensive fringe benefits and quicker promotion. The shortage of engineers was exacerbated by the fact the state's manpower development plans, which also determined the target "output" for university courses, only took into account the demand of state institutions. Also, in previous years, the allocation mechanism for engineering technicians (i.e., graduates of a course for sub-professional engineers) had already shown to be deficient: Those who had been recruited by government institutions often worked in administrative rather than engineering positions in line with their training; at the same time, the ministries had not enforced the bonding contract so that those who had gone to the private sector remained there.[23] At university, for the sake of having more Tanzanian lecturers, the faculty enforced bonding. When some of the best graduates were headhunted by private companies in the late 1970s, they were usually required to remain at the faculty as junior teaching staff, even when they would have preferred to work for private sector companies.[24]

The second intervention into career trajectories was the leadership code of the Arusha Declaration, the central document of Tanzania's socialist path agreed upon by the party in 1967. Apart from charting principles of self-reliance and calling for a focus on rural rather than industrial development, the Arusha Declaration also contained a "leadership code" which applied to all higher party cadres, government officers, and civil servants. In a bid to disentangle political and economic elites and reduce leverage for material accumulation, the leadership code precluded officials—including university lecturers—from earning two or more salaries, owning shares of private businesses or renting out private property. This issue of having more than one source of income would become highly relevant at the faculty. The third intervention was the 1974 Musoma Resolution which introduced universal primary education and changed the admission criteria for higher learning, adding character

[23] URT, *Annual Manpower Report 1969*, 12–14.
[24] Interview #40, Tanzanian engineer and professor.

and socialist attitudes to pure merit.[25] This resolution also led to tensions with donors at the faculty, as will be shown further below.

The fourth intervention was the transmission of ideology via the state's ideological apparatuses, including the media and educational institutions. At university, this became evident with the introduction of obligatory courses in development studies to students of all disciplines in 1971. The proclaimed task of the Institute of Development Studies in 1976 was "to instil into the students of this University […] the commitment to the Ideals [sic] of the Party by giving them proper tools of analysis."[26] Despite the sound of it, classes offered were not necessarily doctrinaire, but rather oriented toward providing an overview of socialist experiences and approaches in the world. Lecturers represented a mixture of *ujamaa* adherents, Maoists, Western neo-Marxists as well as East Germans who fought to defend the "purity" of Marxist–Leninist teachings. All these groups pulled into different directions as far as their vision of socialism was concerned, but they shared the conviction that education needed to be inserted into a political and historical framework. Interviewees noted that as would-be engineers in the 1970s and 1980s, they generally appreciated their exposure to development studies and were proud that Tanzania had her very own national ideology and identity.[27] The nationalist aspect apparently trumped the socialist elements in this appropriation of the ideology.

These measures—bonding, the leadership code, the Musoma Resolution, and political education—became enmeshed with political and ideological struggles on campus. On the one hand, the University of Dar es Salaam was a hotspot of transnational radical activism and intellectual exchange.[28] At the same time, sparks of leftist mobilization were

[25] Cf. Julius Nyerere, *The Arusha Declaration: Ten Years After* (Dar es Salaam: Government Printer, 1977), 13.

[26] CCMA, THQ/C/E.20/7, I.D.S. Board Paper No. B/14/1975, Statement on Institute of Development Studies 1976/77 Estimates; cf. Interview with Pius Msekwa, Dar es Salaam, 23 November 2014.

[27] Ibrahim Kaduma, who was head of the institute and vice-chancellor of the university in the late 1970s, made it his task to personally teach and politicize engineering students. Interview #40, Tanzanian engineer.

[28] Andrew Coulson, *Tanzania: A Political Economy*. Second Edition (Oxford: Oxford University Press, 2013), ix–x; Andrew M. Ivaska, "Movement Youth in a Global Sixties Hub: The Everyday Lives of Transnational Activists in Postcolonial Dar es Salaam," in *Transnational Histories of Youth in the Twentieth Century*, ed. by Richard I. Jobs and David M. Pomfret (Hampshire/New York: Palgrave Macmillan, 2015), 188–210.

tramped out by authorities as soon as these crystallized into organizational forms rivaling the party or its youth wing. The autonomy of the university from the political field was significantly reduced by the political leadership. President Nyerere was the chancellor, and from 1970 to 1979, a high-level party functionary and an *ujamaa*-adhering civil servant (Pius Msekwa, 1970–1977, and Ibrahim Kaduma, 1977–1979) served as vice-chancellors to oversee the nationalization of the university and adherence to party principles.

The results of this politicization in terms of attitudes were not clearcut. Despite several efforts of leftist academics as well as some party cadres to further politicize academia, the university remained an institution geared first and foremost toward producing graduates to realize the state's "manpower development plans." The first generation of Tanzanian engineers was trained overseas. The second generation of engineers was trained in Nairobi (until 1973) and the third in Dar es Salaam (after 1973), although overseas stays remained indispensable, especially for the M.Sc. and Ph.D. levels. India, China, the Soviet Union, and Eastern bloc countries such as Romania and East Germany also offered scholarships for engineering degrees, yet the vast majority of those recruited by the faculty had graduated from British and US universities—not least because those pursuing higher degrees usually opted for Western institutions.[29]

While the transformation of political views during overseas stays was fairly unpredictable, most Tanzanians who studied engineering were exposed to similar technocratic views geared toward plannability and industrialization. Although Tanzanian history boasted a variety of impressive techniques and technologies such as iron smelting—the famous "Dar school" historians were publishing widely on these precolonial achievements—the curriculum at the faculty remained fully centered on Western technology and standards. According to two lecturers from the university's Institute of Development Studies, engineering students that were being introduced to technological achievements

---

[29] Of 281 Tanzanians enrolled in overseas engineering courses in 1975/76, 170 were in India, 24 in China, 22 in East Germany, 16 in Cuba, 15 in Romania, 11 in Italy, 9 in Poland and 8 in Ghana. URT, *Annual Manpower Report to the President 1975* (Dar es Salaam: Government Printer, 1976), 36. Note that these statistics do only include students who received their scholarship through the Ministry of National Education; also, students' courses in the USSR given as "other" very likely include many engineering students.

from precolonial East African usually did not believe that such complex technologies had indeed existed in Tanzania.[30]

Engineering students also clung to a hierarchical vision in which university-trained engineers were white-collar elites overseeing blue-collar technicians. According to a 1978 study on the attitudes of engineering students, students saw the *mhandisi* (engineer) in sharp contrast to the *fundi* (mechanic, technician), charging the former vocation with "an excessively academic meaning, which in turn colours their expectations of engineering employment," freed by obligations to do manual labor.[31] Nyerere personally felt it necessary to emphasize (in one of his well-known homilies addressed to professional cadres) at a meeting of the Institution of Engineers that an engineer in Tanzania needed to be ready to supervise or even execute the most basic tasks like greasing machines and turning screws himself.[32] Tanzanian and expatriate staff at the faculty saw students' expectations of an exclusively managerial job as a serious "confusion of identity."[33] In the case of both technicians and engineers, their identity was coded as a male one: The first two female students at the faculty enrolled as late as 1978.

The expatriates at the faculty—who made up eighty percent of the teaching staff in the late 1970s—did not help to overcome the techno-Eurocentrism, either. The West German engineers who staffed (and, initially, led) the faculty overwhelmingly belonged to the technocratic faction and were far from embracing socialist ideals of Tanzania or any other kind. Only few had been mildly politicized in the wake of the movement of '68. One engineer, who identified as a member of that movement and who also had a degree in sociology, described himself as

---

[30] David Wield and Carol Barker, "Science, Technology and Development: Part of a Course in Development Studies for First and Second Year Engineering and Medical Students at the University of Dar es Salaam, Tanzania," *Social Studies of Science* 8 (1978): 385–395.

[31] A. S. Mawenya and S. B. Lwakamba, "The Indigenisation of Engineering Manpower Capability in Africa—Issues and Problems," 1978, cited in Bundearchiv Koblenz (henceforth: BArch Koblenz), B 213/33074, Report of an International Study Team on the FoE at the UDSM, Mai 1979, 25.

[32] Julius Nyerere, "The Tanzanian Engineer," *Bulletin of Tanzanian Affairs*, no. 21 (1985): 12.

[33] Mawenya and Lwakamba, "The Indigenisation," cited in BArch Koblenz, B 213/33074, Report of an International Study Team on the FoE at the UDSM, Mai 1979, 25.

an "exotic" appearance at the faculty, seen as an "arrogant [...] know-it-all" by his conservative colleagues and unable to find support for his ideas. This even applied to relations with his students: As he tried to introduce them to participatory management styles and workers' self-management, he was cut short with the hint of a student that this would be "arts, not science."[34] But actually, such progressive ideas were not foreign to Tanzania.

Tanzanian workers' struggles (including wildcat strikes and lockouts of owners and managers) to take over private and state-owned companies to introduce cooperative self-management between 1971 and 1973 had been crushed by the authorities. These initiatives had been instigated, in a somewhat absurd turn of events, by the party guidelines (*Mwongozo*) issued in 1971. These party guidelines had called for Tanzanians to exert control over their leaders and as such exhibited a clearly anti-elitist bend, directed particularly against the corrupt behavior, arrogance and bureaucratic authority of cultural and managerial elites. The guidelines encouraged people to speak up against "arrogant, extravagant, contemptuous and oppressive" leaders.[35] Technocratic elites were stripped of their aura of authority: "'It is not correct for leaders and experts to usurp the peoples' right to decide on an issue just because they have the expertise."[36] While activist students quoted the *Mwongozo* in a serious conflict with the university leadership in 1971 (the *Akivaga Crisis*),[37] most of the engineering students who began studying after 1973 seem not to have taken these anti-elite demands to heart to an extent that it would have changed their ambitions. For them as for most other young Tanzanians, there were few possibilities for social mobility through economic accumulation during *ujamaa*, meaning that education remained the most important mechanism of upward mobility. Engineering

---

[34] Interview #122, GTZ expert.

[35] Cited in Issa G. Shivji, *Class Struggles in Tanzania* (London: Heinemann, 1978), 121.

[36] Cited in P. L. Raikes, "Ujamaa and Rural Socialism," *Review of African Political Economy*, no. 3 (1975): 33–52, here: 38. On political vs. technocratic decision-making in Tanzania confer also Gerhard Tschannerl, "Rural Water Supply in Tanzania: Is Politics or Technique in Command?" in *African Socialism in Practice: The Tanzanian Experience*, ed. by Andrew Coulson (Nottingham: Spokesman, 1979), 86–105.

[37] Michelle E. Bourbonniere, "Debating Socialism on the Hill: The University of Dar es Salaam, 1961–1971," MA Thesis (Dalhousie University, 2007); Munene D. Njagi, "The Upheaval Against Bureaucratic Arrogance," *Maji Maji*, no. 3 (1971): 1–6.

students, thus, expected a prestigious office job with good pay and remained at a distance to both zealous party functionaries and student politics. When engineering students complained or even turned to activism, this was closely related to the technocratic image of the vocation and career goals—even when the complaints were framed in politicized terms, as was the case in the mid-1970s.

Engineering Education Under Conditions of Dependency

One year after the inauguration of the faculty, in 1974, thirteen students were at the brink of being dismissed due to poor performance. Trying to avoid their expulsion, student representatives penned an open memorandum addressed to the university senate. This memorandum is one of the few instances in which the "voice" of students appears in the archive. Significantly, the students chose to couch their concerns in the language of dependency, explicitly problematizing the faculty's asymmetric relation to West Germany:

> [W]e are almost totally depe[n]dent on the good will, staff, the expertise and machinery of West Germany in the creation of this important faculty. It is for this reason that this is yet another technological dependence which will tie Tanzania to the technologies and the machines of West Germany[38] and which will produce Tanzanians capable of servicing imported technologies rather than of producing locally designed and locally built technologies.[39]

This was not the students' own words but a quote from a text by Amon J. Nsekela, then chairman of the university council.[40] Dependency

---

[38] Indeed, as the technological equipment was imported from West Germany, Tanzania had to purchase the spare parts from West German companies as well. BArch Koblenz, B 213/33056, Küper (GTZ), Minutes of a meeting at the Faculty of Engineering, Dar es Salaam, 29 November 1975, p. 2.

[39] Amon J. Nsekela (Chairman of the University Council), Communication from the Chair Council Memorandum No. 18.9, cited in BArch Koblenz, B 213/33043, An Open Memorandum to the Senate Regarding the Faculty of Engineering, 2 April 1974, p. 1.

[40] On Nsekela's biography, including many leading positions in state institutions, see Amon S. Nsekela, *Socialism and Social Accountability in a Development Nation: Problems in the Transformation of the Tanzanian Economy and Society* (Nairobi: Kenya Literature Bureau, 1978).

theory had arrived at the helm of its influence in Tanzania, shaping the country's development plans and sharpening the awareness of multiple relations of inequality between "developed" and "underdeveloped" countries. In addition to Nsekela, several neo-Marxist scholars at the university including Walter Rodney, Issa Shivji, and Gerhard Tschannerl had publicly raised their concerns against West German support. They pointed to economic and political strings attached and the Federal Republic of Germany being a close NATO ally of imperial Portugal and important trading partner of apartheid South Africa—while Tanzania actively supported liberation movements like the ANC, the MPLA, and FRELIMO, many of which had their offices in Dar es Salaam and ran refugee camps and training institutions in the country.[41]

While not all students were ardent supporters of these liberation movements, they did react strongly against displays of racial superiority in their own field. Their aspirations and modernist visions of industrializing Tanzania clashed with the demeaning comments of some West German mechanics and lecturers, as was mentioned in the memorandum:

> The attitudes expressed by some staff members of the faculty are unacceptable as regards our aspirations. Their attitudes are biased against the students' capability to perform any duty or 'create' independently. One workshop instructor told a group of students [...] that 'It is impossible for Tanzanians to manufacture complicated machines. The best we can do is to train the students such that they can maintain and repair these machines and we should prepare them for making spare parts for these machines'. The implication is that such an instructor has a belief that an African student is incapable of performing or pursuing technical jobs or procedures.[42]

These beliefs were not only at odds with the proclaimed technocratic objectives of the academic training—"To train engineers, who shall be able to solve Tanzania's problems," "to instil a capacity for leadership and for independent and creative activity"[43]—they were also received as

---

[41] Politisches Archiv des Auswärtigen Amtes, Berlin (PAAA), MfAA, B 279/74, GDR expert B. to GDR-Rep, Dar es Salaam, 30 August 1973.

[42] BArch Koblenz, B 213/33043, An Open Memorandum to the Senate Regarding the Faculty of Engineering, 2 April 1974, p. 6.

[43] BArch Koblenz, B 213/33043, GTZ, University of Dar es Salaam. Faculty of Engineering, Eschborn 1979, p. 14; ibid., B 213/33074, Report of an International Study Team on the FoE at the UDSM, May 1979, p. 52.

racist insults. Still, Western expatriate lecturers routinely emphasized cultural differences and inadequate intellectual capacities (most commonly a supposed lack of three-dimensional thinking and analytical skills) to explain unsatisfying student performances. Some framed the difficulties they experienced in knowledge transfers in terms of civilizational difference, feeling that they had to bridge a "gap of centuries" between their habitus, shaped by the requirements of industrial society, and students' thinking from rural and traditional backgrounds that supposedly lacked concepts of measured time, machines (and the necessity to maintain them properly), or the right angle, all of which were figured as symbols of modernity alien to Tanzania.[44] Even beyond conceptualizing this gap as a difference between rural and urban lifestyles,[45] they often framed it as a difference between Europeans and Africans.

The memorandum was not the product of an isolated (or even radical) minority of students unfairly putting the blame for their failure on expatriate teachers. Quite the opposite, the concerns brought forward in the memorandum resonated with widespread discontent at the faculty. In 1975, several lecturers faced student boycotts, the major reason for which seem to have been insufficient language skills of expatriate staff (note that strikes were an established strategy of Tanzanian students of all political colors at secondary and tertiary level to protest against inadequate teaching or learning conditions; this is not to be confused with radicalism or activism).[46] Students also aired grievances that lecturers showed no understanding for their personal problems and the socioeconomic setting of studies. As mentioned above, German lecturers saw cultural differences as the major cause of inadequate performance, blaming the students rather than themselves for failing to bridge these differences. According to the few Tanzanian lecturers that were at the faculty, however, the relevant factors that negatively affected performance were

---

[44] Interview #122, GTZ expert; BArch Koblenz, B 213/33056, Dietrich Goldschmidt, Die Errichtung der Ingenieurfakultät an der Universität Dar-es-Salaam und Probleme ihres Curriculums, November 1975, S. 3.

[45] BArch Koblenz, B 213/33074, Report of an International Study Team on the FoE at the UDSM, May 1979, pp. 52, 61.

[46] BArch Koblenz, B 213/33043, Kreuser, Projektbericht Nr. 14, Dar es Salaam, 1 November 1975; GTZ, *Bildung und Wissenschaft in Entwicklungsländern. Die Maßnahmen der staatlichen deutschen Bildungs- und Wissenschaftsförderung* (Eschborn: GTZ, 1975), 190.

living conditions which were not conducive for learning, including uncertain career prospects, a lack of funds and family pressures.[47] Family pressure applied particularly to those students who did not come from privileged backgrounds, students which had excelled academically and owed their rise, at least partially, to *ujamaa*'s social policy and meritocratic mechanisms.[48]

Still, while there were tensions between students and faculty staff, these were not based on diverging political outlooks but rather centered around the promise of engineering education as an avenue to a better future—both for the country and individual students. Protests in which Tanzanian students or lecturers employed the rhetoric of dependency theories were short-lived and always connected to grievances about material conditions and the inability of expatriate lecturers to transmit technical knowledge, rather than educational concepts and political questions as such.

Engineering Socialism: Economization and the Undermining of Egalitarianism

The 1974 Musoma Resolution stipulated that only those secondary school leavers who had worked at least two years and were able to produce a recommendation by their employer and their local party branch could enter university. This new regulation has widely been interpreted as a means not only to transmit practical experience and the right attitude toward the working population, but also to ensure academics' loyalty, thus producing "a docile university population."[49] The Musoma Resolution's impact was quickly felt at the faculty: Instead of the 120 students expected, only 65 took up their studies in 1975.

This reduction in student numbers did not go down well with the donors. The West German Federal Ministry of Economic Cooperation argued that the under-utilization of the faculty's capacities would lead to serious problems in legitimizing the enormous costs to the German

---

[47] BArch Koblenz, B 213/33043, Hartmut Glimm (DSE), Evaluation of Participants Questionnaire No. 1, pp. A2, D2, May 1974.

[48] Göran Hydén, *Beyond Ujamaa in Tanzania: Underdevelopment and an Uncaptured Peasantry* (London: Heinemann, 1980), 161.

[49] Arnold Temu and Bonaventure Swai, *Historians and Africanist History: A Critique* (London: Zed Books, 1981), 168; cf. Coulson, *Tanzania*, 273–274.

public (in total, the project would cost over 100 million Deutschmark), which in turn might lead to a reduction of funding available to the project. Representatives flexed the economic muscle and exerted pressure on the university leadership to bend national policies. They proposed that the faculty be granted an exemption to the Musoma Resolution or take in students from other African countries, financed by West German scholarships—a proposal that contradicted Tanzania's drive toward nationalization and self-reliance. In a direct conversation, the responsible minister bluntly refused any exemption to the Musoma Resolution; the university leadership also received the demands coldly and seemed "not particularly touched" by the West German concerns.[50] As such, it came as a surprise to the donors that an exceptional rule was granted to the faculty shortly after. In 1976, courses were filled with young students directly entering after their graduation from secondary school.[51] It is very likely that many Tanzanians—including the minister and university leadership—generally sympathized with the substance of the donor demand for technocratic reasons but resented the interventionist character of the demand. Also, they had little leverage to challenge a measure that had just been introduced with Nyerere's blessings.[52]

In the same year, in 1976, Nairobi- and UK-trained engineer Awadhi Mawenya took over as the first Tanzanian dean of the faculty and served in this function until 1982. As Mawenya emphasized retrospectively, the faculty's concentration of "talent" (i.e., expertise) and "very sophisticated equipment," mostly from Germany, was unique in the country—and opened up commercial opportunities. Already in 1975, the Civil Engineering Consultancy Office (CIVECO, replaced by the Bureau of Industrial Cooperation, BICO, in 1990) had been established to link the faculty to practical projects. Mawenya remembered the establishment of

---

[50] BArch Koblenz, B 213/33056, Küper (GTZ), Vermerk über ein Gespräch mit dem Chief Academic Officer der UDSM Prof. Kimambo am 27.11.1975, Nairobi, 3 December 1975, p. 4.

[51] BArch Koblenz, B 213/33056, Kreuser, Projektbericht Nr. 16, Dar es Salaam, 29 April 1976. Another exemption was made for women, whose share of new entrants had sunken as a result of the Musoma Resolution. The women's wing of the party had been instrumental in pushing for this exception. Buluda Itandala, "University of Dar es Salaam's Immediate Response to Musoma Resolution," in *In Search of Relevance: A History of the University of Dar es Salaam*, ed. by Isaria N. Kimambo, Bertram B. Mapunda, and Yusufu Q. Lawi, 193–205 (Dar es Salaam: Dar es Salaam University Press, 2008), 200.

[52] Cf. Nyerere, *The Arusha Declaration: Ten Years After*, 13.

these links to the industry in terms of personal advancement rather than in terms of usefulness for the faculty or the country's development at large:

> We did many things which could help staff members to progress. [...] Of course you faced a lot of problems with the university administration because the very concept of getting a second income was not allowed [...]. I personally spent a lot of time with the vice chancellor to explain. I said, "We are engineers. You should treat us like medical people. You cannot say you are a teaching engineer when you don't practice engineering. Just like a doctor. You cannot teach doctors when you don't have patients."[53]

The reference to doctors was not coincidental: similar to engineers at the university, doctors responded to decreasing real income with the demand for the right to practice privately in 1981. Similar to engineers, doctors began leaving the country in the late 1970s and early 1980s. Private practice was partially legalized but also repeatedly attacked as driver of "crypto-capitalist" developments.[54] Resistance against similar changes for professionals at the Faculty of Engineering also came on ideological grounds. A West German lecturer who described himself as a central figure in the establishment of consultancy services at the faculty remembered that he was summoned by the university leadership and accused of "introducing capitalist practices."[55] He emphasized that these worries were not present at the faculty itself. The argument at hand was that the economic opportunities provided would also ensure that staff remained at the faculty. Another committee at the faculty, made up only of Tanzanians, had voiced demands for additional incentives including higher salaries, more opportunities for advancement and bonus payments for those who incremented the faculty's income through consulting services.[56]

As the struggle for more incentives continued, three of the still few Tanzanian lecturers (there had only been eight in 1978) quit right after

---

[53] Interview with Awadhi Mawenya, Dar es Salaam, 7 October 2014.

[54] John Iliffe, *East African Doctors: A History of the Modern Profession* (Cambridge/New York: Cambridge University Press, 1998), 208.

[55] Interview #105, West German lecturer (local contract with top-ups).

[56] BArch Koblenz, B 213/33077, Ad Hoc Committee Report on Measures to Address Dissatisfaction of Tanzania Staff, 23 August 1979.

their three-year bonding period had ended and went to work for parastatal or private companies.⁵⁷ The "Tanzanization" of the faculty seemed to become an open-ended project. A team of eighteen evaluators (including both Tanzanians and expatriates from various countries) recommended to tackle the situation of competition with the economic sector head-on, recognizing that the suggested measures to improve the staff situation "might create problems of equity for the University," but were "probably unavoidable [...] in a market situation in which individual employment choices beyond the bonding period are respected."⁵⁸

The proposed measures included—still recognizing that a second income was precluded by the leadership code—the provision of funds for international conference visits, an allocation of resources for membership fees in professional associations and scientific literature as well as a new loan scheme (in addition to already existing schemes for motorbikes and fridges) that should allow Tanzanian staff to build their own houses, taking into account the housing crisis on campus. The representative of the West German aid agency GTZ (*Gesellschaft für Technische Zusammenarbeit*) also demanded, in 1979, further measures to stop the exodus.⁵⁹ He was backed by the West German government which shortly thereafter included a clause in an aid agreement that the faculty "shall undertake special efforts to ensure that the Tanzanian academic and non-academic staff at the Faculty of Engineering remain employed there in line with demand."⁶⁰ With pressure from the faculty's most important donor, initiatives from Tanzanian staff also stood a better chance of success.

Eventually, Mawenya got a Swiss lecturer to write a proposal that was subsequently approved by the university's senate and council. As a result, engineers were now practically exempted from the leadership code: "We were then able to do what other people what call private work at university, but we didn't see it systematically as private work, it was official, because

---

⁵⁷ BArch Koblenz, B 213/33077, Hartmann (GTZ/FoE) to Füllenbach (GTZ), Dar es Salaam, 10 October 1979. In 1978, there had been 69 academic posts, only 8 of which were filled by Tanzanians, 44 by expatriates, and 17 vacancies.

⁵⁸ BArch Koblenz, B 213/33074, Report of an International Study Team on the FoE at the UDSM, May 1979, p. 100.

⁵⁹ BArch Koblenz, B 213/33077, Küper and Füllenbach (GTZ) to Mawenya (Dean of the Faculty of Engineering), Eschborn, 1 October 1979.

⁶⁰ BArch Koblenz, B 213/33088, Entwurf zum Regierungsabkommen, no date, p. 6.

the income was divided into three portions" (thirty percent for individuals, thirty percent for the faculty, forty percent for the facilities that were being used).[61]

It is important to point out here that extra income did by no means automatically mean economic accumulation. Beginning with the mid-1970s and until the late 1980s, real income from regular salaries was melting away. As inflation spiraled further, fringe benefits offered in the parastatal and private sector outcompeted whatever the faculty had to offer; even Mawenya left in 1984 as the official salary did not suffice to make ends meet. As the government was forced (due to budget constraints and structural adjustment programs) to further cut down university funding, donor resources and fringe benefits remained crucial to keep the operations of the faculty going. The monthly salary hardly lasted for a week and extra activities were indispensable to eke out a living. Donor representatives estimated in 1989 that the unofficial consulting services of Tanzanian staff amounted to five to ten times of what they offered through the faculty's institutions.[62] Consequently, teaching in these years was mostly done by those who received top-ups or expatriate salaries, while Tanzanians' side activities were tolerated.

More quickly than any other group at the university, engineers forged close contacts with the economic sector and were trailblazers of both legitimate and illicit paths to convert their knowledge into financial gains. With their networks[63] and professional associations (which guarded the symbolic capital of university graduates against engineers without academic training), they were well-prepared for the post-socialist era and the neoliberalization of the university and the economic sector.

Conclusion: The Legacies and Inequalities of Technocraticizing Socialism

Despite many problems encountered, the establishment of the faculty has been widely regarded as a success. Until 1990, 1300 students had graduated with a B.Sc. and 21 students had finalized the newly introduced

---

[61] Interview with Awadhi Mawenya, Dar es Salaam, 7 October 2014.

[62] BMZ, B 213/48207, Bericht über Besprechung zum Thema Ingenieurfakultät und IPI, Bonn, 30 March 1989.

[63] Cf. for the 1990s: Tom Hewitt and David Wield, "Tanzanian Networks: Networks in Tanzanian Industrialisation," *Science and Public Policy* 24, no. 6 (1997): 395–404.

Master of Science curriculum. Academic engineering education in Dar es Salaam as well as abroad led to the emergence of a new professional group that has ever since claimed a special role in the country's development aspirations. The concrete shape of engineering education was not uncontested, however. In the 1970s and 1980s, the faculty was an arena of struggles in which diverse groups—including students, Tanzanian and expatriate lecturers, donor organizations and the university leadership—took part.

Academic engineers had a particular interest in reforming Tanzanian socialism: more often than other professional groups, they switched between academia and consultancy work and thus had two paid jobs rather than the one allowed by the leadership code. They advocated for salaries larger than that of their colleagues at university and profitted from straddling the line between university and the economic sector. An outcome of these struggles was that the faculty received a special status that contradicted national policies. To be sure, official policies were undermined through a number of groups as the economic crisis intensified and forced people to eke out a living with all kinds of strategies. The particularity of the faculty is that here, this could be done *formally*, while the leadership code itself was not renounced until 1991 with the Zanzibar Declaration.[64]

As this chapter has shown, this was not a natural process. The slight changes eventually leading to larger transformations were the outcome of struggles by an alliance of national and expatriate staff of the faculty with the university leadership. Only thanks to this alliance were engineers capable to change the rules. More generally, international cooperation in educational development has significantly contributed to the universalization and globalization of Western standards and attitudes—definitely so in the realm of engineering. Many of the policy changes were reactions to historically particular problems rather than long-term strategies guided by *ujamaa* principles. The economization at the faculty was a result of the economic-cum-social crisis that gathered momentum shortly after the establishment of the faculty. Given the political as well as economic constraints, Tanzanian as well as German actors saw few other

---

[64]The accompanying statement of the National Executive Committee of the ruling party CCM (the successor to TANU) even encouraged party leaders to engage in trade in production, signaling a clear ideological shift in the party leadership. Aili M. Tripp, *Changing the Rules: The Politics of Liberalization and the Urban Informal Economy in Tanzania* (Berkeley: University of California Press, 1997), 187–188.

options than pushing for more economic incentives to curb the exodus of Tanzanian faculty staff.

Transnational linkages, including overseas education, the recruitment of expatriate personnel and donor relations gave these struggles over the education and careers of engineers a character that clearly transcended the national. The economic crisis was a catalyst for introducing material incentives in an official institution even before Tanzania was openly pressured by the IMF (after 1979) and other donors (all of which joined the IMF's rallying cry for conditionality until 1985) to implement structural adjustment policies. The academic engineers succeeded in turning their specific cultural and symbolic capital into the basis for economic opportunities, a strategy of appropriation that was necessary to mitigate the brain drain from the faculty to parastatals in Tanzania and private companies abroad. Better working conditions in the economic sector legitimized changes at the faculty; in many ways, procedures and incentives at the faculty were economized.

In a long-term view, the Faculty of Engineering helped to uphold the status and privileges of academically trained engineers from colonial to socialist and post-socialist times. But the legacy of the asymmetric global relations under which the engineering profession in Tanzania emerged still shapes careers and engineering education. Although, according to official figures, the country meanwhile boasts over 30,000 engineers, compared to one or two at the eve of political independence,[65] aid and investment contracts continue to stipulate that expatriate engineers be employed to lead and implement larger projects, even in fields in which local expertise is available.[66] The complaints echo the grievances of the six engineering students who objected in 1959 to the fact that they were being trained to serve as aides. The hierarchies that became reinstated through donor policies in the 1980s mirrored the racialized pattern established during the colonial era: West Germany paid top-ups for expatriates on a private contract basis (i.e., not in the framework of bilateral cooperation), many of whom originated from India. Top-ups for Tanzanians were not paid

---

[65] URT, *National Five Year Development Plan 2016/17–2020/21*, 30 March 2016, p. i, http://www.mof.go.tz/mofdocs/msemaji/Five%202016_17_2020_21.pdf.

[66] According to John Masuha, chair of the Engineering Registration Board, around 200 Tanzanian engineers failed to be employed in 1999 because the vacancies were filled with "unqualified" expatriates. Ronald Aminzade, *Race, Nation, and Citizenship in Post-colonial Africa: The Case of Tanzania* (Cambridge: Cambridge University Press, 2013), 306.

(only Switzerland would later do so to reduce informal activities and ensure staff presence at the faculty) with the argument that this would be detrimental to achieving the goal of sustainability.[67] The engineering profession with its transnational networks and ethos remained marked by power differences and larger structures of dependency which go back to the colonial era and could not be overcome by technocratic education alone.

Bibliography

Aminzade, Ronald. *Race, Nation, and Citizenship in Post-colonial Africa: The Case of Tanzania*. Cambridge: Cambridge University Press, 2013.

Andreas, Joel. *Rise of the Red Engineers: The Cultural Revolution and the Origins of China's New Class*. Stanford: Stanford University Press, 2009.

Antoniou, Yiannis, Michalis Assimakopoulos, and Konstantinos Chatzis. "The National Identity of Inter-war Greek Engineers: Elitism, Rationalization, Technocracy, and Reactionary Modernism." *History and Technology* 23, no. 3 (2007): 241–261.

Augustine, Dolores L. *Red Prometheus: Engineering and Dictatorship in East Germany, 1945–1990*. Cambridge, MA: MIT Press, 2007.

Bierschenk, Thomas. "Development Projects as Arenas of Negotiation for Strategic Groups: A Case Study from Bénin." *Sociologia Ruralis* 28, nos. 2–3 (1988): 146–160.

Bourbonniere, Michelle E. "Debating Socialism on the Hill: The University of Dar es Salaam, 1961–1971." MA Thesis, Dalhousie University, 2007.

Buchert, Lene. *Education in the Development of Tanzania, 1919–90*. London: James Currey, 1994.

Burton, Eric. "African Manpower Development During the Global Cold War: The Case of Tanzanian Students in the Two German States." In *Africa Research in Austria: Approaches and Perspectives*, edited by Andreas Exenberger and Ulrich Pallua, 101–134. Innsbruck: Innsbruck University Press, 2016.

———. "Navigating Global Socialism: Tanzanian Students in and Beyond East Germany." *Cold War History* 19, no. 1 (2019): 63–83.

Coulson, Andrew. *Tanzania: A Political Economy*. Second Edition. Oxford: Oxford University Press, 2013.

---

[67] BArch Koblenz, B 213/33099, Füllenbach (GTZ), Besprechungsbericht, Dar es Salaam, 13 July 1982; BMZ, B 213/48210, Gesprächsvermerk über Gespräch mit Vertretern der schweizerischen Direktion für EZA und humanitäre Hilfe (DEH), Bonn, 12 December 1989.

Crehan, Kate, and Achim von Oppen. "Understandings of 'Development': An Arena of Struggle: The Story of a Development Project in Zambia." *Sociologia Ruralis* 28, nos. 2–3 (1988): 113–145.

Eckert, Andreas. *Herrschen und Verwalten: Afrikanische Bürokraten, staatliche Ordnung und Politik in Tanzania, 1920–1970.* München: Oldenbourg, 2007.

Edwards, Sebastian. *Toxic Aid: Economic Collapse and Recovery in Tanzania.* Oxford: Oxford University Press, 2014.

El-Sayed, Osman L., Juan Lucena, and Gary L. Downey. "Engineering and Engineering Education in Egypt." *IEEE Technology and Society* 25, no. 2 (2006): 17–24.

Evers, Hans-Dieter. "Globale Macht: Zur Theorie strategischer Gruppen." Working Paper No. 322, Sociology of Development Research Centre Universität Bielefeld, Bielefeld, 1999.

Fitzpatrick, Sheila. "Stalin and the Making of a New Elite." *Slavic Review* 38, no. 3 (1979): 377–402.

GTZ. *Bildung und Wissenschaft in Entwicklungsländern. Die Maßnahmen der staatlichen deutschen Bildungs- und Wissenschaftsförderung.* Eschborn: GTZ, 1975.

Hewitt, Tom, and David Wield. "Tanzanian Networks: Networks in Tanzanian Industrialisation." *Science and Public Policy* 24, no. 6 (1997): 395–404.

Huber, Valeska. "Planning Education and Manpower in the Middle East, 1950s–60s." *Journal of Contemporary History* 52, no. 1 (2017): 95–117.

Hydén, Göran. *Beyond Ujamaa in Tanzania: Underdevelopment and an Uncaptured Peasantry.* London: Heinemann, 1980.

Iliffe, John. *East African Doctors: A History of the Modern Profession.* Cambridge: Cambridge University Press, 1998.

———. *A Modern History of Tanganyika.* Cambridge: Cambridge University Press, 1979.

Itandala, Buluda. "University of Dar es Salaam's Immediate Response to Musoma Resolution." In *In Search of Relevance: A History of the University of Dar es Salaam*, edited by Isaria N. Kimambo, Bertram B. Mapunda, and Yusufu Q. Lawi, 193–205. Dar es Salaam: Dar es Salaam University Press, 2008.

Ivaska, Andrew M. "Movement Youth in a Global Sixties Hub: The Everyday Lives of Transnational Activists in Postcolonial Dar es Salaam." In *Transnational Histories of Youth in the Twentieth Century*, edited by Richard I. Jobs and David M. Pomfret, 188–210. Hampshire/New York: Palgrave Macmillan, 2015.

———. "Of Students, 'Nizers,' and a Struggle Over Youth: Tanzania's 1966 National Service Crisis." *Africa Today* 51, no. 3 (2005): 83–107.

Katsakioris, Constantin. "Creating a Socialist Intelligentsia: Soviet Educational Aid and Its Impact on Africa (1960–1991)." *Cahiers d'Études Africaines* LVII, no. 2 (2017): 259–287.

Lal, Priya. *African Socialism in Postcolonial Tanzania: Between the Village and the World*. Cambridge: Cambridge University Press, 2015.

Miethe, Ingrid. *Bildung und soziale Ungleichheit in der DDR: Möglichkeiten und Grenzen einer gegenprivilegierenden Bildungspolitik*. Opladen: Barbara Budrich, 2007.

Njagi, Munene D. "The Upheaval Against Bureaucratic Arrogance." *Maji Maji*, no. 3 (1971): 1–6.

Nsekela, Amon S. *Socialism and Social Accountability in a Development Nation: Problems in the Transformation of the Tanzanian Economy and Society*. Nairobi: Kenya Literature Bureau, 1978.

Nyerere, Julius. *The Arusha Declaration: Ten Years After*. Dar es Salaam: Government Printer, 1977.

———. "The Tanzanian Engineer." *Bulletin of Tanzanian Affairs*, no. 21 (1985): 12.

Raikes, P. L. "Ujamaa and Rural Socialism." *Review of African Political Economy*, no. 3 (1975): 33–52.

Shivji, Issa G. *Class Struggles in Tanzania*. London: Heinemann, 1978.

United Republic of Tanzania (URT). *National Five Year Development Plan 2016/17–2020/21*, 30 March 2016. http://www.mof.go.tz/mofdocs/msemaji/Five%202016_17_2020_21.pdf.

University of Dar es Salaam. *A Report on the Activities of the University of Dar es Salaam for the Year 1970–71*. Dar es Salaam: University of Dar es Salaam, 1971.

URT. *Annual Manpower Report to the President 1969*, Dar es Salaam 1970, 18–19.

———. *Annual Manpower Report to the President 1975*. Dar es Salaam: Government Printer, 1976.

Temu, Arnold, and Bonaventure Swai. *Historians and Africanist History: A Critique*. London: Zed Books, 1981.

Tripp, Aili M. *Changing the Rules: The Politics of Liberalization and the Urban Informal Economy in Tanzania*. Berkeley: University of California Press, 1997.

Tschannerl, Gerhard. "Rural Water Supply in Tanzania: Is Politics or Technique in Command?" In *African Socialism in Practice: The Tanzanian Experience*, edited by Andrew Coulson, 86–105. Nottingham: Spokesman, 1979.

Valderrama, Andrés, Juan Camargo, Idelman Mejía, Antonio Mejía, Ernesto Lleras, and Antonio García. "Engineering Education and the Identities of Engineers in Colombia, 1887–1972." *Technology and Culture* 50, no. 4 (2009): 811–838.

Wield, David, and Carol Barker. "Science, Technology and Development: Part of a Course in Development Studies for First and Second Year Engineering and Medical Students at the University of Dar es Salaam, Tanzania." *Social Studies of Science* 8 (1978): 385–395.

Open Access This chapter is licensed under the terms of the Creative Commons Attribution 4.0 International License (http://creativecommons.org/licenses/by/4.0/), which permits use, sharing, adaptation, distribution and reproduction in any medium or format, as long as you give appropriate credit to the original author(s) and the source, provide a link to the Creative Commons license and indicate if changes were made.

The images or other third party material in this chapter are included in the chapter's Creative Commons license, unless indicated otherwise in a credit line to the material. If material is not included in the chapter's Creative Commons license and your intended use is not permitted by statutory regulation or exceeds the permitted use, you will need to obtain permission directly from the copyright holder.

PART III

Entanglements and Competing Projects

CHAPTER 9

Enlightened Developments? Inter-imperial Organizations and the Issue of Colonial Education in Africa (1945–1957)

Miguel Bandeira Jerónimo and Hugo Gonçalves Dores

PROCLAIMING AN "ENLIGHTENED" COLONIALISM

From the mid-1940s onward, the prime colonial powers initiated mutual contacts for the purpose of reflecting on the main challenges to their continued colonial projects in Africa. In some cases, like Anglo-French relations, there proceeded a long genealogy of debates on the

---

This research was co-financed by FEDER—Fundo Europeu de Desenvolvimento Regional through COMPETE 2020—Programa Operacional Competitividade e Internacionalização (POCI) and by national funds through FCT—Fundação para a Ciência e a Tecnologia, in association with the research project "The worlds of (under) development: processes and legacies of the Portuguese colonial empire in a comparative perspective (1945–1975)" (PTDC/HAR-HIS/31906/2017 | POCI-01-0145-FEDER-031906).

M. B. Jerónimo (✉) · H. G. Dores
Center for Social Studies, University of Coimbra, Coimbra, Portugal

H. G. Dores
e-mail: hugodores@ces.uc.pt

© The Author(s) 2020
D. Matasci et al. (eds.), *Education and Development in Colonial and Postcolonial Africa*, Global Histories of Education, https://doi.org/10.1007/978-3-030-27801-4_9

advantages and limits of bilateral and multilateral cooperation centered on the administration of colonial territories. The aim was to surpass the constraints and disagreements dictated by the war, especially regarding competition for human and material resources on the African continent. From concerns rooted in how to achieve a "common policy" that would be instrumental in raising the "natives" standard of living to proposals for establishing "direct contact" on a variety of technical subjects, there were numerous initiatives which made 1945 the moment to resume collaboration started in the previous decade. The number of topics under discussion was considerable, and they were gradually organized around a unifying idea of "development" in the colonial context: sanitary and medical research, labor and agricultural issues and, further, aspects concerning colonial education. As a result of these conversations, arguments in favor of establishing an *entente néo-coloniale* were wielded. These arguments persisted over the following decade, growing more frequent and important, and paved the way for a series of common political initiatives for colonial powers, some more public than others and some more effective than others.[1]

The old tradition of inter-imperial cooperation—exhibited within organizations like the International Colonial Institute (ICI) since 1894 and in the corridors of inter-war international organizations, notably the League of Nations (LoN), its specialized agencies, and its commissions— was renewed and took on new vigor in the post-war period. To sum up, legislation and general policy guidelines on the management of territories, resources, and colonial populations was gathered and shared, always citing science and technical—not predominantly political—concerns as their inspiration. These practices were given continuity[2] and the focus moved onto advancing the production of information with a common and de facto comparable matrix, employing similar methodologies and purposes. Deployment on these fronts took place in innumerable epistemic communities: experts grew in influence and were no longer limited

---

[1] John Kent, *The Internationalisation of Colonialism* (Oxford: Clarendon Press, 1992), 152–153 and 156; Anne Deighton, "Entente Neo-Coloniale?: Ernest Bevin and the Proposals for an Anglo–French Third World Power, 1945–1949," *Diplomacy & Statecraft* 17, no. 4 (2006): 835–852.

[2] The ICI's statutes declared that it was imperative to avoid political discussions in order not to affect its collaborative purpose. The same would happen in its successor, the International Institute of Differing Civilizations (INCIDI).

essentially to those who had made a career in the colonial context or had experience in the administration of colonial matters. The menu of themes studied, around which collaboration and the transfer of expert knowledge took place, extended. What did not change was a willingness to influence the way colonial affairs were discussed, both domestically and externally.

In the first case, that of the ICI, the comparison of colonial legislation had predominated, partly due to the intervention of experts on emerging international colonial law, who followed and tried to condition the dynamics of the internationalization of colonial issues, then undergoing intensification. From work and labor migration to the problem of land and property regimes, via irrigation, alcohol, and opium trafficking and issues of infrastructure development, the ICI sparked a number of debates and fueled a number of publications. The *International Colonial Library* compiled minutes and recommendations of the collective meetings and some reports by experts appointed for this purpose, circulating them internationally. On receiving inside information directly from the colonial ministries of the member states, it sent it back out in another, synthetic and comparable way.[3] The issue of education was one of the topics addressed and merited its own special session, held in Paris in May 1931.[4]

In the second case, the LoN's "forcefield" attracted various projects for internationalizing colonial issues, from work to nutrition and education, the latter especially in the mandates committee. Efforts toward international normative regulation of these issues, based on attempts to gain a thorough knowledge of how they were dealt with in the colonies and on the advancement of common parameters, were significant,

---

[3] Ulrike Lindner, "New Forms of Knowledge Exchange Between Imperial Powers: The Development of the Institut Colonial International (ICI) Since the End of the Nineteenth Century," and Florian Wagner, "Private Colonialism and International Co-operation in Europe, 1870–1914", both in *Imperial Co-operation and Transfer, 1870–1930: Empires and Encounters*, ed. by Volker Barth and Roland Cvetkovski (London: Bloomsbury Academic, 2015), 57–78 and 79–103; Benoit Daviron, "Mobilizing Labour in African Agriculture: The Role of the International Colonial Institute in the Elaboration of a Standard of Colonial Administration, 1895–1930," *Journal of Global History* 5 (2010): 479–501.

[4] Institut Colonial International, *L'Enseignement aux indigènes: rapports préliminaires. XXIe session de l'Institut colonial international, Paris, 5-8 mai 1931* (Bruxelles: Établissements généraux d'imprimerie, 1931).

though their effects were nonetheless much less obvious. The LoN and its specialized agencies also attracted a very considerable set of imperial and colonial interests that sought to curtail the reach and direction of this internationalization, in particular through collaborative strategies which were more or less official. The case of forced labor in the colonial context is a good example of this.[5]

After World War II, the practices of collecting and comparing information on the most pressing colonial issues continued but took on a new dimension and direction. In May 1946, a first conference was held that made the conclusions of the Anglo-French meetings of November 1945 materialize: a conference on veterinary medicine, held in Dakar, followed by another in November in Accra, focusing on medical and sanitary issues. Both recognized the need to emphasize means of cooperation, be it via the exchange of information or the joint use of facilities. That same year, Belgium was also included in technical cooperation projects, and it was decided that a Portuguese observer should join the discussions. Meanwhile, further consideration was given to addressing the problem of including South Africa; this caused great apprehension for many, due to the political resonance which it entailed.[6]

From the outset, the aim was to *regularly* discuss a number of topics, some of them mentioned above, from the point of view of the opportunities they presented for collaboration. Avoiding discussion of the merits of each partner in each of these topics was seen as fundamental, as the Belgian ambassador in London reported to his superior in Brussels in May 1946. These topics together constituted "development," a central factor for the purpose of encouraging cooperation and information exchange between partners. At the end of 1946, apropos of a bilateral meeting between the French and Belgians, the issue of "indigenous affairs" was highlighted as a clear priority. On the one hand, there was "indigenous policy," which referred to issues such as the formation of administrative authorities, the "fight against religious sects," and

[5] Susan Pedersen, *The Guardians: The League of Nations and the Crisis of Empire* (Oxford: Oxford University Press, 2015); Miguel Bandeira Jerónimo, "A League of Empires: Imperial Political Imagination and Interwar Internationalisms," in *Internationalism, Imperialism and the Formation of the Contemporary World*, ed. by Miguel Bandeira Jerónimo and José Pedro Monteiro (London: Palgrave Macmillan, 2017), 87–126.

[6] Kent, *The Internationalisation of Colonialism*, 200–201.

management of the issue of *evolués* or the detribalized; on the other hand arose the issue of "indigenous education," from primary education to the "opportunities for creating higher education." Another central topic, that of agriculture, saw educational aspects resumed, including, for example, a French–Belgian exchange of trainee agricultural technicians, who were to rotate through each country's scientific institutions, both in the metropole and the colonies. Revealingly, the "organization of indigenous welfare" was included as an aim under the topic of agriculture.[7]

From 1947 on, several occasions arose for bipartite, tripartite, and later quadripartite, "conversations." They focused not only on trying to outline a framework of understanding regarding policy-making or expert knowledge exchange and mobility of experts; but also acted as laboratories for common strategies to be adopted in international fora, notably within United Nations (UN) committees or specialized agencies, from the International Labour Organization (ILO) to UNESCO (see Chapter 3 by Brooke Durham in this book).[8] The "conversations" and the myriad of meetings and conferences that took place with remarkable constancy from the late 1940s were also opportunities for preparing alternative development projects within the colonial context; these touched on various issues, from "rural welfare" to nutrition, from housing to medical–sanitary issues, or forestry and soils. At the very first tripartite meeting, for example, the problem of a common position on the UN's way of dealing with (or the way in which it appeared to want to address) the issue of "dependent territories" was taken very seriously. In addition to the splintering of "conversations," numerous regular meetings on technical cooperation were held, from the aforementioned on medical and health matters to others on education, nutrition, and work. The French and the Belgians, especially, saw these as important tools for demonstrating, particularly at the international level, that their imperial arrays were places of social, technical, and scientific progress, combining

[7] Belgian Embassy, London, to Paul-Henri Spaak, Belgian minister of Foreign Affairs, 27.5.1946; Gorlia, Directorate-General of the Ministry of the Colonies to the Ministry of Foreign Affairs, 13.12.1946, in Archives Diplomatiques, Brussels [AD, Brussels], 18729/I.

[8] For the ILO, see Daniel R. Maul, *Human Rights, Development, and Decolonization* (Basingstoke: Palgrave Macmillan, 2012); José Pedro Monteiro, *Portugal e a Questão do Trabalho Forçado* (Lisbon: Edições 70, 2018). For the UNESCO, see Damiano Matasci, "Une 'UNESCO africaine'? Le ministère de la France d'Outre-mer, la coopération éducative intercoloniale et la défense de l'Empire, 1947–1957," *Monde(s)* 13, no. 1 (2018): 195–214.

experience on the ground, dictated by history and capable of informed intervention. So important was it, they saw in these meetings a way of minimizing what they presaged as a trend toward an increased UN intrusion into colonial issues. The Belgian authorities, in particular, celebrated the meeting planned for Paris, as this would enable a "common approach" to be established, "as was desirable," one which would be able to obstruct the UN's request for information under Article 73 (e) of the Charter drawn up in San Francisco (1945), a very sensitive issue at the time. At the same meeting in Paris, twelve conferences were scheduled up to 1950, many in an African context, with two objectives: on the one hand, to involve local administration and society, maintaining political discourse on integration or decentralization; on the other, to demonstrate a capacity for local intervention that was beyond the reach of international organizations.[9]

The new (geo)political circumstances and the direct and indirect effects of the global conflict had brought about a new appreciation and understanding of the motivations, methods, and purposes of the colonial enterprise that should guide metropolitan and colonial authorities. These challenges constrained the rejuvenation of post-war European societies and the reconstruction of imperial projects in different ways, both politically and economically, with the emergence of programs like Truman's Point IV, and also from a symbolic point of view as well as in terms of reputation (for the British case, see Chapter 10 by Hélène Charton).[10] The public projection and proclamation of an "enlightened neo-colonialism," supported by an "imperialism of knowledge," were notable in this process.[11] From development and welfare plans to the

[9] Godding, Directorate-General of the Ministry of the Colonies to the Ministry of Foreign Affairs, 13.4.1947, in AD, Brussels, 18729/I; Kent, *The Internationalisation of Colonialism*, 163, 201–202. For the Belgian context, see Guy Vanthemsche, *Belgium and the Congo, 1885–1980* (Cambridge: Cambridge University Press, 2012), 138–140.

[10] Frederick Cooper, "Reconstructing Empire in British and French Africa," and Nicholas J. White, "Reconstructing Europe through Rejuvenating Empire: The British, French and Dutch Experiences Compared," in *Post-War Reconstruction in Europe: International Perspectives, 1945–1949*, ed. by Mark Mazower, Jessica Reinisch, and David Feldman (Oxford: Oxford University Press, 2011), 196–210 and 211–236.

[11] Marc Michel, "La cooperation intercoloniale en Afrique noire, 1942–1950: un neo-colonialisme eclairé?" *Relations Internationales* 34 (1983): 155–171; Frederick Cooper, "Modernizing Bureaucrats, Backward Africans, and the Development Concept," in *International Development and the Social Sciences*, ed. by Frederick Cooper and Randall Packard (Berkeley: University of California Press, 1997), 64–92, at 64.

redefinition of legal and constitutional frameworks, via new *indigenous policies*, there were various moments where imperial policies were significantly redirected. This was in part marked by a dynamic of collaboration, to varying degrees and levels, and had distinct consequences.[12] Thus, this dynamic also affected the *ends* of the European colonial empires, significantly affecting their various historical paths.[13] Much of this was crucial to the shaping of the various forms of "repressive developmentalism" that mapped the disintegration of European colonial empires.[14]

This chapter explores some of these issues and problems and focuses on how an international, inter-imperial organization created in 1950— the Commission for Technical Cooperation in Africa South of the Sahara (CCTA)—addressed the problem of education in the colonial context. By reconstructing the way in which the educational question was addressed within the institution after 1947, this text focuses on a particular moment, namely the occasion of the 1957 Inter-African Conference on Industrial, Commercial, and Agricultural Education, held in Luanda (Angola), which grew out of the conference held in Tananarive (Madagascar) in November 1954.

Education: "Moral Character," the Political Problem

In June 1947, as we have seen, a Franco-Anglo-Belgian conference took place. According to reports, there was no "divergence" of views on any matter. Recognition of the opportunity and the (certainly political) usefulness for in-depth and permanent inter-imperial technical cooperation

---

[12] For a seminal overview, see Frederick Cooper, *Africa since 1940* (Cambridge: Cambridge University Press, 2002). For the question of development in Africa, see Joseph M. Hodge, Gerald Hodl, and Martina Kopf (eds.), *Developing Africa. Concepts and Practices in Twentieth-Century Colonialism* (Manchester: Manchester University Press, 2014).

[13] Martin Shipway, *Decolonization and Its Impact* (Oxford: Blackwell, 2008); Martin Thomas, Bob Moore, and Larry Butler, *Crises of Empire* (London: Hodder Education, 2008); Miguel Bandeira Jerónimo and António Costa Pinto (eds.), *The Ends of European Colonial Empires* (Basingstoke: Palgrave, 2015).

[14] Miguel Bandeira Jerónimo, "Repressive developmentalisms: idioms, repertoires, trajectories in late colonialism," in *The Oxford Handbook of the Ends of Empire*, ed. by Andrew Thompson and Martin Thomas (Oxford: Oxford University Press, 2017 online; 2018 print). See also Martin Thomas and Gareth Curless (eds.), *Decolonization and Conflict: Colonial Comparisons and Legacies* (London: Bloomsbury, 2017).

was unanimous and was extended into the field, although with caution. It was thus agreed that cooperation in Africa should merely be suggested and recommended, not imposed. Portugal's right to inclusion was also discussed at the meeting and was delayed only by the indecision of the British. As previously mentioned, the challenges placed by the UN were duly discussed, and a prudent position was sketched out which attempted to avoid politicizing the debates in the committee which had labored over compliance with Article 73. The relations to be established with specialized UN agencies were given special consideration, the aim being to mitigate any potential intrusion into colonial affairs. For example, the idea was put forward that whenever its specialized agencies wanted to establish a regional bureau in Africa, on a variety of topics, colonial entente should anticipate and propose proprietary structures for this purpose. The objective therefore became focused on creating institutional spaces centered on the main issues affecting the African continent and led by the existing colonial powers and their experts.[15]

On the question of education, a meeting of "experts" took the first step on a long path of sharing perspectives and strategies for action on the issue. In keeping with the aims that governed the colonial axis, the meeting was held before the Mexico UNESCO Conference, in November and December 1947. As Colonial Office representative Hilton Poynton stated, "the union of the African powers is mostly necessary after UNESCO started to deal with the question of mass education in Africa." Albert Charton (Directeur de l'Enseignement et de la Jeunesse at ministère de la France d'outre-mer, from 1946) underlined the "great interest in confronting and balancing the ideas regarding UNESCO's work," stating that the "pilot experiences" sponsored by this body that were being announced for Haiti could be extended to Africa. One of the most active representatives at the meeting, Charton reflected at length on the central importance of "education for the masses" for promoting better economic, "political," cultural, and "hygiene" conditions in the colonial context. Without it, the ambitions for development would be most unlikely to come about and projects aimed at

---

[15] "Rapport—Conférence africaine anglo-franco-belge ténue à Paris du 20 au 24 mai 1947," 2.7.1947, AD, Brussels, 18729/I.

domesticating undesirable tendencies in the internationalization of issues of "non-autonomous" territories would be less effective.[16]

In accordance with these concerns, one of the conclusions of the meeting was that the problems of education should be examined in light of the general policy of "fundamental education," which the governments present were committed to implementing. This policy, considered as having "moral character," implied a program composed of three essential elements. First, extending school education to a universal primary education system. Second, a campaign for adult education. Third, there were a number of measures designed to stimulate the "désir d'un niveau de vie plus élevé dans les domaines tels que la santé, le logement, l'agriculture, l'artisanat, l'art et la musique." Success was held to be dependent on the development of female education, as well as vocational education and arts and crafts. It required appreciable economic development, as it required the education of a large number of specialized and semi-skilled artisans and technicians. In this sense, undertaking studies on the problem of technical education was seen to be fundamental, both from an economic and pedagogical point of view. Participants of the three governments present also concluded that the closest possible collaboration should be established as a matter of urgency, encouraging an exchange of educational materials, information, surveys, experiences, points of view, and teaching staff. Just as important as consensus on the general guidelines to follow was the question of how to begin to contribute to political reorientation at the grass-roots level in each colony. David Rees-Williams, British Under-Secretary of State for the Colonies, was clear in this regard: "fully recognise the difficulties of any common policy in educational matters," given the diversity of colonial contexts and dynamics it was crucial that the chance for greater standardization be studied by the respective authorities, both in the metropole and the colonies. By any means, it was crucial to ensure "close discussion" between those involved and also "the full and regular exchange of information and ideas." And that was, indeed, what occurred.[17]

[16] Report on Paris' tripartite conversations (20–24 May 1947) to the head of office of the Belgian Minister of Foreign Affairs, 5.6.1947, AD, Brussels, 18729/I. Memo for the Belgian Secretary General of the Colonies, 24.6.1947, in Archives Africaines, Brussels [AA, Brussels], AE (3105).

[17] CCTA, "Conférence Franco-Anglo-Belge de Juin 1947," in *Enseignment. Conférence Interafricaine et Conférences Regionales* (London: CCTA, 1954), 33; Dispatch by Rees-Williams, 25.2.1948, in AA, Brussels, AE (3105).

Following decisions taken at a tripartite conference held in London at the beginning of January of that year, in which relations with UNESCO were once again discussed, the heads of French, Belgian, and British education services met in Paris in March 1949. On the agenda was a reassessment of the conclusions reached in 1947 and an examination of the UN resolutions on the *Educational Advancement in Trust Territories* (Resolution A/RES/225(III)), passed in 1948. The aim was to make cooperation in this field "a reality," which was increasingly urgent in light of the "numerous pressures made by international organizations about the spreading of education in trusteeship territories, and, in a general way, in the non-self-governing territories," as the French representative stated. UNESCO was invited, but only for the last day. The conclusions of the meeting were considered "confidential" and the final report, expressing a "common" position, was "sweetened" for UNESCO and the UN Trusteeship Council. As previously stated, the various suggestions made to UNESCO aimed to promote the colonial powers' experts and institutions, for example, in the area of "pedagogical research." The option of setting up a university in the territories under colonial guardianship, a process sponsored by UNESCO, was considered "inopportune" and a "utopian and dangerous project," according to an assessment published in a report of the Colonial Office by the Inter-University Council for Higher Education in the Colonies. A survey was also carried out on the need for teaching material (primary, secondary, and technical) in overseas territories. More importantly, Regional Conferences on education in West and East Africa were suggested and supported by local political authorities.[18]

One year later, in 1950, the newly convened CCTA met in Accra (Gold Coast) for the Regional Conference on Education. Top of the agenda was to examine the conclusions of the 1947 conference, and to revisit the conclusions again in 1957. The following year, organized by the East African High Commission and the General Government of the Belgian Congo, Nairobi (Kenya) hosted a second Regional Conference on Education, that only delegates from the British and Belgian colonies

---

[18] Ministry of Overseas France to the Belgian Ministry of the Colonies, 16.2.1949, 7.3.1949, 18.3.1949; Colonial Office to the Belgian Ministry of the Colonies, 29.12.1949; all in AA, Brussels, AE (3105).

attended.[19] One of the main recommendations of the conference was the need to insist upon, to colonial ministries in Brussels, Lisbon, London, and Paris, a conference on education for Central, West, and East Africa as well as the exchange of information on debates and resolutions taken at regional conferences and the dissemination of information to other territories. On the other hand, it was accepted that combating illiteracy could not be done in isolation but should be made part of a campaign designed to promote the general objectives of education, such as improving social and health conditions, or soil conservation. This would be further strengthened in the conclusions and recommendations of the Inter-African Conference on Rural Welfare, organized by the CCTA in Lourenço Marques in 1953.

"Basic education" campaigns, including those with the aim of eradicating illiteracy, would target adults especially, distinct from child illiteracy. The programs and administration of each education campaign were to take local conditions and the respective political and technical authorities into account.[20] Consideration had to be given to the possible assistance provided by UNESCO in promoting education in Africa. Lloyd Hughes, who was sent as an observer to Nairobi from that institution's Department of Education, proposed that UNESCO could provide support via technical assistance for economic development. This would be a special project to create a network of regional centers for basic education or the creation of a pedagogical documentation center, among other aspects. However, in spite of the opportunities for institutional collaboration offered by UNESCO, colonial representatives believed that no resolution could be tabled without careful consideration of the issue, especially its implications.[21] As the Belgian consul general in Nairobi, W. Stevens, wrote, "the clearest thing to remember from this first contact is, it seems, that the field for a cooperation in this matter is very large, but everything is yet to be organized. UNESCO's intervention will contribute a lot, it is believed, to the success of this cooperation." Another aspect which Stevens emphasized was the agreement among those

---

[19] CCTA, *Education: Inter-African and Regional Conferences—Tananarive 1954, Accra 1950, Nairobi 1951* (London: CCTA, 1954).

[20] CCTA, *Conférence Inter-africaine sur le Bien-Être rural. Première Session. Lourenço Marques—Septembre 1953* (Lisbon: Secretariado da Conferência Inter-Africana do Bem-estar rural, 1953).

[21] "CCTA, *Education: inter-african and regional conferences*," CCTA [1954], 39–42.

present that education designed for the indigenous population should be essentially directed toward the learning of manual crafts and less particularly academic teaching. This observation indicates the overwhelming tendency in colonial administrations and among colonial experts toward providing practical education for indigenous populations.[22]

Creating the Conditions: Old Principles, New Drive, New Challenges

Two years after Nairobi, during the 8th session of the CCTA in Lisbon, the colonial powers arranged two new conferences on education, continuing the inter-imperial cooperative goals that had begun in the late 1940s. Initially the conferences were to follow the regional model used in Accra and Nairobi, but it was then decided to organize themed meetings. The first meeting would discuss issues related to primary education and the next would focus on technical and agricultural education. In the case of agricultural education, the forthcoming conference was to take into account the conclusions and recommendations arising from the Lourenço Marques Conference on Rural Welfare.[23] The first inter-African conference was announced for Tananarive in 1954. At the preparatory meeting in Paris (December 1953) the option was raised of inviting Liberia to send one observer to each conference, and any specialized institutions which were interested in attending. Thus, UNESCO could be invited to the conference on primary education, and the ILO to the

---

[22] W. Stevens to the Belgian Ministry of the Colonies, 21.8.1950, in AA, Brussels, AE (3105).

[23] Among other issues, the Committee III—Social Services and the organization of the community, had discussed "educational facilities" (social and moral training, primary and post-school teaching, vocational training) and adult education (fundamental education, social centers), where it was assumed that the school should give an important contribution to rural welfare, "teaching to students to be more useful to the community, both in economic and social spheres." The CCTA stated that universal primary education ("instruction primaire," in French; and "ensino rudimentar," in Portuguese) was the "first goal" in the African territories south of the Sahara. It recommended to the participants at the Conference on education scheduled for 1954 the establishment of a link between school and the community in development programs. CCTA, *Conférence Inter-africaine sur le Bien-Être rural*, 123–125.

conference on technical education.[24] The question of inviting specialized agencies raised serious doubts at the heart of CCTA governments from the outset. For example, the Belgian Ministry of Foreign Affairs shared the concern of the Minister of the Colonies on the issue, arguing that any interference in African affairs from those bodies should be avoided.[25]

UNESCO was invited to Tananarive; the head of the Department of Education, Lionel Elvin, stated that having an observer from the agency present at the conference had a number of advantages, since he could "open the door to the important development of our action" in non-autonomous territories. The instructions given to the observer, André Lestage (who had been an inspector of education in Madagascar in the 1930s), stated that this was an "excellent occasion" for closer collaboration with the CCTA. Lestage's report on the conference was, however, extremely critical of the organization and proceedings of the meeting and showed his disappointment with the poor technical quality of the information presented. He went so far as to conclude that no advantage could be seen for UNESCO's participation in the next conference (at that time planned for 1955), or at least not under the same conditions granted to the agency by the organizers. Lestage warned that the aim of the CCTA, "not the only one, but the most important," was to gather all kinds of activities related to education, science, culture, and technology—UNESCO's domains—intending to "keep its monopoly in Africa south of the Sahara." He foresaw enormous difficulties in realizing the idea, declared in the UNESCO 1955/1956 program, of preparation taking place in 1956 for a conference to be held in 1958 on a free and compulsory education for Africa.[26] He added that he would not be surprised if the Tananarive conference was cited for "'showing' the uselessness of our project." Within UNESCO, it was clearly apparent that the imperial governments sought to use the CCTA and its agencies to block

[24] Document CCTA (53) 60—"Proces-Verbal de la Reunion Preliminaire aux Conférences de la CCTA sur l'enseignment, Paris, 1–2 Décembre 1953," in Arquivo Histórico–Diplomático do Ministério dos Negócios Estrangeiros (Lisbon) [AHD-MNE], 2P/A17/M45, Pasta [...] Conferências regionais sobre o Ensino.

[25] N.º Aff.Col./588, Belgian Ministry of Foreign Affairs (4 Section, 1st Directorate of the Directorate General of Politics) to the minister of the Colonies, 1.2.1954, in AA, Brussels, AE (3105). Enseignment I. 5. Conférence Paris décembre 1953.

[26] UNESCO, "UNESCO. Proposed Programme and Budget for 1955 and 1956. Education. (C) Regional Conference on Free and Compulsory Education" (Paris: UNESCO, 1954).

any attempt by specialized international agencies to intervene in African territories. They were right, as we have seen.[27]

The Tananarive Inter-African Conference on Education began on November 8, 1954, with the main objective being to "lead to the exchange of reciprocal and confident information" among technicians on issues regarding first-grade teaching. The aim was to study the practical means to achieve this, as well as to reflect on issues related to the principle of organizing education in each territory, avoiding discussion of "purely doctrinal" matters. Each participant would present the solutions which had been found in their country in answer to questions related to primary education, teacher training, and adapting educational methodologies to local circumstances. Unlike other meetings, the Tananarive conference drew no conclusions nor did it make recommendations, and it issued only one final vote; this expressed the wish that the contacts that had been initiated should be continued via an exchange of documentation and visits, and that the upcoming conferences on education should confirm "the spirit" of international cooperation exhibited at the meeting.[28]

But the spirit of cooperation to which the delegates appealed was not echoed among the British, although they had been one of the main drivers of the formation of the CCTA and the concentration of inter-imperial cooperation. The British delegation sent to the tenth session of the CCTA in Paris in early 1955 was under instruction to propose that the second part of the conference on education (originally scheduled for 1955) should be postponed "sine die" and that the other participants should know that there was no option of a British territory hosting it. The United Kingdom had not been in favor of holding the conference and had only accepted it under pressure from the French and so as not to block the goodwill of the other members of the CCTA, since the

---

[27] Elvin (Director of UNESCO's Department of Education) to UNESCO's Assistant Director General, 9.8.1954; Jean Thomas (UNESCO's acting Director General) to Lestage, 6.10.1954; Lestage to the Director General of UNESCO, 15.12.1954, in UNESCO Archive—62 A81/01 (6-13) CTCASS "-66" Commission for Technical Cooperation in Africa—South of the Sahara. Part IIa—from 1/1/1950 up to 30/XII/1955.

[28] Document CCTA (54) 102—"Lettre de Fournier, inspecteur général adjoint e secretário-geral da Conferência aux fonctionnaires de liaison," 30.7.1954, in AHD-MNE, 2P/A17/M45, Pasta [...] *Conferências regionais sobre o Ensino.* CCTA, *Education: inter-african and regional conferences* (London: CCTA, 1954).

committee's decisions were taken unanimously. Since the Conference on African Education held in Cambridge (September 1952), the Colonial Office had taken the position that new conferences on education would have no "useful purpose" at that time, and would only disrupt the work of people who should be busy implementing an educational policy that had been agreed upon by and for all British territories. In the instructions sent to the head of the British delegation to Tananarive, John Attenborough, the Colonial Office had stated that the United Kingdom's "basic policy document" was the report that resulted from the proceedings of the Cambridge conference.[29] Thus, the British were inclined to resist new CCTA proposals for conferences devoted to general aspects of education, but were prepared to consider specialized conferences in areas such as technical or vocational/professional education.[30]

After months of discussing the possibility of establishing cooperation mechanisms between the CCTA and UNESCO, the governments of the CCTA met in London in late 1955 in a working group to continue cooperation on educational matters. Upon analysis of the topics of the proposals for future conferences presented by each delegation, the group recommended a conference focusing on technical and agricultural education, which had already been planned at the 1953 meeting. The Portuguese government offered to host the meeting in 1957.[31]

During the meeting of the working group, it was decided that a panel of liaison officers in the field of education should be set up. This was a possible conciliation between the members of CCTA and the Portuguese proposal to set up an inter-African committee for education, similarly to other existing committees (such as the Inter-African Bureau for Soils and

[29] The Cambridge *Conference on African Education* was sponsored by the Nuffield Foundation and the Colonial Office, which promoted field trips for educationalists to Africa, where they studied the existing colonial systems of education. The conference's final report *African Education* was organized by W. E. F. Ward, *African Education* (London: Oxford University Press, 1953). In this regard, see Alan Peshkin, "Educational Reform in Colonial and Independent Africa," *African Affairs* 64, no. 256 (1965): 210–216; R. J. Harvey (Colonial Office) to John Attenborough, 20.10.1954, in National Archives (Kew), CO 859.628 Regional CCTA Conference on Education (1954–1956).

[30] "Brief for the United Kingdom delegation. CCTA Tenth Session. Education. Paris, 1955," in National Archives (Kew), CO 859.628 Regional CCTA Conference on Education (1954–1956).

[31] Document CCTA/CSA (55) 203—"Working Party on Regional Co-operation in the Field of Education," in AHD-MNE—2P/A62/M152.

the Inter-African Labour Institute). But while the Belgians and French supported the Portuguese suggestion, the remaining governments were clearly reluctant for various reasons. The South African delegation, while supporting the proposal, believed that it would not "take root" and therefore suggested expanding the functions of the CCTA Committee for Social Sciences to include educational issues. The Federation of Rhodesia and Nyasaland felt that the creation of such a body was premature and inappropriate and had only one political meaning: "fear of UNESCO." It suggested instead that a panel of liaison officers be established which would maintain contact between the different national commissions (to be created by each member state) and the CCTA. The main resistance to the Portuguese idea came from the British, who reiterated their opposition (the proposal had already been presented at the special meeting of the CCTA in July[32]), taking the position that the results of the committee would be null and void, and that it would be yet another organism that produced "theoretical papers that nobody would read." What was important was to establish greater contact between technicians, to carry out more visits, and to convene more conferences, and they requested that the list of upcoming conferences be reviewed. One of the Portuguese delegates, Franco Nogueira, stated that the British delegation had shown "absolute intransigence, even treating the Portuguese proposal with a certain irony." The British and Portuguese did, however, agree on a final solution along the lines of the proposal of the federal government. Franco Nogueira accepted that this solution was "insufficient," but "the risk of nothing being done," resulting in "inconvenient consequences regarding UNESCO," would be much worse. The proposed education committee had a political purpose and a cause: to block UNESCO.[33] The Belgian point of view was that while the British did not want to "hurt" UNESCO, the French supported the Portuguese proposal with the aim to "roll out or contain" the organization.[34]

---

[32] Document CCTA/CSA (55) 114—"Liaison Permanent dans le Domaine de l'Enseignement. Memorandum reçu du Gouvernement Portugais," 29.6.1955, in AHD-MNE—2P/A62/M152.

[33] Report by the Portuguese representative at the Working Party (London, 1955) to the Portuguese Ministry of Foreign Affairs, in AHD-MNE—2P/A62/M152.

[34] "Note de Mission. Groupe de Travail sur la coopération régionale dans le domaine de l'enseignment. Londres 12 au 14.12.1955," in AA, Brussels, AE (3105). Enseignment I. 8. Groupe de Travail Lisbonne 1956.

The panel of liaison officers in the field of education would be responsible for organizing and encouraging contact and exchange of information on education between African territories. Each government would appoint officials at governmental and local levels who would function as intermediaries for those at the level of colonial government. The main objective was to develop collaboration at a regional level. Staff could also be invited to assist in the technical preparation of the CCTA's inter-African and regional teaching conferences.[35] In order to reconcile their efforts, the first meeting of liaison officers was scheduled for Lisbon in June 1956, the same time the preparatory meeting for the second inter-African conference was held in Luanda.

The focus of one of the first debates to emerge at the Lisbon meeting concerned the terms of the theme proposed for the conference and their meanings: "technical education and agricultural education." The Belgian delegation drew attention to the fact that, in its view, industrial and agricultural training came under the common name of technical education, so the aim of the conference could not be technical education and agricultural education. The South Africans questioned whether agricultural training could be included in technical training. The British suggested that the committee of experts define the terms "technical education" and "agricultural education" and that it would be more appropriate to replace "technical education" with "commercial and industrial training," which the Secretary General of the CCTA supported. The French proposed two distinct sets of meetings: one for industrial and commercial training and another for agricultural education.[36] The discussion of the scope of the conference was symptomatic of the complexity and diversity of the theme of education within the CCTA. The definition of one term gave rise to additional explanations that came from the different systems of education that existed in each country of the commission. For example, when the Belgians proposed that the theme of the conference should be "industrial and agricultural education at primary and secondary level," the representative of the Federation questioned where secondary school ended, and the South

---

[35] Document CCTA/CSA (55) 203—"Working Party on Regional Co-operation in the Field of Education."

[36] Document CCTA/CSA (56) 103—"Report on the Preliminary Meeting of Experts for the Inter-African Conference on Education, Lisbon, from 4th June 1956. Record of Proceedings No. 1," in AHD-MNE—2P/A62/M152.

African delegation stated that all institutions counted as secondary education institutions if they were not operating at university level.[37]

In the end, it was decided that the aim of the meeting would be to study industrial, commercial, and agricultural education in schools up to, but not including, university level, with a view to practical cooperation on the problems emerging in the different countries of sub-Saharan Africa. The program of the forthcoming conference included a set of general topics for discussion in a plenary session that included the general aspects of industrial, commercial, and agricultural training in relation to social conditions; adapting industrial, commercial, and agricultural training to the needs of rural, industrial, and urban communities; or the general problem of vocational training. For each of the themes of the conference (industrial, commercial, and agricultural), specialized committees would be established: Committee I—industrial training; Committee II—commercial training; and Committee III—agricultural training.[38]

In addition to potential invitations to the Inter-African Labour Institute and other CCTA organizations (such as the Inter-African Bureau on Rural Welfare and the Inter-African Bureau for Soils and Rural Economy-BIS), the option of inviting the FAO (Food and Agriculture Organization), the ILO, and UNESCO was pondered, as they would be interested in the conference themes from a technical point of view.[39] However, on the eve of the meeting, the Portuguese organization clarified that UNESCO should only be present in the role of an observer, not only because it was impossible to change the conference program, increasing the number of participants, but also because it was preferable "to limit their interference in Africa." This was the line consistently held, as we have seen.[40]

---

[37] "Preliminary Meeting of Experts for the Inter-African Conference on Education, Lisbon, from 4th June 1956. Record of Proceedings No. 1," in AHD-MNE—2P/A62/M152.

[38] Document CCTA/CSA (56) 103—"Report on the Preliminary Meeting of Experts [...]," in AHD-MNE—2P/A62/M152.

[39] Later on, FAO would inform that it would not be possible to send an observer since the conference at Luanda would be held at the same time of FAO's conference. "Nota da CCTA, 20 de Junho de 1957," in AHD-MNE—2P/A62/M157.

[40] Henrique Queiroz, Director General of the Portuguese Ministry of Foreign Affairs, to João de Lucena, charge d'affaires at Portugal's embassy in London, 22.8.1957, in AHD-MNE—2P/A62/M157.

New Data for a New Policy

In preparation for the conference, the preliminary meeting commissioned the cadre of education officers to organize a prior exchange of information on the conference subjects. It was based on a questionnaire, including a detailed description of the current structure and objectives of education and industrial, commercial, and agricultural training, while at the same time highlighting the main difficulties encountered in the field of education. The questionnaire was divided into two parts. The first asked for a set of issues related to the general aspects of education in each territory, adapting education to rural needs and a description of systems for vocational guidance. The second part was divided into four points. The first presented general and common questions about the three types of education, from administrative organization to the relationship between industry, trade, and agriculture with different types of education, and—an important topic for colonial administrations—the language of instruction. The remaining three points focused on the different areas of education to be discussed at the conference. There was a need to gather new data on all these issues to enhance the possibility of setting a new policy for cooperation and also a common framework for education policies in an African context.

Between 1956 and 1957, the questionnaire sent by governments to the African territories was answered and returned to the metropoles, forwarded to the General Secretariat of the CCTA, and sent on to the other members. To a greater or lesser extent, the documentation submitted presents an important insight into the state of the colonial educational scenario in the mid-1950s, although whether the data presented in each report corresponds to the actual situation of education is questionable. However, the questionnaire did not aim simply to gather statistical data. The questions posed requested a description of the rationale, objectives, and education systems in place. It was not enough just to indicate only the number of schools, pupils, or graduates. In order to draw up the final report of each committee to be presented for discussion, a presentation of the different educational systems and their methods of delivery was required. Thus, answers to the questionnaire allow an understanding of how the colonial authorities looked at the problem of education in Africa, even though the questionnaire targeted a well-defined area of education. Each of the British, French, and Belgian colonies sent individual replies, while the Federation of Rhodesia and Nyasaland, South Africa, and Portugal sent joint reports from their territories.[41]

As a means of complementing the information provided by the questionnaires, spokespeople from each commission made trips to different African territories. This experience received praise from the steering committee of the conference; in its view, it was a "useful basis for discussion," and one of its conclusions was a recommendation that the practice should continue, fostering one of the initial ideas of the cooperation strategies that had been established from the moment of the first tripartite meetings of the 1940s: an exchange of expertise as a means of bringing together forms of knowledge, training, and delivery. Before the conference, the participants visited the Léopoldville pilot-center for vocational guidance. As part of the meeting, some work was done outside Luanda, as the program included visits to see agropastoral activity in Huíla, the Tchivinguiro Agricultural School, and the settlement at Cela. These visits were not only intended to publicize local progress in education, with their projection of an image of a colonial society in "development" and modernization[42]; they also sought to exemplify and encourage the exchange of experiences among experts in order to contribute to the discussion of commissions and to the establishment of common strategies to be shared by members of the CCTA.[43]

In order to make this exchange of knowledge more thorough, it was recommended by the conference that experts travel before the conferences, that documentation and staff be exchanged, and that there be mutual assistance of experts on education and work. Examples of the work and intense activity generated by the Inter-African Labour Institute and various inter-African labor conferences were given, as well as research on "rural welfare" in order to underline the importance of collaborating with experts from other fields. On the other hand, the panel of liaison officials was to implement the recommendations collaboratively

---

[41] Document CCTA/CSA (56) 103. Annex: "Questionnaire. Industrial, Commercial and Agricultural Education."

[42] For the Portuguese case, see Miguel Bandeira Jerónimo and António Costa Pinto, "A Modernizing Empire? Politics, Culture and Economy in Portuguese Late Colonialism," in *The Ends of European Colonial Empires*, ed. by Jerónimo and Pinto, 51–80.

[43] CCTA, *Conferência Interafricana do Ensino. 2.ª sessão. Programa e Informações* (Luanda: CCTA, 1957), 19.

as a joint secretariat of the CCTA and the Scientific Council for Africa South of the Sahara (CSA), and while it did not have all the functions of an autonomous committee, it could work toward establishing mechanisms for cooperation between CCTA governments; information could be collected, analyzed, and produced, to be circulated among experts and, if possible, have an influence on the policy decision-making process.[44]

At the end of the conference, the work still to be done was unclear, and some of the plans put forward raised innumerable doubts. The lack of qualified staff or the idea that there was no human mass that could meet the expectations of the strategies outlined were just two of the reasons for reservations. A few months later, at the 13th session in Brussels (May 1958), CCTA officials declared themselves satisfied with the outcome of the conference, stating that proposals should be put forward to implement its recommendations.[45]

As on other occasions, the results of the Luanda conference focused mainly on recommendations that emphasized the exchange of information and experience between CCTA members and their experts, without seriously engaging in defining a common strategy which could be practiced in each territory. Luanda, however, proved a tremendous improvement over previous conferences, notably that of Tananarive, in which "recommendations" were not even made. Preparations for the 1957 meeting were made with great care. The preparatory meeting drew up an extensive questionnaire on the state of education at the time, to cater for the general requests for educational data prior to the conferences. The information collected would be analyzed by spokespeople appointed by different governments, who were also able to travel to Africa to add *in loco* observations to the documentation submitted. To a certain extent, the preparatory process for the conference, which culminated in a pedagogical and publicity visit to the Leopoldville pilot-center for vocational guidance, as a means of furthering the extension of its model to other

---

[44] CCTA, "Comissão Geral. Recomendações," in *Ensino. Conferência Interafricana. 2.ª sessão* (Luanda: CCTA, 1957).

[45] CCTA/CSA (55) 203—"Working Party on Regional Co-operation in the Field of Education."

territories, was to substantiate the suggestions made in the years leading up to the meeting in Luanda: visits, information exchanges, preparation of reports, and discussion among experts.[46]

Conclusion

This text shows how the study of the evolution of educational programs in late colonialism in Africa, which were important for the overall developmentalist strategies tentatively enacted by European empire-states in the period, must not ignore the key role played by instances and modalities of inter-imperial cooperation that had their highest institutional expression with the Commission for Technical Cooperation in Africa South of the Sahara.[47] The main colonial powers strove to find means of exchanging and producing information, sharing and transferring knowledge, and training and mobilizing technicians and experts in various areas, in both the metropoles and colonial worlds. They organized numerous "conversations," meetings, and conferences for this purpose. They did so bilaterally and multilaterally, at an international and regional level, always striving to establish a developmental alternative to the nascent programs of the UN and its specialized agencies. One of the main results of CCTA cooperation in educational matters was the systematic and, in a way, successful blockade of UNESCO's attempts to enter sub-Saharan African space, or to establish any form of effective collaboration with the CCTA in the field of education. UNESCO never held the conference planned for 1958 on free and compulsory education and postponed the course on technical and vocational education which had been recommended at the 9th General Conference (New Delhi, 1956). This was also scheduled for 1958, not only due to the postponement

---

[46] The impact of these processes in the elaboration of educational policies in colonial contexts is yet to be properly studied. Nevertheless, among other aspects, the dynamics of knowledge production on those issues and of self-scrutiny of existing policies were certainly relevant.

[47] For a study that explores the connection between imperial projects and education in Africa, from a comparative point of view, see Peter Kallaway and Rebecca Swartz (eds.), *Empire and Education in Africa* (New York: Peter Lang, 2016). See also Joyce Goodman, Gary McCulloch, and William Richardson (eds.), "Empires at Home and Empires Overseas: Postcolonial and Transnational Perspectives on Social Change in the History of Education," *Paedagogica Historica* 45, no. 6 (2010): 695–706; Barnita Bagchi, Eckhardt Fuchs, and Kate Rousmaniere (eds.), *Connecting Histories of Education* (New York/London: Berghahn Books, 2014).

of the conference on the same theme in the Arab countries, but also because of the CCTA conference in Luanda.[48]

In May 1961, UNESCO organized the Addis Ababa Conference of African States on the development of education, making a definitive mark in the area of education in Africa, at a time when the map of the continent was undergoing reformulation with the process of decolonization and reordering of the CCTA.[49] CCTA member governments exposed and discussed their differences, seeking an understanding around colonial policies. The case of education in colonial contexts is an excellent example of these dynamics, the effects of which are largely still to be determined. This work addresses the attempts to establish and intensify efforts toward cooperation in education, from the end of the Second World War to the late 1950s and at the same time signals the key moments of these efforts—from the bilateral meetings of 1945 to the remarkable Inter-African Conference on Education of 1957—and the crucial topics and problems that characterized them. It shows how and why the CCTA was a fundamental piece in the historical evolution of educational dynamics and policies in the colonial context.

Archival Sources

Archives Africaines, Brussels [AA, Brussels].
    AE (3105). Enseignment I. 5. Conférence Paris décembre 1953.
    AE (3105). Enseignment I. 8. Groupe de Travail Lisbonne 1956.
Archives Diplomatiques, Brussels [AD, Brussels].
18729/I.
Arquivo Histórico-Diplomático do Ministério dos Negócios Estrangeiros (Lisbon) [AHD-MNE].
    2P/A62/M152.
    2P/A62/M157.
    2P/A17/ M45.
National Archives (Kew).
    CO 859.628 Regional CCTA Conference on Education (1954–56).
UNESCO Archive.
    62 A81/01 (6–13) CTCASS "-66" Commission for Technical Cooperation in Africa – South of the Sahara. Part IIa – from 1/1/1950 up to 30/XII/1955.

---

[48] CCTA/CSA Circular 327, 9.10.1957, in AHD-MNE—2P/A62/M157.

[49] See United Nations, *Conference of African States on the Development of Education in Africa: Addis Ababa, 15–25 May 1961: Final Report* (Paris: UNESCO, 1961).

Bibliography

Bagchi, Barnita, Eckhardt Fuchs, and Kate Rousmaniere, eds. *Connecting Histories of Education*. New York/London: Berghahn Books, 2014.

CCTA. *Conférence Inter-africaine sur le Bien-Être rural. Première Session. Lourenço Marques – Septembre 1953*. Lisbon: Secretariado da Conferência Inter-Africana do Bem-estar rural, 1953.

———. *Education: Inter-African and Regional Conferences—Tananarive 1954, Accra 1950, Nairobi 1951*. London: CCTA, 1954.

———. *Enseignment. Conférence Interafricaine et Conferences Regionales*. London: CCTA, 1954.

———. *Ensino. Conferência Interafricana do Ensino. 2.ª sessão. Programa e Informações*. Luanda: CCTA, 1957.

———. *Ensino. Conferência Interafricana. 2.ª sessão*. Luanda: CCTA, 1957.

Cooper, Frederick. "Modernizing Bureaucrats, Backward Africans, and the Development Concept." In *International Development and the Social Sciences*, edited by Frederick Cooper and Randall Packard, 64–92. Berkeley: University of California Press, 1997.

———. "Reconstructing Empire in British and French Africa." In *Post-War Reconstruction in Europe: International Perspectives, 1945–1949*, edited by Mark Mazower, Jessica Reinisch, and David Feldman, 196–210. Oxford: Oxford University Press, 2011.

———. *Africa Since 1940: The Past of the Present*. Cambridge: Cambridge University Press, 2002.

Daviron, Benoit. "Mobilizing Labour in African Agriculture: The Role of the International Colonial Institute in the Elaboration of a Standard of Colonial Administration, 1895–1930." *Journal of Global History* 5 (2010): 479–501.

Deighton, Anne. "Entente Neo-Coloniale?: Ernest Bevin and the Proposals for an Anglo–French Third World Power, 1945–1949." *Diplomacy & Statecraft* 17, no. 4 (2006): 835–852.

Goodman, Joyce, Gary McCulloch, and William Richardson, eds. "Empires at Home and Empires Overseas: Postcolonial and Transnational Perspectives on Social Change in the History of Education." *Paedagogica Historica* 45, no. 6 (2010): 695–706.

Hodge, Joseph M., Gerald Hodl, and Martina Kopf, eds. *Developing Africa. Concepts and Practices in Twentieth-Century Colonialism*. Manchester: Manchester University Press, 2014.

Institut Colonial International, *L'Enseignement aux indigènes: rapports préliminaires. XXIᵉ session de l'Institut colonial international, Paris, 5–8 mai 1931*. Bruxelles: Établissements généraux d'imprimerie. 1931.

Jerónimo, Miguel Bandeira, and António Costa Pinto. "A Modernizing Empire? Politics, Culture and Economy in Portuguese Late Colonialism." In *The Ends of European Colonial Empires: Cases and Comparisons*, edited by Jerónimo and Pinto, 51–80. Basingstoke: Palgrave, 2015.

———, eds. *The Ends of European Colonial Empires: Cases and Comparisons*. Basingstoke: Palgrave, 2015.

Jerónimo, Miguel Bandeira. "A League of Empires: Imperial Political Imagination and Interwar Internationalisms." In *Internationalism, imperialism and the formation of the contemporary world*, ed. by Miguel Bandeira Jerónimo and José Pedro Monteiro, 87–126. London: Palgrave Macmillan, 2017.

———. "Repressive Developmentalisms: Idioms, Repertoires, Trajectories in Late Colonialism." In *The Oxford Handbook of the Ends of Empire*, edited by Andrew Thompson and Martin Thomas, 337–354. Oxford: Oxford University Press, 2017 online; 2018 print.

Kallaway, Peter, and Rebecca Swartz, eds. *Empire and Education in Africa*. New York: Peter Lang, 2016.

Kent, John. *The Internationalisation of Colonialism: Britain, France, and Black Africa, 1939–1956*. Oxford: Clarendon Press, 1992.

Lindner, Ulrike. "New Forms of Knowledge Exchange Between Imperial Powers: The Development of the Institut Colonial International (ICI) Since the End of the Nineteenth Century." In *Imperial Co-operation and Transfer, 1870–1930: Empires and Encounters*, edited by Volker Barth and Roland Cvetkovski, 57–78. London: Bloomsbury Academic, 2015.

Matasci, Damiano. "Une 'UNESCO africaine'? Le ministère de la France d'Outre-mer, la coopération éducative intercoloniale et la défense de l'Empire, 1947–1957." *Monde(s)* 13, no. 1 (2018): 195–214.

Maul, Daniel R. *Human Rights, Development, and Decolonization: The International Labour Organization, 1940–1970*. Basingstoke: Palgrave Macmillan, 2012.

Michel, Marc. "La cooperation intercoloniale en Afrique noire, 1942–1950: un neo-colonialisme eclairé?" *Relations Internationales* 34 (1983): 155–171.

Monteiro, José Pedro. *Portugal e a Questão do Trabalho Forçado. Um império sob escrutínio (1944–1962)*. Lisbon: Edições 70, 2018.

Pedersen, Susan. *The Guardians: The League of Nations and the Crisis of Empire*. Oxford: Oxford University Press, 2015.

Peshkin, Alan. "Educational Reform in Colonial and Independent Africa." *African Affairs* 64, no. 256 (1965): 210–216.

Shipway, Martin. *Decolonization and Its Impact: A Comparative Approach to the End of the Colonial Empires*. Oxford: Blackwell, 2008.

Thomas, Martin, and Gareth Curless, eds. *Decolonization and Conflict: Colonial Comparisons and Legacies*. London: Bloomsbury, 2017.

Thomas, Martin, Bob Moore, and Larry Butler. *Crises of Empire. Decolonization and Europe's Imperial States*. London: Hodder Education, 2008.

UNESCO, "UNESCO: Proposed Programme and Budget for 1955 and 1956. Education. (C) Regional Conference on Free and Compulsory Education." Paris: UNESCO, 1954.

United Nations. *Conference of African States on the Development of Education in Africa: Addis Ababa, 15–25 May 1961: Final Report*. Paris: UNESCO, 1961.

Vanthemsche, Guy. *Belgium and the Congo, 1885–1980*. Cambridge: Cambridge University Press, 2012.

Wagner, Florian. "Private Colonialism and International Co-operation in Europe, 1870–1914." In *Imperial Co-operation and Transfer, 1870–1930: Empires and Encounters*, edited by Volker Barth and Roland Cvetkovski, 79–103. London: Bloomsbury Academic, 2015.

Ward, W. E. F. *African Education*. London: Oxford University Press, 1953.

White, Nicholas J. "Reconstructing Europe through Rejuvenating Empire: The British, French and Dutch Experiences Compared." In *Post-War Reconstruction in Europe: International Perspectives, 1945–1949*, edited by Mark Mazower, Jessica Reinisch, and David Feldman, 211–236. Oxford: Oxford University Press, 2011.

Open Access This chapter is licensed under the terms of the Creative Commons Attribution 4.0 International License (http://creativecommons.org/licenses/by/4.0/), which permits use, sharing, adaptation, distribution and reproduction in any medium or format, as long as you give appropriate credit to the original author(s) and the source, provide a link to the Creative Commons license and indicate if changes were made.

The images or other third party material in this chapter are included in the chapter's Creative Commons license, unless indicated otherwise in a credit line to the material. If material is not included in the chapter's Creative Commons license and your intended use is not permitted by statutory regulation or exceeds the permitted use, you will need to obtain permission directly from the copyright holder.

CHAPTER 10

The Fabric of Academic Communities at the Heart of the British Empire's Modernization Policies

Hélène Charton

This chapter underscores the role played by university reforms on the new social and political agenda of the British Empire in the 1940s. The creation of colonial universities in Africa and the multiplying number of scholarships to study in Great Britain that were offered to colonial people, were at the heart of post-war modernization policies. Indeed, the modalities of training a modern educated elite shed light on the nature and range of new links that the home country intended to forge with its African colonies. While the colonial order was based on racial distinctions, the new imperial paradigm, that emerged from the social and political crises of the 1930s, tended to reverse these hierarchies in favor of class relationships, embodied in the new modern elites, sharing a common set of practices and values, entrenched in Great Britain's culture.

The work of American historian Frederick Cooper on the politics of the modernization of empires provides a theoretical framework for this

H. Charton (✉)
CNRS, Les Afriques dans le Monde, University of Bordeaux, Bordeaux, France
e-mail: h.charton@sciencespobordeaux.fr

© The Author(s) 2020
D. Matasci et al. (eds.), *Education and Development in Colonial and Postcolonial Africa*, Global Histories of Education,
https://doi.org/10.1007/978-3-030-27801-4_10

analysis, which also draws upon the New Imperial History approach to bring forward connections and interactions between colonies and home countries.[1] A number of scholars have explored the way in which modernization programs have been implemented in various sectors, such as in urban or social policies.[2] As shown in many chapters of this edited volume, the training of an educated African elite has also been the subject of historical and sociological research,[3] something that we will examine here, in conjunction with global imperial dynamics, in order to bring out the political dimensions.

Such an approach must allow us to revisit the notion of modernization, in broaching the intertwining social, political, and economic dimensions of this educational engineering. In fact, analysis of the ways these training programs were implemented in East Africa, and in Kenya

[1] Frederick Cooper, *Decolonization and African Society: The Labour Question in French and British Africa* (Cambridge: Cambridge University Press, 1996); Ann Laura Stoler and Frederick Cooper (eds.), *Tensions of Empire: Colonial Cultures in a Bourgeois World* (Berkeley: California Press, 1997); Catherine Hall, *Cultures of Empire: Colonizers in Britain and the Empire in the Nineteenth and Twentieth Centuries: A Reader* (Manchester: Manchester University Press, 2000); Frederick Cooper, *Colonialism in Question: Theory, Knowledge, History* (Berkeley: University of California Press, 2005); Catherine Hall and Sonya O. Rose (eds.), *At Home with the Empire: Metropolitan Culture and the Imperial World* (Cambridge: Cambridge University Press, 2006); Hélène Charton, "Produits d'Empires: expériences universitaires coloniales britanniques et françaises en Asie et en Afrique aux XIXᵉ et XXᵉ siècles," *Outre-Mers, Revue d'histoire* 394–395 (2017): 5–13.

[2] Johanna Lewis, *Empire State Building: War and Welfare in Kenya 1925–52* (Oxford: James Currey, 2000); Séverine Awenengo Dalberto, Hélène Charton, and Odile Goerg, "Urban Planning, Housing, and the Making of 'Responsible Citizens' in the Late Colonial Period: Dakar, Nairobi, Conakry," in *Governing Cities in Africa: Politics and Policies*, ed. by Simon Becker and Laurent Fourchard (Cape Town: HSRC Press, 2013), 43–64.

[3] James Anthony Mangan (ed.), *Benefits Bestowed, Education and British Imperialism* (Manchester: Manchester University Press, 1988); Apollo O. Nwauwa, *Imperialism, Academe and Nationalism: Britain and University Education for Africans 1860–1960* (London: Frank Cass, 1997); Katia Leney, *Decolonisation, Independence and the Politics of Higher Education in West Africa* (London: Edwin Mellen Press, 2003); Joyce Goodman, Gary McCulloch and William Richardson, "'Empires Overseas' and 'Empires at Home' Postcolonial and Transnational Perspectives on Social Change in the History of Education," *Paedagogica Historica* 45 (2009): 695–706; Pascale Barthélémy, *Africaines et diplômées à l'époque coloniale (1918–1957)* (Rennes: Presses universitaires de Rennes, 2010); Peter Kallaway and Rebecca Swartz (eds.), *Empire and Education: The Shaping of a Comparative Perspective* (New York: Peter Lang, 2016); Hélène Charton, "Homo Africanus academicus. Les limites de la fabrique d'une élite universitaire africaine en Afrique de l'Est," *Outre-Mers, Revue d'histoire* 394–395 (2017): 127–148.

in particular, reveals the processes of acculturation underpinning these measures, and their obvious political goal. While imperial domination was at that time strongly criticized, these new elites were greatly sought after by emerging powers, such as the Soviet Union, the United States, and India (for detailed case studies, see Chapter 8 by Eric Burton and Chapter 11 by Alexandra Piepiorka, both in this book).[4] For British authorities, it was a matter of maintaining control over these new elites despite stiff resistance from both colonial administrators, attached to the preservation of a colonial order based on a strict racial differentiation, and African students denouncing the violence of domination.

UNIVERSITIES TO REINVENT THE EMPIRE

The development of universities in the British colonies and the intensification of training programs in the home country were part of a global project aiming to rebuild the Empire, then facing a major social, economic, and geopolitical crisis.

Establishing New Links Within the Empire

The British world system emerged severely weakened from the Second World war. In terms of territory, the Empire lost its Asian possessions, and the two great world powers, the United States and the Soviet Union, did not mask their hostility to colonialism.[5] From the

---

[4] William Roger Louis, "American Anti-colonialism and the Dissolution of the British Empire," *International Affairs* 61, no. 3 (Summer 1985): 395–420; Hakim Adi, *West Africans in Britain 1900–1960, Nationalism, Panafricanism and Communism* (London: Lawrence and Wishart, 1998); Hélène Charton, "La genèse ambiguë de l'élite kenyane, origine, formation et intégration, de 1945 à l'indépendance," Ph.D. dissertation, Université Paris 7—Denis Diderot, 2002; Vladimir Bartenev, "L'URSS et l'Afrique noire sous Khrouchtchev: la mise à jour des mythes de la coopération," *Outre-mers* 354–355 (2007): 63–82; Constantin Kastakioris, "Transferts Est-Sud. Échanges éducatifs et formation de cadres africains en Union soviétique pendant les années soixante," *Outre-mers* 354–355 (2007): 83–106; Monique de Saint Martin, Grazia Scarfò Ghellab, and Kamal Mellakh (dir.), *Étudier à l'Est. Expériences de diplômés africains* (Paris: Karthala 2015); Patrice Yengo and Monique de Saint-Martin, "Quelles contributions des élites 'rouges' au façonnement des États post-coloniaux?" *Cahiers d'études africaines* 226 (2017): 231–258.

[5] Gabriel Olakunle Olusanya, *The West African Students Union and the Politics of Decolonization, 1935–1958* (Ibadan: Daystar Press, 1982); Posser Gifford and William Roger Louis (eds.), *The Transfer of Power in Africa: Decolonization 1940–1960* (Harvard: Harvard University Press, 1982); Marc Michel, *Décolonisations et émergence du*

end of the 1930s onward, commissions of inquiry, established after social and political crises in the West Indies and Africa, had brought to light the British colonial model's loss of impetus. In an article published in 1942, following the fall of Singapore, Margery Perham publicly denounced the failure of Great Britain to meet the social and political aspirations of colonial populations but, above all, the violence of colonial racism behind the pauperization of these territories, characterized as "Tropical East Ends."[6] It is in this context that the Labour government of Clement Attlee (1945–1951) attended to the reform of the Empire, in an attempt to save it:

> British leaders began to think enthusiastically about the need for imperial unity and a common foreign policy to which Britain, the dominions and the rest of the empire, including India, would be tied.[7]

This new vision of the British world system confronted the Victorian conception of empire based on a sharp distinction between its former white colonies which had become dominions, and its tropical territories. Erasing this differentiation involved, in fact, the deracialization of the imperial link which found its expression in the redefinition and enlarging of the Commonwealth, from then on conceived as an alliance of nations sharing a history and common economic interests.[8] The integration of African colonies into the sterling zone was the cornerstone of the reconstruction and restoration of the Empire's prestige. It occurred due to the implementation of voluntarist modernization policies in the economic, social, and political fields.

The Colonial Development and Welfare Act (CDWA), adopted in 1940 and revised in 1945, was the main vehicle of these reforms.

---

tiers-monde (Paris: Hachette, 1993); Ode Arne Westad, *The Global Cold War: Third World Interventions and the Making of Our Times* (New York: Cambridge University Press, 2005).

[6] Margery Perham, "The Colonial Empire: Capital, Labour and the Colonial Colour Bar," *The Times*, 14 March 1942.

[7] John Darwin, *The Empire Project: The Rise and Fall of the British World System, 1830–1970* (Cambridge: Cambridge University Press, 2009), 520.

[8] The Commonwealth was created in 1931 around four dominions: New Zealand, South Africa, Canada, and Australia.

Granted a budget of £100 million over 10 years, this unprecedented program financed vast modernization projects over a wide range of domains. Education represented 20% of the budget of the CDWA, much of which was devoted to the creation of colonial universities and to programs offering scholarships in the United Kingdom. These measures aimed to train a qualified workforce, able to occupy senior positions with, in 1945, the still vague and distant prospect of self-government. A memorandum, published in 1946 by the Colonial Office under the title *Education for Citizenship*, explicitly linked political emancipation with the prior training of colonized people.[9] Whereas France established a common (but still unequal) citizenship within the newly created Union Française (1946),[10] the new British imperial strategy was not explicitly political. It rested upon a voluntarist influence policy that could be spread through the building up of new imperial communities sharing a collection of common representations.

The academic communities which arose from post-war training programs were deeply involved in this new political project. The expression "academic community" had been employed in 1912 during the first congress of universities of the British Empire, organized at the University of London on July 2, 1912, to designate its 158 delegates. These British white men (women and the colonized being excluded), had come to celebrate the vitality of British cultural imperialism. Indeed, the universities founded in the former colonies at the end of the nineteenth century were shaped along the same patterns as the homeland institutions with which they maintained close relations (including visiting scholars and student grants).[11] The establishment of universities in tropical territories reveals the outline of a renewed cultural imperialism that would contribute to rebuilding and fostering the Empire. In fact, the opening up of university training to African people appears a cornerstone of these policies, as colonial people had remained, until that point, at the margins of a solely white imperial history.

[9] Public Record Office (PRO), London, CO/859/89/8. *Education for Citizenship*, 1946.

[10] Frederick Cooper, *Citizenship Between Empire and Nation* (Princeton: Princeton University Press, 2014).

[11] Tamson Pietsch, *Empire of Scholars, Universities, Networks and the British Academic World (1850–1939)* (Manchester: Manchester University Press, 2013).

The way in which this African educated elite was trained through post-war modernization programs highlights the features of the new links forged by London with its colonies. It was believed that the promotion of British values, practices, and cultural references in the whole Empire would foster and unite imperial communities that would, in time, overcome dominant racial distinctions in favor of class relations. The processes of acculturation underlying these training arrangements suggest they were part of a broader project aiming to deracialize the Empire.

Training Academic Elites in and for the Colonies

The Colonial Office started to consider the opportunity of establishing universities in its African colonies in the middle of the 1930s. The project, however, only took shape in 1943, when a commission was established, presided over by Sir Cyril Asquith. Its task was to define a common model of universities for the colonies.[12] Asquith universities were meant to build bridges between London and its African colonies through the spreading of British university culture.[13] Thanks to CDWA grants, the first colonial universities were established in Africa after the war. Thus, in West Africa, where education was most developed, the University College of Legon (formerly Achimota), in the Gold Coast, welcomed its first 100 students in 1948. That same year, the University College of Ibadan, in Nigeria, opened its doors to 210 students.

The Inter-University Council, formed with British university representatives, responsible for ensuring the equivalence of diplomas within the Special Relationship Scheme with the University of London, paid its first visit in 1946 to Makerere, Uganda. The Native Technical College of Makerere had been created in 1922 to train African subordinates for colonial administration in the four British territories of East Africa (i.e., Uganda, Tanganyika, Kenya, and Zanzibar) in the fields of health, agriculture, animal husbandry, and education. To become a university, the training college first had to symbolically endorse its new status. When the Inter-University Council visited the college for the second time in

---

[12] Kenya National Archives (KNA), Nairobi, ED/3/3181.

[13] Eric Ashby, *British, Indians, African Universities: A Study in the Ecology of Higher Education* (London: Weidenfeld & Nicolson, 1966); John D. Hargreaves, "The Idea of a Colonial University," *African Affairs* 72 (1973): 26–36.

1949, the school uniforms of shorts, green socks with red bands, and caps with tassels had been replaced by blazers and long trousers. Sport was no longer obligatory and school prefects had disappeared. At a more academic level, three university chairs and two lecturer positions were created; expatriate stipends and adaptable teaching schedules made these positions highly attractive.[14] In addition, the honorary college member status enabled eminent British professors to regularly visit the college; Margery Perham from Oxford University was one of them.[15] In 1950, Makerere was able to offer two full-fledged two years' curricula in sciences (higher science) and arts (higher arts), corresponding to the intermediate level of the British bachelor's degree. A £400,000 CDWA grant for the first five years and £200,000 for the following five years allowed the college to build new classrooms, science laboratories, and university residences, including one for women only (Mary Stuart Hall), as well as lodgings for academic staff. Thus, between 1948 and 1955, its student body grew from 177 to 558.[16]

Scholarships in the United Kingdom were also awarded to colonial students under the CDWA, for a total of £1 million over ten years.[17] African colonies received 41%, with 16% going to East Africa (a total of £160,000 of which £43,000 went to Kenya).[18] To make sure this program would not hinder the development of colonial universities, applicants were required to have exhausted local educational resources first. Bursaries were first awarded to members of the public service, especially teachers, who would in turn contribute to the modernization project. However, at an average cost of £1500 per year (£1100 after the deduction of the salary of the bursar) versus £500 for Makerere students, the number of scholarships given to one territory remained limited. Thus, between 1946 and 1956, 28 CDWA bursaries were granted to Kenyan students.

---

[14] Leney, *Decolonisation*, 94.

[15] Carol Sicherman, *Becoming an African University: Makerere 1922–2000* (Trenton: Africa World Press, 2005).

[16] Margaret Macpherson, *They Built for the Future: A Chronicle of Makerere College 1922–1962* (Cambridge: Cambridge University Press, 1964), 47.

[17] PRO, London, WO95/2043. *Rules Governing the Award of Scholarships Tenable in the United Kingdom Under the Colonial Development and Welfare Acts*, January 1947.

[18] KNA, Nairobi. ED/1/2522, 10 November 1951.

Colonial governments were also encouraged to finance scholarships from their own budgets with, however, huge discrepancies in the way such programs were administered. Consistent with its segregated educational system, the Government Overseas Bursaries Scheme of Kenya was broken down into three different programs depending on the racial origin of students (Indians, Europeans, and Africans). While four-fifths of the 1948 colony budget, allocated to the higher education of Africans, went to Makerere, African students received only a limited number of scholarships.[19] In Kenya, only two Africans benefited from this program in 1947 versus 46 in Nigeria.[20] For the period between 1947 and 1950, 20 Africans were government bursars while there were 38 Europeans and 24 Indians.[21] Racial discrimination against Kenyan government bursars was the subject of a question raised in Parliament in 1950. The Secretary of State claimed that this situation was due to the weakness of African secondary education in the colony and the limited number of suitable candidates trained in Makerere.[22] Indeed, African applicants were asked to have completed their studies in Makerere and to have worked for at least two years for government services. They also had to demonstrate that they had insufficient resources to pay for their studies abroad. Such requirements were not raised for European students.

Such racial bias also affected scholarship costs. Married students were given additional stipends to compensate for their loss of salary and allow their wives and families to meet their needs in the colony. According to the common scale issued by the Colonial Office, married students could claim £110 a year, to which a further £40 would be added for the first two children, with £27 added for each subsequent child. The government of Kenya ignored these recommendations, aimed at stopping racial differentiation, and continued to apply its own scales. A European married student's stipend would be, on average, £600 a year, versus £400 for an Indian and £60 for an African. Such racial scales which also applied to salaries, were justified by colonial authorities by quoting discrepancies

---

[19] PRO, London. CO/ 533/558/6.

[20] PRO, London. CO/544/61. Kenya Colony and Protectorate, *Education Department. Annual Report*, 1947.

[21] In total, between 1946 and 1955, the government of Kenya financed scholarships for 38 Africans.

[22] PRO, London. CO/876/133. Parliamentary debates.

in the living standards and lifestyles of each community.[23] While Uganda increased its family stipends for African students, Kenya refused on the grounds that Kenyan women were less educated than their neighbors.[24] In 1953, the government increased allocations by 50% but they remained far below those established by London, which had also increased in January 1953.[25]

These examples highlight the inherent contradiction between the objectives of London's modernization programs and the conservatism of colonial administrators and white colonists. While the post-war reforms endeavored to reconfigure the imperial space around its former tropical margins, the emergence of an educated elite acculturated to the British model, at the heart of this new paradigm, presupposed the elimination of racial distinctions. Yet resistance in Kenya made it impossible to overturn these racial hierarchies, dominated by powerful white settlers, on which the colonial order was established. Their hegemony was based on tight control of an educated African elite. This constraint was clearly identified by the newly appointed African representative of the Legislative Council of the colony, who demanded imperial recognition and protection:

> Unless Kenya is to be reserved in Africa as a whole as a quarry for museum specimens of ancient Africa, there cannot be any justification in such overdue controls. (…) Africans ought to be trained, not just because one office or institution needs such a one, but for the general welfare of the whole country (…) If we make the future development of Kenya the central theme of our consideration, it is the African students whose backward conditions require them to go for studies overseas, for then assimilation of the Western culture would be ensured. It is the Europeans who have little need to go overseas, for they already have the Western culture in their homes and in their blood (…) We are also British heirs and have a right to claim the best that the Empire can afford for the progress of her peoples.[26]

These training programs precisely sought to develop and bring to life the new imperial academic communities, in encouraging the spread of common values, references, and practices.

---

[23] KNA, Nairobi. ED/3/3165, 19 December 1947.
[24] KNA, Nairobi. ED/1/2297. Report of the liaison officer.
[25] KNA, Nairobi. ED/3/564, 29 July 1953.
[26] KNA, Nairobi. PC/NZA/3/6/162, Owino, 30 June 1945.

The Fabric of Imperial Academic Communities

The Asquith Universities: Agents of a New Cultural Imperialism

During the 1950s, Makerere became a university college, hosting an academic community. It adopted codes and practices common to British universities, which contributed to forging the group's collective identity, and to distinguishing it from the rest of the population.

The first official graduation ceremony for those receiving bachelor's degrees in arts and in sciences was organized in Makerere in 1953. For this occasion, five armchairs covered in green leather on which was written the motto of the establishment, that is, *Pro futuro aedificamus*,[27] were ordered from England. The choice of Latin, a language not taught in East Africa, but required for entry into Oxford or Cambridge, reveals invisible ties to the British template. The red academic gowns, worn by this first group of graduates, although those of British students were black, reflected the group's distinctiveness, while still attaching it to the larger British academic family. Indeed, exporting to the colonies traditions practiced by prestigious universities, such as Oxford, Cambridge, or Durham, for example, that of the High Table, reinforced its members' feelings of belonging to the same community. This idea was emphasized by the former director of Makerere, who witnessed these transformations:

> Friends at home tell me that academic dress such as ours was irrational and so it is. The students wanted it, felt the better for it and perhaps many needed all the boosts they could get to their self-confidence. They needed recognition.[28]

The reproduction of British university rites and traditions that permeate college life helped to create social practices and imaginaries, contributing to the identity of the community, while initiating young Africans into Western codes of appropriate behavior and respectability. At the first ball in 1947, students were expected to follow a painstaking protocol before and after each dance: engaging in pleasant conversation with their

---

[27] "We build for the future," KNA, Nairobi, MAA/8/140, A. G. Macpherson, 1 July 1952, 3.

[28] Bernard de Busen, *Adventures in Education* (London: Titus Wilson Kendal, 1995), 93.

partners and being sure to accompany them back to their seats once the dance was over. The creation in 1949 of an association of former students fostered the Makerereans' esprit de corps, long after they had left the college and abandoned the practice of *Lunamakerere*.[29]

These university practices, drawing upon a range of ancient European traditions, and incorporating codes of Englishness, contributed to the fabric of imperial academic communities. Indeed, they provided models of behavior for the educated elites who were considered to be at the cutting edge of colonial modernization policies. In that, they can be seen as part of the neo-traditions identified by Ranger and Hobsbawm, the principal function of which was to restructure relations between the dominant and the dominated in periods of change.[30] The first official reunion of former students was held in 1952 under the double patronage of His Majesty the Kabaka (King) and the governor of Uganda. In his closing speech, the Kabaka stressed the universal nature of university communities, notably, in comparing Makerere with Cambridge, his alma mater, while the governor reminded the audience that Makerere remained, first and foremost, a colonial institution.[31] This example illustrates the ambivalence of university reforms in a changing colonial context. The Asquith universities, to which Makerere was attached were, indeed, based on a narrow European centrism, as Eric Ashby reminds us:

> The doctrine was a vivid expression of British cultural parochialism: its basic assumption was that a university system appropriate for Europeans brought up in London and Manchester and Hull was also appropriate for Africans brought up in Lagos and Kumasi and Kampala.[32]

Yet the acculturation of African elites did not stop at the borders of colonies; it continued in Great Britain, as the way of handling scholarship students demonstrates.

---

[29] Name attributed to Daniel Wako who studied the specifics of this university slang. Macpherson, *They Built for the Future*, 168.

[30] Eric Hobsbawm and Terence Ranger (eds.), *The Invention of Tradition* (Cambridge: Cambridge University Press, 2006).

[31] KNA, Nairobi, ED/1/2317. Newsletter, n°10, 10 September 1952.

[32] Eric X. Ashby, *African Universities and Western Tradition* (London: Oxford University Press, 1964), 19.

Integrating, Supporting, and Controlling Colonial Students in Great Britain

The creation in February 1942 of the post of Director of Colonial Scholars and Advisor to Colonial Students, followed in November by the designation of an Advisory Committee on the Welfare of Colonial People in the United Kingdom, demonstrates the attention given by the Colonial Office to welcoming and integrating colonial students to Great Britain.[33] Faced with the church's vague desire to extend its educational mission in the home country and to continue to exercise its moral authority over the educated and Christianized elites, such initiatives allowed it to reaffirm direct responsibility for the British administration of colonial students.[34] One of the principal issues of these training programs was specifically to keep educated elites within the imperial fold.

After the war, the influx of colonial students, whose numbers grew from 1000 to 5000 between 1945 and 1951,[35] led to the Director of Colonial Scholars and Advisor to Colonial Students delegating some responsibilities to the British Council. Thus, in 1950, agents of the British Council welcomed more than 1700 colonial students to Great Britain. At that time, there were 2000 colonial students present in London and its surroundings and 2200 in the provinces; of this number, 750 were not scholarship recipients. Besides welcoming students at the airport, the British Council offered training sessions to familiarize newcomers with daily life in Great Britain. These included visits to stores, restaurants, the underground, etc.[36] Prior to their departure, preparation sessions were sometimes organized by local branches of the British Council who also distributed a regularly updated brochure entitled *How to Live in Britain*. Thus, in 1951, 17 Kenyans participated in a three-day training program in Nairobi during which former students came to talk about their experiences. Some were occasionally invited to stay with a

---

[33] PRO, London. CO/876/21. *Welfare of Colonial Students in the UK, 1942–1943*; London School of Economics (LSE), London. Archives of A. Carr-Saunders, B/3/12, n°26, J. L. Keith, 29 November 1943.

[34] Church of England Record Center, London. MC/AAC/1. AAC meeting, 3 July 1942.

[35] PRO, London. CO/1028/12. *Conference of Voluntary Societies on the Welfare of Colonial Students in London: Appendix A*, 1952.

[36] PRO, London. CO/876/265. *British Council Report on the Welfare of Students*, September 1950, 6.

British family to prepare themselves for their new way of life.[37] These initiatives were designed to give newcomers a positive image of Great Britain and the British:

> The first impressions which colonial students have formed on arrival in this country have often, in the past, been of bewilderment and discouragement, and sometimes of resentment at the apparent unfriendliness of their reception.[38]

The social fund (Amenity Fund), created in 1947, also aimed to enrich the student experience in Great Britain. The *pro-rata* contribution of each colony, according to the number of students it had in the United Kingdom, allowed for subsidies to clubs and associations offering colonial students recreational and cultural activities. These measures were designed to encourage immersion in British society, while both providing support and orienting leisure time toward what were considered useful activities. The Victoria League and Christian organizations, such as the YMCA and the YWCA, for example, proposed cultural outings (visits to Eton and Windsor), as well as recreational activities: Saturday evening dances, study groups, weekly meetings, etc. Training sessions were also offered to students during their holidays around carefully chosen themes such as "local government" or "England and the British." The Amenity Fund also contributed to financing holiday camps organized by the Workers' Educational Association (WEA).[39] All these initiatives had the same goal: to promote the image of the Empire to new colonial elites. Actually, colonial students faced countless difficulties during their stay in Great Britain. Finding lodgings was frequently a serious challenge in light of the housing shortage and persistent racial prejudice.

Distinguishing Colonial Students from the Immigrant Population

Ideally, colonial students were placed in the traditional residential colleges of Oxford, Cambridge, Saint Andrews, Durham, Aberdeen, Exeter, or Cardiff, to both steep them in British culture and allow them to

---

[37] KNA, Nairobi. CNC/8/42. *British Council Report on the Welfare of Students*, May 1952.
[38] PRO, London. BW/3/25. *Colonial Students in Britain*, PEP Report, 9/12 1954, 3.
[39] PRO, London. CO/876/72. Arthur Creech Jones to J. L. Keith, 26 June 1946.

benefit from a stimulating academic environment, while sparing them the temptations of the big cities.[40] Nevertheless, since the capacity of these establishments was limited, in 1952, most colonial students still ended up in London, where they had the greatest difficulty finding lodgings. With insufficient resources, students often found themselves in far-flung and notorious neighborhoods, such as Camden Town or Morning Crescent in London.[41] The Colonial Office considered this situation dangerous and alarming:

> The present housing shortage, coupled with the prejudice of the public against giving accommodation to Africans, constitutes the root of the trouble. This is accentuated by the rather exacting demand from the Africans. It is apparent, however, that whatever the cause of the trouble, if steps are not taken quickly to remedy it, there may be serious repercussions as a result of the Africans becoming disillusioned.[42]

To address these problems, a five-year program of construction and renovation of London, Edinburgh, and Newcastle residences—up to that point reserved for colonial students—was launched in 1951, thanks to a subsidy of £450,000 from the Colonial Development and Welfare Fund.[43] The new residences were intended for temporary stays by both British and colonial students. Indeed, the objective was to encourage the formation of contacts, intermingling, and the integration of students within the same community, following the model of classic university colleges, and suppressing the racial and colonial characteristics of such residences. The temporary closing of former residences in London (Crescent Hall), Edinburgh, and Newcastle, where 460 students were lodged, caused grave concern among colonial students who were afraid of not finding any accommodation or suffering rental increases.[44] Approximately thirty of them refused to leave the residence of Crescent

---

[40] PRO, London. BW/3/25. *Colonial Students in Britain, PEP report*, 1954, 9.

[41] PRO, London. CO/537/2574. J. L. Keith, *Colonial Students in the UK and Eire*, 25 February 1948.

[42] PRO, London. CO/876/69. *Welfare of Colonial People on UK Advisory Council, 1944-46*.

[43] Ade Ajayi, *The African Experience with Higher Education* (London: James Currey, 1996), 154.

[44] PRO, London. CO/876/240. Parliamentary debate, 19 July 1950.

Hall in July 1951, despite threats to cancel their scholarships.[45] The event, covered extensively in the colonies' newspapers, was perceived as a form of collective student mobilization.[46] Eventually, a consultative committee was established to coordinate the action of associations, universities, and the British Council on the question of student housing.[47]

Despite these initiatives and efforts conducted by the British Council's Accommodation Unit to identify private lodgings and convince owners to rent to colonial students at reasonable prices,[48] the latter always faced the same racial prejudices. The influx of colonial people (who had come to participate in the war effort) to the big cities had reinforced racist sentiment among some of the British population. The students suffered from the same bullying and other expressions of suspicion and hostility as the rest of the colonial population, and had to submit to the color bar that was in effect in certain public places (hotels, restaurants, and stores).[49] The Colour Bar Bill, condemning all forms of racial discrimination as well as authors of racist acts, tabled by Labour Member of Parliament Sorenson, was rejected in the spring of 1951, despite receiving support from the West African Students' Union (WASU) and the League of Colored People (LCP), both having denounced similar situations for many years.[50]

However, a number of the Colonial Office reports had identified rising racism in Great Britain and the threat this posed to its colonial policy, especially with regard to colonial students. They underlined the risk of students succumbing to communist anticolonial propaganda and engaging in activities considered undesirable.[51] Failing to eliminate

---

[45] PRO, London. CO/876/265.

[46] Faced with the influx of students, provincial centers finally remained open and the construction of a new 200-bed residence was initiated in London, thanks to a subsidy of £85,000 from the CDWA.

[47] PRO, London. CO/1028/28. *Consultative Committee on Welfare of Students*, 1952–1953.

[48] PRO, London. CO/876/265. *Welfare Department, Report on Student Accommodations*, 8.

[49] KNA, Nairobi. ED/3/3161. *A Bow Group Pamphlet, Coloured People in Britain*, November 1952.

[50] PRO, London. CO/876/197. *Colour Prejudice in the UK*.

[51] PRO, London. BW/3/25. *Colonial Students in Britain, PEP Report*, 1954; PRO, London. CO/876/252. Interdepartmental committee on Welfare of Colonial People, *The Coloured Population of London*.

racial prejudices, the British authorities specifically focused on colonial students, distinguishing them from the rest of the immigrant population. For example, the brochure, *An Appeal to Londoners*, encouraged Londoners to establish personal contacts with colonial students. In 1955, 3500 booklets entitled *Far from home: Overseas students in London* were distributed by various associations to inhabitants of the capital.

In total, numerous acculturation efforts, undertaken jointly by the colonies and home country, reveal the mechanisms and limitations of the social engineering accompanying post-war training programs. Clearly, the entire new British imperial project was based on the capacity to create fresh links between its different territories, for which students immersed in British culture were planned as flag-bearers. In the post-war context, when British leadership was being seriously questioned by both emerging powers and nationalist movements in the colonies, convincing the educated elites of the legitimacy of the Empire, making sure they would become lasting allies, seemed an eminently political undertaking.

Training Allies—Academic Communities Serving the New British Imperial Project

The assumptions underlying these training programs, the spectrum of activity of which extended significantly beyond merely the academic field, are clearly political. In offering colonial students as many opportunities as possible to absorb British culture, as well as excellent study conditions in both the colonies and the United Kingdom, the Colonial Office hoped to favorably carve relations that future ruling elites would nurture and, above all, that would divert them from the anticolonial ideologies that existed after the war. However, numerous obstacles encountered along the way revealed flaws in the new British imperial project.

The Specter of Communism

The African elites' possible acceptance of the anti-racist and anticolonial discourse of the Communist International was one of the obsessions of imperial powers. In January 1948, the Colonial Office brought together a working group to investigate the degree of political commitment of colonial students in Great Britain, in particular considering their receptivity to communist propaganda seeking to exploit their discontent and anti-British sentiment. With fewer than 12 students being official Communist Party members, of the 3200 colonial students at that time present in Great Britain, such fears were the product of rumor and fantasy.[52] Nonetheless, in 1949 the government of Kenya decided to investigate the apparently suspicious political activities of the son of a chief, Charles Njonjo, then a law student in London. The inquiry finally revealed that such fears were baseless.[53]

Like other political groups based in the home country, the Communist Party organized political clubs and offered summer university programs, open to colonial students.[54] Close to certain student organizations, like WASU,[55] at times it also organized lectures, such as those held in London on the 2nd and 3rd of October 1948, entitled *The Crisis of British Imperialism*. In addition, the Monthly Colonial Socials, organized by activists, allowed for exchanges and informal contacts with British members.

The risk of politicization of colonial students stemmed more from their disappointment with respect to the colonial policy of the Labour Party. Nonetheless, the government did all in its power to organize propaganda efforts through clubs, discussion forums in certain universities, films, or most commonly the presentation of lectures on its imperial policy in student residences in London. It even arranged meetings between students and government-associated agents. On the left, the Fabian Colonial Bureau, founded in 1940 within the Fabian Society by individuals close to the Labour Party, provided colonial students many opportunities for dialogue and expression.[56] For its part, the Independent Labour Party of Fenner Brockway echoed colonial students' claims in public and Parliament. Long considered the party of the Empire, Conservative Party authorities also sought to rehabilitate their negative image among colonial students. The Conservative Commonwealth Council organized political debates with students on the future of their colonial territories and on their associated problems. Picking up again on the previous

---

[52] Rhodes House Library, Oxford. Mss Brit EMP.s. 468. 725/1. *Colonial Student Political Problems*, Confidential Note, 1948.

[53] PRO, London. CO/537/4312, J. L. Keith to Ph. Mitchell, 11 February 1949.

[54] PRO, London. BW/3/25. *Colonial Students in Britain, PEP Report*, 1954, 12.

[55] PRO, London. CO/537/4312. *Communist Influences Amongst Students in the UK*, 1948.

[56] Ajayi, *The African Experience*, 141.

government's rhetoric on the new Empire, in one of its pamphlets published in 1952, the Bow Group, founded in 1951 by Conservative students, castigated the racism of colonial emigrants and officers:

> The emigrant who plays the petty aristocrat, the Colonial Office official who makes up for any social inferiority experienced at home by a good dose of colour consciousness in the colonies; all these and worse have, in the mind of the coloured man, been connected with Conservatism.[57]

Highly Sought-After Colonial Elites

Various British political organizations attempted to seduce colonial students to keep future African ruling elites in the imperial fold when other powers were trying to weigh in on the political future of the colonial territories.

The Eastern Bloc, from the end of the 1940s, had established scholarship programs for colonial students. Thus, Czechoslovakia had welcomed 70 West African students in 1949 and the movement continued throughout the following decades.[58] Also, immediately after the war, the United States consolidated its tradition of welcoming colonial students to its universities. In the 1930s, a number of West African nationalist leaders, such as Kwame Nkrumah and Nnamdi Azikiwe, were trained in the United States. In 1948, 154 African students were studying in the United States, of whom 103 came from British colonies—twice the number in 1946, thanks to various scholarship programs offered by the government (Fulbright), private philanthropic foundations (Ford, Carnegie Corporation, and the Phelps Stokes Fund), and African–American colleges and churches. These different scholarships, administered by the Institute of International Education (IIE), permitted 22 Kenyans to study in the United States between 1948 and 1953.[59]

---

[57] KNA, Nairobi. ED/3/3161. *A Bow Group Pamphlet*, 11.

[58] PRO, London. CO/537/4312, 20 July 1949.

[59] Kenneth King, *Panafricanism and Education: A Study of Race Philanthropy and Education in the Southern States of America and East Africa* (Oxford: Clarendon Press, 1971); Ade Ajayi, *The American Factor in the Development of Higher Education in Africa* (Los Angeles: University of California, 1988); John C. Stoner, "Anti-communism, Anti-colonialism and African Labor, the AFL-CIO, 1955–1975," Ph.D. thesis, Columbia University, 2000; Charton, *La naissance ambiguë*; Robert F. Stephens, *Kenyan Student*

Great Britain closely followed these initiatives and, in 1947, named a Colonial Attaché to the British Embassy in Washington to support colonial students, that is, the British Information Service (BIS), created the previous year, tasked to disseminate British colonial propaganda on American soil. However, despite its efforts, London did not manage to take control of the Committee on Africans studying in North America (CASNA), created in 1946 to coordinate the actions of the Colonial Office, colonial governments, and American organizations interested in colonial students in America. In 1949, its activities were attached to the IIE, which fulfilled the same welcoming and information missions for colonial students in the United States as did the British Council in Great Britain.[60] From 1945 onward, the institute published and distributed an information guide for foreign students entitled: *Meet the US, Handbook for Foreign Students and Specialists*.

Colonial students were also of interest to newly independent countries like India. From 1947 onward, this young republic offered 70 scholarships to students from Commonwealth and British colonies, 30 of which were reserved for students of Indian origin and four for students from East African colonies. Thus, this new state intended to affirm its role as a role model and leader in the fight for the national liberation of countries still under colonial domination, while claiming a central place within the new Commonwealth.

The British authorities did not look at all kindly upon such initiatives since they were in direct competition with their own strategies for controlling and integrating colonial students.[61] They also had to deal with resistance from some colonial governments that were trying to obstruct the implementation of modernization programs.

Airlifts to America 1959–1961: An Educational Odyssey (Nairobi: East African Publishers, 2013).

[60] Columbia University, Special collections, Archives of the Carnegie Corporation, Box 117, 10 January 1947, and note of 3 November 1949.

[61] PRO, London. CO/537/3646. *Report of the Information Services of Kenya*, November 1948.

Colonial Resistance

The reforms imposed by London, were received with considerable reluctance in Kenya, where the government strove to slow them or bypass them altogether. This was symptomatic of the dissonance between the reform-minded pragmatism of "War Time babies," based in London, and followers of an archaic colonial order that needed to be sacrificed to save the Empire. The historian Ronald Hyam interpreted this hiatus as a major factor in the fall of the British Empire.[62]

The Kenyan government rejected the global schedule suggested for these reforms, pleading that reforms should follow at the pace most suitable to each territory. For instance, the secretariat of the colony reminded everyone that, while certain families in West Africa already comprised (in 1944) three generations of graduates, the education of those in East Africa was only in its infancy. Makerere's changeover to a university was also vehemently denounced by the Kenyan Director of Education, who regretted the loss of the former professional school and deplored the development of general training when the colony, first and foremost, needed doctors, assistant veterinarians, and teachers.[63] All these criticisms were actually nurtured by the severe racism of a colonial order guaranteeing white hegemony that felt threatened by modernization projects. The Governor of Kenya, Sir Philip Mitchell, who had already served 37 years in the colonies, expressed the same feeling when he stated:

> Instead of facing the unhappy but at present undeniable facts of African dishonesty, unreliability, untruthfulness and sloth which are to—day among the major—perhaps they are the major—difficulties which confront us in Kenya, a pathetic and romantic picture is conjured out of the writers imaginations.[64]

The Principal of the Alliance High School (AHS), the main high school in Kenya, where the vast majority of Kenyan students were trained, never missed an opportunity to castigate the academic reforms designed in London. Carrey Francis virulently denounced the ambitions

---

[62] Ronald Hyam, *Britain's Declining Empire: The Road to Decolonisation, 1918–1968* (Cambridge: Cambridge University Press, 2006).

[63] KNA, Nairobi. ED/3/3181, 6 March 1944.

[64] PRO, London. CO/859/171/1, 19 May 1949.

of Makerere university which, in his view, inflated student pride and undermined the entire enterprise of colonial education in Kenya that he was promoting, which was based on obedience and submission to a basically racist colonial order. In his judgment, the team of young inexperienced teachers recruited for Makerere, without knowing anything of the realities of East Africa, encouraged dangerous practices, almost debauchery (e.g., in occasionally proposing a drop of sherry to students, which was a common practice in Great Britain at the time).[65] Refusing to consider the Africans as anything other than big school children, he could not accept that students at Makerere should be treated like British undergraduates. In fact, African teachers at AHS were paid one quarter the salary accorded their European colleagues, while trousers and shoes were banned in the name of preservation of traditional lifestyles. As for studies in Great Britain, he considered them both inappropriate and dangerous:

> The best educated Africans in Kenya—those who have obtained school certificates and especially those who have studied at Makerere—are seldom doing real work. This is to be deplored. The chief reason is that these men, instead of getting down to work, go to continual "courses" overseas. When one course is completed, they ask for another. Some courses are unsuitable, a waste of time or worse, a very great waste of money; because of them, men are kept from, and sometimes incapacitated for, the plain ordinary jobs which they might have done, and which so greatly need to be done. I know of no one who has clearly benefited from an overseas course. Some have clearly been harmed, some ruined. Even those who are unsuccessful in getting overseas are damaged; they long to go and their minds are taken from their work.[66]

These lines reveal how much this perspective, steeped in the racist paternalism of Carey Francis, who for over twenty years, trained the educated elite of the colony, was so far removed from approaches underpinning modernization programs. Unable to block them, the colonial authorities tried to bypass them, by controlling the activities of students in the home country.

---

[65] KNA, Nairobi. CNC/7/257. *Higher Education for Non-European Students in East Africa*, 28 August 1948.
[66] KNA, Nairobi. ED/1/2743, 30 December 1953.

Worried about the living and studying conditions of African students, and more specifically about the "bad influences" to which they might be exposed, the Government of Kenya soon asked for the creation of a position of Supervisor of African Bursars.[67] The Colonial Office rejected such a demand based on racial distinctions, and suggested naming a liaison agent (following the example of the Gold Coast and Nigeria since 1946)[68] for all students from East Africa. The officer in charge was chosen for his good knowledge of Kenya's social environment and his capacity to defend colonial interests against the Colonial Office, all while being capable of gaining the confidence of students, so as to exercise a "positive influence" over them. The liaison officer was actually caught between the contradictory requirements of the colonial government and the Colonial Office. He was to submit quarterly reports to colonial authorities about student progress and lifestyle as well as the company students kept, and was encouraged to make regular contact with them. For students, he represented merely a spying government agent; one of them frankly told him that there was something sinister about his job.[69]

Despite all the Colonial Office's efforts, colonial racism sometimes expressed itself in the home country, for example, during the inauguration, accompanied by great fanfare, of East African House in London in 1951. This club was in fact very restricted, at the time having only 6 Africans amongst its 720 mostly European members.[70] For African students, it was hard to differentiate between the policies of colonial governments and those of the Colonial Office. In their publications, members of the Kenya African Students Association continuously denounced the violent repression of the Mau Mau in Kenya during its state of emergency and, especially, the propaganda disseminated to justify such violence.[71] Examples from the Gold Coast, Malaysia, and Kenya all demonstrated the same degree of brutality, and were actually underscoring the schizophrenic nature of the modernization policies of the British Empire.

[67] PRO, London. CO/537/4270, 6 April 1949.
[68] PRO, London. CO/537/1222.
[69] PRO, London. CO/537/4270, March 1949.
[70] KNA, Nairobi. ED/1/2297, 20 July 1951.
[71] KNA, Nairobi. ED/1/2295, October 1955.

Conclusion

Higher education programs, which were thought of as imperial modernization instruments, certainly contributed to the creation of an educated African elite. However, they seemed to have failed to bring together an imperial community, embodied in these new elites. When they returned to Kenya, students confronted the inertia and racism of a conservative colonial society. They were also sometimes cruelly faced with direct competition from a new wave of expatriates sent to the colonies to implement social and economic modernization programs. Thus, the number of Europeans established in Kenya rose from 30,000 to 50,000 between 1948 and 1952. These employees were hired by international companies or by the administration, and occupied posts that should have theoretically been available to the new African educated elites. Such a situation accentuated the pressure on an already tight labor market.

Above all, such programs revealed the limitations and paradoxes of post-war modernization policies. The persistence of racial hierarchies and differentiated treatment in certain colonies like Kenya, stemming from unabashed racist paternalism, contradicted the spirit of post-war reforms. Indeed, these voluntarist programs aimed to put a new face on the Empire, backed by a community of interests, of history, and of values which would relegate racial distinctions to the backburner, and for which the educated Africans, emblematic figures of this modernity, were to spearhead. The mitigated success of these reforms, contested on all fronts, ultimately revealed that it was certainly easier to reform the idea of the Empire than to reform the Empire itself.

Bibliography

Adi, Hakim. *West Africans in Britain 1900–1960, Nationalism, Panafricanism and Communism*. London: Lawrence and Wishart, 1998.

Ajayi, Ade J. F. *The American Factor in the Development of Higher Education in Africa*. Los Angeles: University of California, 1988.

———. *The African Experience with Higher Education*. London: James Currey, 1996.

Ashby, Eric X. *African Universities and Western Tradition*. London: Oxford University Press, 1964.

———. *British, Indians, African Universities: A Study in the Ecology of Higher Education*. London: Weidenfeld and Nicolson, 1966.

Awenengo Dalberto, Séverine, Hélène Charton, and Odile Goerg. "Urban Planning, Housing, and the Making of 'Responsible Citizens' in the Late Colonial Period: Dakar, Nairobi, Conakry." In *Governing Cities in Africa: Politics and Policies*, edited by Simon Becker and Laurent Fourchard, 43–64. Cape Town: HSRC Press, 2013.

Bartenev, Vladimir. "L'URSS et l'Afrique noire sous Khrouchtchev: la mise à jour des mythes de la coopération." *Outre-mers* 354–355 (2007): 63–82.

Barthélémy, Pascale. *Africaines et diplômées à l'époque coloniale (1918–1957)*. Rennes: Presses universitaires de Rennes, 2010.

Charton, Hélène. "La genèse ambiguë de l'élite kenyane, origine, formation et intégration, de 1945 à l'indépendance." Ph.D. dissertation, Université Paris 7—Denis Diderot, 2002.

———. "Homo Africanus academicus. Les limites de la fabrique d'une élite universitaire africaine en Afrique de l'Est." *Outre-Mers, Revue d'histoire* 394–395 (2017): 127–148.

———. "Produits d'Empires: expériences universitaires coloniales britanniques et françaises en Asie et en Afrique aux XIXe et XXe siècles." *Outre-Mers, Revue d'histoire* 394–395 (2017): 5–13.

Cooper, Frederick. *Decolonization and African Society: The Labour Question in French and British Africa*. Cambridge: Cambridge University Press, 1996.

———. *Colonialism in Question: Theory, Knowledge, History*. Berkeley: University of California Press, 2005.

———. *Citizenship Between Empire and Nation*. Princeton: Princeton University Press, 2014.

Darwin, John. *The Empire Project: The Rise and Fall of the British World System, 1830–1970*. Cambridge: Cambridge University Press, 2009.

de Busen, Bernard. *Adventures in Education*. London: Titus Wilson Kendal, 1995.

de Saint Martin, Monique, Grazia Scarfò Ghellab, and Kamal Mellakh (dir.). *Étudier à l'Est. Expériences de diplômés africains*. Paris: Karthala, 2015.

Gifford, Posser, and William Roger Louis, eds. *The Transfer of Power in Africa: Decolonization 1940–1960*. Harvard: Harvard University Press, 1982.

Goodman, Joyce, Gary McCulloch, and William Richardson. "'Empires Overseas' and 'Empires at Home' Postcolonial and Transnational Perspectives on Social Change in the History of Education." *Paedagogica Historica* 45 (2009): 695–706.

Hall, Catherine. *Cultures of Empire: Colonizers in Britain and the Empire in the Nineteenth and Twentieth Centuries: A Reader*. Manchester: Manchester University Press, 2000.

Hall, Catherine, and Sonya O. Rose, eds. *At Home with the Empire: Metropolitan Culture and the Imperial World*. Cambridge: Cambridge University Press, 2006.

Hargreaves, John D. "The Idea of a Colonial University." *African Affairs* 72 (1973): 26–36.
Hobsbawm, Eric, and Terence Ranger, eds. *The Invention of Tradition.* Cambridge: Cambridge University Press, 2006.
Hyam, Ronald. *Britain's Declining Empire: The Road to Decolonisation, 1918–1968.* Cambridge: Cambridge University Press, 2006.
Kallaway, Peter, and Rebecca Swartz, eds. *Empire and Education: The Shaping of a Comparative Perspective.* New York: Peter Lang, 2016.
Kastakioris, Constantin. "Transferts Est-Sud. Échanges éducatifs et formation de cadres africains en Union soviétique pendant les années soixante." *Outre-mers* 354–355 (2007): 83–106.
King, Kenneth. *Panafricanism and Education: A Study of Race Philanthropy and Education in the Southern States of America and East Africa.* Oxford: Clarendon Press, 1971.
Leney, Katia. *Decolonisation, Independence and the Politics of Higher Education in West Africa.* London: Edwin Mellen Press, 2003.
Lewis, Johanna. *Empire State Building: War and Welfare in Kenya 1925–52.* Oxford: James Currey, 2000.
Louis, William Roger. "American Anti-colonialism and the Dissolution of the British Empire." *International Affairs* 61, no. 3 (1985): 395–420.
Macpherson, Margaret. *They Built for the Future: A Chronicle of Makerere College 1922–1962.* Cambridge: Cambridge University Press, 1964.
Mangan, James Anthony, ed. *Benefits Bestowed, Education and British Imperialism.* Manchester: Manchester University Press, 1988.
Michel, Marc. *Décolonisations et émergence du tiers-monde.* Paris: Hachette, 1993.
Nwauwa, Apollo O. *Imperialism, Academe and Nationalism: Britain and University Education for Africans 1860–1960.* London: Frank Cass, 1997.
Olusanya, Gabriel Olakunle. *The West African Students Union and the Politics of Decolonization, 1935–1958.* Ibadan: Daystar Press, 1982.
Pietsch, Tamson. *Empire of Scholars, Universities, Networks and the British Academic World (1850–1939).* Manchester: Manchester University Press, 2013.
Sicherman, Carol. *Becoming an African University. Makerere 1922–2000.* Trenton: Africa World Press, 2005.
Stephens, Robert F. *Kenyan Student Airlifts to America 1959–1961: An Educational Odyssey.* Nairobi: East African publishers, 2013.
Stoler, Ann Laura, and Frederick Cooper, eds. *Tensions of Empire: Colonial Cultures in a Bourgeois World.* Berkeley: California Press, 1997.
Stoner, John C. "Anti-communism, Anti-colonialism and African Labor, the AFL-CIO, 1955–1975." Ph.D. dissertation, Columbia University, 2000.
Westad, Ode Arne. *The Global Cold War: Third World Interventions and the Making of Our Times.* New York: Cambridge University Press, 2005.
Yengo, Patrice, and Monique de Saint-Martin. "Quelles contributions des élites 'rouges' au façonnement des États post-coloniaux?" 226 (2017): 231–258.

Open Access This chapter is licensed under the terms of the Creative Commons Attribution 4.0 International License (http://creativecommons.org/licenses/by/4.0/), which permits use, sharing, adaptation, distribution and reproduction in any medium or format, as long as you give appropriate credit to the original author(s) and the source, provide a link to the Creative Commons license and indicate if changes were made.

The images or other third party material in this chapter are included in the chapter's Creative Commons license, unless indicated otherwise in a credit line to the material. If material is not included in the chapter's Creative Commons license and your intended use is not permitted by statutory regulation or exceeds the permitted use, you will need to obtain permission directly from the copyright holder.

CHAPTER 11

Exploring "Socialist Solidarity" in Higher Education: East German Advisors in Post-Independence Mozambique (1975–1992)

Alexandra Piepiorka

On the eve of its independence, Mozambique was among the last of the colonial territories in Africa. After the proclamation of the People's Republic of Mozambique by the liberation movement FRELIMO (Mozambican Liberation Front) in 1975, it gradually became evident

---

The findings presented here are derived from the research project "Globalization of an Educational Idea: Workers' Faculties in Cuba, Mozambique and Vietnam" at Giessen University (2013–2017), carried out by Prof. Dr. Ingrid Miethe. See https://www.uni-giessen.de/fbz/fb03/institute/ifezw/prof/allgemeine/forschung/globfak.

A. Piepiorka (✉)
University of Giessen, Giessen, Germany
e-mail: Alexandra.Piepiorka@erziehung.uni-giessen.de

that Mozambique's new government would follow a socialist path.[1] However, material and financial resources, as well as qualified national cadres, to contribute to the envisioned post-independence development were scarce.[2] Popular hopes for economic progress and social advancement were high after independence, and education was politically perceived as the driving force for social and economic progress.[3] Tragically though, its educational institutions were lacking the skilled personnel required to train Mozambican citizens.[4] To overcome this educational shortcoming, largely inherited from the colonial era, the FRELIMO government chose to build upon its own experiences in popular education, as initiated during the struggle for independence. Moreover, the government also heavily relied on foreign aid for education, preferentially—but never exclusively—from socialist countries.[5] Subsequently, socialist aid agencies from all over the world offered to play a role in Mozambique's educational history as well as in the running of its only institution of higher learning, the *Eduardo-Mondlane-University* (Universidade Eduardo Mondlane—UEM). Within the socialist bloc, the German Democratic Republic (GDR) was one of the major providers of so-called "socialist solidarity" to Mozambique, especially in the arena of education.[6] Accordingly, numerous East German aid workers took up "solidarity" tasks at the UEM in the 1970s and 1980s.

This chapter seeks to retrace the spirit of "socialist solidarity" in the context of educational aid, dwelling on the historical example of cooperation in higher education between Mozambique and the GDR during the first decades of Mozambican independence. The concept of

[1] Malyn Newitt, *A Short History of Mozambique* (London: Hurst & Company, 2017), 154–155.

[2] Michael Cross, *An Unfulfilled Promise: Transforming Schools in Mozambique* (Addis Ababa: Organization for Social Science Research in Eastern and Southern Africa, OSSREA, 2011), 61.

[3] Anton Johnston, "Adult Literacy and Development in Mozambique," *African Studies Review* 33, no. 3 (1990): 83–96.

[4] Barbara Barnes, "Education for Socialism in Mozambique," *Comparative Education Review* 26, no. 3 (1982): 441; also see Anton Johnston, "The Mozambican State and Education," in *Education and Social Transition in the Third World*, ed. by Martin Carnoy and Joel Samoff (Princeton/Oxford: Princeton University Press, 1990), 306–307.

[5] Cross, *An Unfulfilled Promise*, 50–59, 74.

[6] Tanja Müller, *Legacies of Socialist Solidarity: East-Germany in Mozambique* (London/New York: Lexington, 2014).

"socialist solidarity" from the East German perspective was generally "based on solidarity combined with what in official parlance was called cooperation for mutual advantage"[7] in relation to countries following a socialist path of development. This implied a complex mixture of ideological, economic, and developmentalist goals in GDR–Mozambican cooperation.[8] Accordingly, educational aid offered to Mozambican partners was of little material benefit to the GDR initially—it was rather meant to foster "an 'emotional disposition' towards socialism in general and the GDR in particular"[9] in Mozambican minds, which in turn was meant to prepare the ground for envisioned economic ties between the two parties. At the same time, solidarity engagement in developing countries played an intriguing role in the GDR's self-perception as an internationally acknowledged socialist player in the Cold War world, and seemingly contributed to foster a corresponding feeling of pride in GDR citizens, many of whom shared "a strong belief in a more just and equitable world order."[10]

Although the abovementioned socialist aid endeavors surely marked the post-independence development of education in Mozambique, scientific knowledge about the actual scope and day-to-day practices of Euro-socialist engagement in southern African higher education is still limited. As part of the current research on foreign aid experts and their possible impact on African education, a study conducted by Koch and Weingart was instructive. Yet, Koch and Weingart's focal interest did not reside in the history of socialist aid endeavors.[11] This is true for most of the literature reviewed. An inspiring exception is the concept of (post-)socialism as discussed in the field of comparative education, which has been introduced to re-evaluate (post-)socialist educational transfers within the (former) Socialist "Bloc," and also with reference to Africa.[12]

---

[7] Ibid., 24.

[8] Hans-Joachim Döring, *"Es geht um unsere Existenz"*. *Die Politik der DDR gegenüber der Dritten Welt am Beispiel von Mosambik und Äthiopien* (Berlin: Ch. Links, 1999).

[9] Müller, *Legacies*, 27.

[10] Ibid., 26.

[11] Susanne Koch and Peter Weingart, *Delusion of Knowledge Transfer: The Impact of Foreign Aid Experts on Policy-Making in South Africa and Tanzania* (Stellenbosch, SA: African Minds, 2016).

[12] Iveta Silova, *Post-Socialism Is Not Dead: (Re)Reading the Global in Comparative Education* (Bingley: Emerald, 2010); Diane Brook Napier, "African Socialism, Post-Colonial Development, and Education: Change and Continuity in the Post-Socialist Era," in ibid., 369–399.

Recently, a corresponding strand of research has focused on student experience and personal accounts of socialist education, thereby contributing an actor-centered perspective to the (post-)socialist discourse prevalent in history of education and educational sciences (for a detailed case study, see Chapter 8 by Eric Burton in this book).[13] Moreover, sophisticated historical studies on GDR–Mozambican cooperation in the educational sector do exist, but reviewed studies mostly concentrate on educational aid projects located within the GDR, like the "School of Friendship" (*Schule der Freundschaft*) in Stassfurt.[14] For an overview of GDR–Mozambican cooperation and the official motifs of the GDR's educational aid toward Mozambique, studies by Müller and Döring prove insightful,[15] as do some studies published in the GDR.[16] Besides this, publications by former GDR aid workers have been consulted, even though these sources contain rather personal descriptions of work in Mozambique, with only a fraction of publications concentrating on the education sector.[17]

Summing up I would argue that overall visibility appears to lean toward the East German perspective, as a donor country, in research

---

[13] Iveta Silova, Nelli Piattoeva, and Zsuzsa Millei, *Childhood and Schooling in (Post)Socialist Societies: Memories of Everyday Life* (Cham: Springer, 2018).

[14] Lutz R. Reuter and Annette Scheunpflug, *Die Schule der Freundschaft. Eine Fallstudie zur Bildungszusammenarbeit zwischen der DDR und Mosambik* (Münster: Waxmann, 2006); Jane Schuch, *Mosambik im pädagogischen Raum der DDR. Eine bildanalytische Studie zur 'Schule der Freundschaft' in Staßfurt* (Wiesbaden: Springer, 2013); Jason Verber, "True to the Politics of Frelimo? Teaching Socialism at the *Schule der Freundschaft*, 1981–1990," in *Comrades of Color: East Germany in the Cold War World*, ed. by Quinn Slobodian (Oxford/New York: Berghahn, 2015), 188–210.

[15] Hans Mathias Müller, *Die Bildungshilfe der Deutschen Demokratischen Republik* (Frankfurt: Peter Lang, 1995); Döring, "*Es geht um unsere.*"

[16] Klaus Willerding, "Zur Afrika-Politik der DDR," *Deutsche Aussenpolitik* 24, no. 8 (1979): 5–19; Rosemarie Lewin et al., *Die Herausbildung eines nationalen höheren Bildungswesens in Ländern mit sozialistischem Entwicklungsweg* (Berlin: Zentralinstitut für Hochschulbildung, 1986).

[17] Matthias Voß, *Wir haben Spuren hinterlassen! Die DDR in Mosambik. Erlebnisse, Erfahrungen und Erkenntnisse aus drei Jahrzehnten* (Münster: LIT, 2005); Rainer Grajek, *Berichte aus dem Morgengrauen. Als Entwicklungshelfer der DDR in Mosambik* (Grimma: Ute Vallentin, 2005); Helmut Dora, *Kokos und bitterer Tee. Tage und Nächte in Mosambik* (Rostock: BS-Verlag, 2009).

concerned with the GDR's involvement in Africa. This perspectival imbalance will be perpetuated in this chapter, because the views of donors on development processes in Mozambique seem relatively well documented and accessible for matters of research.[18] In comparison, the perspectives of Mozambican counterparts, involved in the East German "solidarity" project in Mozambique, are less overtly expressed in the historical documents evaluated. Keeping this in mind, I will try to highlight reciprocal exchanges between Mozambican and East German actors whenever possible.

This case study seeks to contribute to the further exploration of historical trajectories of East German "socialist solidarity" at the UEM. Historical sources for the analysis were collected from archives in Germany (*Bundesarchiv*, BArch) and Mozambique (*Arquivo Histórico de Moçambique*, AHM),[19] as well as from interviews with contemporaries from the former GDR and Mozambique.[20] In the following sections I will first examine the relevance of "socialist solidarity" for educational cooperation between East Germany and Mozambique. Second, I will summarize FRELIMO'S vision of the post-independence development in higher education, and then contrast it by reviewing the GDR's educational aid agenda for higher education in Mozambique. Third, I will retrace the everyday practices of GDR teaching staff at the UEM by offering micro-insights into their work. Finally, I will draw conclusions on East German "solidarity" engagement in Mozambique's higher education sector, relying on the empirical material presented in the chapter.

---

[18] A rich body of East German reports on GDR–Mozambican cooperation in Maputo was obtained from the Federal Archive (BArch). For further information on GDR expatriate cadres, see Astrid Hedin, "Die Reiseorganisation der Hochschulen der DDR. Ein Reisekadersystem sowjetischen Typus," in *Die DDR in Europa – zwischen Isolation und Öffnung*, ed. by Heiner Timmermann (Münster: LIT, 2005), 280–290; Jens Niederhut, *Die Reisekader. Auswahl und Disziplinierung einer privilegierten Minderheit in der DDR* (Leipzig: Evangelische Verlagsanstalt, 2005), esp. pp. 115–130.

[19] All consulted archive holdings were not paginated. All quotations from documents translated by author.

[20] Ten semi-structured interviews were conducted in Riesa (2013), Rostock, Lisbon, Maputo (2014), and Berlin (2015). All interviewees worked at the UEM during the 1970s and 1980s. All quotations from interviews translated by author.

How Does "Socialist Solidarity" Integrate into the Mozambican History of Education?

To evaluate the aid provided by the GDR to Mozambique it is useful to assess the notion of "solidarity" inherent in the East German concept of aid.[21] In general terms, the East German aid provided to developing countries was related to the concept of "antiimperialist solidarity," and was formally defined in opposition to the non-socialist concept of "development aid," current in the Western world.[22] From the GDR's point of view, Western aid endeavors resembled international dominance between the wealthy and industrialized countries in the North and West and the poorer, less developed countries of the Southern Hemisphere, ultimately leading to new dependencies on capitalist goods and services (imperialism), and not to independent (socialist) development.[23] Accordingly, GDR officials were keen to emphasize the concept of "mutual benefit" and "socialist solidarity" in reference to foreign trade relations, rather than highlight economic motifs.[24] Moreover, the GDR was offering a range of partly cost-free education and training programs to socialist-orientated partners in the framework of "solidarity," both in the GDR and befriended developing countries.[25] For the most part however, both variants of aid pursued goals linked to the modernization of recipient countries, and almost unanimously, in most African countries, promises connected to

---

[21] Article 6 of the GDR constitution established a solidarity-driven mode of conduct in relation to countries and nations struggling against colonialism or imperialism, see Döring, "*Es geht um unsere,*" 37.

[22] Berthold Unfried, "Instrumente und Praktiken von 'Solidarität' Ost und 'Entwicklungshilfe' West: Blickpunkt auf das entsandte Personal," in *Create One World. Practices of 'International Solidarity' and 'International Development'*, ed. by Berthold Unfried and Eva Himmelstoss (Wien: Akademische Verlagsanstalt, 2012), 73–98.

[23] Maria Magdalena Verburg, *Ostdeutsche Dritte-Welt-Gruppen vor und nach 1989/90* (Göttingen: V&R unipress, 2012), 21–24.

[24] Whether GDR's foreign trade relations were liberal in motive or dominant toward developing countries is a contested question in German historiography; e.g., compare the perspectives of Ulrich van der Heyden, *GRD Development Policy in Africa: Doctrine and Strategies Between Illusions and Reality, 1960–1990: The Example (South) Africa* (Münster: LIT, 2013) and the rather critical account by Verburg, *Ostdeutsche Dritte-Welt-Gruppen*, 30–31.

[25] Verburg, *Ostdeutsche Dritte-Welt-Gruppen*, 25–27.

(European) modernity were integrated into the overall imaginary of post-independence development by local governments.[26]

While belief in progress was true for both capitalist- and socialist-aligned countries in Africa, a set of designated features characterized socialist-orientated states. Extended discussions on the scope of socialist development and modernity in Africa have been conducted elsewhere.[27] Therefore, for our context a brief summary of the Mozambican vision of socialist modernity shall be sufficient: "FRELIMO opted for a modernization project that entailed mechanization of farming, collectivization of peasant production through communal villages (*aldeias communais*), spread of industries and an expansion of the commercial network in the countryside. The success of such project, it was argued, depended on universal literacy. Literacy campaigns were undertaken at the national level with a great deal of enthusiasm."[28] Such enthusiastic development plans, however, were affected by exigencies of the "transition state"[29] in the aftermath of colonialism, and correspondingly the burden to deal with colonial legacies in education was a major challenge for most new governments across Africa. In dealing with this burden, African governments often chose to link development plans to school expansion plans in the transitional phase following independence. This was especially true for governments that opted for socialism: "The revolutionary state generally makes mass basic education its first priority because those peasants and workers and their children who have been denied access to such schooling are potentially the most important supporters of transition reforms."[30] But simultaneously, state bureaucracy and economy registered a high demand for qualified cadres, so that higher and technical education became equally crucial for socialist development policies, since

---

[26] Hubertus Büschel, "In Afrika helfen. Akteure westdeutscher 'Entwicklungshilfe' und ostdeutscher 'Solidarität' 1955–1975," in *Dekolonisation. Prozesse und Verflechtungen 1945–1990*, ed. by Anja Kruke (Bonn: Dietz, 2009), 333–365; Unfried, "Instrumente und Praktiken"; Verburg, *Ostdeutsche Dritte-Welt-Gruppen*, 30.

[27] Elíso Salvado Macamo, *Negotiating Modernity: Africa's Ambivalent Experience* (London/New York: ZED, 2005); Napier, "African Socialism."

[28] Cross, *Unfulfilled Promise*, 70.

[29] Martin Carnoy, "Education and the Transition State," in *Education and Social Transition in the Third World*, ed. by Marin Carnoy and Joel Samoff (Princeton: Princeton University Press, 1990), 63–96.

[30] Ibid., 81.

skilled personnel were "more directly related to capital accumulation and filling short-term needs for administrative cadres."[31] The balancing act between educational expansions at different levels was momentous for Mozambique's post-independence development—actually this quest has not lost its relevance in present-day Mozambique.[32]

Another feature in Frelimo's strategy of coping with its past in terms of education, was its wish to overcome certain traditions—those stemming from its colonial past as well as other certain African traditions. In this context, Frelimo opted for a modernity-driven discourse that would reflect Euro-socialist societal standards, composed of "'modern' norms and values, including the ideal of the nuclear family, monogamy, scientific knowledge, and rationality,"[33] in a somewhat idealized manner. In accordance with this, from the point of view of a (Swedish) foreign aid agency, the Mozambican education sector in the 1980s was described as "a 'modern', job-intensive sector, which provides employment for thousands of teachers, administrators and subsidiary personnel of all kinds."[34] In how far this post-independence development in education was triggered by foreign-induced impulses, stemming from "socialist solidarity," shall be discussed in the following text.

While the Mozambican government was struggling to redesign the post-colonial state apparatus and the social system, the wider context of the Cold War gained relevance to the local context. Referring explicitly to higher education, Katsakioris highlights that "with decolonialization, higher education became one of the most important issues in

---

[31] Ibid., 82.

[32] Cross, *Unfulfilled Promise*, 75–78; José Manuel Flores, *Das Problem der gleichzeitigen Sicherung von Bildungsbeteiligung und Bildungsqualität in Mosambik. Kritische Rekonstruktion einer bildungspolitischen Entscheidung und ihrer Folgen* (Hamburg: Dr. Kovač, 2014).

[33] Esther Miedema, "'Let's Move, Let's Not Remain Stagnant': Nationalism, Masculinism, and School-Based Education in Mozambique," in *Childhood and Nation: Interdisciplinary Engagements*, ed. by Zsuzsa Millei and Robert Imre (New York: Palgrave Macmillan, 2015), 189.

[34] Anton Johnston et al., *Education and Economic Crisis: The Cases of Mozambique and Zambia* (Stockholm: SIDA, 1987), 33.

the international culture politics of the global Cold War."[35] In their competition for "soft" or cultural influence on the African continent, educational actors and agencies of both ideological camps agitated in the field of African education and interfered in local development discourses.[36] In this framework, and with the explicit intent to support socialist development in Mozambique, the GDR delivered "solidarity" services to the Mozambican education sector in the 1970s and 1980s, ranging from the printing of schoolbooks to the training of Mozambican cadres in GDR institutions. Such services were embedded in bilateral agreements[37] and included sending GDR cadres to Mozambique where they worked as educational advisors for the Ministry of Education, as schoolteachers, curriculum planners, or lecturers at university.[38] For the higher education sector, estimations suggest that about 115 lecturers from the GDR alone worked at the UEM during the period between 1976 and 1989,[39] while many other socialist *cooperantes*[40] from the East and West collaborated.

[35] Constantin Katsakioris, "Creating a Socialist Intelligentsia: Soviet Educational Aid and Its Impact on Africa, 1960–1991," *Cahiers d'études africaines*, no. 226 (2017): 260.

[36] Gita Steiner-Khamsi, "The Development Turn in Comparative Education," *European Education* 38, no. 3 (2006): 19–47; Hubertus Büschel and Daniel Speich, *Entwicklungswelten. Globalgeschichte der Entwicklungszusammenarbeit* (Campus: Frankfurt, 2009); Ragna Boden, "Globalisierung sowjetisch: Der Kulturtransfer in die Dritte Welt," in *Globalisierung imperial und sozialistisch*, ed. by Martin Aust (Frankfurt: Campus, 2013), 425–442.

[37] The agreement on cultural and scientific cooperation between the GDR and Mozambique entered into force on 23 September 1976 (BArch DR3/21775).

[38] Müller, *Bildungshilfe*; Matthias Tullner, "Die Zusammenarbeit der DDR und Mosambiks auf dem Gebiet der Bildung und die Tätigkeit der Bildungsexperten der DDR in Mosambik," in *Wir haben Spuren hinterlassen! Die DDR in Mosambik. Erlebnisse, Erfahrungen und Erkenntnisse aus drei Jahrzehnten*, ed. by Matthias Voß (Münster: LIT, 2005), 399.

[39] Holger Hegewald, "Berlin, Maputo und zurück – Dozent an der Eduardo-Mondlane-Universität 1989–1990," in *Wir haben Spuren hinterlassen!* ed. by Matthias Voß, 471.

[40] The term "*cooperante*" was a current label for foreign aid workers in Mozambique and was applicable for expatriates from socialist countries as well as from Western Europe, the United States, Canada, or Nordic countries, see Allen and Barbara Isaacman, *Mozambique: From Colonialism to Revolution, 1900–1982* (Boulder: Westview Press, 1993), 185.

Mozambican Ideas for Post-Independence Development in Higher Education

The vision of development through education that the FRELIMO government chose to pursue was deeply intertwined with the country's colonial past. Considering that at the time of independence more than 90% of the Mozambican population were illiterate,[41] educational policy primarily concentrated on countrywide literacy campaigns for children and adults to address the overwhelming patterns of exclusion inherited from the colonial education system.[42] With regard to under-representation in higher education, it might be helpful to note that, although in 1970 about 98% of Mozambique's population were of African origin,[43] by 1975 only 1–2% of university students were African.[44] Such figures illustrate the unequal access to higher education that existed during the colonial period, resulting in a severe lack of academically and technically qualified Mozambican cadres. In addition, the colonial administration and economy had heavily relied on Portuguese and immigrant personnel to fulfil leadership positions. This meant that the FRELIMO government inherited a state apparatus with mostly underqualified Mozambican cadres in 1975. Furthermore, by 1976 about 200,000–250,000 Portuguese citizens left the country, resulting in a dramatic loss of expertise and technical knowledge in the young nation state's administration and economy.[45] Consequently, the

---

[41] Estimations range from 85 to 97% of the population, see Barnes, "Education for Socialism," 406; Mário Mouzinho and Deborah Nandja, "Literacy in Mozambique: Education for all Challenges," paper commissioned for the "Education for All" (EFA) Global Monitoring Report 2006, Paris: UNESCO; Maputo: UEM, Faculty of Education, http://unesdoc.unesco.org/images/0014/001462/146284e.pdf.

[42] Agneta Lind, *Adult Literacy Lessons and Promises: The Mozambican Literacy Campaigns, 1978-1982* (Stockholm: Institute of International Education, 1988).

[43] The source reports that 2% of the population in Mozambique were "whites" in 1970 and mentions a decline of the white population after 1974–1975, to a level of 0.2% in 1983, see Statistisches Bundesamt, *Länderbericht Mosambik* (Stuttgart: Metzler-Poeschel, 1989), 23.

[44] Peter Fry and Rogério Utui, "Promoting Access, Quality and Capacity-Building in African Higher Education: The Strategic Planning Experience at the Eduardo Mondlane University" (Washington: ADEA Working Group on Higher Education, The World Bank, 1999), 2–3, http://www.adeanet.org/adea/publications/wghe/wghe_uem_en.pdf.

[45] Barnes, "Education for Socialism," 406; Statistisches Bundesamt, *Länderbericht*, 18; Newitt, *Short History*, 151.

lack of local clerks and functionaries became a major problem facing the state-building process after independence, and a key obstacle to the prosperous development envisioned by FRELIMO.

In response to this twofold colonial legacy, FRELIMO's priority was the education of a national intelligentsia, alongside the general goal of introducing education for all.[46] Education was perceived as a prerequisite to securing national independence; this somewhat heroic stance on education was vividly demonstrated in slogans like "study, combat, produce!"[47] Unfortunately, FRELIMO had to build up its leadership cadres and "prepare the 'working class for the control of the economy' [...] without an adequate social base,"[48] while facing a serious lack of financial resources. In such a situation, FRELIMO resolved to rely on the experience it gained during its struggle for independence from Portugal (1964–1974), during which, the areas under its control (*zonas libertadas*) successfully introduced an embryonic education system for liberation fighters and their children.[49] Besides this experience for self-reliance[50] in education, FRELIMO relied on educational aid from socialist states, as well as from supporting actors from around the non-socialist world, to realize its educational goals.[51]

Gradually, nationwide educational policies were introduced by the FRELIMO government, starting with the nationalization of all educational institutions as decreed in September 1975, and followed by the foundation of the Mozambican Education Ministry (MEC), which

---

[46] Johnston, *Mozambican State*.

[47] Anthon Johnston, *Study, Produce, and Combat! Education and the Mozambican State 1962–1984* (Stockhom: Institute of International Education, University of Stockholm, 1989).

[48] Cross, *Unfulfilled Promise*, 61.

[49] Johnston, *Mozambican State*, 280–282; Salvador André Zawangoni, *A FRELIMO e a Formação do Homem Novo, 1964–1974 e 1975–1982* (Maputo: CIEDIMA, 2007).

[50] The first FRELIMO-led schools were run by exiles in Tanzania, and FRELIMO's struggle for independence benefited from the generous hospitality that the Tanzanian government granted to anti-imperialist liberation movements. Therefore, it is likely that FRELIMO educators were at least partly inspired by the concept of African *self-reliance*, as propagated by the Tanzanian president Nyerere; see Cross, *Unfulfilled Promise*, 52–53, 61–62.

[51] José P. Castiano, *Das Bildungssystem in Mosambik (1974–1966): Entwicklungen, Probleme und Konsequenzen* (Hamburg: Institut für Afrika-Kunde, 1997), 128.

started to function in February 1976.[52] In May 1976, the country's only institution of higher learning was renamed *Eduardo Mondlane University* (UEM), after the founding member and first president of FRELIMO.[53] A year later, the decision for socialism as a state ideology was officially confirmed during the III FRELIMO Congress, during which FRELIMO turned from a liberation movement into a "vanguard party" (called the Frelimo Party) with a Marxist–Leninist political orientation.[54] As a consequence of the congress of 1977, "Education for Socialism"[55] became the leitmotif in the following orchestration of educational policies. Nevertheless, in 1979 the majority of students in most UEM faculties still originated from middle-class backgrounds[56]; in the mid-1980s only about 11% of university students were from families with worker–peasant backgrounds.[57] These statistics did not fit the socialist outlook of the university as planned by the Frelimo Party, because it was doubted that middle-class members would support Frelimo's path of socialist development. To counteract trends labeled as "petit bourgeois" at the UEM, Frelimo introduced regulations favoring students with worker–peasant backgrounds for entry to university, hoping that they would naturally align themselves with the socialist project.[58] Thus, the educational goals set by Frelimo involved "an education system to cater for workers and their children at all levels, the development of an education system at the service of society [...], and the breakdown of the barriers between theory

[52] Ibid., 85–86.

[53] The institution was founded in 1962 in the city of Lourenço Marques (today Maputo) and acquired the status of a university in 1968. The name of the colonial *University of Lourenço Marques* referred to a Portuguese "discoverer" of the sixteenth century. Therefore, the post-independence renaming of the university after a pioneer of the liberation struggle was as symbolic act highlighting the history of anticolonial resistance. See Frey and Utui, "Promoting Access," 2–3; Mouzinho Mário et al., *Higher Eduaction in Mozambique: A Case Study* (Oxford: James Currey; Maputo: Imprensa & Livraria Universitária UEM, 2003), 7.

[54] FRELIMO, "Ökonomische und soziale Direktiven," in *Dokumente des 3. Kongresses der FRELIMO*, ed. by Informationsstelle Südliches Afrika (Bonn: Issa, 1978), 139–190.

[55] Cross, *Unfulfilled Promise*, 76.

[56] See report "Halbjahresbericht 2/79 der DDR-Lehrkräfte an der Universität "Eduardo Mondlane" signed by Dora on 30 January 1980 (BArch/DR3/II.Schicht/1540).

[57] Lewin et al., *Die Herausbildung*, 43.

[58] FRELIMO, *Direktiven*, 187.

and practice or study and production."⁵⁹ These post-independence socialist goals were integrated into the first Mozambican national education system (*Sistema Nacional de Educação*, SNE), which only came into effect in 1983.⁶⁰

In the field of higher education, the SNE regulated that the UEM should, first and foremost, educate scientific and technical cadres to meet the demands of the state, economy, and society. The teaching conducted at the UEM was meant to contribute to the overall (socialist) development of the country, by providing politically, culturally, and not least ideologically educated graduates. Furthermore, Frelimo's development goals did materialize in the organizational structure of the UEM when, for instance, two new faculties were created: one exclusively devoted to the new state ideology of Marxism–Leninism, and another meant for the explicit qualification of adult students with worker–peasant backgrounds. Curiously, from 1983 onward, this later faculty was also in charge of training former FRELIMO fighters and experienced workers (worker students), who actually did not have an adequate educational background for entry to university.⁶¹ Another such exception was made for students applying for minor teacher-training courses at the Faculty of Education, where nine years of prior schooling was accepted as a pre-requisite to university entry.⁶² Despite offensives to promote university access, graduate numbers stagnated, while the demand for national and loyal cadres in state apparatus and state enterprises remained high throughout the post-independence period.⁶³

---

⁵⁹ Cross, *Unfulfilled Promise*, 76.

⁶⁰ For a detailed description of the post-independence development of Mozambique's education sector see Johnston, *Mozambican State*; Brazão Mazula, *Educação, Cultura e Ideologia em Moçambique: 1975–1985. Em busca de fundamentos filosófico-antropológicos* (Porto: Edições Afrontamento, 1995); Castiano, *Bildungssystem*; Buendía Miguel Gómez, *Educação Moçambicana. História de um processo: 1962–1984* (Maputo: Livraria Universitária, UEM, 1999); Cross, *Unfulfilled Promise*.

⁶¹ See leaflet "O que é o Curso Pré-Universitário da Faculdade de Antigos Combatentes e Trabalhadores de Vanguarda," UEM, Maputo, November 1985 (AHM/documentation Ganhão/box 16); Castiano, *Bildungssystem*, 112.

⁶² It was usually required to pass the 10th and 11th grade of regular schooling before entry to university. Ibid., 102.

⁶³ Anton Johnston, *Educação em Moçambique: 1975–1984* (Stockholm: SIDA, 1986).

Ironically enough, while the UEM was responsible for educating university-trained personnel, the university itself suffered from a severe lack of academic staff. To enhance national university staff qualifications, a practice of "training on the job" became widespread at the UEM; Mozambican assistants, so-called *monitores,* were included within the teaching staff. Such *monitores* were mostly undergraduate students of Mozambican origin, who were already delivering lectures to younger fellow students and assisting regular—mostly foreign—lecturers at the UEM.[64] In that light, the massive employment of foreign advisors and teaching staff served first as a relief mechanism to keep the university functioning, and second, contributed to the training of local UEM staff. This was especially true for the ad hoc qualification of national cadres, as exemplified in the case of Mozambican *monitores*. Nevertheless, by 1980 this employment policy led to a situation in which 79% of the teaching staff employed at the UEM were of foreign origin.[65] We will later see that the recruitment of foreign cooperators "had serious political and pedagogical implications"[66] for the whole education sector. Still, a partial success in the "Mozambicanization" process of UEM structures was reported by East German cooperators in 1981, when leadership of three university faculties was handed over to Mozambican cadres.[67] Details in East German reports reveal that the cooperators were well aware of their "mission" to improve the level of qualification of Mozambican staff; such reports also hint that East German cooperators perceived themselves as supportive colleagues at the UEM.

[64] Hegewald, "Berlin, Maputo," 470, 476.

[65] See statistical chart "Evolução dos docentes da UEM de 1980 a 1983" (BArch/DR3/II.Schicht/1539).

[66] Cross, *Unfulfilled Promise*, 74.

[67] See report "Halbjahresbericht I/1981, Bereich Gesellschaftswissenschaften" by the GDR teaching staff at the UEM, signed by Schlauch, Maputo, 10 June 1981 (BArch/DR3/II.Schicht/1540), concerning the following faculties: Law, Education, and Marxism–Leninism (p. 7).

East German Involvement in Mozambique's (Socialist) Development and International Cooperation in Higher Education

While exerting their "socialist solidarity" duties on campus, East German lecturers were formally embedded in a wider system of bilateral cooperation. Notably, educational cooperation between Mozambican and East German protagonists began during the struggle for liberation, namely in a FRELIMO school based in Tanzania set up by Mozambican exiles in 1967.[68] Before that, FRELIMO President Mondlane visited the GDR in 1966,[69] looking for support for Mozambican liberation.[70] FRELIMO was not yet a political party, but an anticolonial movement, therefore, an intergovernmental basis for regulating services of "socialist solidarity" was temporarily missing. Nevertheless, on behalf of GDR's "Solidarity Committee" (*Solidaritätskomitee*) a handful of GDR teachers and educational advisers were sent to Tanzania, and later to the "liberated zones" in northern Mozambique, to support FRELIMO's educational programs prior to independence.[71] Interestingly, at that time knowledge about Mozambique and the liberation movement FRELIMO was very limited in the GDR, illustrated by the East German authorities' uncertainty about Portuguese as lingua franca within FRELIMO.[72] The first GDR "expert" sent to a FRELIMO-run school,[73] for instance, only spoke

---

[68] For a more sophisticated report on this early stage of GDR–Mozambican cooperation in education see Hans-Jochen Roos, "Unterrichten unter Palmen. Als Biologielehrer an der FRELIMO-Schule in Bagamoyo," in *Wir haben Spuren hinterlassen!* ed. by Matthias Voß, 407–425.

[69] Tullner, "Zusammenarbeit," 389.

[70] During the liberation struggle, FRELIMO succeeded to mobilize a wide network of international supporters in socialist and non-socialist countries, and was engaged in the non-alignment movement. See António da Costa Gaspar, "Frente Diplomática," in *História da Luta de Libertação Nacional*, vol. 1, ed. by Joel de Neves Tembe (Maputo: Ministério dos Combatentes, 2014), 87–188.

[71] Matthias Voß and Achim Kindler, "Um de nós – einer von uns! Gespräch mit Achim Kindler, der als Lehrer im Auftrag des Solidaritätskomitees der DDR als erster DDR-Bürger bei der FRELIMO arbeitete," in *Wir haben Spuren hinterlassen!* ed. by Matthias, 34–46.

[72] Tullner, "Zusammenarbeit," 389.

[73] This secondary school (*Instituto Mozambicano*) was run in Dar-es-Salaam, Tanzania.

English. As no suitable Portuguese language course was available in the GDR, he brought a Spanish dictionary with him to improvise communication. Official instructions concerning the mission of GDR cooperators in FRELIMO-run schools appeared to be rather vague during that period.[74] This initial situation changed over time and Mozambique became a priority in the framework of the GDR's solidarity engagement in Africa, and educational aid came to play a major role within the concept of "socialist solidarity" for the young People's Republic.[75] In the field of higher education, at times, up to 42 GDR cooperators were simultaneously working at the UEM, distributed among all twelve faculties.[76]

Concerning the practice of recruiting at the UEM, it is relevant to mention that the GDR sent advisors and lecturers only on the request of its Mozambican counterparts. East German cooperators were then contracted to carry out specific tasks that were defined by the Frelimo government.[77] One such project was the creation of a special "workers' faculty" at the UEM.[78] Although the creation of this faculty represented a comparatively small part in the overall scope of responsibilities carried out by GDR cooperators at the UEM, its founding process may serve as an interesting example of the practice of international cooperation

---

[74] Voß and Kindler, "Um de nós," 35–36, 39; Tullner, "Zusammenarbeit," 389.

[75] Müller, *Bildungshilfe*; Schuch, *Mosambik*, 22–23.

[76] Highest number of GDR staff at the UEM registered in the period 1976–1989; the source does not reveal the concrete date, but it states that most of the GDR cooperators in that group worked for the Faculty of Engineering (28), followed by the Faculty of Education and the Faculty of Economy (both 15), and the Faculty of Medicine (12). In 1984, for instance, 30 GDR cooperators were working in the higher education sector. See Hegewald, "Berlin, Maputo," 467, 471.

[77] Corresponding working plans were agreed upon in special annexes to signed treaties of friendship and cooperation, which in the case of Mozambique was signed on February 24, 1979 (BArch/DR3/II.Schicht/B 1542). Also see Hans-Georg Schleicher, "Spurensuche im Süden Afrikas. Die Zusammenarbeit mit den Befreiungsbewegungen wirkt nach," in *Ostalgie international. Erinnerungen an die DDR von Nicaragua bis Vietnam*, ed. by Thomas Kunze and Thomas Vogel (Berlin: Ch. Links, 2010), 49.

[78] See report "Bericht zur Einrichtung einer ABF-ähnlichen Einrichtung an der UEM" by Strobel 1981 (BArch, DR3, II. Schicht, 1540); see also "Bericht über die Arbeit der Ökonomischen Fakultät (II. Halbjahr/1980) der AG-Universität Maputo" by Dora, including "Anlage zum Halbjahresbericht II/1980 der AG der DDR-Lehrkräfte an der UEM" to the MHF, Maputo, 14 November 1980 (BArch, DR3, II. Schicht, 1540).

at the university. To begin with, the requested faculty was supposed to take in adult students from the working class at pre-university level and prepare them in an accelerated manner for entry to university.[79] Comparable institutions called "worker–peasant faculties" existed in East German universities until 1963,[80] and cooperators from the GDR brought with them their own ideas about how a similar faculty could be implemented into the Mozambican context.[81] The actual founding process of the Mozambican "workers' faculty" lasted from 1979 to its opening in 1983 and personnel from Mozambique, the GDR, as well as Portugal and Chile were prominently involved in the conception of the faculty throughout the process. Although possible "role model" institutions existed in the GDR—and other socialist countries, such as Cuba or the Soviet Union—cooperators in charge remained reluctant to push through homegrown concepts where they considered them unsuitable. Final decision-making power on the design of a "workers' faculty" at the UEM resided with Mozambican actors, that is, the Frelimo Party.[82] As a result, a rather Mozambican version of a "workers' faculty" was established and fittingly named the "Faculty for Former Combatants and Vanguard Workers," because former liberation fighters constituted one of its target groups. The formation process of this "workers' faculty" exemplifies that educational transfers from abroad did not work in one direction only at the UEM, and that foreign cooperators were not always

---

[79] FRELIMO, "Direktiven," 187.

[80] For the history of worker–peasant faculties in the GDR see Ingrid Miethe, *Bildung und soziale Ungleichheit in der DDR. Möglichkeiten und Grenzen einer gegenprivilegierenden Bildungspolitik* (Opladen: Barbara Budrich, 2007).

[81] It is very likely that all GDR cooperators had a notion of the worker–peasant faculty called "ABF" in the GDR. Even Berthold Brecht devoted a poem to the ABF, and the East German writer Hermann Kant wrote a well-received novel on the ABF. See John Connelly, *Captive University: The Sovietization of East German, Czech, and Polish Higher Education, 1945–1956* (Chapel Hill, London: The University of North Carolina Press, 2000), 281. Kant's book "Die Aula" was "among the most printed books in the GDR," ibid., 397.

[82] See "Zur Einschätzung der Arbeit im Rektorat," report by Hr. Urbanski to MHF, Maputo, 19 June 1981 (BArch/DR3/II. Schicht/1540). For more examples on GDR–Mozambican cooperation see interviews with former UEM lecturers in Lisbon, Maputo, and Rostock, February to November 2014. Also see Dora, *Kokos*, 85–87; Tullner, "Zusammenarbeit," 396–403.

able or willing to assert their homegrown models within the framework of multinational cooperation.[83]

EAST GERMAN ADVISERS AT THE UEM AND INTERNATIONALIST PRACTICES "ON THE GROUND"

The everyday work of East German cooperators at the UEM will be depicted in the following sections of this chapter mainly through examples from three university departments, namely the Faculty of Education (Teacher Training Faculty), the Faculty of Marxism–Leninism, and the Faculty for Former Combatants and Vanguard Workers.[84] The findings collected indicate that "socialist solidarity" at the UEM was accompanied by intercultural misunderstandings and ideological differences. But, besides these rather negative aspects of international cooperation, the remarkable motivation of GDR staff "to make things work" was noticeable.

Intercultural Encounters

In relation to their Mozambican partners, interviews and memoirs produced by GDR cooperators point toward a relative openness for intercultural learning. But GDR cooperators also had to deal with partners from non-socialist countries, and many GDR cooperators encountered some—more or less harsh—diversity shocks during their mission at the UEM. In 1981, for example, the Faculty of Education had "a very international teaching staff with lecturers from socialist countries (USSR, GDR, Cuba, Bulgaria), approx. 26 lecturers from non-socialist countries,

---

[83] Tim Kaiser et al., "Educational Transfers in Postcolonial Contexts: Preliminary Results from Comparative Research on Workers' Faculties in Vietnam, Cuba, and Mozambique," *European Education* 47, no. 3 (2015): 252–255; Alexandra Piepiorka, "Sozialistische Hochschulpolitik im Mosambik der 1980er Jahre. Das Beispiel der Fakultät für ehemalige Kämpfer*innen and Arbeiter*innen," in *Sozialismus & Pädagogik: Verhältnisbestimmungen und Entwürfe*, ed. by Sebastian Engelmann and Robert Pfützner (Bielefeld: Transcript, 2018), 173–196.

[84] All three faculties seem rather unusual when compared with "classic" university structures, but in socialist universities similar departments can be found. In the Soviet Union, for instance, teacher training institutes, departments of Marxism–Leninism, and "workers' faculties" existed in the higher education sector; see Connelly, *Captive University*.

and 8 Mozambicans."[85] In face of this situation most GDR cooperators kept a critical distance to their colleagues from non-socialist countries, even though many of them had left-wing views. Apparently, the left-wing background of people from non-socialist countries was quite different from the experience of state socialism that was familiar to GDR citizens. In official reports, "Western" socialists were sometimes labeled as "left-wing extremists" by GDR cooperators.[86] Nevertheless, GDR cooperators embraced the possibilities of observing the unknown "other" and, in some cases, even chose to befriend some of their left-wing colleagues from the "West."[87]

An anecdote from the Faculty of Combatants seems telling in the context of diversity at the UEM. The pedagogical director of that faculty was a communist Chilean and generally recognized for his expertise in the field of adult education. He was described as a person who had a very positive influence on the students within the faculty, but due to his spontaneity, used to come up with new pedagogical concepts once in a while.[88] His East German colleague, on the other hand, was respected for this systematic working routine and his well-planned course of action. The collaboration of both characters within the international team of the faculty thus lead to frequent quarrels, and to amusement on the side of their Mozambican supervisor: "Jorge and Hans were always discussing with each other, all the time, all the time, all the time. Hans was very German, and Jorge was very Latin … [laughs] so Hans was very organized, and Jorge had a new idea every day. And Hans did not really like new ideas on a daily basis. [laughs] He preferred to bring things to an end. So both of them had [intercultural, AP] shocks, but these were friendly shocks. They hang out together from the beginning until the

---

[85] See report "Gruppe Maputo/UEM – Jahresbericht 1981, Teilbericht Gesellschaftswissenschaftlicher Bereich" signed by Schlauch on 02 December 1981 (BArch/DR3/II.Schicht/1540).

[86] See incomplete report without title (pp. 1, 10–13), no date, no author, in folder "Bilaterale Zusammenarbeit zwischen der DDR – Mosambique auf dem Gebiet des Bildungswesens" (BArch/DR3/II.Schicht/1539).

[87] See interviews; also see Dora, *Kokos*, 23. Unfortunately, sources on the way international colleagues viewed GDR personnel at the UEM were rarely found during the research period.

[88] See interviews with former lecturers at the UEM. In opposite to the generally positive view of the Chilean's work, a negative report was found in: "Bericht über das 1. Semester 1986 an der ABF," signed by Hunecke on 28 June 1986 (BArch/DR3/II.Schicht/1538).

end [of the project, AP] ... And the Russians were kind of Latin, as well. The Bulgarians, too" [all names changed in this quote].[89] Interestingly, both the Mozambican and GDR staff of this faculty partly disapproved of the leadership qualities of their Chilean colleague. But at the same time, all of them respected most of his pedagogical attitudes and teaching methods, which they perceived as being innovative and having a positive effect on students.[90]

Ideological Disputes

The relative diversity of ideas at the UEM resulted in an, at times, ideologically contested campus. Ideological differences between Frelimo functionaries, socialist cooperators, and personnel from non-socialist countries caused sophisticated quarrels between colleagues.[91] Such ideological disputes between members of the teaching staff took place on occasion, but they persisted in the Faculty of Marxism–Leninism (ML). The Faculty of ML came into existence in March 1981 and was directly subordinated to Frelimo, whereas all other faculties were affiliated to the rectorate of the UEM. By June 1981, a Frelimo group started to work on a new concept for teaching ML without consulting the international staff of that faculty.[92] Although GDR and Soviet teachers insisted on their interpretation of ML and tried to instill "correct" interpretations of ML philosophy into their fellow lecturers and students, their overall mission failed dramatically. Students used to mock dogmatic interpretations of ML and humorously renamed the subjects historical materialism and dialectical materialism into "hysteric and diabolic materialism."[93] One Mozambican staff member mockingly compared the quality of ML teaching, concluding that "a Canadian lecturer and an East German

---

[89] Quote from interview 1, Lisbon, 2014.
[90] See interviews 1 and 2, Rostock, 2014; also see all interviews in Maputo, 2014.
[91] See all interviews, 2014.
[92] See report "Halbjahresbericht I/1981, Bereich Gesellschaftswissenschaften" by the GDR teaching staff at the UEM, signed by Schlauch, Maputo, 10 June 1981 (p. 7) (BArch/DR3/II.Schicht/1540).
[93] Quote from interview 2, Maputo, 2014.

lecturer certainly do not teach in the same way."[94] Finally, in 1985, the rector asked GDR staff to make some alterations to their highly theoretical mode of teaching. To sum up, GDR lecturers of ML were openly criticized for their lack of flexibility in the application of ML to the Mozambican context. Furthermore, their focus on theory seemed unsuitable in terms of meeting the country's demand for practical answers.[95] Consequently, events at the Faculty of ML fostered a rather negative perception of GDR lecturers in the field of political and ideological education, and obligatory training in ML was abolished at the UEM.[96]

Dialogue and Cooperative Attitude

Besides their inefficient ideological endeavors at the UEM, the GDR staff were largely respected for their professional knowledge in other fields, and their cooperative behavior in most aspects of collaboration was perceived well by their Mozambican partners.[97] GDR cooperators usually looked to Frelimo's educational guidelines for pedagogical orientation, and a corresponding mode of conduct was officially promoted by the GDR ministries of education (MHF and MfV) when sending staff to the UEM. GDR advisors working at the Faculty of Education, for instance, were instructed "not to copy GDR-plans" and to rather do the "necessary and right" according to Mozambican conditions.[98] Bearing this in mind, GDR cooperators at the UEM proved quite open to acquiring new teaching skills proposed by their Mozambican counterparts or—in some cases—by their international colleagues.[99] Beyond this, more pragmatic factors may also have played a part in the cooperative behavior of GDR staff. Documents indicate that GDR teaching staff were not always

---

[94] Quote from interview 1, Maputo, 2014.
[95] Lewin et al., *Die Herausbildung*, 54–55; Tullner, "Zusammenarbeit."
[96] Ibid., 400; also see all interviews in Maputo, 2014.
[97] See interviews and Voß, *Wir haben Spuren*.
[98] Grajek, *Berichte aus...*, 10.
[99] See interviews; also see Hegewald, "Berlin, Maputo."

sufficiently prepared to meet the Mozambican realities on the ground, consequently, newly arrived GDR cooperators may have been more amenable to follow Frelimo guidelines.[100] In addition, experienced GDR staff members were reportedly keen to maintain a high level of recognition both at the UEM[101] and in relation to the Frelimo Party. Therefore, experienced staff members made some effort to effectively integrate new GDR cadres, in order to prevent losses in working standards.[102]

Available sources reveal a mixed view of GDR cooperators at the UEM. Retrospectively, former GDR cooperators mostly picture rather positive images of their encounters with Mozambican partners.[103] Considering the GDR perspective, "*Cooperantes da RDA*" (cooperators from the GDR) were perceived as "comrades" and accordingly treated in a friendly manner.[104] This affirmative view on "socialist solidarity" is congruent with the views expressed by Mozambican counterparts for the most part.[105] But with reference to ideological divergences, Mozambican contemporaries were very explicit when describing the problems encountered at the faculty of Marxism-Leninism as "wars between socialist countries."[106] Therefore, one can conclude that in terms of organizational tasks and teaching practices "socialist solidarity" worked well at UEM. However, in the field of ideology some major differences between international cadres prevented such a cooperative attitude.

[100] See letter to the MHF "Stellungnahme der MHF-Expertengruppe Maputo zum Schreiben des Genossen Dr. Jürgen du Puits an das Ministerium für Hoch- und Fachschulwesen," May 1983, signed by Urbanski, Dora, Willig (BArch/DR3/II.Schicht/1538); report "Halbjahresbericht II/1988 der MHF-Expertengruppe Maputo," 30 December 1988, signed by Dora (BArch/DR3/II.Schicht/1538).

[101] See report "Jahresbericht – 1981, Teilbericht der naturwissenschaftlichen und technischen Fakultät," by AG der DDR- Lehrkräfte an der UEM, Maputo, 25 November 1981, signed by Welzk (BArch/DR3/II.Schicht/1540).

[102] See report "Rechenschaftsbericht zur Erfüllung des Wettbewerbsprogrammes," by MHF-Expertengruppe, Gewerk- schaftsgruppe, Engenharia, Maputo, June 1987. Annex in letter of the MHF-Expertengruppe (Engenharia) to the political department of the GDR embassy in Mozambique, June 1987 (BArch/DR3/II.Schicht/1538).

[103] See interviews with East German *cooperantes*, and Voß, *Wir haben Spuren*.

[104] Grajek, *Berichte aus...*, 15.

[105] At this point, the limits of retrospective evaluations must be taken into consideration, because personal relations are involved here and interview partners may have been reluctant to express negative feelings about former colleagues.

[106] Quote from interview 2 in Maputo, 2014.

Wind of Change and the Legacy of "Socialist Solidarity" at the UEM

In the late 1980s, changes in educational policies began to manifest, after the Frelimo government started to implement a program of "structural adjustment" as favored by their financial aid agencies (mainly the World Bank and International Monetary Fund). Under these circumstances, the influence of socialist ideology in the Mozambican education system declined, as did the influence of advisors from the GDR within the framework of the UEM. The East German model of "socialist solidarity" came to an end after the GDR's reunification with West Germany in 1990.[107] Two years later, the Frelimo government passed a new law on education, which abstained from socialist goals in education.[108]

Nevertheless, educational projects realized in the framework of "socialist solidarity" seemingly supported a symbolic "Mozambicanization" of the UEM in the aftermath of independence. The history of the Faculty for Former Combatants, for instance, showed that educational ideas "borrowed"[109] from socialist partners were useful for the consolidation of the new education system (SNE) and, thereby, were conducive to the decolonization process of the newly independent country in a broader sense. This faculty not only successfully promoted the education of former independence fighters within the UEM, but also qualified a certain number of Mozambican cadres to contribute to post-colonial state building, as envisioned by the (then Socialist) Frelimo government. Although the design of the faculty combined different foreign as well as local educational concepts, in the end the integration of them all resulted in an educational institution specific to the Mozambican context. Fittingly, the perception of the Faculty for Combatants as a Mozambican institution was highlighted by a former member of the Frelimo Central Committee (Marcelino dos Santos)

---

[107] Jude Howell, "The End of an Era: The Rise and Fall of G.D.R. Aid," *The Journal of Modern African Studies* 32, no. 2 (1994): 305–328.

[108] Castiano, *Bildungssystem*, 124–137; Tullner, "Zusammenarbeit," 401–405.

[109] For further reading on processes of "borrowing and lending" within international cooperation in the field of education see Gita Steiner-Khamsi and Florian Waldow, *World Yearbook of Education 2012: Policy Borrowing and Lending in Education* (London/New York: Routledge, 2012).

when he stressed that within the UEM it was was "truly our faculty."[110] Besides this rather symbolic interpretation of the faculty, the gradually rising number of its Mozambican teaching staff was regarded as a "Mozambicanization" process by the East German advisors at the UEM. GDR cooperators were officially instructed to contribute to the long-term "Mozambicanization of the academic staff" at the UEM,[111] and consequently GDR reports kept track of the proportion of national, in relation to foreign, cadres at the Faculty for Combatants, and regularly delivered statistical data on the faculty's staff development. Finally, in the 1984/1985 academic year, more "national" (17) than foreign (8) lecturers were reported to be teaching at the faculty. GDR cooperators perceived this parameter as an important contribution to the "Mozambicanization" of the UEM.[112]

The tales of everyday cooperation at the UEM exemplify how different notions of socialist education were—sometimes more and sometimes less successfully—reconciled under the overarching category of "socialist solidarity" in post-independence Mozambique. And interestingly, the overall narrative of "socialist solidarity" at the UEM points to a positive way of remembering by protagonists. This retrospective needs to be completed with further critical insight from the international staff at the UEM. Yet, for the time being, this research indicates that Mozambican counterparts perceived most acts of "socialist solidarity," delivered by East German cooperators, as rather friendly contributions to Mozambique's post-independence development.[113] At the same time, the Frelimo government remained eager to channel various inflows of "socialist solidarity" at the UEM toward the Party's envisioned development path. East German actors were thus influential in the first decade

---

[110] See "Mensagem lido pelo sr. Ermelindo Mwya em nome dos ex-alunos da Faculdade," in report on the "Semana de Educação" 13–20 April 1985, UEM, FACOTRAV, Maputo (AHM/documentation Ganhão/box 55).

[111] See Report "Einschätzung zum Stand und zu einigen Entwicklungen an der UEM, Bericht der MHF-Expertengruppe aus Maputo" to the MHF, Abt. Auslandskader/ Experten, Maputo, June 1986, 17 (BArch/DR3/II. Schicht/1538).

[112] "Informationsbericht über die Fakultät für Kämpfer und Arbeiter der Avantgarde," 1984/1985. BArch, DR3, II. Schicht, 1539, not paginated.

[113] In this context, it seems intriguing that three former East German cooperators have been awarded the governmental *Nachingwea Medal* for extraordinary merit many years *after* the Frelimo government's departure from a socialist path of development. See Voß and Kindler, "Um de nós," 46; Schleicher, "Spurensuche," 46.

after the country's independence when Frelimo favored socialist educational policies. But with the introduction of structural adjustment programs in the late 1980s and, related to this, the country's gradual shift toward a market-orientated, multi-party democracy, the overall standing of "socialist solidarity" at the UEM declined, with new sources of educational aid gaining importance.[114]

Conclusion

My preliminary conclusion is that while the post-independence period was marked by "socialist solidarity," and the contribution East German advisors made to the construction of the first Mozambican education system remains recognized, the effects of socialist aid on the development of higher education in Mozambique turned out to be rather sort-lived. It seems that the technical knowledge delivered by East German advisors proved to be more valuable in the long-term, as opposed to their ideological contributions on campus. To sum up, I would argue that Frelimo's attitude toward "socialist solidarity" in higher education was rather receptive, but selective. Mozambican counterparts did not always embrace East German or other foreign advice unanimously. This perceived selectivity may be illustrated by the following statement of a Mozambican university lecturer, commenting on the practice of accepting foreign aid at the UEM during the post-independence period: "You want to support us? Great! But you don't want this, you don't want that ... Well, that's your problem! We will receive your suggestions ... But the steering wheel is ours! In this aspect Mozambique has always been very bold."[115] I find this self-understanding very telling, and I tend to sympathize with Mingolos' view in my interpretation of post-independence events at the UEM. Mingolo reminds us to restrain from categorizing post-colonial developments too fast into liberal or socialist developments, and encourages researchers to challenge epistemic patterns of thought related to modernity and developmentalism, since these ideas were crucial

---

[114]David N. Plank, "Aid, Debt, and the End of Sovereignty: Mozambique and Its Donors," *The Journal of Modern African Studies* 31, no. 3 (1993): 407–430; Howell, "End of an Era."

[115]Quote from interview 2, Maputo, 2014.

for installing the colonial systems at the beginning.[116] This argument is applicable to the Mozambican case, because socialist and liberal aid agencies alike preached a rather developmentalist discourse in terms of Mozambique's higher education since independence.

BIBLIOGRAPHY

Barnes, Barbara. "Education for Socialism in Mozambique." *Comparative Education Review* 26, no. 3 (1982): 406–419.

Boden, Ragna. "Globalisierung sowjetisch: Der Kulturtransfer in die Dritte Welt." In *Globalisierung imperial und sozialistisch*, edited by Martin Aust, 425–442. Frankfurt: Campus, 2013.

Büschel, Hubertus. "In Afrika helfen. Akteure westdeutscher 'Entwicklungshilfe' und ostdeutscher 'Solidarität', 1955–1975." In *Dekolonisation. Prozesse und Verflechtungen 1945–1990*, edited by Anja Kruke, 333–365. Bonn: Dietz, 2009.

Büschel, Hubertus, and Daniel Speich, eds. *Entwicklungswelten. Globalgeschichte der Entwicklungszusammenarbeit*. Campus: Frankfurt, 2009.

Carnoy, Martin. "Education and the Transition State." In *Education and Social Transition in the Third World*, edited by Marin Carnoy and Joel Samoff, 63–96. Princeton: Princeton University Press, 1990.

Castiano, José P. *Das Bildungssystem in Mosambik (1974–1966): Entwicklungen, Probleme und Konsequenzen*. Hamburg: Institut für Afrika-Kunde, 1997.

Connelly, John. *Captive University: The Sovietization of East German, Czech, and Polish Higher Education, 1945–1956*. Chapel Hill/London: The University of North Carolina Press, 2000.

Cross, Michael. *An Unfulfilled Promise. Transforming Schools in Mozambique*. Addis Ababa: Organization for Social Science Research in Eastern and Southern Africa (OSSREA), 2011.

Dora, Helmut. *Kokos und bitterer Tee: Tage und Nächte in Mosambik*. Rostock: BS–Verlag, 2009.

Döring, Hans-Joachim. *"Es geht um unsere Existenz". Die Politik der DDR gegenüber der Dritten Welt am Beispiel von Mosambik und Äthiopien*. Berlin: Ch. Links, 1999.

Flores, José Manuel. *Das Problem der gleichzeitigen Sicherung von Bildungsbeteiligung und Bildungsqualität in Mosambik. Kritische Rekonstruktion einer bildungspolitischen Entscheidung und ihrer Folgen*. Hamburg: Dr. Kovač, 2014.

---

[116]Walter Mingolo, "Epistemic Disobedience and the Decolonial Option," *Transmodernity* 1, no. 2 (2011): 52.

FRELIMO. "Ökonomische und soziale Direktiven." In *Dokumente des 3. Kongresses der FRELIMO*, edited by Informationsstelle Südliches Afrika, 139–190. Bonn: Issa, 1978.

Fry, Peter, and Rogério Utui. *Promoting Access, Quality and Capacity-Building in African Higher Education: The Strategic Planning Experience at the Eduardo Mondlane University*. Washington, DC: ADEA Working Group on Higher Education, The World Bank, 1999. http://www.adeanet.org/adea/publications/wghe/wghe_uem_en.pdf.

Gaspar, António da Costa. "Frente Diplomática." In *História da Luta de Libertação Nacional, Volume 1*, edited by Joel de Neves Tembe, 87–188. Maputo: Ministério dos Combatentes, Direcção Nacional de História, 2014.

Gómez, Buendía Miguel. *Educação Moçambicana. História de um processo: 1962–1984*. Maputo: Livraria Universitária, UEM, 1999.

Grajek, Rainer. *Berichte aus dem Morgengrauen. Als Entwicklungshelfer der DDR in Mosambik*. Grimma: Ute Vallentin, 2005.

Hedin, Astrid. "Die Reiseorganisation der Hochschulen der DDR. Ein Reisekadersystem sowjetischen Typus." In *Die DDR in Europa – zwischen Isolation und Öffnung*, edited by Heiner Timmermann, 280–290. Münster: LIT, 2005.

Hegewald, Holger. "Berlin, Maputo und zurück – Dozent an der Eduardo-Mondlane-Universität 1989–1990." In *Wir haben Spuren hinterlassen! Die DDR in Mosambik. Erlebnisse, Erfahrungen und Erkenntnisse aus drei Jahrzehnten*, edited by Matthias Voß, 463–480. Münster: LIT, 2005.

Howell, Jude. "The End of an Era: The Rise and Fall of G.D.R. Aid." *Journal of Modern African Studies* 32, no. 2 (1994): 305–328.

Isaacman, Allen, and Barbara Isaacman. *Mozambique: From Colonialism to Revolution, 1900–1982*. Boulder: Westview Press, 1983.

Johnston, Anton. *Educação em Moçambique: 1975–1984*. Stockholm: SIDA, 1986.

———. *Study, Produce, and Combat! Education and the Mozambican State 1962–1984*. Stockhom: Institute of International Education, University of Stockholm, 1989.

———. "Adult Literacy and Development in Mozambique." *African Studies Review* 33, no. 3 (1990): 83–96.

———. "The Mozambican State and Education." In *Education and Social Transition in the Third World*, edited by Martin Carnoy and Joel Samoff, 275–314. Princeton/Oxford: Princeton University Press, 1990.

Johnston, Anton, Henry Kaluba, Mats Karlsson, and Kjell Nyström. *Education and Economic Crisis: The Cases of Mozambique and Zambia*. Stockholm: SIDA, 1987.

Kaiser, Tim, Tobias Kriele, Ingrid Miethe, and Alexandra Piepiorka. "Educational Transfers in Postcolonial Contexts: Preliminary Results from Comparative Research on Workers' Faculties in Vietnam, Cuba, and Mozambique." *European Education* 47, no. 3 (2015): 242–259.

Katsakioris, Constantin. "Creating a Socialist Intelligentsia: Soviet Educational Aid and Its Impact on Africa (1960–1991)." *Cahiers d'études africaines* no. 226 (2017): 259–288. http://journals.openedition.org/etudesafricaines/20664. https://doi.org/10.4000/etudesafricaines.20664.

Koch, Susanne, and Peter Weingart. *Delusion of Knowledge Transfer: The Impact of Foreign Aid Experts on Policy-Making in South Africa and Tanzania.* Stellenbosch, SA: African Minds, 2016.

Lewin, Rosemarie, Siegmund Müller, Petra Münch, and Hans-Dieter Schaefer. *Die Herausbildung eines nationalen höheren Bildungswesens in Ländern mit sozialistischem Entwicklungsweg* (Studien zur Hochschulentwicklung, Sonderdruck. Nur für den Dienstgebrauch). Berlin: Zentralinstitut für Hochschulbildung, 1986.

Lind, Agneta. *Adult Literacy Lessons and Promises: The Mozambican Literacy Campaigns, 1978–1982.* Stockholm: Institute of International Education, 1988.

Macamo, Elíso Salvado. *Negotiating Modernity: Africa's Ambivalent Experience.* London/New York: ZED, 2005.

Mário, Mouzinho, Peter Fry, Lisbeth A. Levey, and Arlindo Chilundo. *Higher Eduaction in Mozambique: A Case Study.* Oxford: James Currey/Maputo: Imprensa & Livraria Universitária UEM, 2003.

Mazula, Brazão. *Educação, Cultura e Ideologia em Moçambique: 1975–1985. Em busca de fundamentos filosófico-antropológicos.* Porto: Edições Afrontamento e Fundo Bibliográfico de Língua Portuguesa, 1995.

Miedema, Esther. "'Let's Move, Let's Not Remain Stagnant': Nationalism, Masculinism, and School-Based Education in Mozambique." In *Childhood and Nation: Interdisciplinary Engagements*, edited by Zsuzsa Millei und Robert Imre, 183–206. New York: Palgrave Macmillan, 2015.

Miethe, Ingrid. *Bildung und soziale Ungleichheit in der DDR. Möglichkeiten und Grenzen einer gegenprivilegierenden Bildungspolitik.* Opladen: Barbara Budrich, 2007.

Miethe, Ingrid, Tim Kaiser, Tobias Kriele, and Alexandra Piepiorka. *Globalisation of an Educational Idea: Workers' Faculties in Eastern Germany, Vietnam, Cuba and Mozambique.* Berlin: De Gruyter, 2019.

Mingolo, Walter. "Epistemic Disobedience and the Decolonial Option." *Transmodernity* 1, no. 2 (2011): 44–66.

Mouzinho, Mário, and Deborah Nandja. *Literacy in Mozambique: Education for All Challenges.* Paper commissioned for the "Education for All" (EFA) Global Monitoring Report 2006, Literacy for Life. Paris: UNESCO/Maputo: UEM, Faculty of Education, 2005. http://unesdoc.unesco.org/images/0014/001462/146284e.pdf.

Müller, Hans Mathias. *Die Bildungshilfe der Deutschen Demokratischen Republik.* Frankfurt: Peter Lang, 1995.

Müller, Tanja. *Legacies of Socialist Solidarity: East-Germany in Mozambique.* London/New York: Lexington, 2014.

Napier, Diane Brook. "African Socialism, Post-Colonial Development, and Education: Change and Continuity in the Post-Socialist Era." In *Post-Socialism is Not Dead: (Re)Reading the Global in Comparative Education*, edited by Iveta Silova, 369–399. Bingley, UK: Emerald, 2010.
Newitt, Malyn. *A Short History of Mozambique*. London: Hurst & Company, 2017.
Niederhut, Jens. *Die Reisekader. Auswahl und Disziplinierung einer privilegierten Minderheit in der DDR*. Leipzig: Evangelische Verlagsanstalt, 2005.
Piepiorka Alexandra. "Sozialistische Hochschulpolitik im Mosambik der 1980er Jahre. Das Beispiel der Fakultät für ehemalige Kämpfer*innen and Arbeiter*innen." In *Sozialismus & Pädagogik: Verhältnisbestimmungen und Entwürfe*, edited by Sebastian Engelmann and Robert Pfützner, 173–196. Bielefeld: Transcript, 2018.
Plank, David N. "Aid, Debt, and the End of Sovereignty: Mozambique and Its Donors." *Journal of Modern African Studies* 31, no. 3 (1993): 407–430.
Reuter, Lutz R., and Annette Scheunpflug. *Die Schule der Freundschaft. Eine Fallstudie zur Bildungszusammenarbeit zwischen der DDR und Mosambik*. Münster: Waxmann, 2006.
Roos, Hans-Jochen. "Unterrichten unter Palmen. Als Biologielehrer an der FRELIMO-Schule in Bagamoyo." In *Wir haben Spuren hinterlassen! Die DDR in Mosambik. Erlebnisse, Erfahrungen und Erkenntnisse aus drei Jahrzehnten*, edited by Matthias Voß, 407–425. Münster: LIT, 2005.
Schleicher, Hans-Georg. "Spurensuche im Süden Afrikas. Die Zusammenarbeit mit den Befreiungsbewegungen wirkt nach." In *Ostalgie international. Erinnerungen an die DDR von Nicaragua bis Vietnam*, edited by Thomas Kunze and Thomas Vogel, 47–56. Berlin: Ch. Links, 2010.
Schuch, Jane. *Mosambik im pädagogischen Raum der DDR. Eine bildanalytische Studie zur "Schule der Freundschaft" in Staßfurt*. Wiesbaden: Springer, 2013.
Silova, Iveta. *Post-Socialism Is Not Dead: (Re)Reading the Global in Comparative Education*. Bingley: Emerald, 2010.
Silova, Iveta, Nelli Piattoeva, and Zsuzsa Millei. *Childhood and Schooling in (Post)Socialist Societies: Memories of Everyday Life*. Cham: Springer 2018.
Statistisches Bundesamt. *Länderbericht Mosambik*. Stuttgart: Metzler-Poeschel, 1989.
Steiner-Khamsi, Gita. "The Development Turn in Comparative Education." *European Education* 38, no. 3 (2006): 19–47.
Steiner-Khamsi, Gita, and Florian Waldow. *World Yearbook of Education 2012: Policy Borrowing and Lending in Education*. London/New York: Routledge, 2012.
Tullner, Matthias. "Die Zusammenarbeit der DDR und Mosambiks auf dem Gebiet der Bildung und die Tätigkeit der Bildungsexperten der DDR in Mosambik." In *Wir haben Spuren hinterlassen! Die DDR in Mosambik. Erlebnisse, Erfahrungen und Erkenntnisse aus drei Jahrzehnten*, edited by Matthias Voß, 388–406. Münster: LIT, 2005.

Unfried, Berthold. "Instrumente und Praktiken von 'Solidarität' Ost und 'Entwicklungshilfe' West: Blickpunkt auf das entsandte Personal." In *Create One World: Practices of 'International Solidarity' and 'International Development'*, edited by Berthold Unfried and Eva Himmelstoss, 73–98. Wien: Akademische Verlagsanstalt, 2012.

van der Heyden, Ulrich. *GRD Development Policy in Africa: Doctrine and Strategies Between Illusions and Reality, 1960–1990. The Example (South) Africa*. Münster: LIT, 2013.

Verber, Jason. "True to the Politics of Frelimo? Teaching Socialism at the 'Schule der Freundschaft', 1981–1990." In *Comrades of Color: East Germany in the Cold War World*, edited by Quinn Slobodian, 188–210. Oxford/New York: Berghahn, 2015.

Verburg, Maria Magdalena. *Ostdeutsche Dritte-Welt-Gruppen vor und nach 1989/90*. Göttingen: V&R unipress, 2012.

Voß, Matthias. *Wir haben Spuren hinterlassen! Die DDR in Mosambik. Erlebnisse, Erfahrungen und Erkenntnisse aus drei Jahrzehnten*. Münster: LIT, 2005.

Voß, Matthias, and Achim Kindler. "Um de nós – einer von uns! Gespräch mit Achim Kindler, der als Lehrer im Auftrag des Solidaritätskomitees der DDR als erster DDR-Bürger bei der FRELIMO arbeitete." In *Wir haben Spuren hinterlassen! Die DDR in Mosambik. Erlebnisse, Erfahrungen und Erkenntnisse aus drei Jahrzehnten*, edited by Matthias Voß, 34–46. Münster: LIT, 2005.

Willerding, Klaus. "Zur Afrika-Politik der DDR." *Deutsche Aussenpolitik* 24, no. 8 (1979): 5–19.

Zawangoni, Salvador André. *A FRELIMO e a Formação do Homem Novo (1964–1974 e 1975–1982)*. Maputo: CIEDIMA, 2007.

Open Access This chapter is licensed under the terms of the Creative Commons Attribution 4.0 International License (http://creativecommons.org/licenses/by/4.0/), which permits use, sharing, adaptation, distribution and reproduction in any medium or format, as long as you give appropriate credit to the original author(s) and the source, provide a link to the Creative Commons license and indicate if changes were made.

The images or other third party material in this chapter are included in the chapter's Creative Commons license, unless indicated otherwise in a credit line to the material. If material is not included in the chapter's Creative Commons license and your intended use is not permitted by statutory regulation or exceeds the permitted use, you will need to obtain permission directly from the copyright holder.

Index

A
Agriculture/agricultural, 10, 11, 19, 20, 39, 58, 61–63, 71, 76, 95–97, 110–112, 117–129, 132, 133, 137, 138, 144, 145, 147, 150, 151, 162, 164, 174, 177, 180, 186, 187, 197, 206, 211, 238, 241, 243, 245, 248, 251, 253–256, 268
Aid, 16, 18, 21, 32, 49, 206, 209, 212, 213, 226, 229, 290–294, 296, 297, 299, 304, 311, 313, 314

B
Belgium, 13–15, 34, 240
Britain, 35, 37, 39, 41, 48, 117, 263, 264, 266, 273–275, 277–279, 281, 283

C
Catholic Church, 9, 145, 149, 150, 157, 163

Centres sociaux, 14, 19, 55–58, 60–78
Civilizing mission, 12, 20, 57, 71, 78, 85, 87, 102, 167, 168
Colonialism, 59, 119, 121, 122, 131, 143, 145, 166, 167, 210, 237, 265, 294, 295
Commission for Technical Cooperation in Africa south of the Sahara (CCTA), 21, 243, 245–259
Cooperation, 21, 58, 67, 68, 76, 98, 206, 223, 224, 229, 238, 240, 241, 243, 244, 246, 247, 250, 251, 254–259, 290–293, 303–306, 311, 312

D
Development, 3, 5, 7, 8, 11–16, 18–21, 31–33, 36–41, 47, 48, 50, 56–61, 71, 75, 76, 78, 84–86, 92–94, 97–102, 112, 116, 117, 119–121, 123, 127, 132, 135, 137, 138, 144, 145, 163,

167, 168, 174, 175, 183–185,
206–210, 212, 215–218, 221,
225, 228, 229, 238–242, 244,
245, 247–249, 256, 259, 265,
266, 269, 271, 276, 282, 290,
291, 293–301, 303, 312, 313

E

East Germany, 217, 293
Economy/economic, 2, 3, 5, 7, 8,
10–14, 16, 17, 20, 21, 31, 33,
39, 41, 43, 46, 49, 58, 59, 61,
64–66, 68, 71, 72, 86, 87, 89,
92, 93, 96, 98, 99, 101, 110,
113–117, 119, 122, 124, 125,
127, 129, 133, 135, 152, 165,
166, 174, 175, 177, 179–185,
188, 192–194, 198, 200, 206–
208, 210, 211, 213–215, 219,
221, 223–229, 244, 245, 247,
248, 264–266, 285, 290, 291,
294, 295, 298, 299, 301, 304
Empire, 5, 8, 12, 18, 37, 41, 43, 45,
50, 62, 66, 102, 111, 121, 123,
128, 148, 166, 263–268, 271,
275, 278–280, 282, 284, 285

F

France, 14, 16, 35, 57, 62, 64–67, 70,
71, 75, 78, 101, 121, 128, 174,
175, 183, 191, 193, 195–197,
244, 246, 267
Fundamental education, 15, 19, 57–61,
65–67, 71, 73–78, 245, 248

H

Health, 8, 10, 11, 19, 37, 39, 40, 42,
44, 50, 58, 62, 76, 91, 96, 125,
132, 189, 241, 247, 268

Higher education, 17, 21, 39, 46, 49,
50, 177, 206, 241, 246, 270,
285, 290, 291, 293, 296–298,
301, 303–306, 313, 314

I

Industry/industrial, 10, 33, 45,
73, 127, 177, 183, 184, 186,
187, 192, 196, 199, 200, 211,
213, 215, 222, 224, 225, 243,
253–256
Italy, 144–146, 148, 149, 152, 154,
156, 158, 164, 166, 217

L

Labour, 6–9, 20, 41, 211, 218, 252,
254, 256, 266, 277, 279

M

Mise en Valeur, 5, 8, 12, 57, 71, 86,
98, 99, 101, 102, 119, 121, 127,
175, 183
Missions/missionaries, 4–6, 10, 12, 13,
20, 34, 36, 38, 39, 76, 111, 143,
145–158, 160, 162–165, 168, 281
Modernization, 3, 5, 14, 16, 20,
21, 33, 34, 57, 87, 125, 163,
174, 176, 208, 256, 263, 264,
266–269, 271, 273, 281–285,
294, 295
Morocco, 20, 173–177, 180, 184,
186, 187, 189, 190, 192–199
Mozambique, 18, 21, 145, 289–294,
296–298, 301, 303–306, 310,
312–314

P

Portugal, 221, 244, 254, 256, 299, 305

INDEX 321

Primary schools/education, 135, 180, 191, 192, 194, 195, 207, 215, 241, 245, 248, 250

S

Secondary schools/education, 50, 128, 159, 180, 192, 254, 270
Socialism/socialist, 17, 21, 96, 97, 207–209, 212, 213, 215, 216, 218, 223, 227–229, 290–301, 303–308, 310–314
Somalia, 20, 143–155, 157–159, 163–168
South West Africa, 20, 135
Soviet Union, 17, 206, 212, 217, 265, 305, 306

T

Tanzania, 18, 20, 109, 145, 206, 208–210, 212–216, 218–222, 224, 225, 229, 299, 303
Technical education, 33, 46, 50, 213, 245, 249, 253, 295
Training, 5, 8, 17, 18, 20, 37, 61, 63, 65, 74, 76, 84, 88, 90, 93, 95, 102, 120, 124–128, 137, 150, 174, 177, 180, 181, 183, 185, 186, 190, 206, 211, 215, 221, 227, 248, 250, 253–256, 258, 263–265, 267, 268, 271, 274, 275, 278, 282, 294, 297, 301, 302, 306, 309

U

United Nations Educational, Scientific and Cultural Organization (UNESCO), 15, 57–61, 65, 75–78, 94, 241, 244, 246–249, 251, 252, 254, 258, 259
United States, 10, 17, 131, 136, 167, 206, 211, 265, 280, 281, 297
University/Universities, 1–6, 8–10, 12, 14–18, 21, 32–34, 37, 40, 41, 45, 46, 60, 64, 66, 67, 71, 78, 102, 111, 113, 116, 117, 122, 123, 126, 127, 144, 145, 150, 157, 160, 180, 186, 205–221, 223–229, 240, 242, 243, 246, 251, 254, 263–269, 272, 273, 276, 277, 279, 280, 282, 283, 289, 290, 295, 297–302, 305, 306, 313

V

Vocational education/training, 20, 33, 40, 46, 130, 137, 148, 151, 165, 174–178, 180, 181, 183–186, 189, 191, 193–200, 245, 248, 254, 258

W

Welfare, 13, 14, 19, 32, 33, 37, 39–41, 44, 45, 47, 48, 50, 71, 241, 242, 247, 248, 256, 266, 269, 271, 274, 276
West Germany, 211–213, 220, 229, 311

The manufacturer's authorised representative in the EU is Springer Nature Customer Service Centre GmbH, Europaplatz 3, 69115 Heidelberg, Germany. If you have any concerns regarding our products, please contact ProductSafety@springernature.com

Printed and bound by CPI Group (UK) Ltd, Croydon, CR0 4YY

23/03/2026

02076670-0007